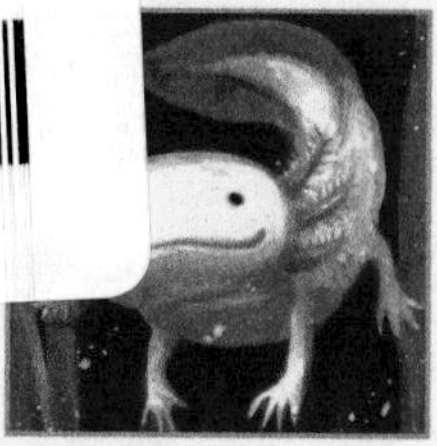

尾田栄一郎

Have you ever thought, ***"I don't wanna be an adult!!"*** If there are no satisfactory role models around children, they'll lose their appetite and refuse to grow. If we could somehow utilize this property, it could unlock the secrets of anti-aging. The more worthless adults there are, the longer those who don't want to be like them can remain young. But these days, there are still plenty of cool adults in their 40s and even their 70s. ***What a shame.*** Now let's get to volume 70!! Here comes volume 68!!!

-Eiichiro Oda, 2012

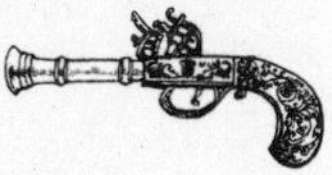

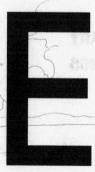

Eiichiro Oda began his manga career at the age of 17, when his one-shot cowboy manga **Wanted!** won second place in the coveted Tezuka manga awards. Oda went on to work as an assistant to some of the biggest manga artists in the industry, including Nobuhiro Watsuki, before winning the Hop Step Award for new artists. His pirate adventure **One Piece**, which debuted in **Weekly Shonen Jump** in 1997, quickly became one of the most popular manga in Japan.

ONE PIECE VOL. 68
NEW WORLD PART 8

SHONEN JUMP Manga Edition

STORY AND ART BY EIICHIRO ODA

Translation/Stephen Paul
Touch-up Art & Lettering/Vanessa Satone
Design/Fawn Lau
Editor/Alexis Kirsch

Printed in the U.S.A.

Published by VIZ Media, LLC
P.O. Box 77010
San Francisco, CA 94107

10 9 8 7 6 5
First printing, September 2013
Fifth printing, December 2016

viz media
www.viz.com

PARENTAL ADVISORY
ONE PIECE is rated T for Teen and is recommended for ages 13 and up. This volume contains fantasy violence and tobacco usage.
RATED T FOR TEEN
ratings.viz.com

SHONEN JUMP MANGA

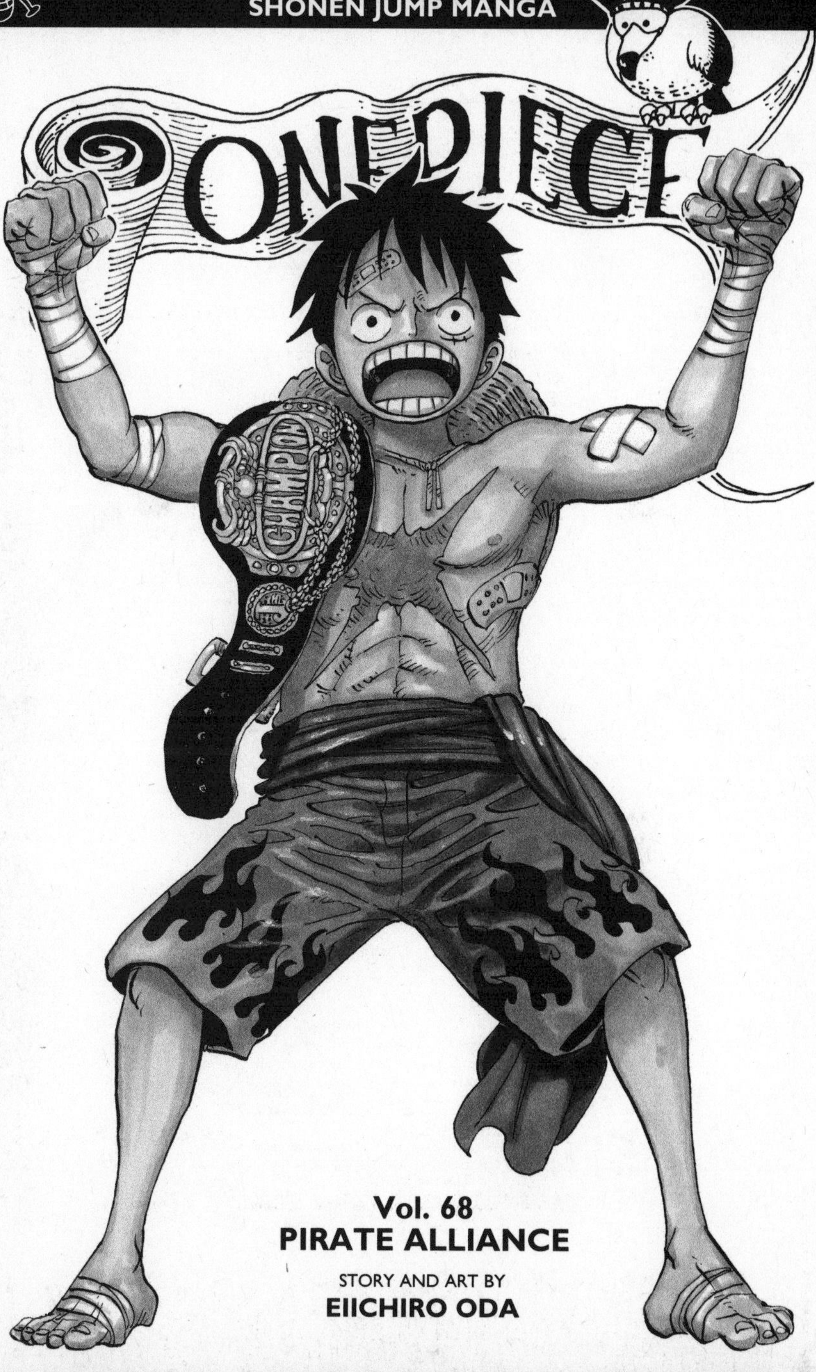
ONE PIECE
CHAMPION

Vol. 68
PIRATE ALLIANCE

STORY AND ART BY
EIICHIRO ODA

The Straw Hat Crew

Monkey D. Luffy

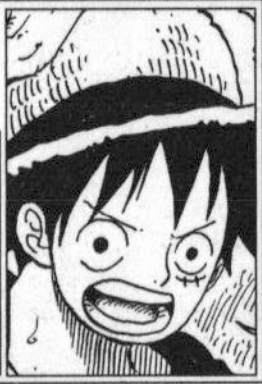

A young man who dreams of becoming the Pirate King. After training with Rayleigh, he and his crew head for the New World!

Captain, Bounty: 400 million berries

Roronoa Zolo

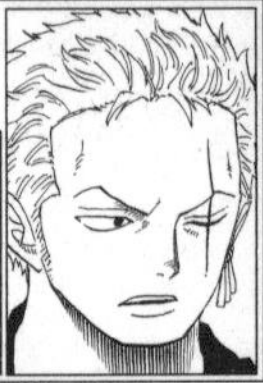

He swallowed his pride and asked to be trained by Mihawk on Gloom Island before reuniting with the rest of the crew.

Fighter, Bounty: 120 million berries

Tony Tony Chopper

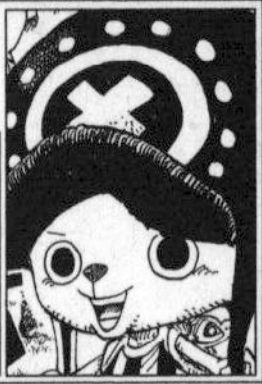

After researching powerful medicine in Birdie Kingdom, he reunites with the rest of the crew.

Ship's Doctor, Bounty: 50 berries

Nami

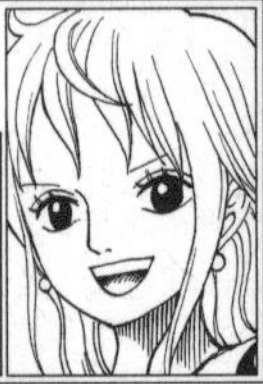

She studied the weather of the New World on the small Sky Island Weatheria, a place where weather is studied as a science.

Navigator, Bounty: 16 million berries

Nico Robin

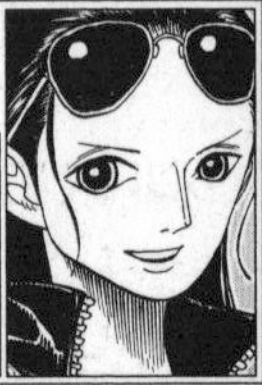

She spent her time in Baltigo with the leader of the Revolutionary Army: Luffy's father, Dragon.

Archeologist, Bounty: 80 million berries

Usopp

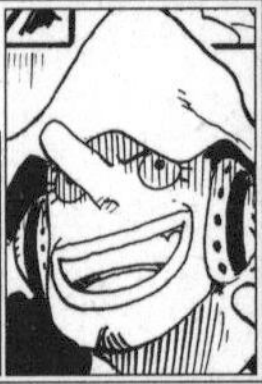

He trained under Heracles at the Bowin Islands to become the King of Snipers.

Sniper, Bounty: 30 million berries

Franky

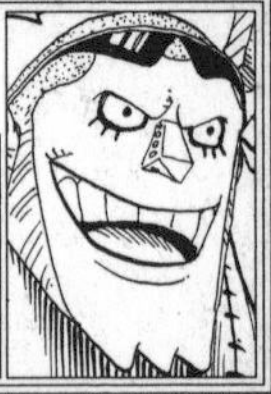

He modified himself in Future Land Baldimore and turned himself into Armored Franky before reuniting with the rest of the crew.

Shipwright, Bounty: 44 million berries

Sanji

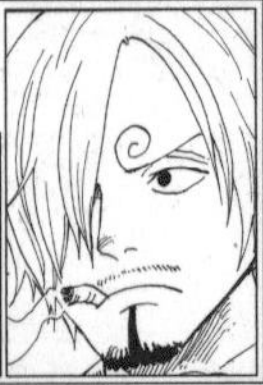

After fighting the New Kama Karate masters in the Kamabakka Kingdom, he returned to the crew.

Cook, Bounty: 77 million berries

Brook

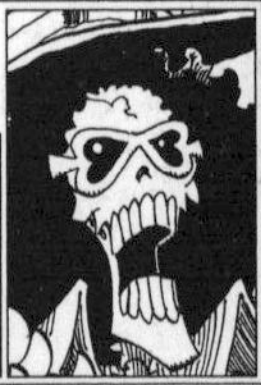

After being captured and used as a freak show by the Longarm Tribe, he became a famous rock star called "Soul King" Brook.

Musician, Bounty: 33 million berries

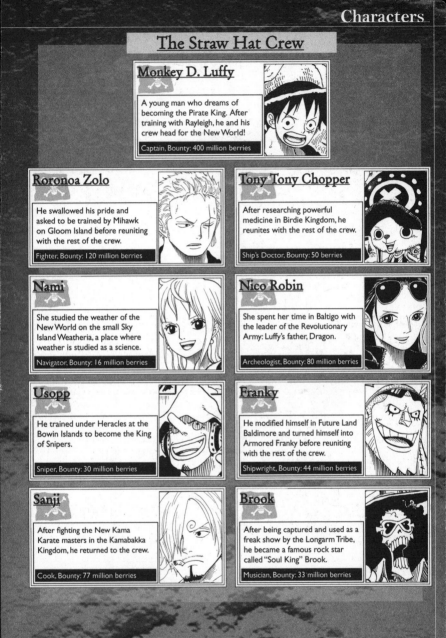

continues to wait for Luffy in the second half of the Grand Line, called the New World.

Captain of the Red-Haired Pirates

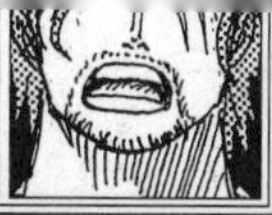

Trafalgar Law

The Surgeon of Death, wielder of the Op-Op Fruit's powers. One of the Seven Warlords of the Sea.

Pirate, Warlord

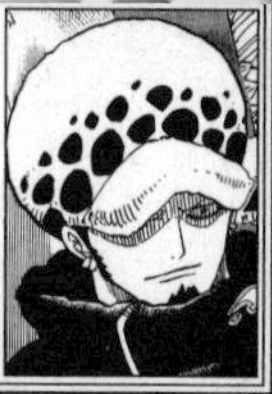

Punk Hazard

Master Caesar Clown

Dr. Vegapunk's former colleague. An authority on weapons of mass-murder, now wanted by the government.

Former gov't scientist

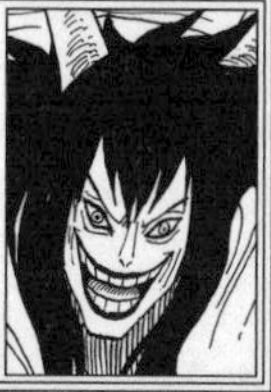

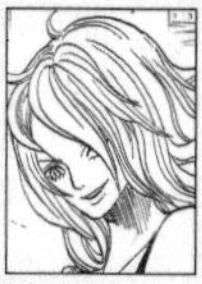

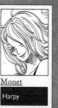

Monet

Harpy

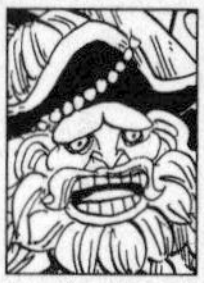

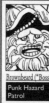

Brownbeard ("Boss")

Punk Hazard Patrol

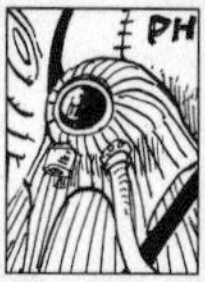
PH

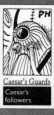

Caesar's Guards

Caesar's followers

Naval G-5: 5th Branch of the Naval Grand Line

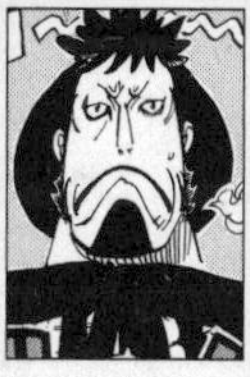

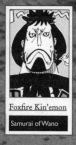

Foxfire Kin'emon

Samurai of Wano

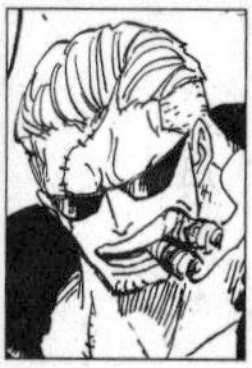

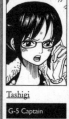

White Chase Smoker

G-5 Vice Admiral

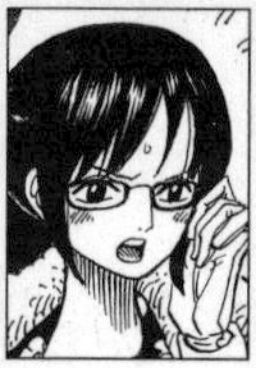

Tashigi

G-5 Captain

Story

Having finished their two years of training, the Straw Hat crew reunites on the Sabaody Archipelago. They finally reached the New World via Fish-Man Island!

The crew lands on Punk Hazard, a mysterious island covered in fire and ice, housing a former government laboratory, and ruled by the mad scientist Caesar Clown. Now it is also host to the Straw Hats, the Navy hot on their heels, and even Trafalgar Law, a newly appointed Warlord of the Sea. When these disparate forces clash, the sparks of battle cover the island!! What is Caesar plotting on Punk Hazard?! Will Kin'emon ever find his son safe and sound?! And will Luffy's pirate alliance with Law really lead him to face off against one of the Four Emperors?!

NEW WORLD

ONE PIECE

Vol. 68
PIRATE ALLIANCE

CONTENTS

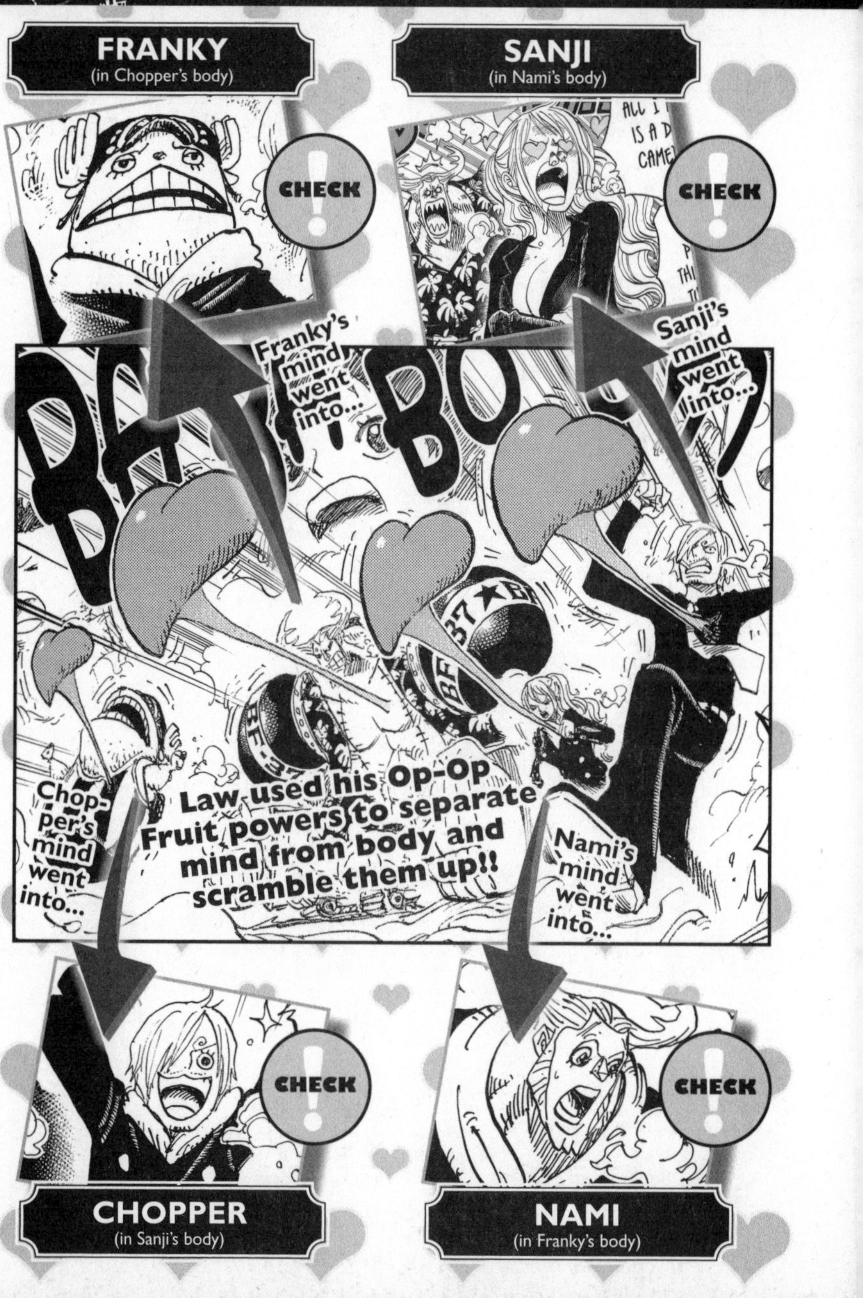
SANJI
(in Nami's body)
CHECK
FRANKY
(in Chopper's body)
CHECK
Sanji's mind went into...
Franky's mind went into...
Nami's mind went into...
Law used his Op-Op Fruit powers to separate mind from body and scramble them up!!
Chop-per's mind went into...
NAMI
(in Franky's body)
CHECK
CHOPPER
(in Sanji's body)
CHECK

SMOKER
(in Tashigi's body)

TASHIGI
(in Smoker's body)

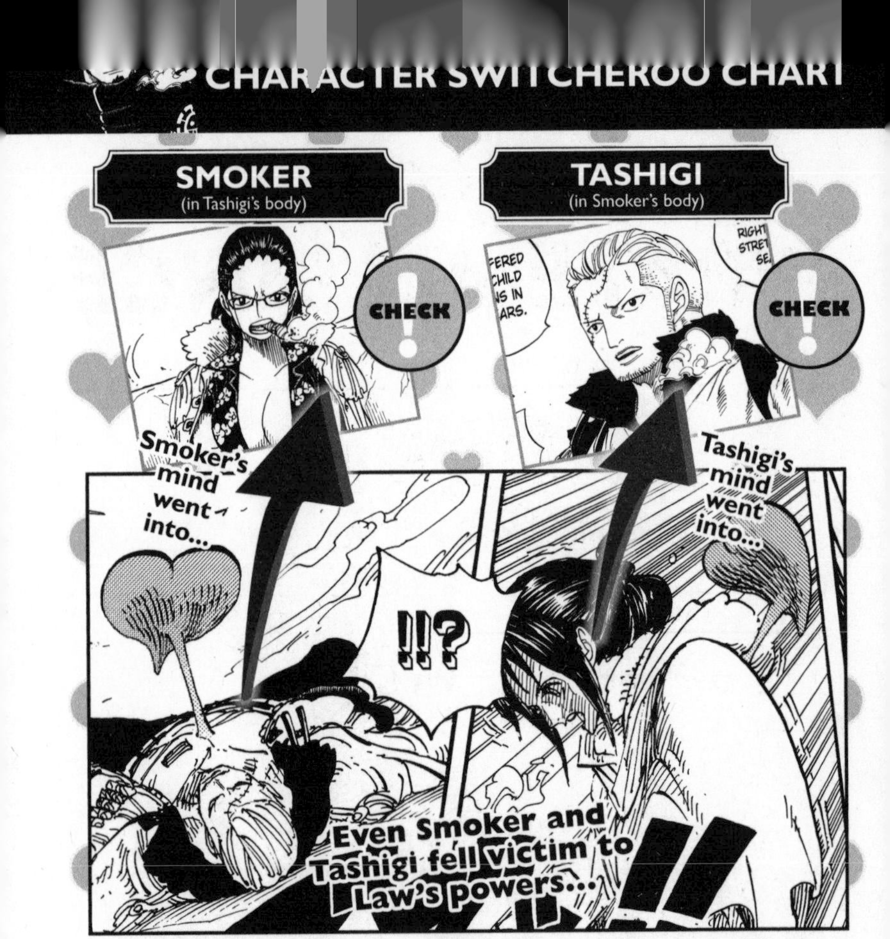
CHECK
CHECK
Smoker's mind went into...
Tashigi's mind went into...
!!?
Even Smoker and Tashigi fell victim to Law's powers...

World Government Recognized Pirate, Warlord of the Sea

TRAFALGAR LAW

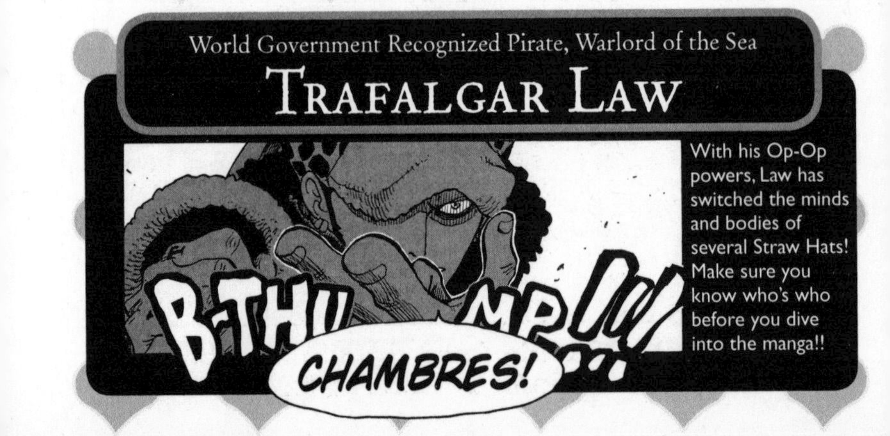
B-THU
MP!!!
CHAMBRES!

With his Op-Op powers, Law has switched the minds and bodies of several Straw Hats! Make sure you know who's who before you dive into the manga!!

Chapter 668:
PIRATE ALLIANCE

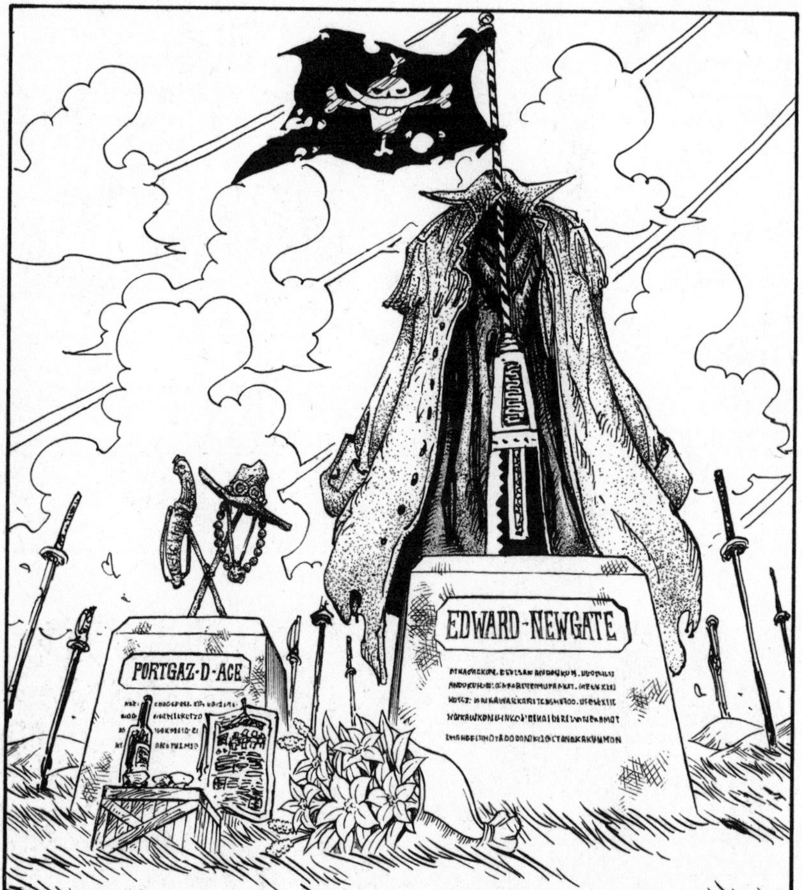
EDWARD-NEWGATE
PORTGAZ-D-ACE

DECKS OF THE WORLD, FINAL VOLUME:
"WHITEBEARD AND ACE'S GRAVES"

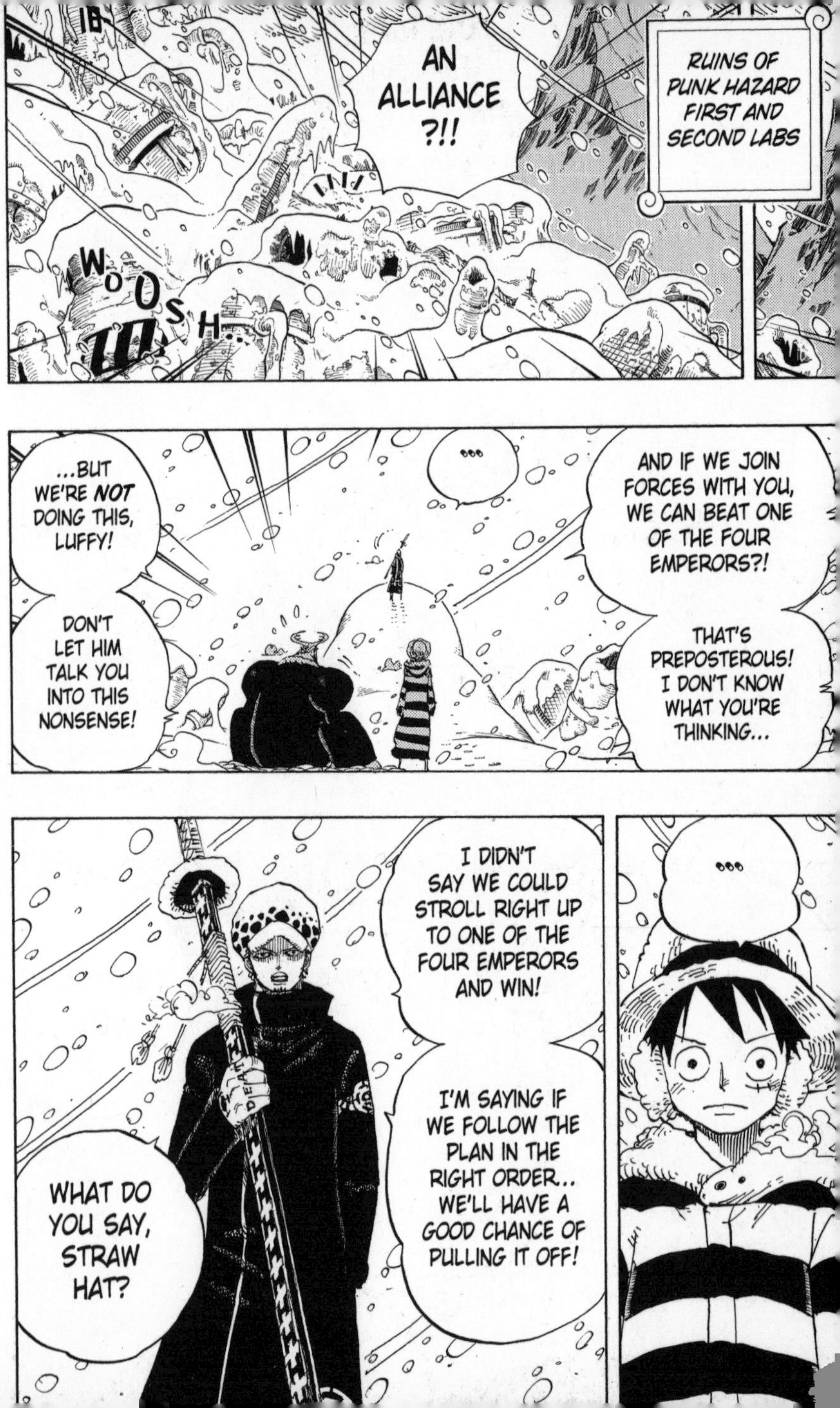
RUINS OF PUNK HAZARD FIRST AND SECOND LABS
AN ALLIANCE ?!!
WOOSH
AND IF WE JOIN FORCES WITH YOU, WE CAN BEAT ONE OF THE FOUR EMPERORS?!
THAT'S PREPOSTEROUS! I DON'T KNOW WHAT YOU'RE THINKING...
...
...BUT WE'RE *NOT* DOING THIS, LUFFY!
DON'T LET HIM TALK YOU INTO THIS NONSENSE!
...
I DIDN'T SAY WE COULD STROLL RIGHT UP TO ONE OF THE FOUR EMPERORS AND WIN!
I'M SAYING IF WE FOLLOW THE PLAN IN THE RIGHT ORDER.. WE'LL HAVE A GOOD CHANCE OF PULLING IT OFF!
WHAT DO YOU SAY, STRAW HAT?

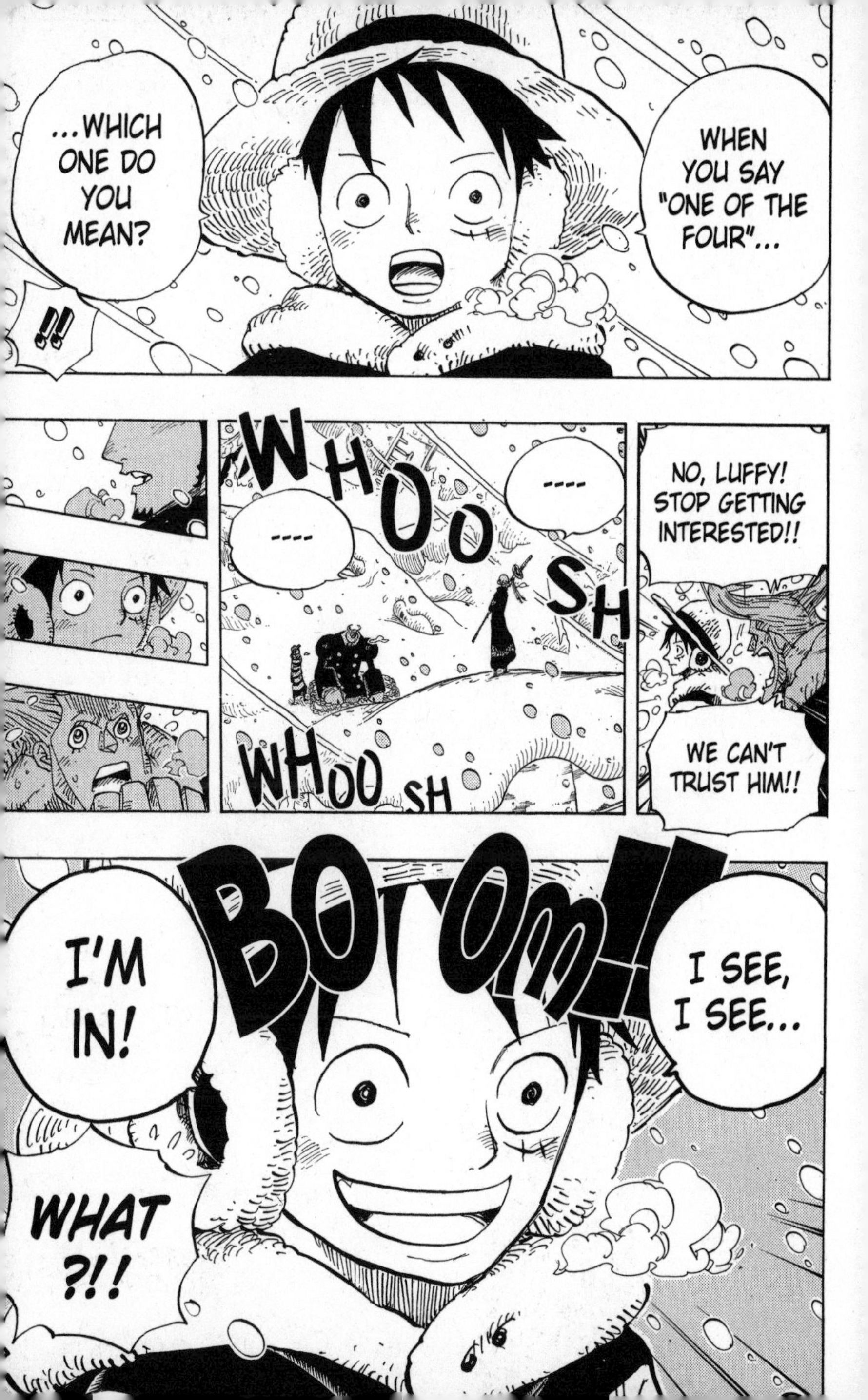
WHEN YOU SAY "ONE OF THE FOUR"...
...WHICH ONE DO YOU MEAN?
!!
NO, LUFFY! STOP GETTING INTERESTED!!
WE CAN'T TRUST HIM!!
WHOOSH

WHOOSH
I SEE, I SEE...
BOOM!!
I'M IN!
WHAT?!!

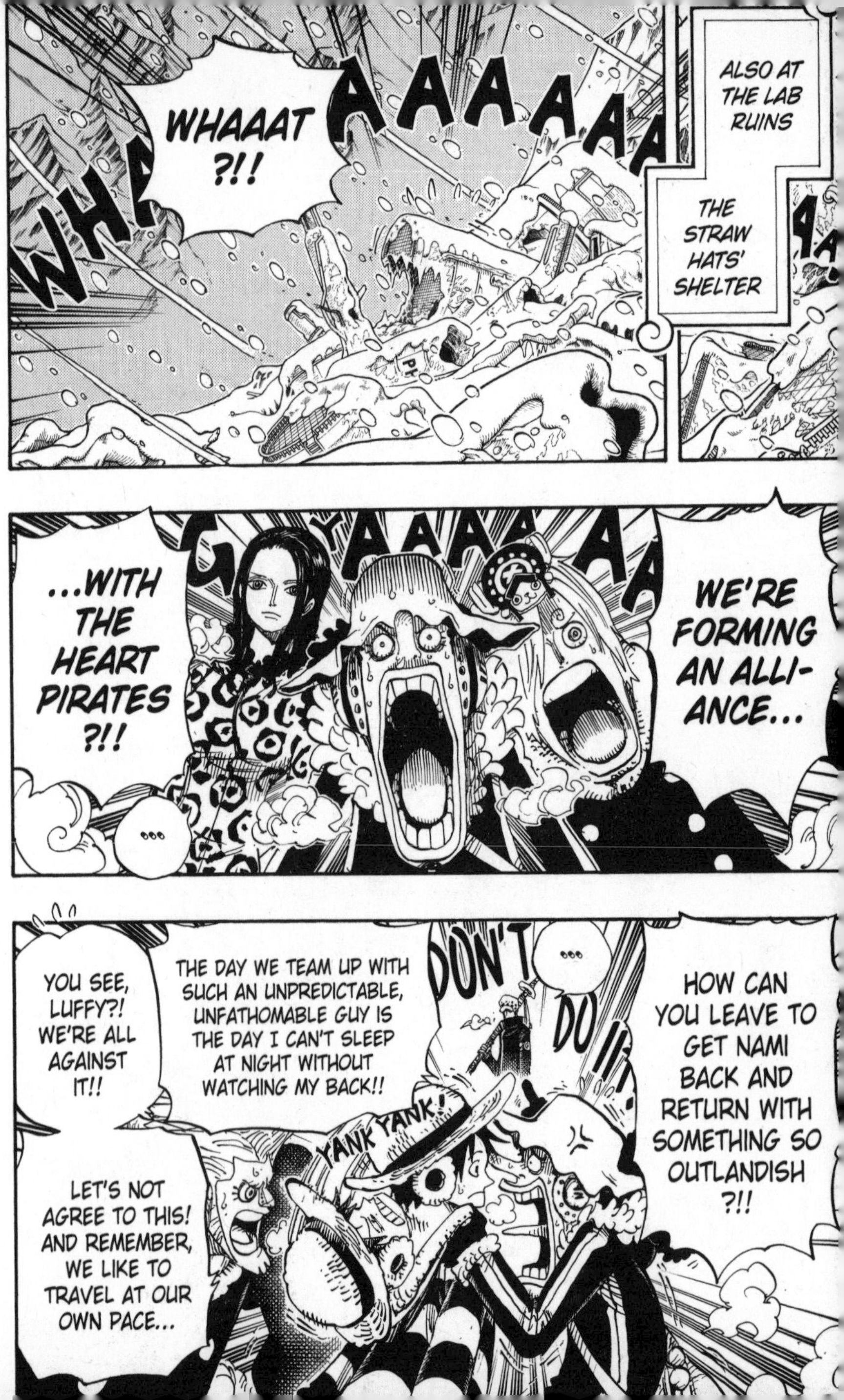

ALSO AT THE LAB RUINS
THE STRAW HATS' SHELTER
WHAAAT ?!!
WHAAAAAAA
WE'RE FORMING AN ALLI-ANCE...
GYAAAAAAA
...WITH THE HEART PIRATES ?!!
...
HOW CAN YOU LEAVE TO GET NAMI BACK AND RETURN WITH SOMETHING SO OUTLANDISH ?!!
...
DON'T DO IT!
YANK YANK!
THE DAY WE TEAM UP WITH SUCH AN UNPREDICTABLE, UNFATHOMABLE GUY IS THE DAY I CAN'T SLEEP AT NIGHT WITHOUT WATCHING MY BACK!!
YOU SEE, LUFFY?! WE'RE ALL AGAINST IT!!
LET'S NOT AGREE TO THIS! AND REMEMBER, WE LIKE TO TRAVEL AT OUR OWN PACE...

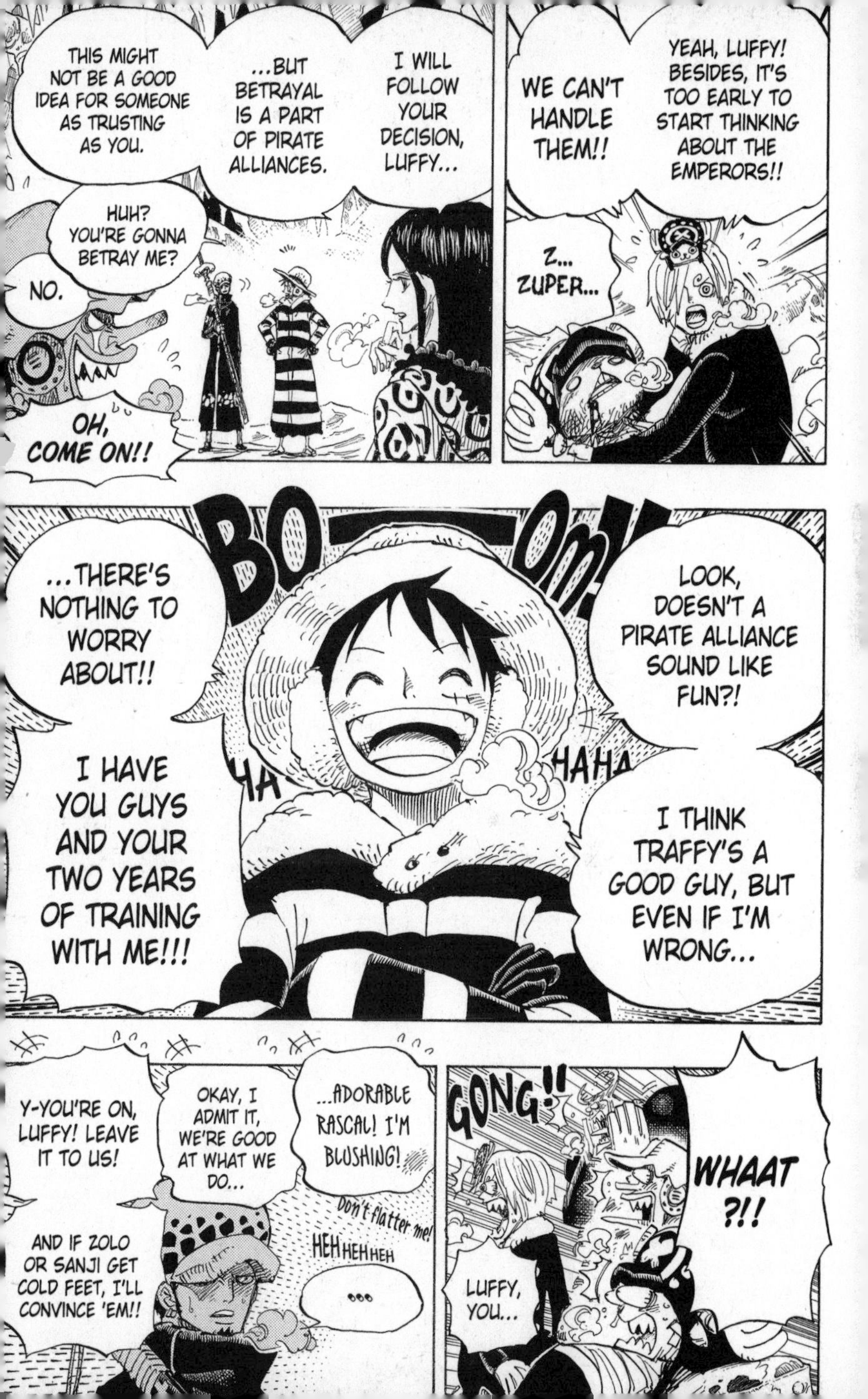
YEAH, LUFFY! BESIDES, IT'S TOO EARLY TO START THINKING ABOUT THE EMPERORS!!
WE CAN'T HANDLE THEM!!
Z... ZUPER...
I WILL FOLLOW YOUR DECISION, LUFFY...
...BUT BETRAYAL IS A PART OF PIRATE ALLIANCES.
THIS MIGHT NOT BE A GOOD IDEA FOR SOMEONE AS TRUSTING AS YOU.
HUH? YOU'RE GONNA BETRAY ME?
NO.
OH, COME ON!!
BO—OM!!
LOOK, DOESN'T A PIRATE ALLIANCE SOUND LIKE FUN?!
I THINK TRAFFY'S A GOOD GUY, BUT EVEN IF I'M WRONG...
HAHA
HA
...THERE'S NOTHING TO WORRY ABOUT!!
I HAVE YOU GUYS AND YOUR TWO YEARS OF TRAINING WITH ME!!!
GONG!!
WHAAT?!!
LUFFY, YOU...
...ADORABLE RASCAL! I'M BLUSHING!
Don't flatter me!
OKAY, I ADMIT IT, WE'RE GOOD AT WHAT WE DO...
Y-YOU'RE ON, LUFFY! LEAVE IT TO US!
HEH HEH HEH
...
AND IF ZOLO OR SANJI GET COLD FEET, I'LL CONVINCE 'EM!!

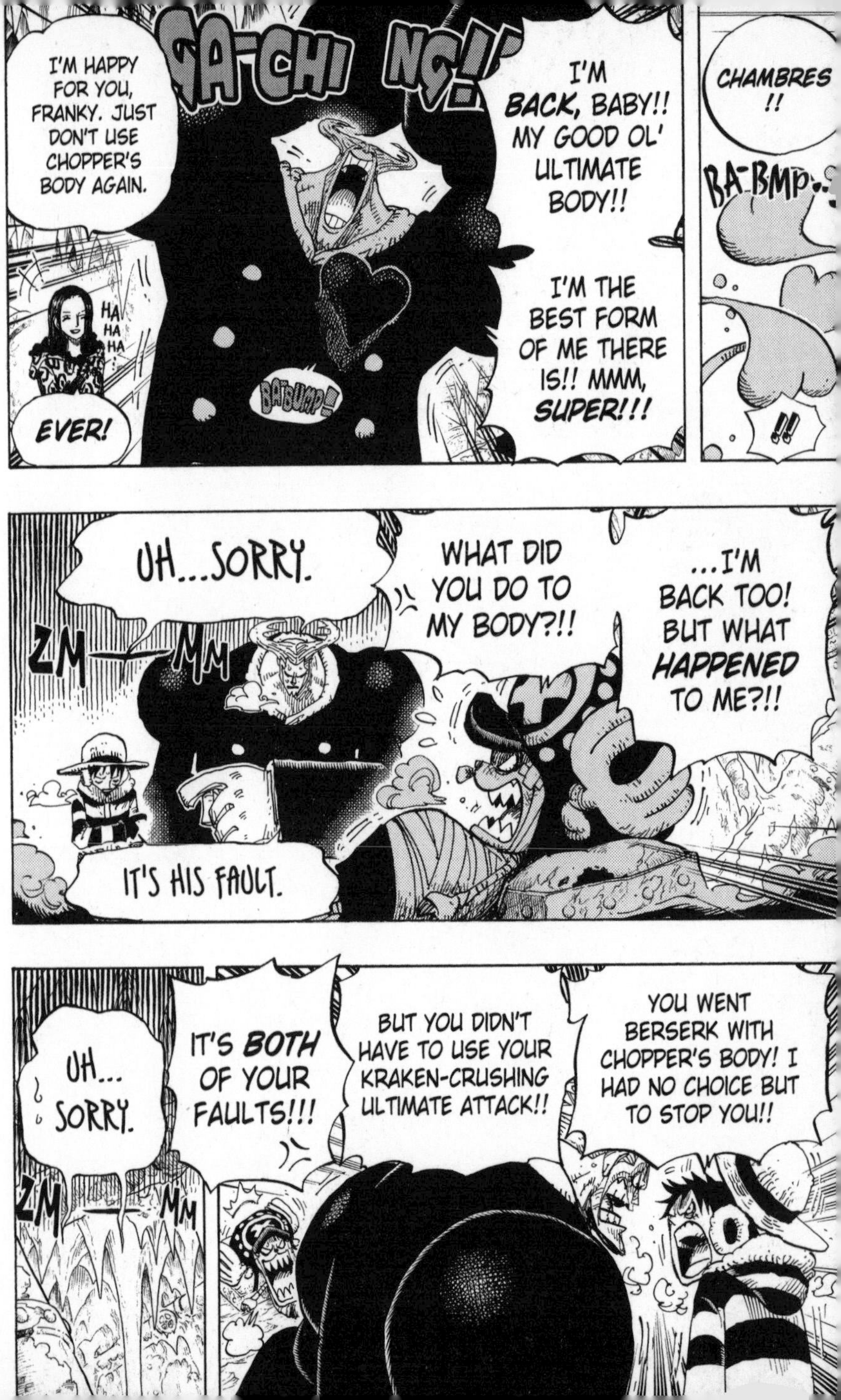
CHAMBRES !!
BA-BMP
!!
GA-CHI NG!!
I'M BACK, BABY!! MY GOOD OL' ULTIMATE BODY!!
I'M THE BEST FORM OF ME THERE IS!! MMM, SUPER!!!
BA-BUMP!!
I'M HAPPY FOR YOU, FRANKY. JUST DON'T USE CHOPPER'S BODY AGAIN.
HA HA HA
EVER!
...I'M BACK TOO! BUT WHAT HAPPENED TO ME?!!
WHAT DID YOU DO TO MY BODY?!!
UH...SORRY.
ZM—MM
IT'S HIS FAULT.
YOU WENT BERSERK WITH CHOPPER'S BODY! I HAD NO CHOICE BUT TO STOP YOU!!
BUT YOU DIDN'T HAVE TO USE YOUR KRAKEN-CRUSHING ULTIMATE ATTACK!!
IT'S BOTH OF YOUR FAULTS!!!
UH... SORRY.
ZM—MM

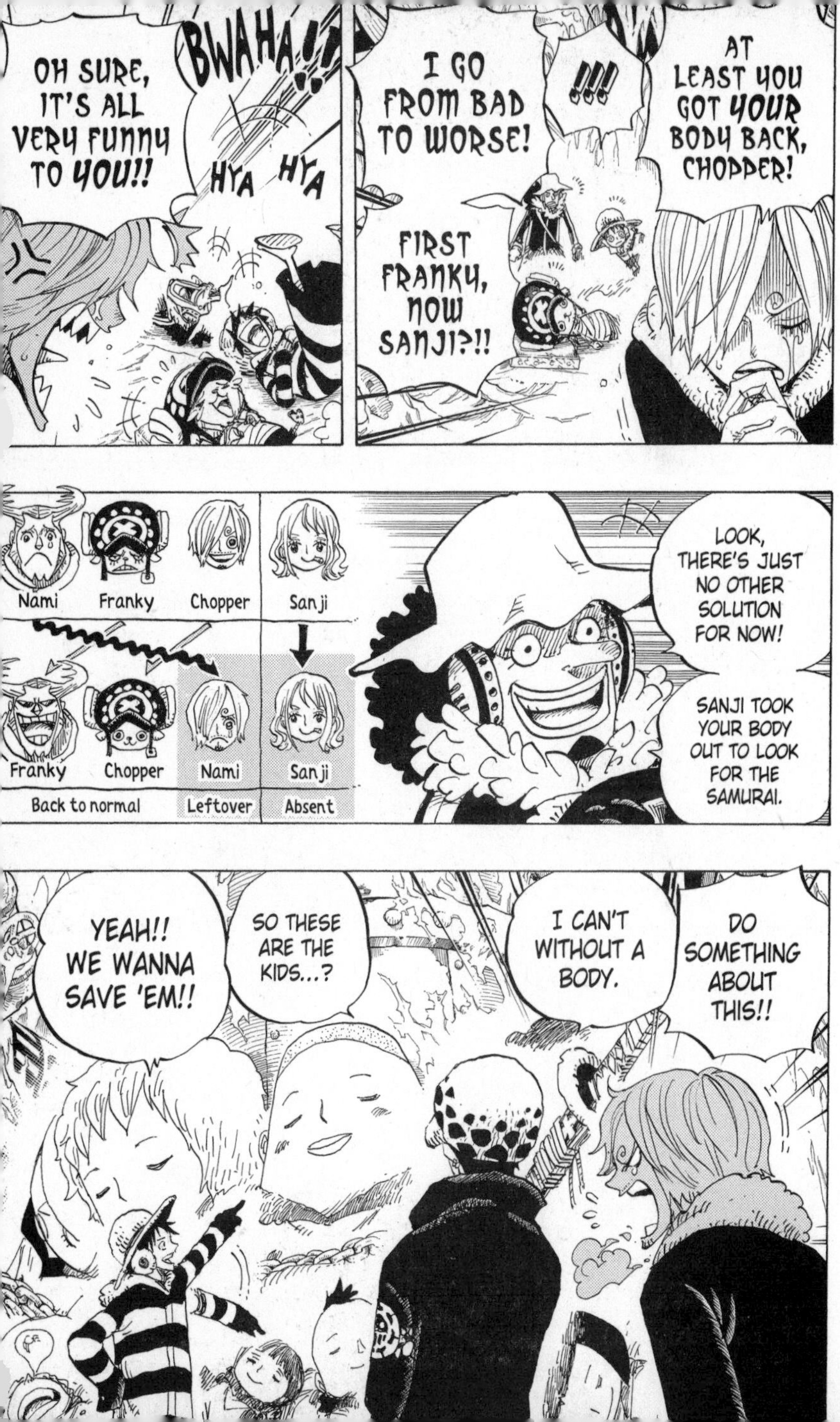
AT LEAST YOU GOT YOUR BODY BACK, CHOPPER!
!!!
I GO FROM BAD TO WORSE!
FIRST FRANKY, NOW SANJI?!!
BWAHA!!
HYA HYA
OH SURE, IT'S ALL VERY FUNNY TO YOU!!
LOOK, THERE'S JUST NO OTHER SOLUTION FOR NOW!
SANJI TOOK YOUR BODY OUT TO LOOK FOR THE SAMURAI.
Nami
Franky
Chopper
Sanji
Franky
Chopper
Nami
Sanji
Back to normal
Leftover
Absent
DO SOMETHING ABOUT THIS!!
I CAN'T WITHOUT A BODY.
SO THESE ARE THE KIDS...?
YEAH!! WE WANNA SAVE 'EM!!

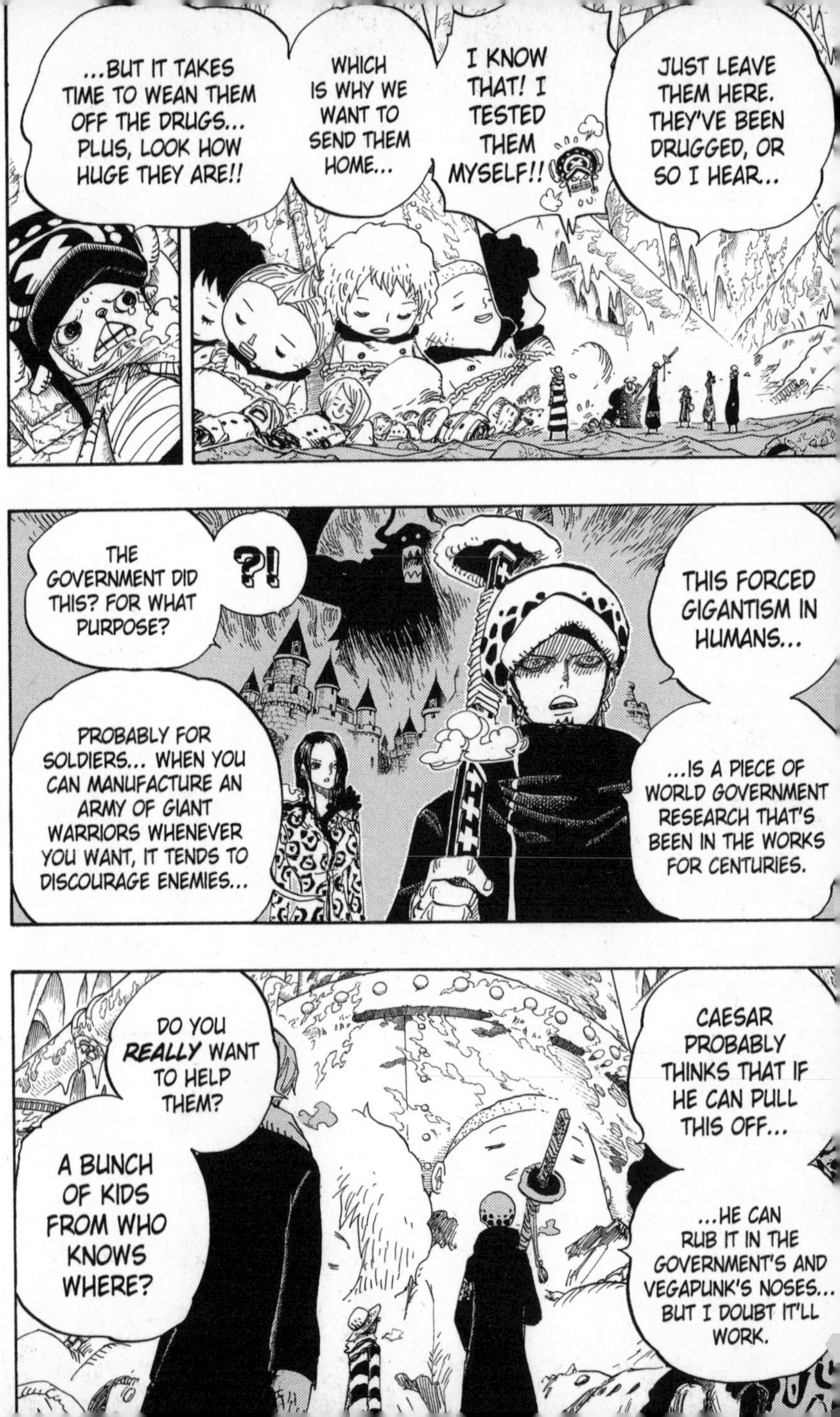
JUST LEAVE THEM HERE. THEY'VE BEEN DRUGGED, OR SO I HEAR...
I KNOW THAT! I TESTED THEM MYSELF!!
WHICH IS WHY WE WANT TO SEND THEM HOME...
...BUT IT TAKES TIME TO WEAN THEM OFF THE DRUGS... PLUS, LOOK HOW HUGE THEY ARE!!
THIS FORCED GIGANTISM IN HUMANS...
...IS A PIECE OF WORLD GOVERNMENT RESEARCH THAT'S BEEN IN THE WORKS FOR CENTURIES.
?!
THE GOVERNMENT DID THIS? FOR WHAT PURPOSE?
PROBABLY FOR SOLDIERS... WHEN YOU CAN MANUFACTURE AN ARMY OF GIANT WARRIORS WHENEVER YOU WANT, IT TENDS TO DISCOURAGE ENEMIES...
CAESAR PROBABLY THINKS THAT IF HE CAN PULL THIS OFF...
...HE CAN RUB IT IN THE GOVERNMENT'S AND VEGAPUNK'S NOSES... BUT I DOUBT IT'LL WORK.
DO YOU ***REALLY*** WANT TO HELP THEM?
A BUNCH OF KIDS FROM WHO KNOWS WHERE?

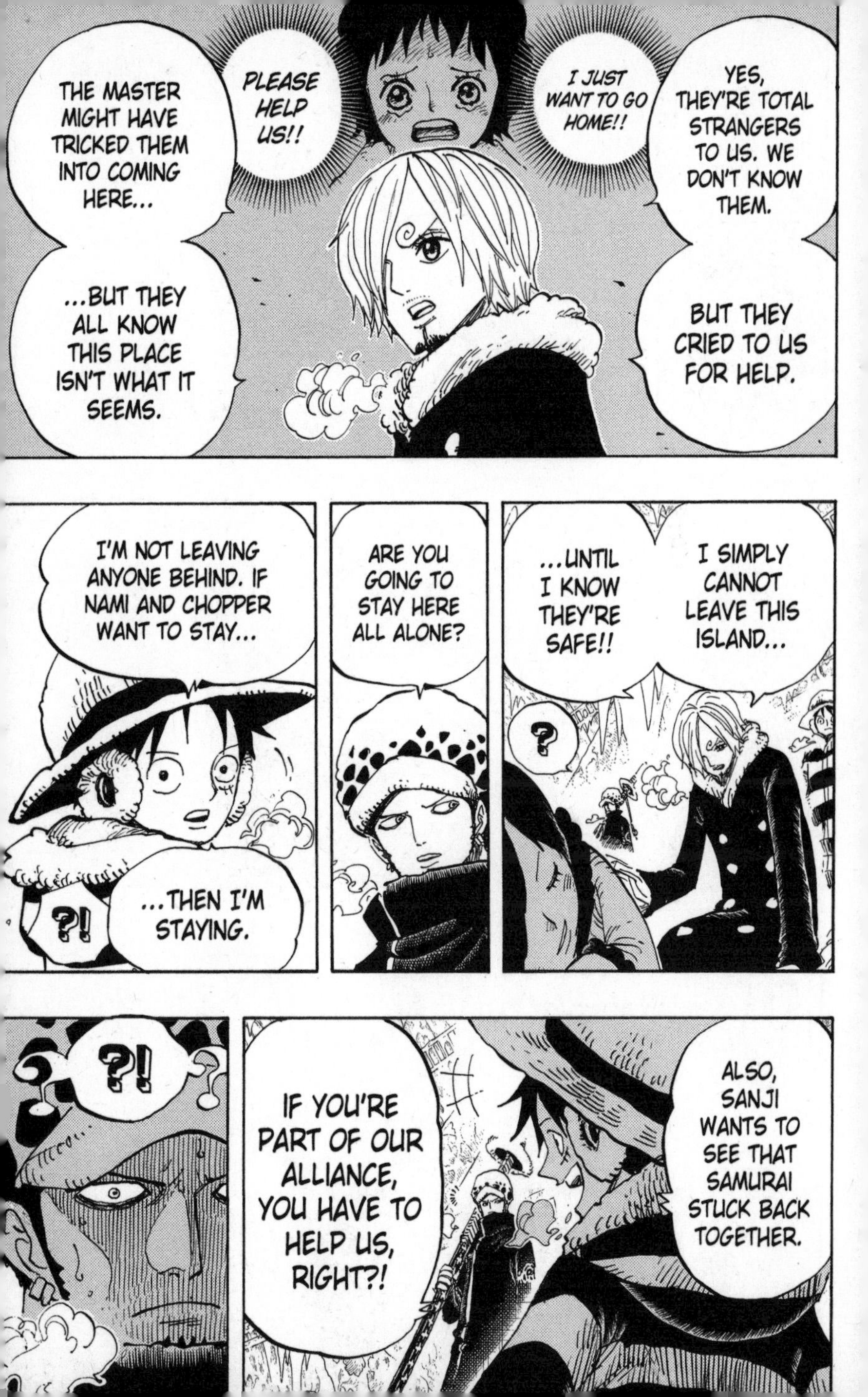
YES, THEY'RE TOTAL STRANGERS TO US. WE DON'T KNOW THEM.
BUT THEY CRIED TO US FOR HELP.
I JUST WANT TO GO HOME!!
PLEASE HELP US!!
THE MASTER MIGHT HAVE TRICKED THEM INTO COMING HERE...
...BUT THEY ALL KNOW THIS PLACE ISN'T WHAT IT SEEMS.
I SIMPLY CANNOT LEAVE THIS ISLAND...
...UNTIL I KNOW THEY'RE SAFE!!
?
ARE YOU GOING TO STAY HERE ALL ALONE?
I'M NOT LEAVING ANYONE BEHIND. IF NAMI AND CHOPPER WANT TO STAY...
...THEN I'M STAYING.
?!
ALSO, SANJI WANTS TO SEE THAT SAMURAI STUCK BACK TOGETHER.
IF YOU'RE PART OF OUR ALLIANCE, YOU HAVE TO HELP US, RIGHT?!
?!

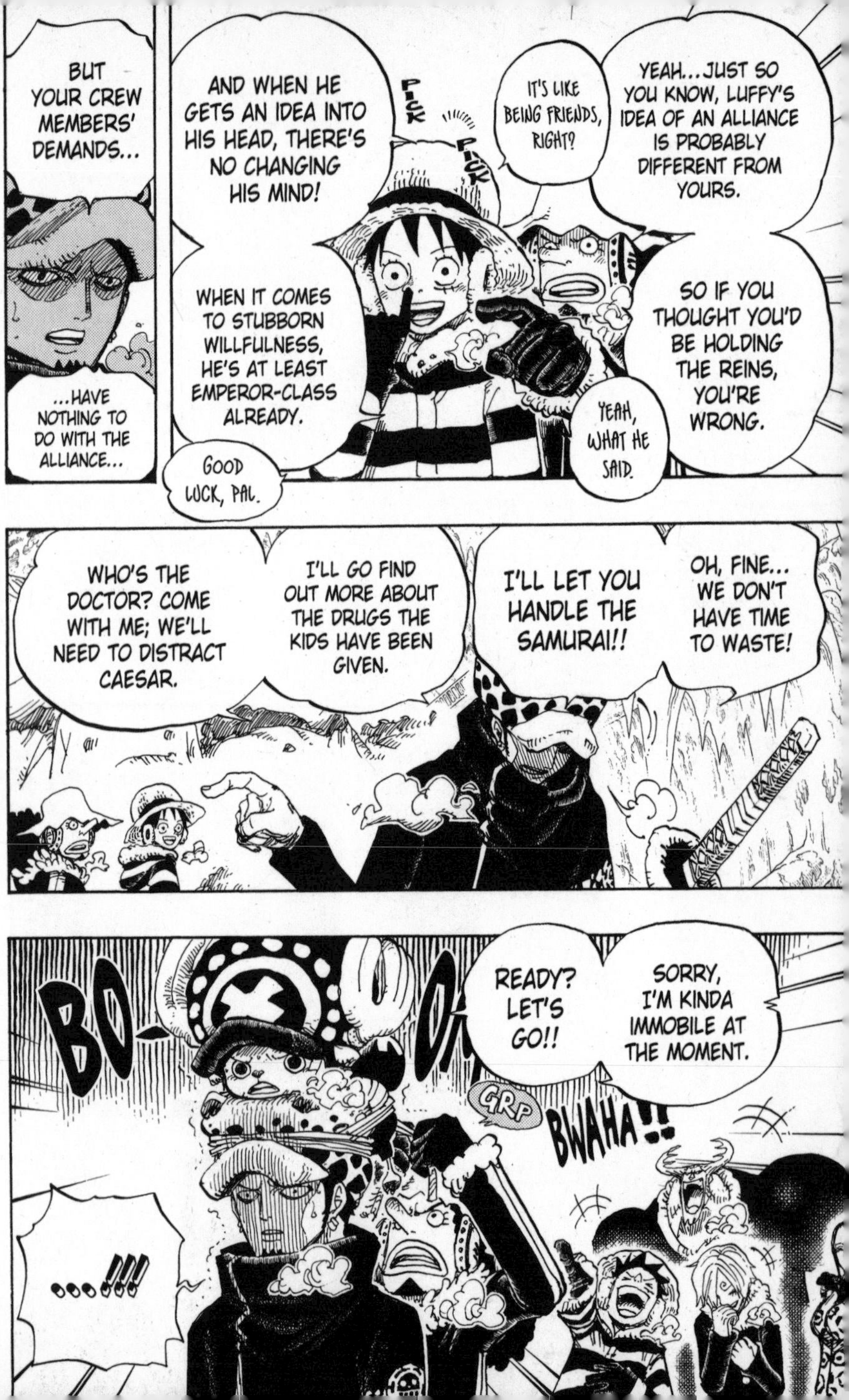
YEAH...JUST SO YOU KNOW, LUFFY'S IDEA OF AN ALLIANCE IS PROBABLY DIFFERENT FROM YOURS.
IT'S LIKE BEING FRIENDS, RIGHT?
PICK
PICK
AND WHEN HE GETS AN IDEA INTO HIS HEAD, THERE'S NO CHANGING HIS MIND!
SO IF YOU THOUGHT YOU'D BE HOLDING THE REINS, YOU'RE WRONG.
YEAH, WHAT HE SAID.
WHEN IT COMES TO STUBBORN WILLFULNESS, HE'S AT LEAST EMPEROR-CLASS ALREADY.
GOOD LUCK, PAL.
BUT YOUR CREW MEMBERS' DEMANDS...
...HAVE NOTHING TO DO WITH THE ALLIANCE...
OH, FINE... WE DON'T HAVE TIME TO WASTE!
I'LL LET YOU HANDLE THE SAMURAI!!
I'LL GO FIND OUT MORE ABOUT THE DRUGS THE KIDS HAVE BEEN GIVEN.
WHO'S THE DOCTOR? COME WITH ME; WE'LL NEED TO DISTRACT CAESAR.
SORRY, I'M KINDA IMMOBILE AT THE MOMENT.
READY? LET'S GO!!
BO-
GRP
BWAHA!!
...!!!

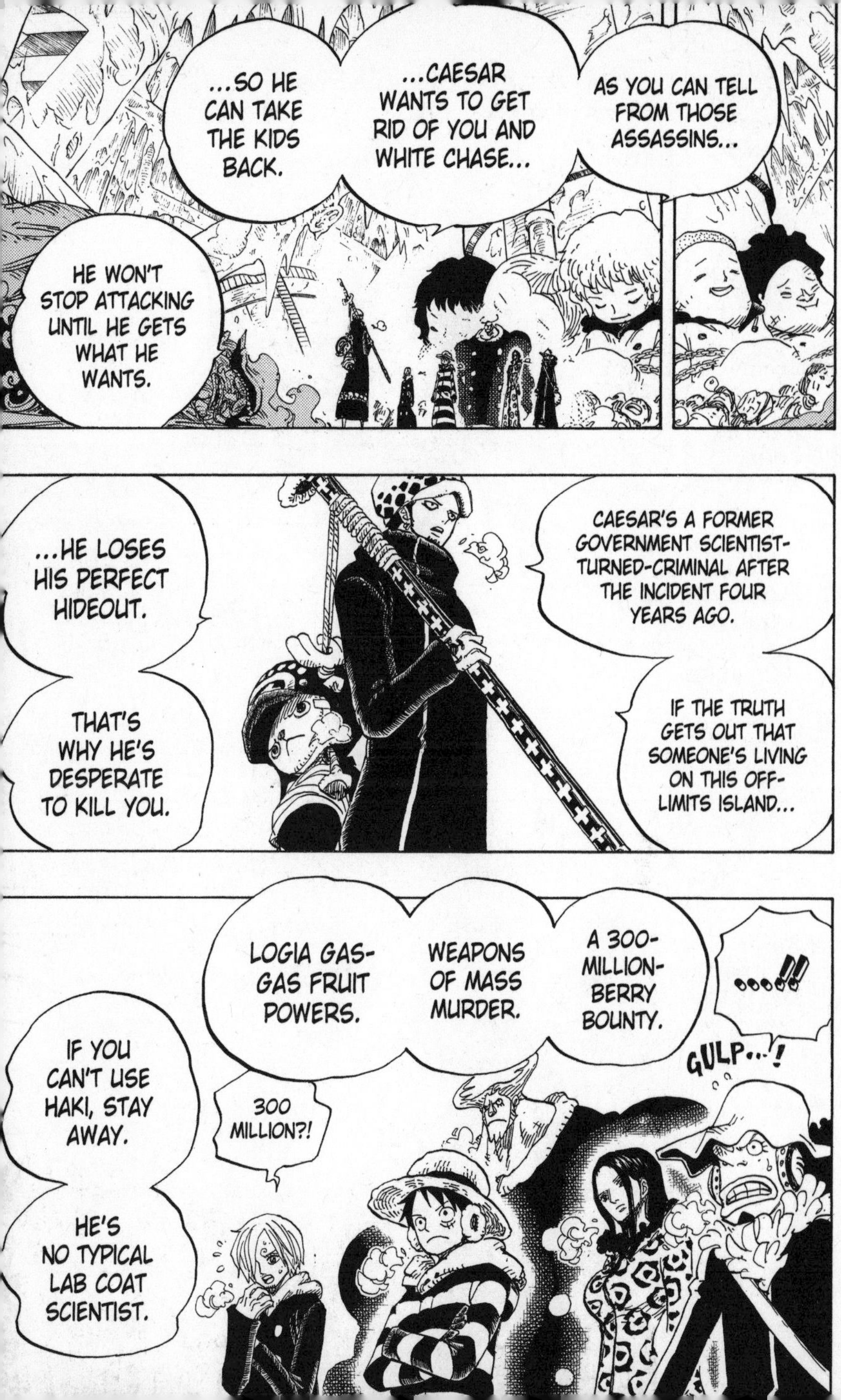
AS YOU CAN TELL FROM THOSE ASSASSINS...
...CAESAR WANTS TO GET RID OF YOU AND WHITE CHASE...
...SO HE CAN TAKE THE KIDS BACK.
HE WON'T STOP ATTACKING UNTIL HE GETS WHAT HE WANTS.
CAESAR'S A FORMER GOVERNMENT SCIENTIST-TURNED-CRIMINAL AFTER THE INCIDENT FOUR YEARS AGO.
IF THE TRUTH GETS OUT THAT SOMEONE'S LIVING ON THIS OFF-LIMITS ISLAND...
...HE LOSES HIS PERFECT HIDEOUT.
THAT'S WHY HE'S DESPERATE TO KILL YOU.
.....!!
GULP...!
A 300-MILLION-BERRY BOUNTY.
WEAPONS OF MASS MURDER.
LOGIA GAS-GAS FRUIT POWERS.
300 MILLION?!
IF YOU CAN'T USE HAKI, STAY AWAY.
HE'S NO TYPICAL LAB COAT SCIENTIST.

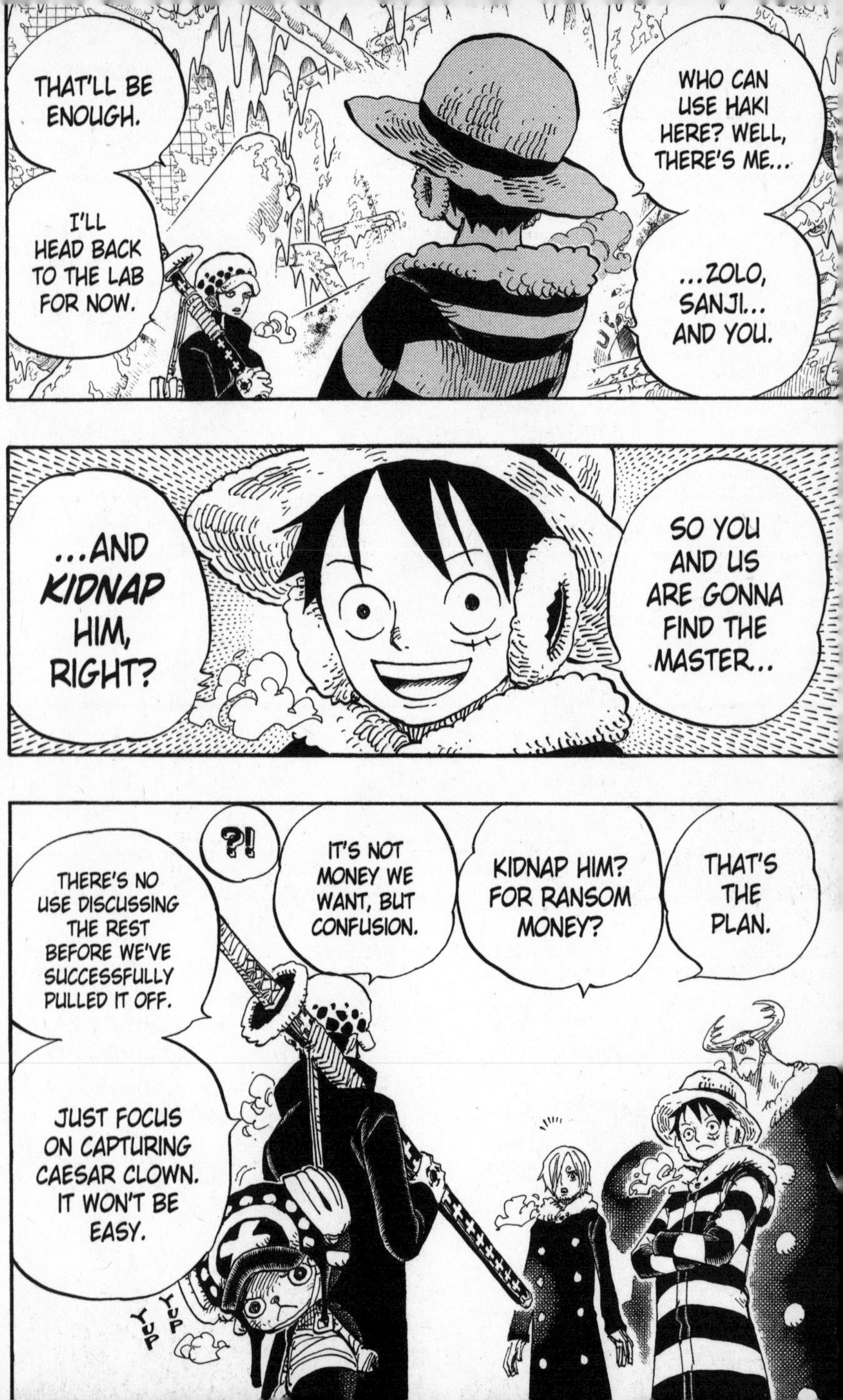
WHO CAN USE HAKI HERE? WELL, THERE'S ME...
...ZOLO, SANJI... AND YOU.
THAT'LL BE ENOUGH.
I'LL HEAD BACK TO THE LAB FOR NOW.
SO YOU AND US ARE GONNA FIND THE MASTER...
...AND *KIDNAP* HIM, RIGHT?
THAT'S THE PLAN.
KIDNAP HIM? FOR RANSOM MONEY?
IT'S NOT MONEY WE WANT, BUT CONFUSION.
?!
THERE'S NO USE DISCUSSING THE REST BEFORE WE'VE SUCCESSFULLY PULLED IT OFF.
JUST FOCUS ON CAPTURING CAESAR CLOWN. IT WON'T BE EASY.
YUP YUP

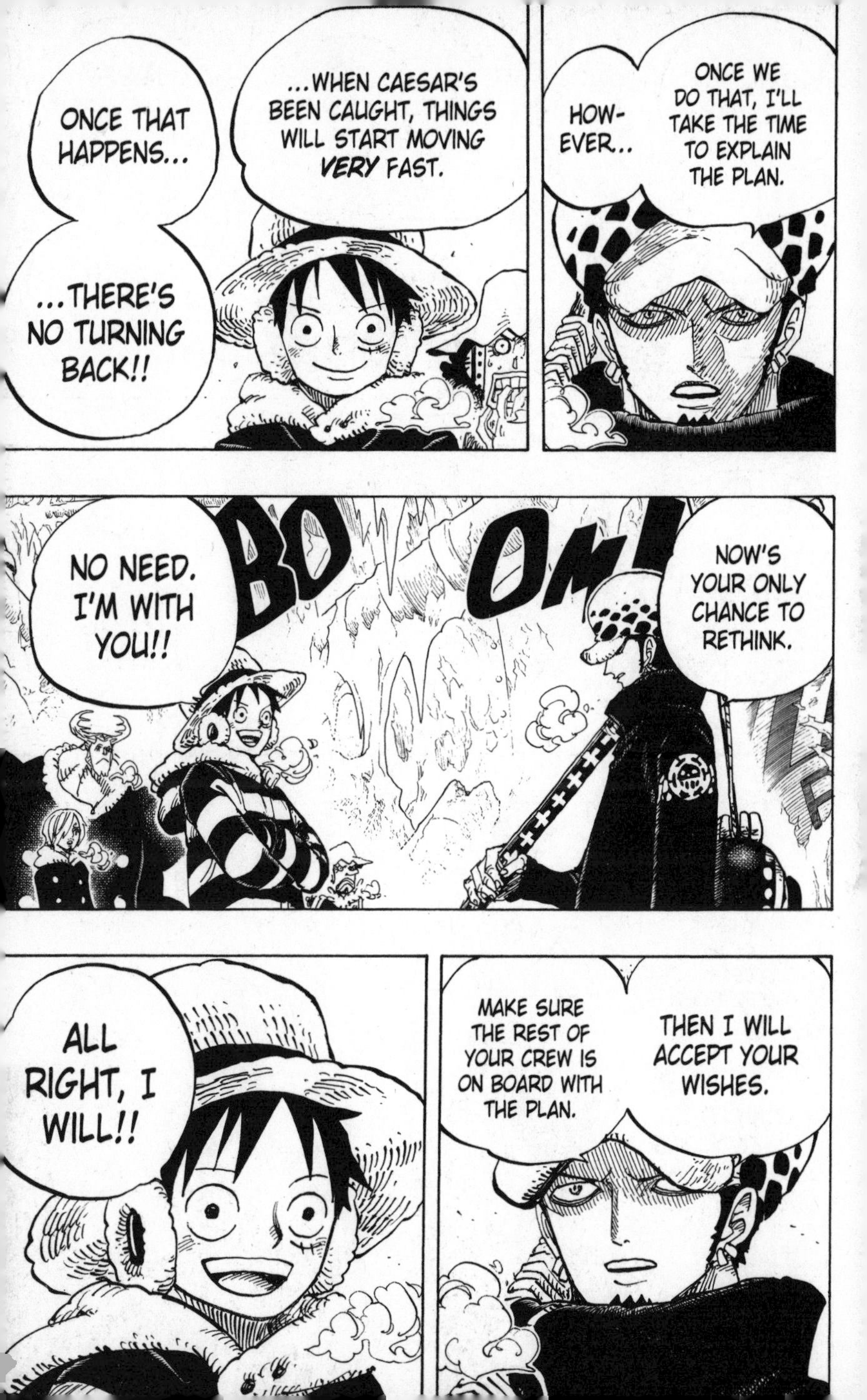
HOW-EVER...
ONCE WE DO THAT, I'LL TAKE THE TIME TO EXPLAIN THE PLAN.
...WHEN CAESAR'S BEEN CAUGHT, THINGS WILL START MOVING *VERY* FAST.
ONCE THAT HAPPENS...
...THERE'S NO TURNING BACK!!
NOW'S YOUR ONLY CHANCE TO RETHINK.
BOOM!
NO NEED. I'M WITH YOU!!
MAKE SURE THE REST OF YOUR CREW IS ON BOARD WITH THE PLAN.
THEN I WILL ACCEPT YOUR WISHES.
ALL RIGHT, I WILL!!

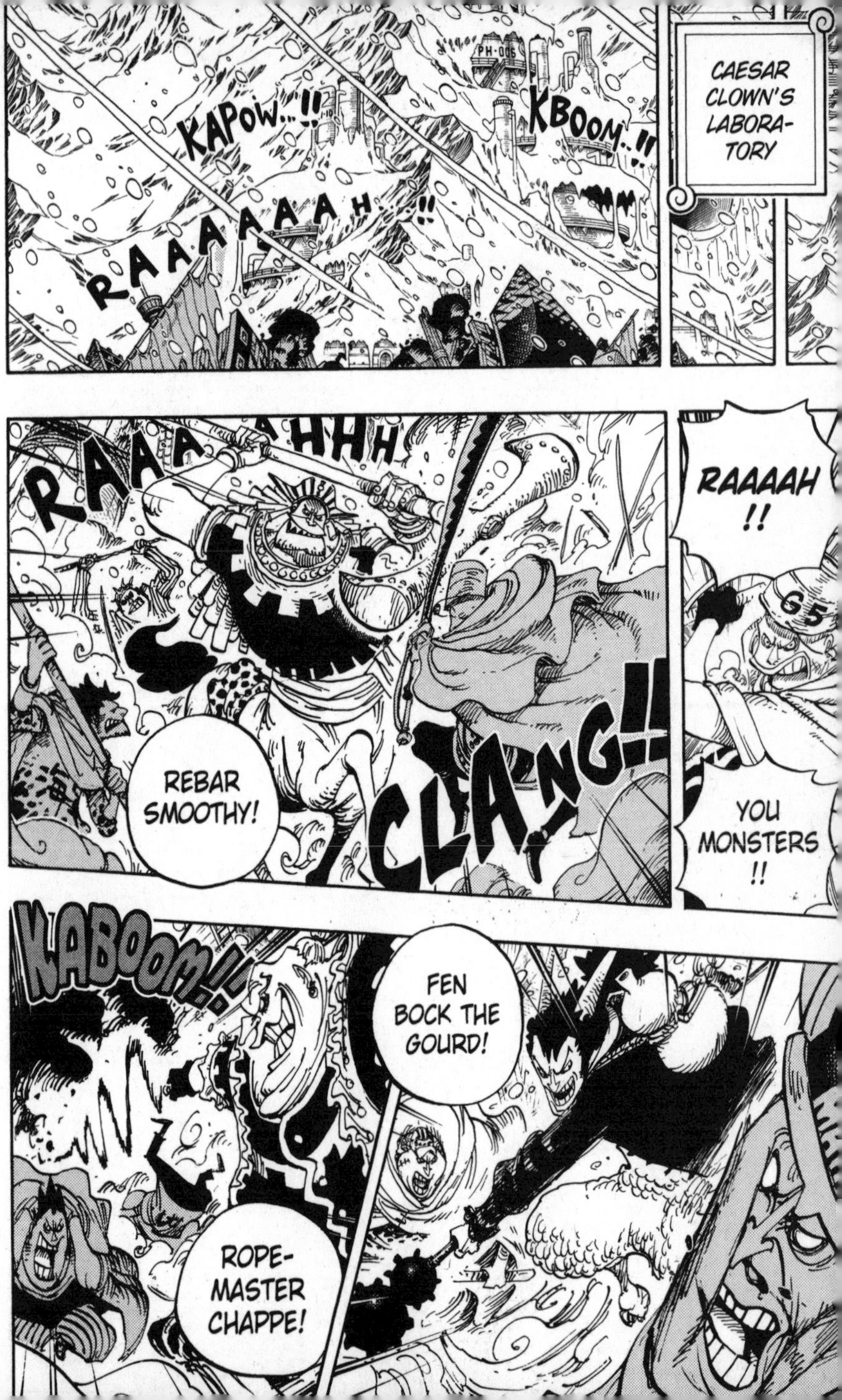
CAESAR CLOWN'S LABORA-TORY
KBOOM..!!
KAPOW...!!
RAAAAAAH..!!
RAAAAH!!
YOU MONSTERS!!
RAAAHHHH
CLANG!!
REBAR SMOOTHY!
FEN BOCK THE GOURD!
KABOOM!!
ROPE-MASTER CHAPPE!

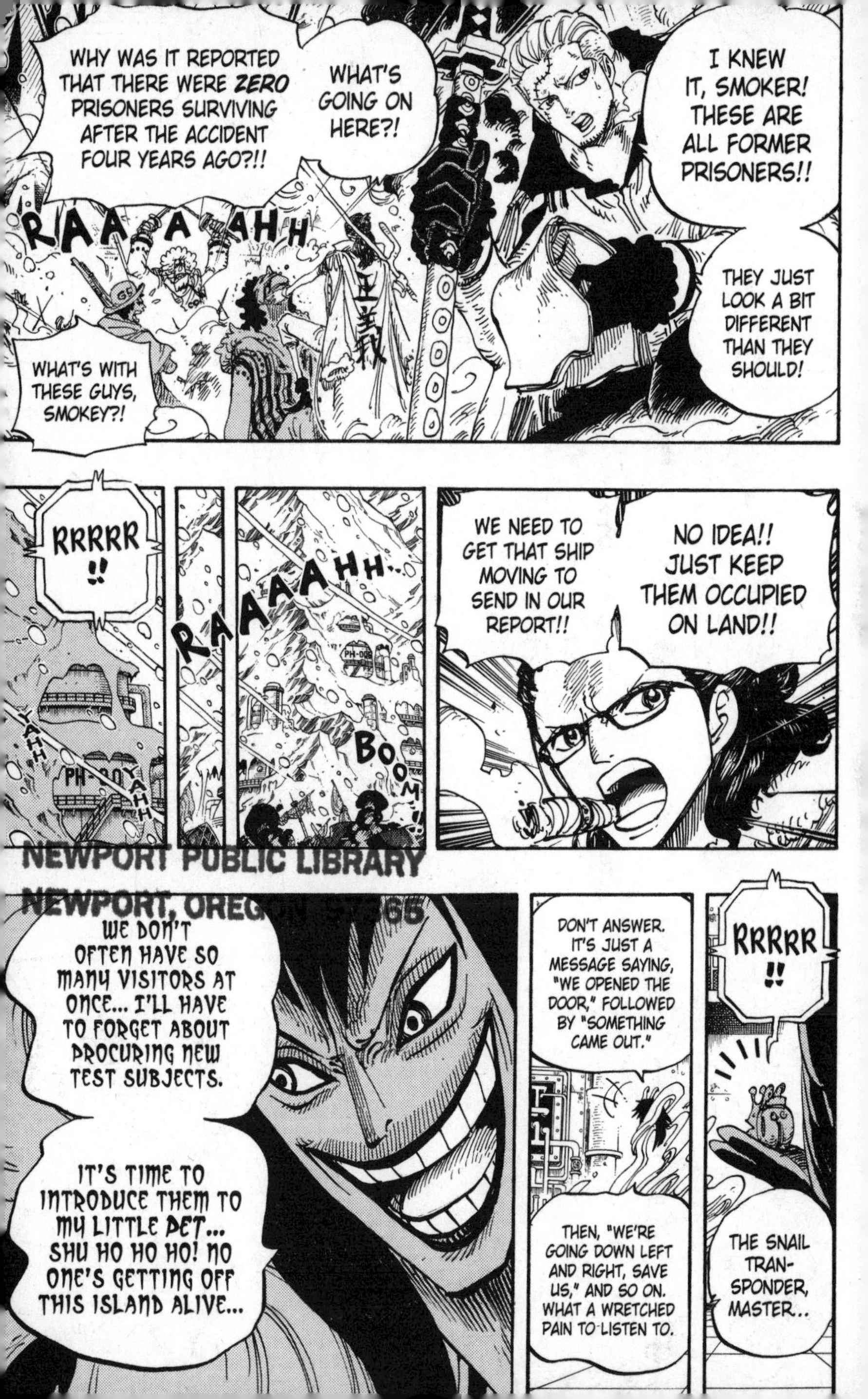
I KNEW IT, SMOKER! THESE ARE ALL FORMER PRISONERS!!
THEY JUST LOOK A BIT DIFFERENT THAN THEY SHOULD!
WHAT'S GOING ON HERE?!
WHY WAS IT REPORTED THAT THERE WERE ZERO PRISONERS SURVIVING AFTER THE ACCIDENT FOUR YEARS AGO?!!
RAAAAHH
WHAT'S WITH THESE GUYS, SMOKEY?!
NO IDEA!! JUST KEEP THEM OCCUPIED ON LAND!!
WE NEED TO GET THAT SHIP MOVING TO SEND IN OUR REPORT!!
RAAAAHH...
BOOOM
RRRRR!!
YAHH
YAHH
RRRRR!!
THE SNAIL TRAN-SPONDER, MASTER...
DON'T ANSWER. IT'S JUST A MESSAGE SAYING, "WE OPENED THE DOOR," FOLLOWED BY "SOMETHING CAME OUT."
THEN, "WE'RE GOING DOWN LEFT AND RIGHT, SAVE US," AND SO ON. WHAT A WRETCHED PAIN TO LISTEN TO.
WE DON'T OFTEN HAVE SO MANY VISITORS AT ONCE... I'LL HAVE TO FORGET ABOUT PROCURING NEW TEST SUBJECTS.
IT'S TIME TO INTRODUCE THEM TO MY LITTLE PET... SHU HO HO HO! NO ONE'S GETTING OFF THIS ISLAND ALIVE...

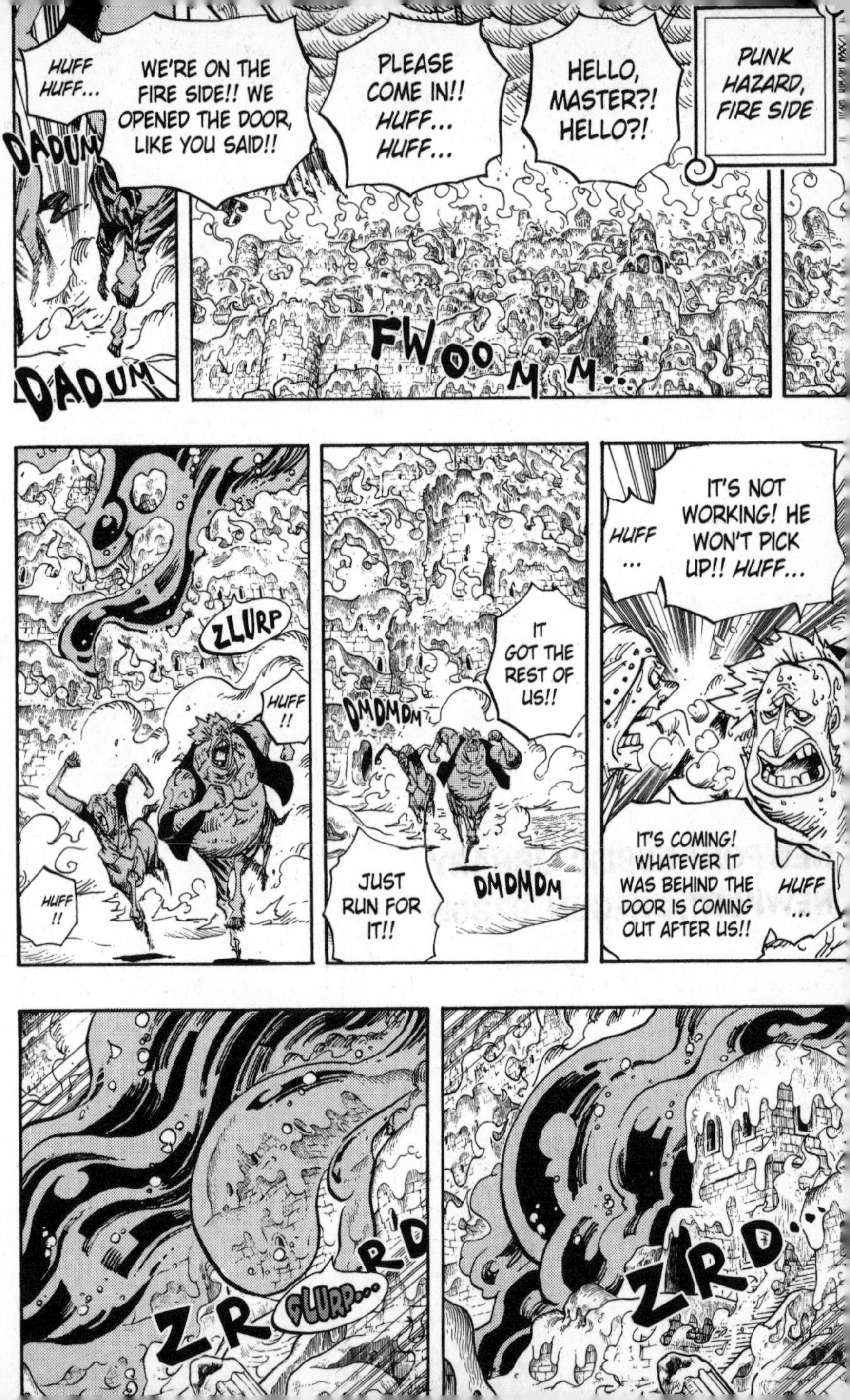

PUNK HAZARD, FIRE SIDE
HELLO, MASTER?! HELLO?!
PLEASE COME IN!! HUFF... HUFF...
FWOOMM...
WE'RE ON THE FIRE SIDE!! WE OPENED THE DOOR, LIKE YOU SAID!!
HUFF HUFF...
DADUM
DADUM
IT'S NOT WORKING! HE WON'T PICK UP!! HUFF...
HUFF ...
IT'S COMING! WHATEVER IT WAS BEHIND THE DOOR IS COMING OUT AFTER US!!
HUFF ...
IT GOT THE REST OF US!!
DMDMDM
DMDMDM
JUST RUN FOR IT!!
ZLURP
HUFF !!
HUFF !!
ZRD
RD
ZR
GLURP...

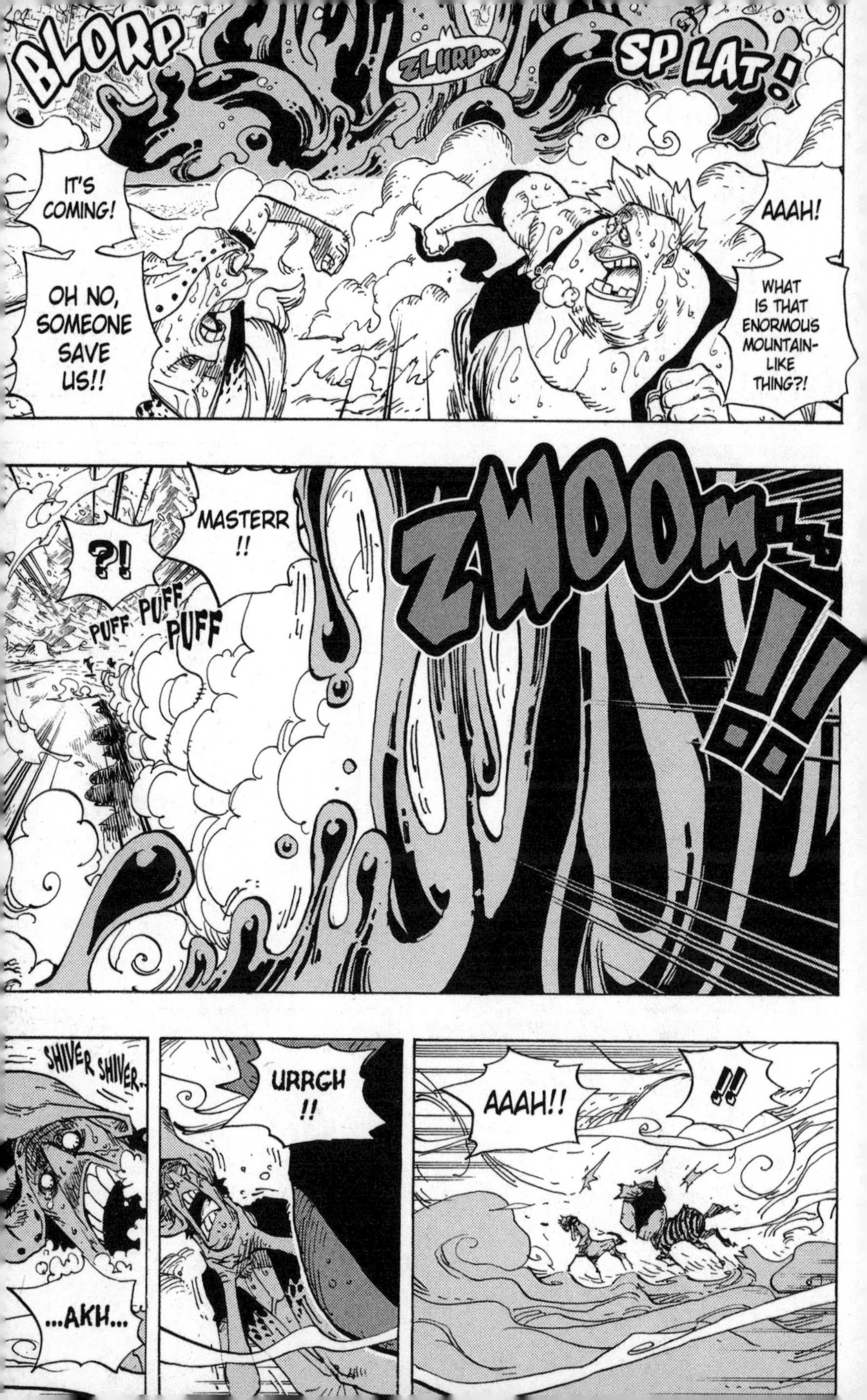
SPLAT!
ZLURP...
BLORP
AAAH!
WHAT IS THAT ENORMOUS MOUNTAIN-LIKE THING?!
IT'S COMING!
OH NO, SOMEONE SAVE US!!
ZWOOM!!!
MASTERR!!
?!
PUFF PUFF PUFF
!!
AAAH!!
URRGH!!
SHIVER SHIVER...
...AKH...

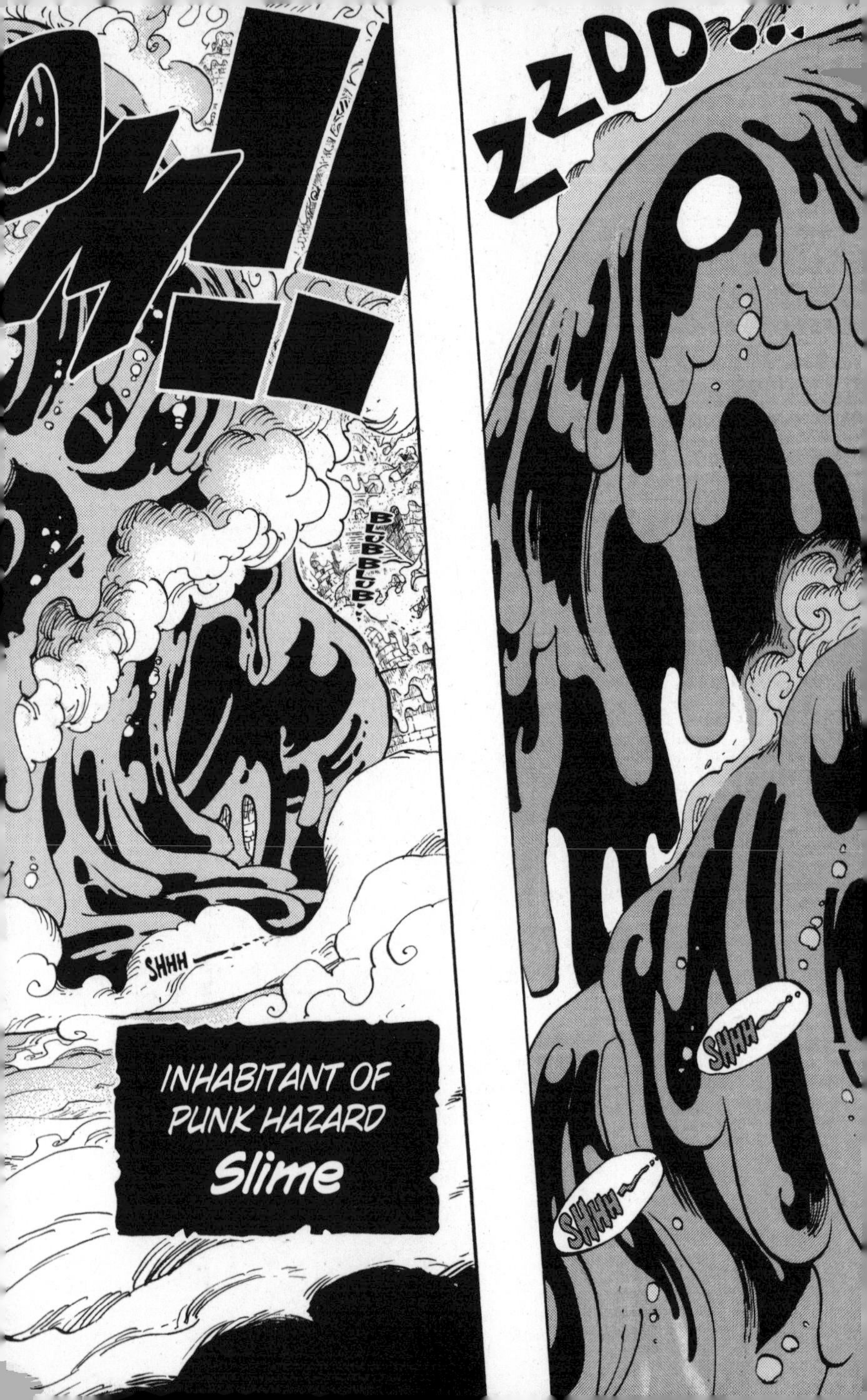
ZZDD...
SHHH
SHHH
BLUB BLUB
SHHH
INHABITANT OF PUNK HAZARD
Slime

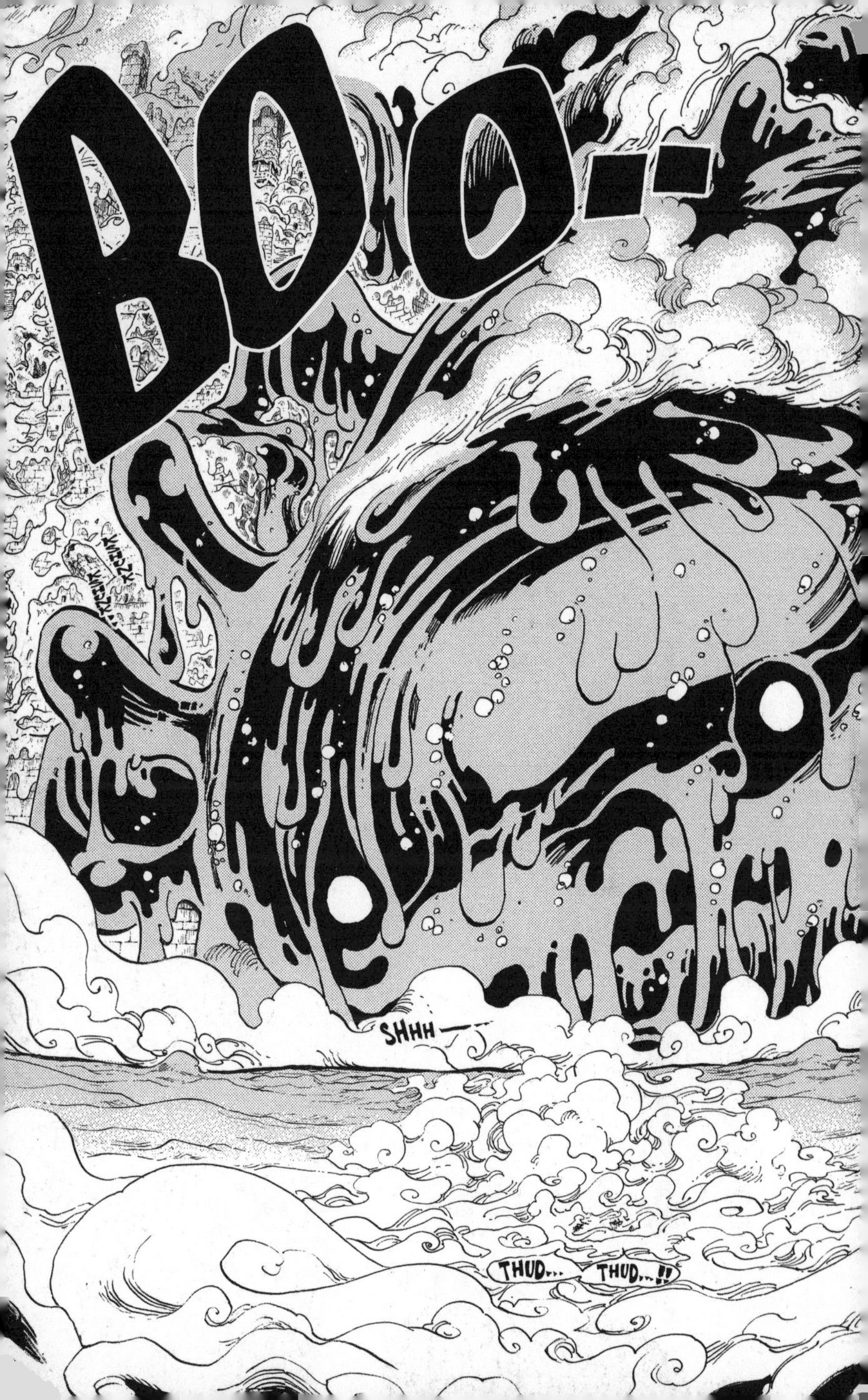
BOO--
KSHUNK
KSHUNK...
SHHH--
THUD...
THUD...!!

SBS Question Corner

(Ponio, Aichi)

Q: Odacchi, good mornooneevening. I've noticed you haven't started the SBS on your own recently. Well, I'm here to continue the trend!!

Shall we begin! The SBS??
--Tatsumi

A: What's the plan?!!‽ Are we starting? Or not? Hey, get Back here!!‽

Q: Mr. Oda, I've been practicing day and night to say the title of my favorite part of my favorite manga. Please hear my call!

Start the SB-poot!!!
--Takuya D. Matsumura

A: He was speaking in fart-ese!! Talk about raising a stink...

Q: Hello there! Quick, say "wiener" ten times fast! Hurry up!! You're running out of time!!
--Atsuma

A: Wiener wienerwienerwienerwienerwiener wiener noodle wiener wiener.

Q: Here's your question. 🖊 Who is this?
--Atsuma

A: Hmm? Who could it be...? Some famous character? He's got a Big nose... Maybe a figure from a high-brow Ryunosuke Akutagawa novel? Let's see what the answer is...

Mr. Twiggan Berries

How would I know that?!! What the heck?!‽

Q: Hello, Mr. Oda!!! Could you tell me what you're thinking about right now?
--Chiko

A: Well...I'm thinking about politics. In a sexy way.

Chapter 669:
COMMENCE OPERATION

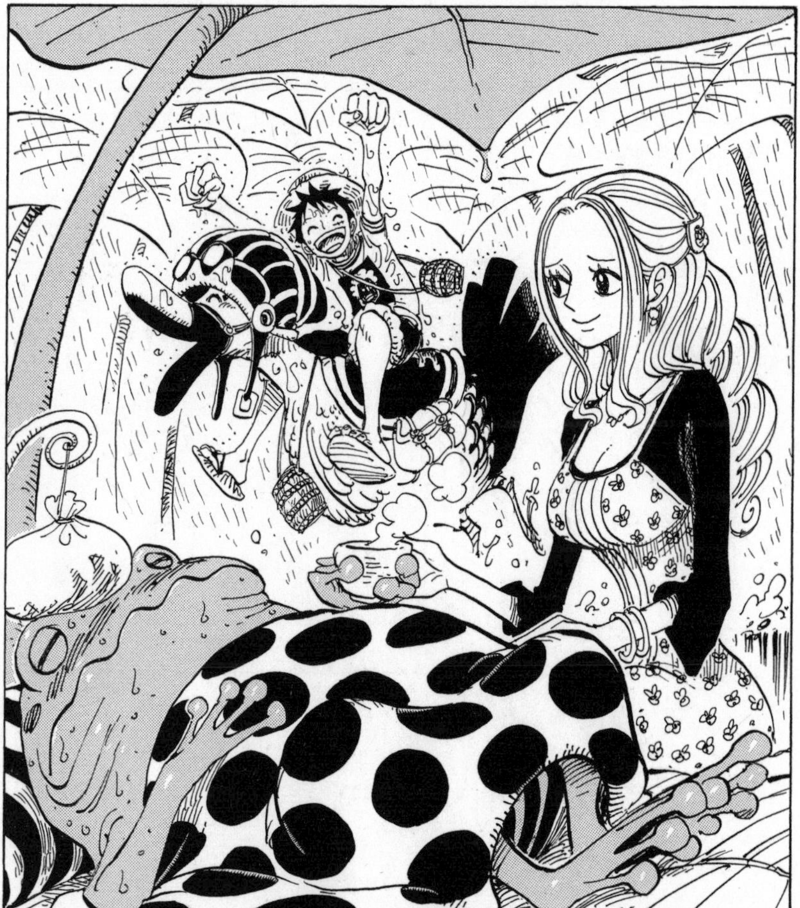

REQUEST: "LUFFY AND KAROO PLAY IN THE RAIN AS VIVI TENDS TO A SICK FROG" BY YUSAKU SHIBATA FROM SAITAMA

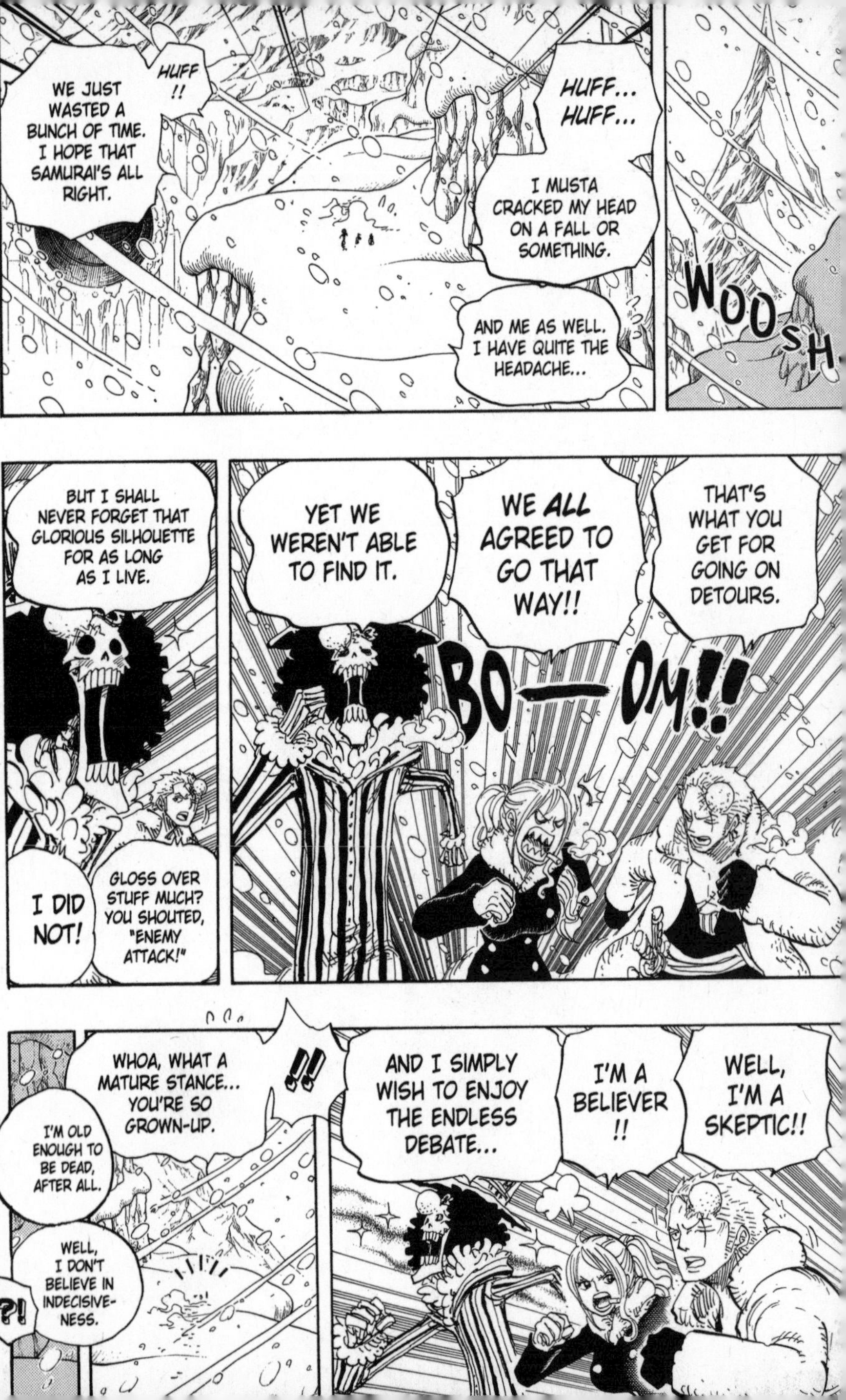
WOOSH
HUFF... HUFF...
I MUSTA CRACKED MY HEAD ON A FALL OR SOMETHING.
AND ME AS WELL. I HAVE QUITE THE HEADACHE...
HUFF !!
WE JUST WASTED A BUNCH OF TIME. I HOPE THAT SAMURAI'S ALL RIGHT.
THAT'S WHAT YOU GET FOR GOING ON DETOURS.
WE ALL AGREED TO GO THAT WAY!!
YET WE WEREN'T ABLE TO FIND IT.
BO—OM!!
BUT I SHALL NEVER FORGET THAT GLORIOUS SILHOUETTE FOR AS LONG AS I LIVE.
GLOSS OVER STUFF MUCH? YOU SHOUTED, "ENEMY ATTACK!"
I DID NOT!
WELL, I'M A SKEPTIC!!
I'M A BELIEVER !!
AND I SIMPLY WISH TO ENJOY THE ENDLESS DEBATE...
!!
WHOA, WHAT A MATURE STANCE... YOU'RE SO GROWN-UP.
I'M OLD ENOUGH TO BE DEAD, AFTER ALL.
WELL, I DON'T BELIEVE IN INDECISIVE-NESS.
?!

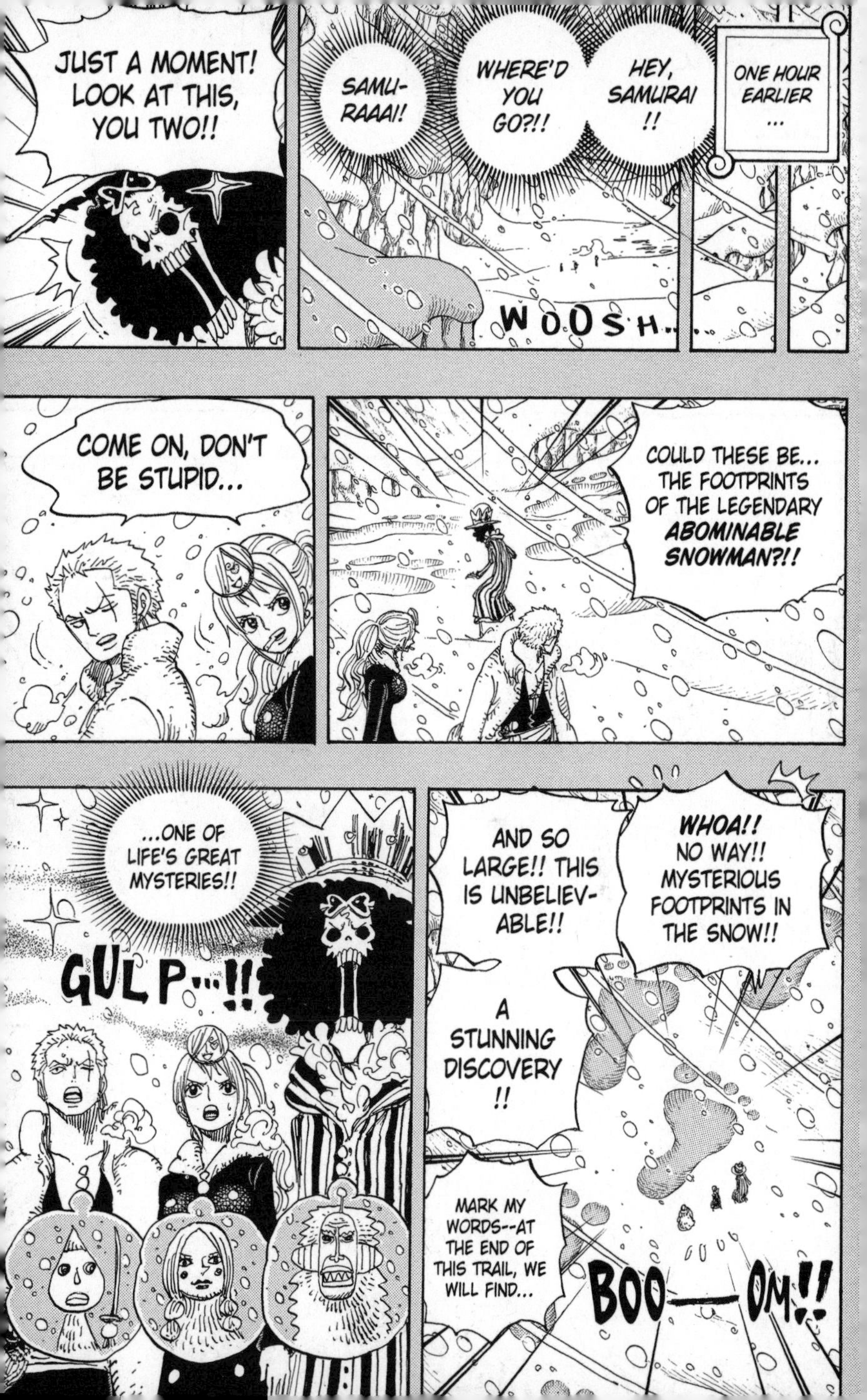
ONE HOUR EARLIER ...
HEY, SAMURAI !!
WHERE'D YOU GO?!!
SAMU-RAAAI!!
WOOSH...
JUST A MOMENT! LOOK AT THIS, YOU TWO!!
COULD THESE BE... THE FOOTPRINTS OF THE LEGENDARY ABOMINABLE SNOWMAN?!!
COME ON, DON'T BE STUPID...
WHOA!! NO WAY!! MYSTERIOUS FOOTPRINTS IN THE SNOW!!
AND SO LARGE!! THIS IS UNBELIEV-ABLE!!
A STUNNING DISCOVERY !!
MARK MY WORDS--AT THE END OF THIS TRAIL, WE WILL FIND...
BOO—OM!!
...ONE OF LIFE'S GREAT MYSTERIES!!
GULP...!!

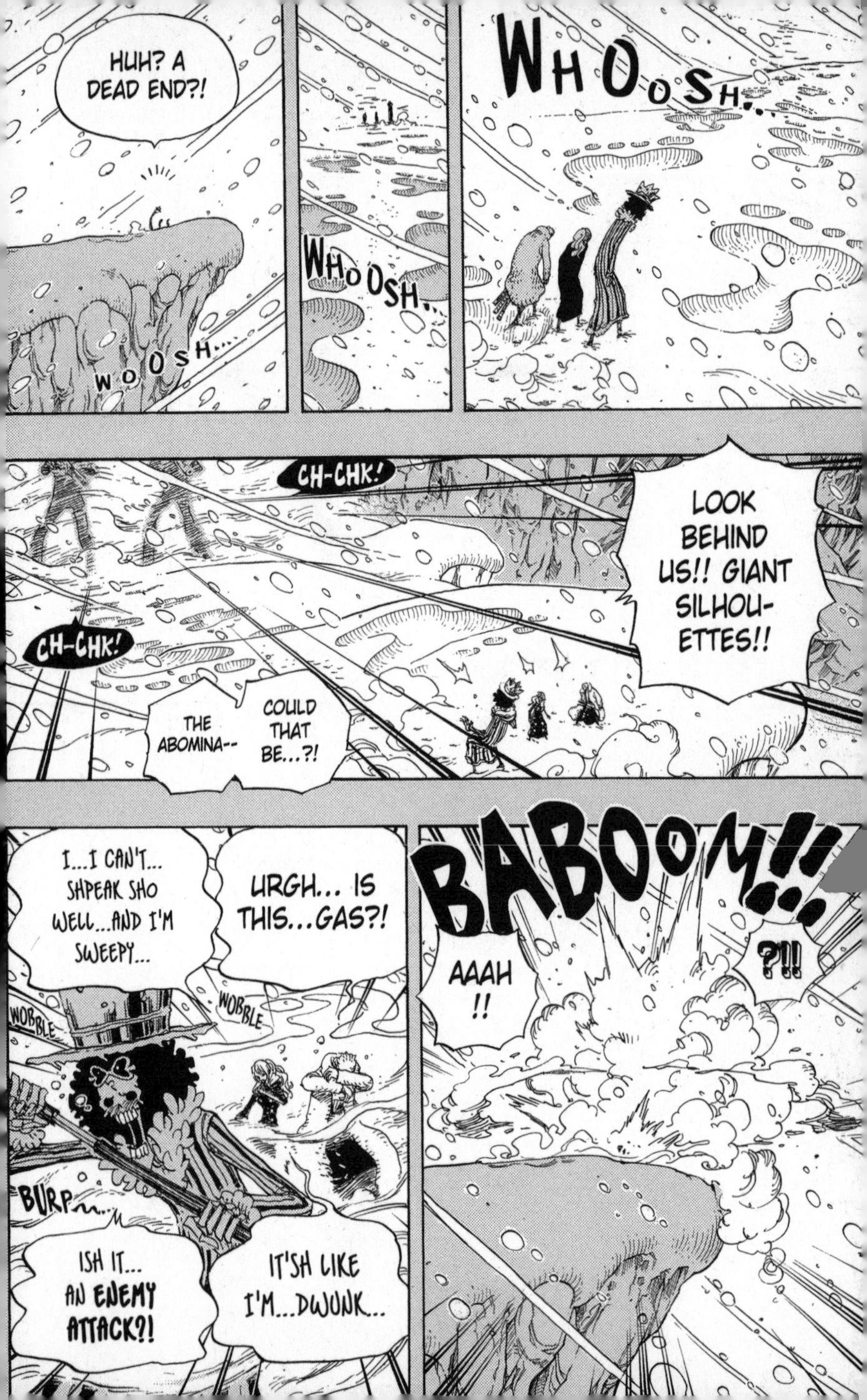
WHOOSH...
WHOOSH...
HUH? A DEAD END?!
WOOSH...
LOOK BEHIND US!! GIANT SILHOU-ETTES!!
CH-CHK!
CH-CHK!
COULD THAT BE...?!
THE ABOMINA--
BABOOM!!
?!!
AAAH !!
URGH... IS THIS...GAS?!
I...I CAN'T... SHPEAK SHO WELL...AND I'M SWEEPY...
WOBBLE
WOBBLE
BURP...
IT'SH LIKE I'M...DWUNK...
ISH IT... AN ENEMY ATTACK?!

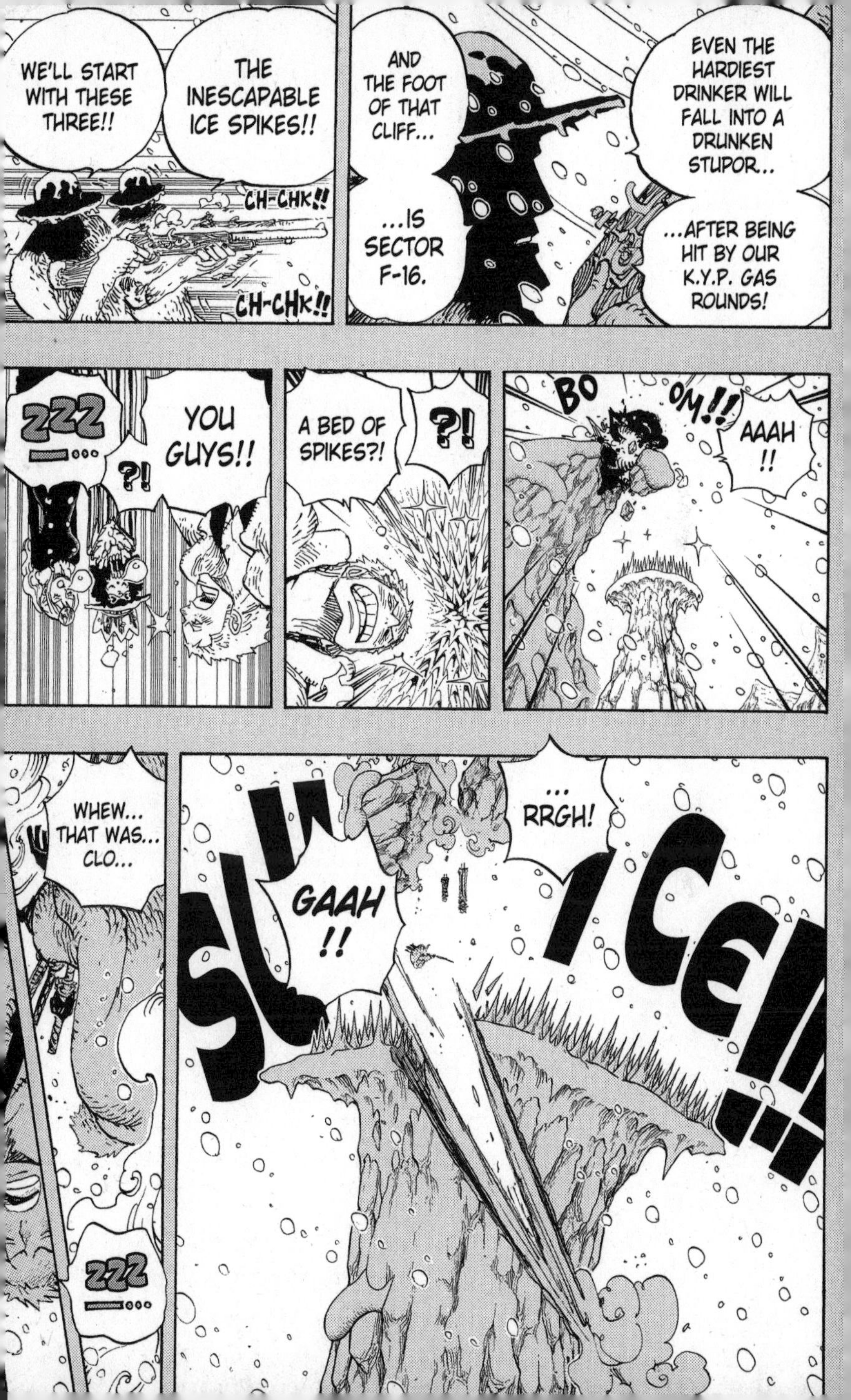
EVEN THE HARDIEST DRINKER WILL FALL INTO A DRUNKEN STUPOR...
...AFTER BEING HIT BY OUR K.Y.P. GAS ROUNDS!
AND THE FOOT OF THAT CLIFF...
...IS SECTOR F-16.
THE INESCAPABLE ICE SPIKES!!
WE'LL START WITH THESE THREE!!
CH-CHK!!
CH-CHK!!
BOOM!!
AAAH !!
?!
A BED OF SPIKES?!
YOU GUYS!!
?!
ZZZ
...RRGH!
GAAH !!
WHEW... THAT WAS... CLO...
ZZZ

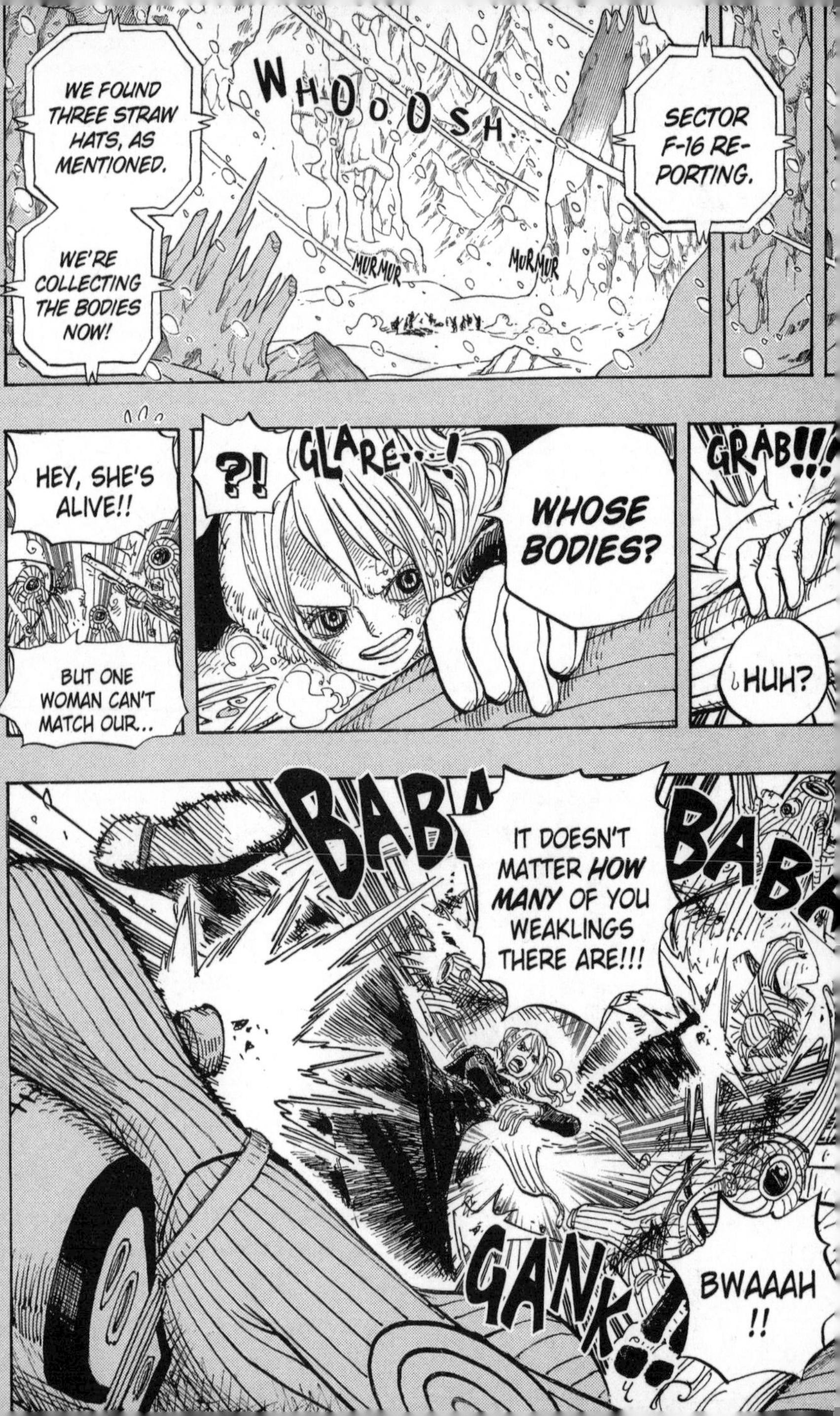
SECTOR F-16 REPORTING.
WHOOOSH
MURMUR
MURMUR
WE FOUND THREE STRAW HATS, AS MENTIONED.
WE'RE COLLECTING THE BODIES NOW!
GRAB!!!
HUH?
GLARE...!
?!
WHOSE BODIES?
HEY, SHE'S ALIVE!!
BUT ONE WOMAN CAN'T MATCH OUR...
BABA
IT DOESN'T MATTER *HOW MANY* OF YOU WEAKLINGS THERE ARE!!!
BABA
BWAAAH !!
GANK

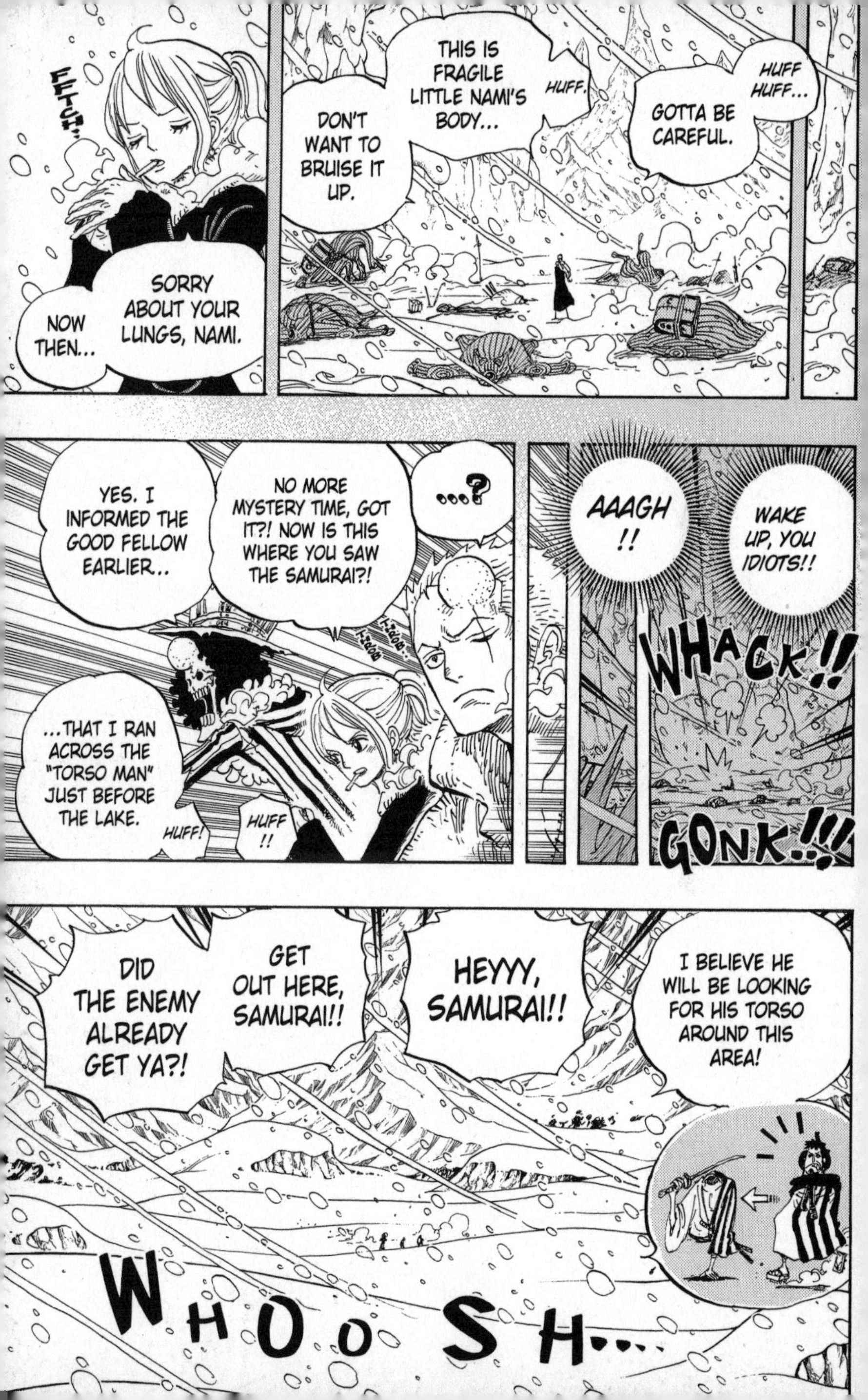
HUFF HUFF...
GOTTA BE CAREFUL.
HUFF.
THIS IS FRAGILE LITTLE NAMI'S BODY...
DON'T WANT TO BRUISE IT UP.
FETCH
SORRY ABOUT YOUR LUNGS, NAMI.
NOW THEN...
WAKE UP, YOU IDIOTS!!
AAAGH!!
WHACK!!
GONK!!!
...?
NO MORE MYSTERY TIME, GOT IT?! NOW IS THIS WHERE YOU SAW THE SAMURAI?!
YES. I INFORMED THE GOOD FELLOW EARLIER...
...THAT I RAN ACROSS THE "TORSO MAN" JUST BEFORE THE LAKE.
HUFF !!
HUFF!
I BELIEVE HE WILL BE LOOKING FOR HIS TORSO AROUND THIS AREA!
HEYYY, SAMURAI!!
GET OUT HERE, SAMURAI!!
DID THE ENEMY ALREADY GET YA?!
WHOOSH...

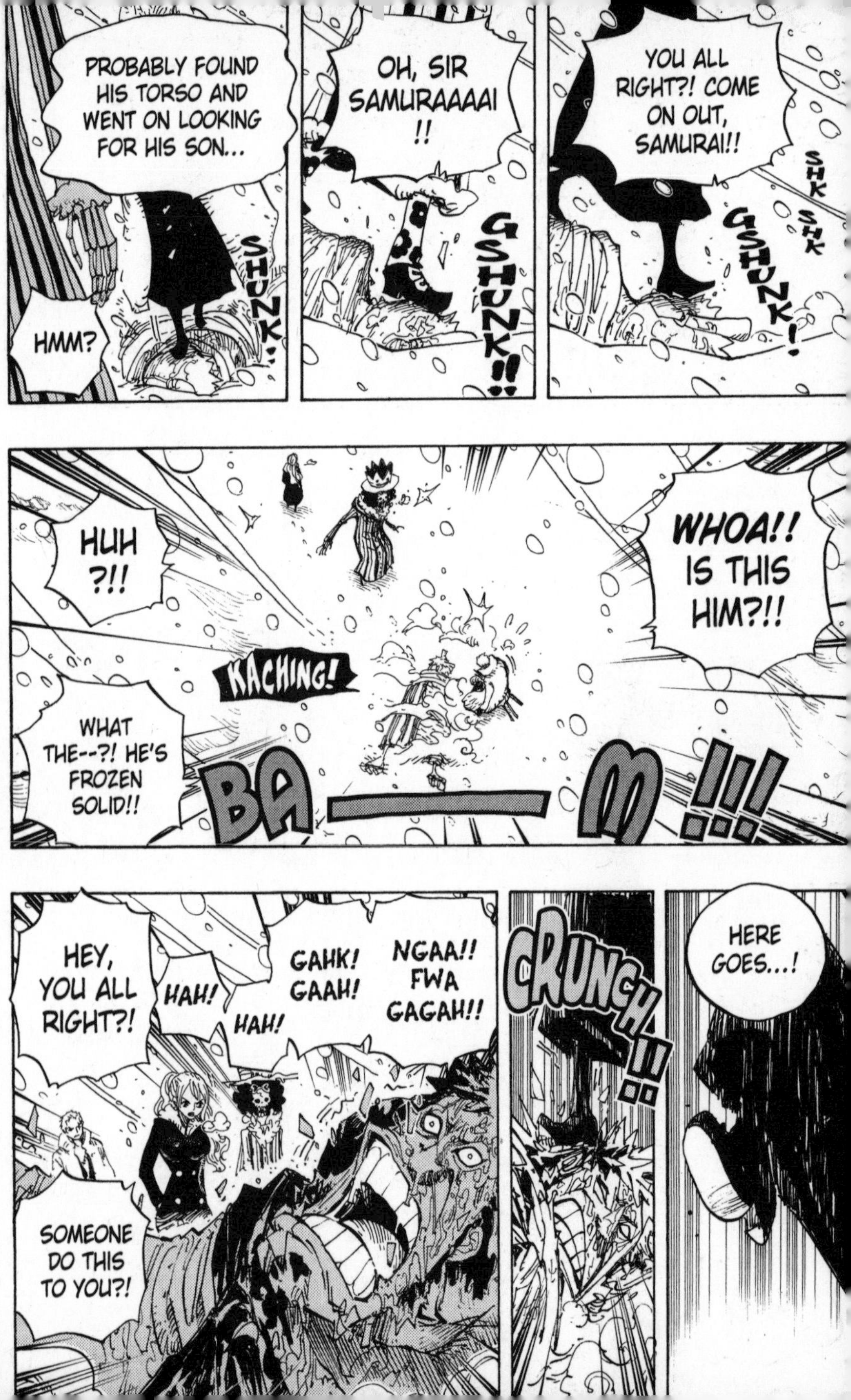
YOU ALL RIGHT?! COME ON OUT, SAMURAI!!
SHK SHK
GSHUNK!
OH, SIR SAMURAAAAI!!
GSHUNK!!
PROBABLY FOUND HIS TORSO AND WENT ON LOOKING FOR HIS SON...
SHUNK!
HMM?
WHOA!! IS THIS HIM?!!
HUH?!!
KACHING!
WHAT THE--?! HE'S FROZEN SOLID!!
BA—M!!!
HERE GOES...!
CRUNCH!!
NGAA!! FWA GAGAH!!
GAHK! GAAH!
HAH!
HAH!
HEY, YOU ALL RIGHT?!
SOMEONE DO THIS TO YOU?!

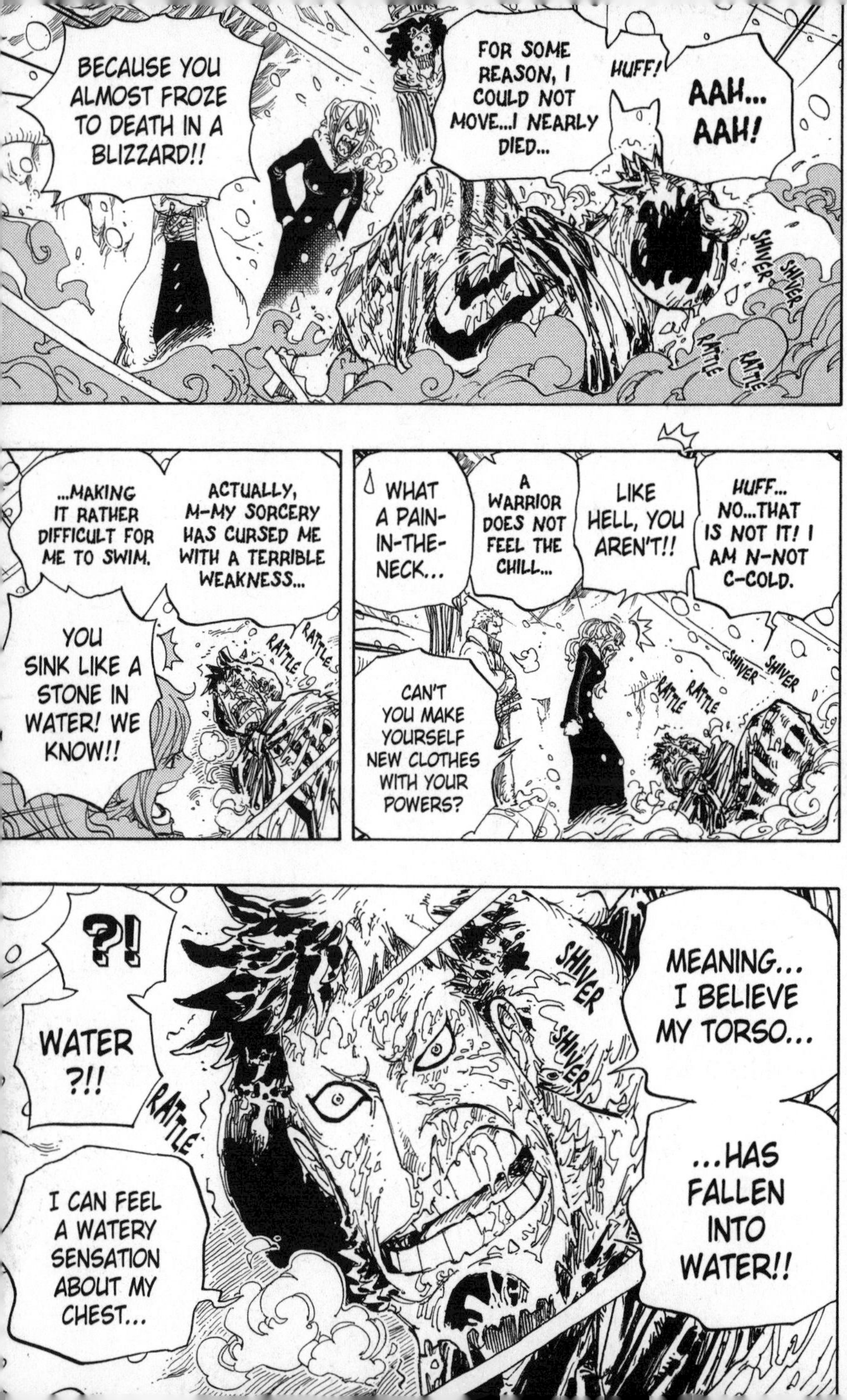
AAH... AAH!
HUFF!
FOR SOME REASON, I COULD NOT MOVE...I NEARLY DIED...
BECAUSE YOU ALMOST FROZE TO DEATH IN A BLIZZARD!!
SHIVER SHIVER
RATTLE RATTLE
HUFF... NO...THAT IS NOT IT! I AM N-NOT C-COLD.
LIKE HELL, YOU AREN'T!!
A WARRIOR DOES NOT FEEL THE CHILL...
WHAT A PAIN-IN-THE-NECK...
SHIVER SHIVER
RATTLE RATTLE
CAN'T YOU MAKE YOURSELF NEW CLOTHES WITH YOUR POWERS?
ACTUALLY, M-MY SORCERY HAS CURSED ME WITH A TERRIBLE WEAKNESS...
...MAKING IT RATHER DIFFICULT FOR ME TO SWIM.
RATTLE RATTLE
YOU SINK LIKE A STONE IN WATER! WE KNOW!!
MEANING... I BELIEVE MY TORSO...
SHIVER SHIVER
?!
WATER?!!
...HAS FALLEN INTO WATER!!
RATTLE
I CAN FEEL A WATERY SENSATION ABOUT MY CHEST...

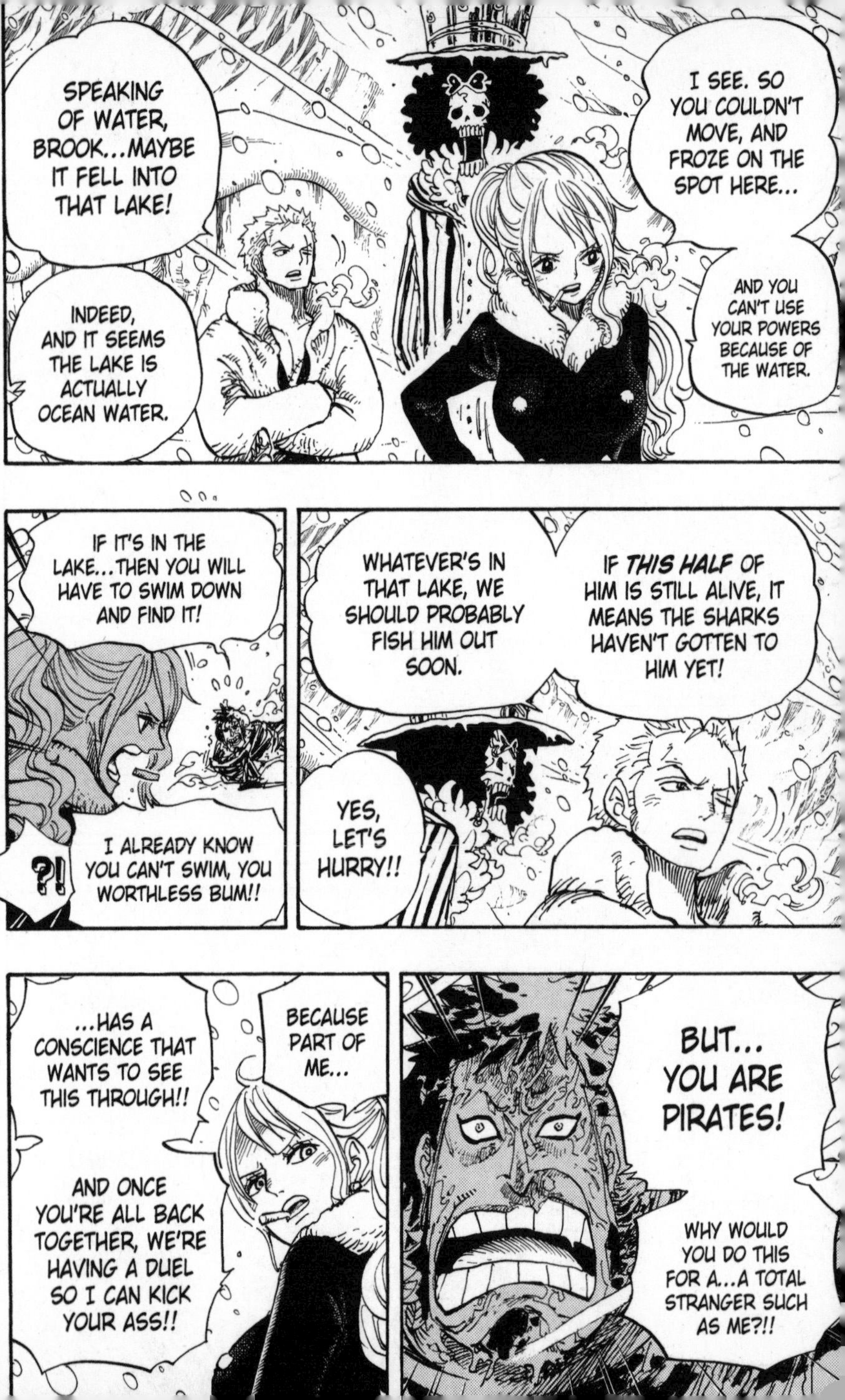
I SEE. SO YOU COULDN'T MOVE, AND FROZE ON THE SPOT HERE...
AND YOU CAN'T USE YOUR POWERS BECAUSE OF THE WATER.
SPEAKING OF WATER, BROOK...MAYBE IT FELL INTO THAT LAKE!
INDEED, AND IT SEEMS THE LAKE IS ACTUALLY OCEAN WATER.
IF *THIS HALF* OF HIM IS STILL ALIVE, IT MEANS THE SHARKS HAVEN'T GOTTEN TO HIM YET!
WHATEVER'S IN THAT LAKE, WE SHOULD PROBABLY FISH HIM OUT SOON.
YES, LET'S HURRY!!
IF IT'S IN THE LAKE...THEN YOU WILL HAVE TO SWIM DOWN AND FIND IT!
?!
I ALREADY KNOW YOU CAN'T SWIM, YOU WORTHLESS BUM!!
BUT... YOU ARE PIRATES!
WHY WOULD YOU DO THIS FOR A...A TOTAL STRANGER SUCH AS ME?!!
BECAUSE PART OF ME...
...HAS A CONSCIENCE THAT WANTS TO SEE THIS THROUGH!!
AND ONCE YOU'RE ALL BACK TOGETHER, WE'RE HAVING A DUEL SO I CAN KICK YOUR ASS!!

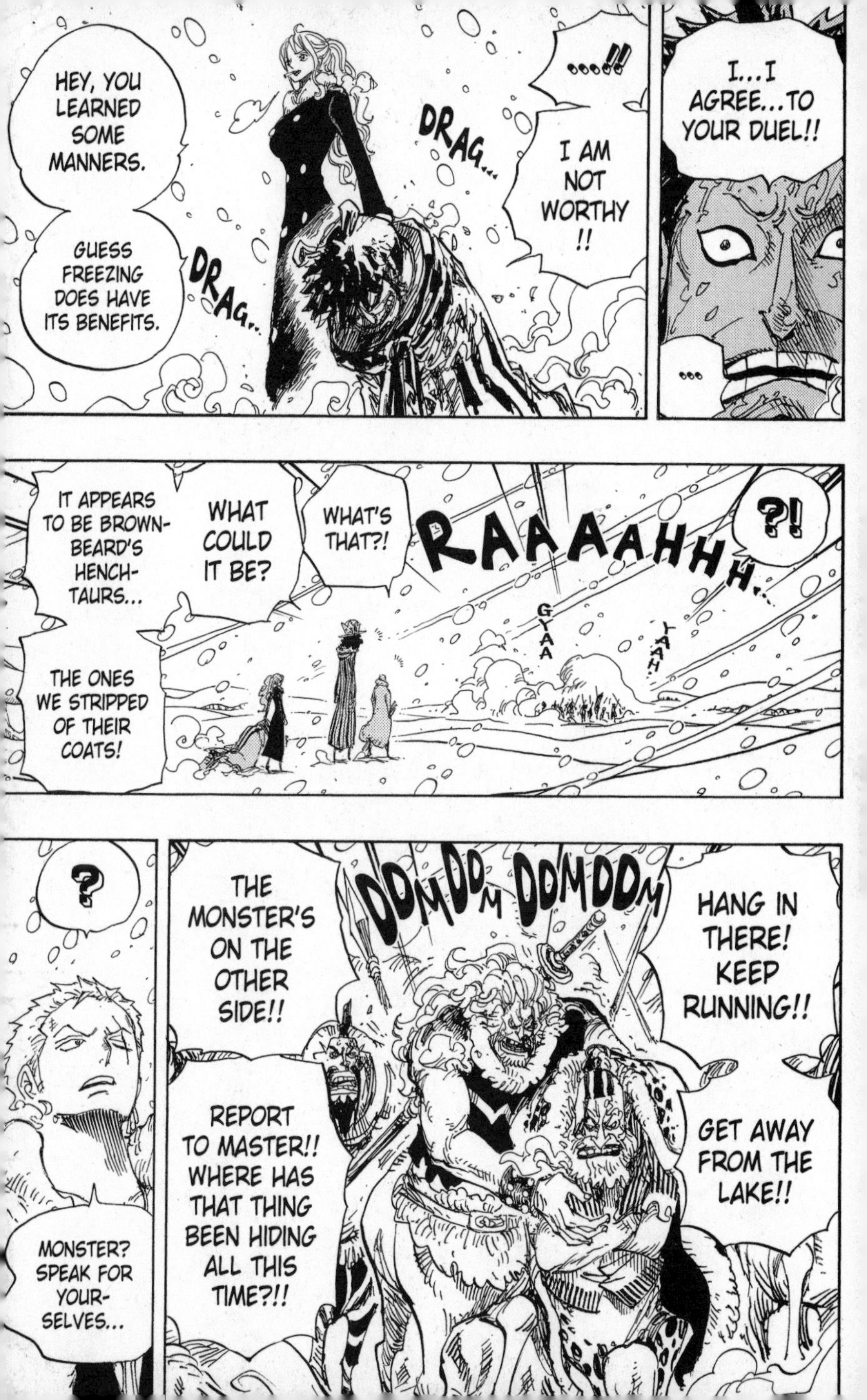
I...I AGREE...TO YOUR DUEL!!
...
....!!
I AM NOT WORTHY !!
DRAG...
DRAG..
HEY, YOU LEARNED SOME MANNERS.
GUESS FREEZING DOES HAVE ITS BENEFITS.
?!
RAAAAAHHHH..
GYAA
YAAH
WHAT'S THAT?!
WHAT COULD IT BE?
IT APPEARS TO BE BROWN-BEARD'S HENCH-TAURS...
THE ONES WE STRIPPED OF THEIR COATS!
HANG IN THERE! KEEP RUNNING!!
DOMDOM DOMDOM
THE MONSTER'S ON THE OTHER SIDE!!
GET AWAY FROM THE LAKE!!
REPORT TO MASTER!! WHERE HAS THAT THING BEEN HIDING ALL THIS TIME?!!
?
MONSTER? SPEAK FOR YOUR-SELVES...

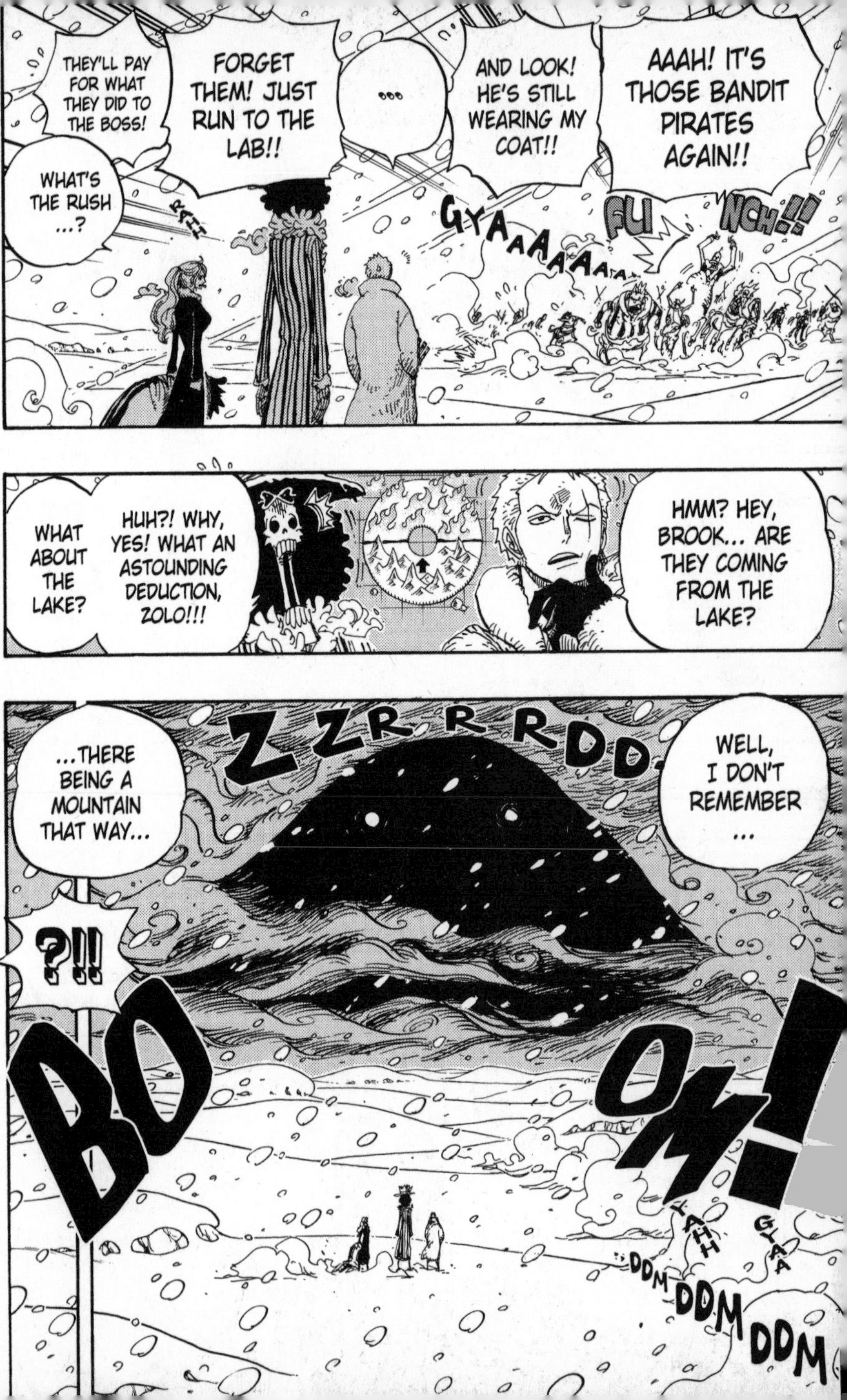
AAAH! IT'S THOSE BANDIT PIRATES AGAIN!!
AND LOOK! HE'S STILL WEARING MY COAT!!
...
FORGET THEM! JUST RUN TO THE LAB!!
THEY'LL PAY FOR WHAT THEY DID TO THE BOSS!
FUNCH!!
GYAAAAAAA
WHAT'S THE RUSH ...?
RAH
HMM? HEY, BROOK... ARE THEY COMING FROM THE LAKE?
HUH?! WHY, YES! WHAT AN ASTOUNDING DEDUCTION, ZOLO!!!
WHAT ABOUT THE LAKE?
WELL, I DON'T REMEMBER ...
...THERE BEING A MOUNTAIN THAT WAY...
ZZRRRRDD
?!!
BOOM!
GYAA
YAHH
DDM DDM DDM

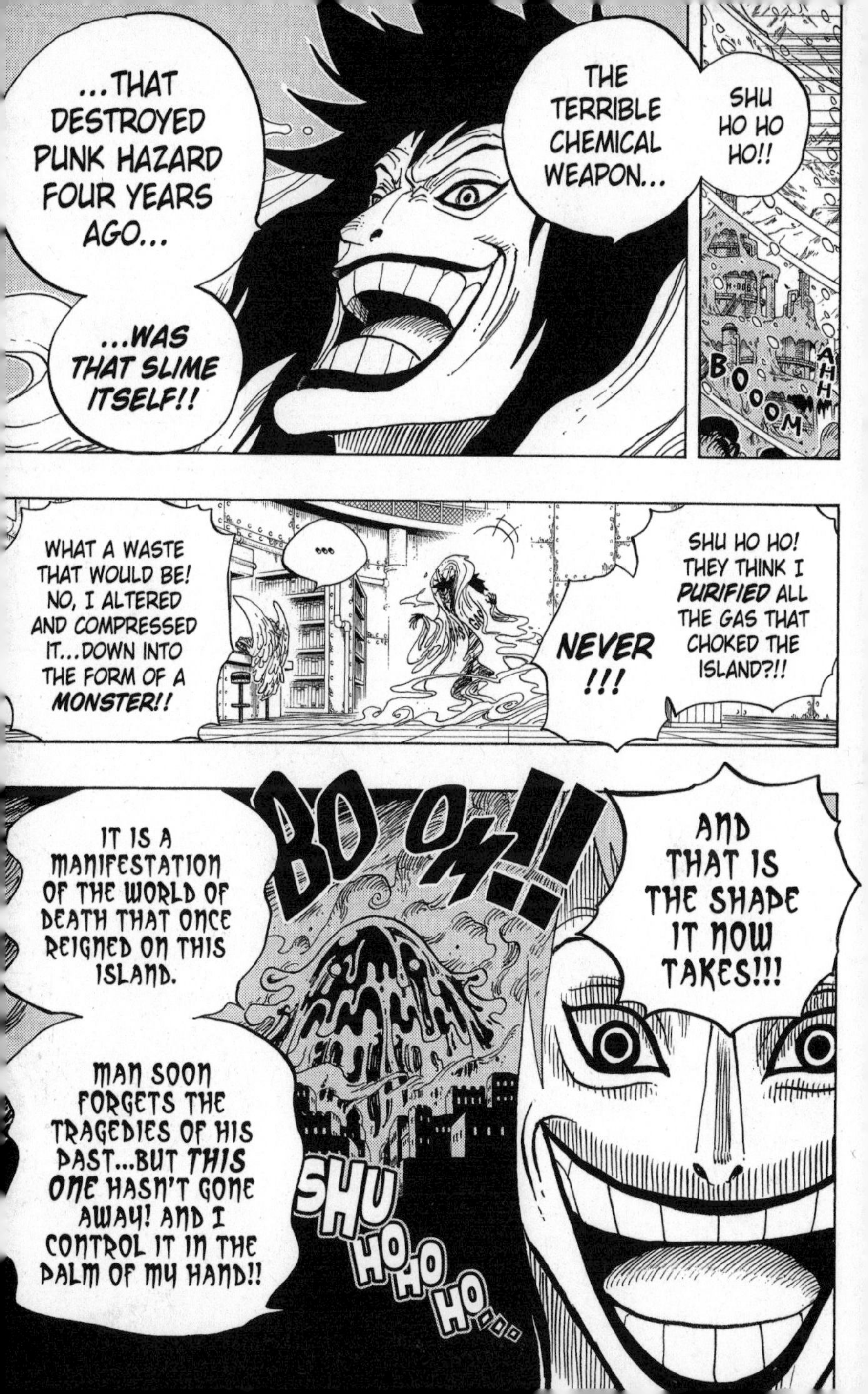
SHU HO HO HO!!
BOOOM
AHH
THE TERRIBLE CHEMICAL WEAPON...
...THAT DESTROYED PUNK HAZARD FOUR YEARS AGO...
...WAS THAT SLIME ITSELF!!
SHU HO HO! THEY THINK I PURIFIED ALL THE GAS THAT CHOKED THE ISLAND?!!
NEVER!!!
...
WHAT A WASTE THAT WOULD BE! NO, I ALTERED AND COMPRESSED IT...DOWN INTO THE FORM OF A MONSTER!!
AND THAT IS THE SHAPE IT NOW TAKES!!!
BOOM!!
IT IS A MANIFESTATION OF THE WORLD OF DEATH THAT ONCE REIGNED ON THIS ISLAND.
MAN SOON FORGETS THE TRAGEDIES OF HIS PAST...BUT THIS ONE HASN'T GONE AWAY! AND I CONTROL IT IN THE PALM OF MY HAND!!
SHU HO HO HO...

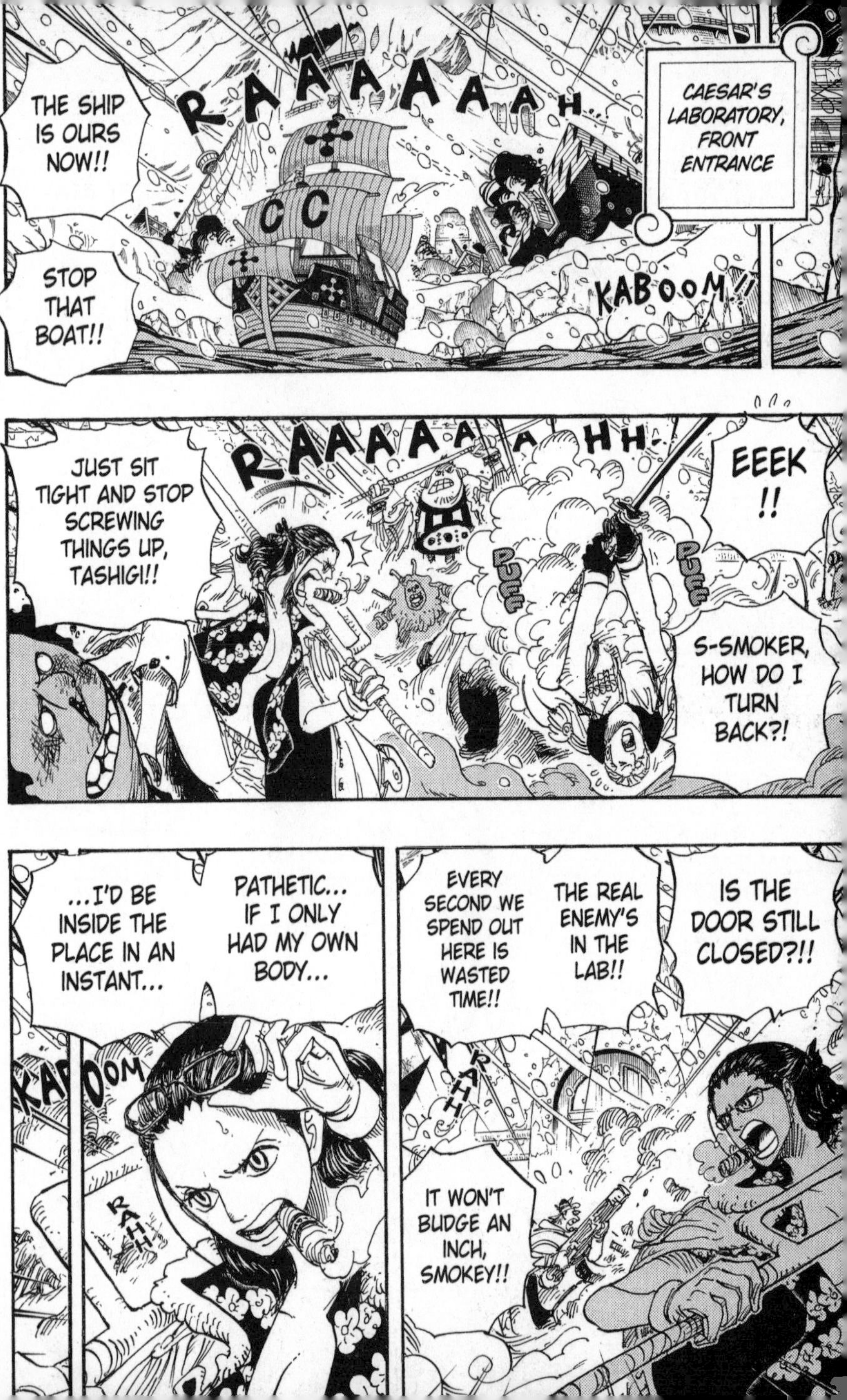
CAESAR'S LABORATORY, FRONT ENTRANCE
RAAAAAAH
KABOOM!!
THE SHIP IS OURS NOW!!
STOP THAT BOAT!!
EEEK!!
S-SMOKER, HOW DO I TURN BACK?!
PUFF
PUFF
RAAAAAAAHH
JUST SIT TIGHT AND STOP SCREWING THINGS UP, TASHIGI!!
IS THE DOOR STILL CLOSED?!!
THE REAL ENEMY'S IN THE LAB!!
EVERY SECOND WE SPEND OUT HERE IS WASTED TIME!!
RAHH
IT WON'T BUDGE AN INCH, SMOKEY!!
PATHETIC... IF I ONLY HAD MY OWN BODY...
...I'D BE INSIDE THE PLACE IN AN INSTANT...
KABOOM
RAHH

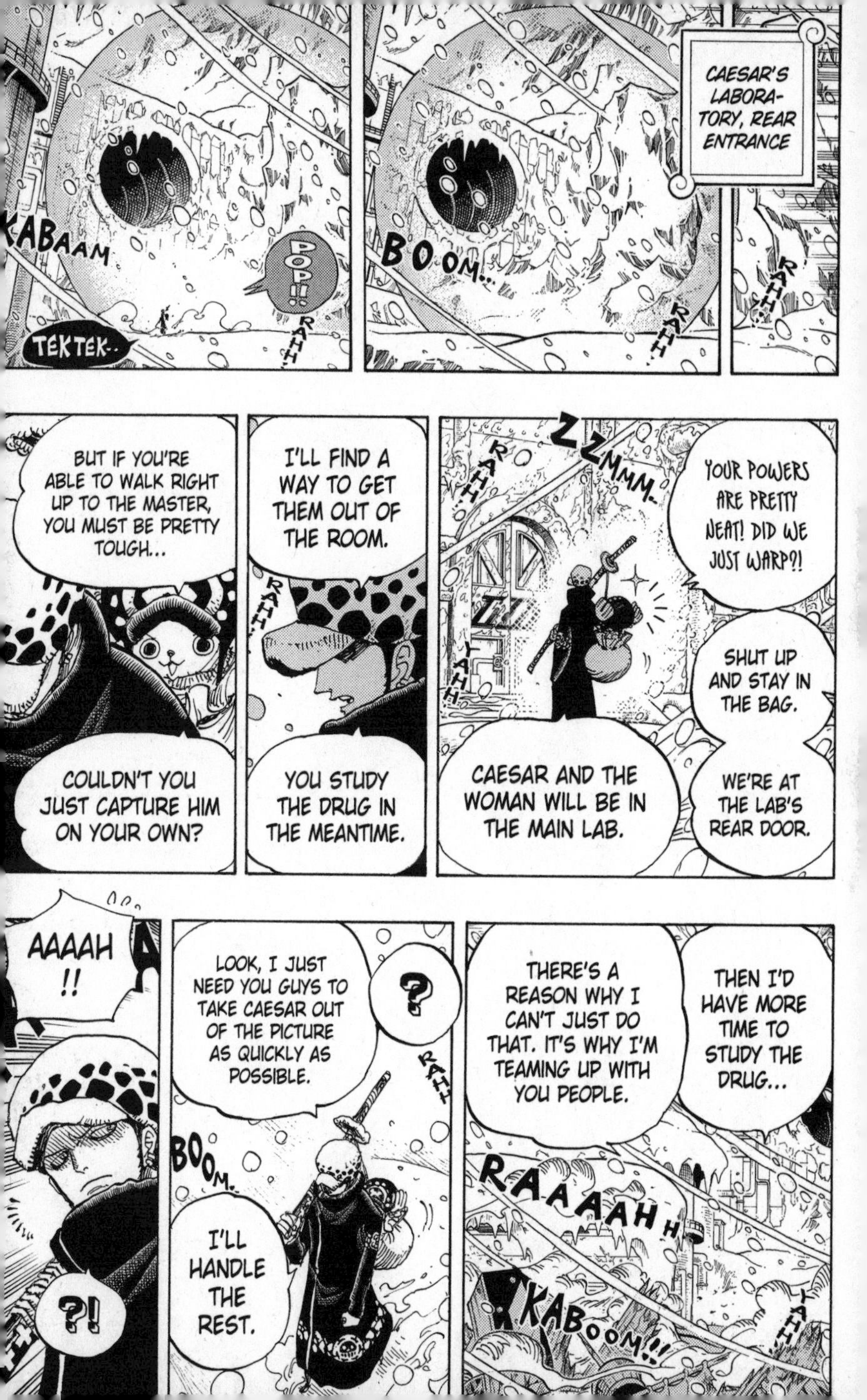

CAESAR'S LABORA-TORY, REAR ENTRANCE
RAHH
BOOOM...
RAHH
KABAAM
POP!!
RAHH
TEKTEK-.
ZZMMM-
RAHH
YOUR POWERS ARE PRETTY NEAT! DID WE JUST WARP?!
SHUT UP AND STAY IN THE BAG.
WE'RE AT THE LAB'S REAR DOOR.
CAESAR AND THE WOMAN WILL BE IN THE MAIN LAB.
YAHH
I'LL FIND A WAY TO GET THEM OUT OF THE ROOM.
RAHH
YOU STUDY THE DRUG IN THE MEANTIME.
BUT IF YOU'RE ABLE TO WALK RIGHT UP TO THE MASTER, YOU MUST BE PRETTY TOUGH...
COULDN'T YOU JUST CAPTURE HIM ON YOUR OWN?
THEN I'D HAVE MORE TIME TO STUDY THE DRUG...
THERE'S A REASON WHY I CAN'T JUST DO THAT. IT'S WHY I'M TEAMING UP WITH YOU PEOPLE.
RAAAAHH
KABOOM!!!
YAHH
?
LOOK, I JUST NEED YOU GUYS TO TAKE CAESAR OUT OF THE PICTURE AS QUICKLY AS POSSIBLE.
RAHH
BOOOM..
I'LL HANDLE THE REST.
AAAAH !!
?!

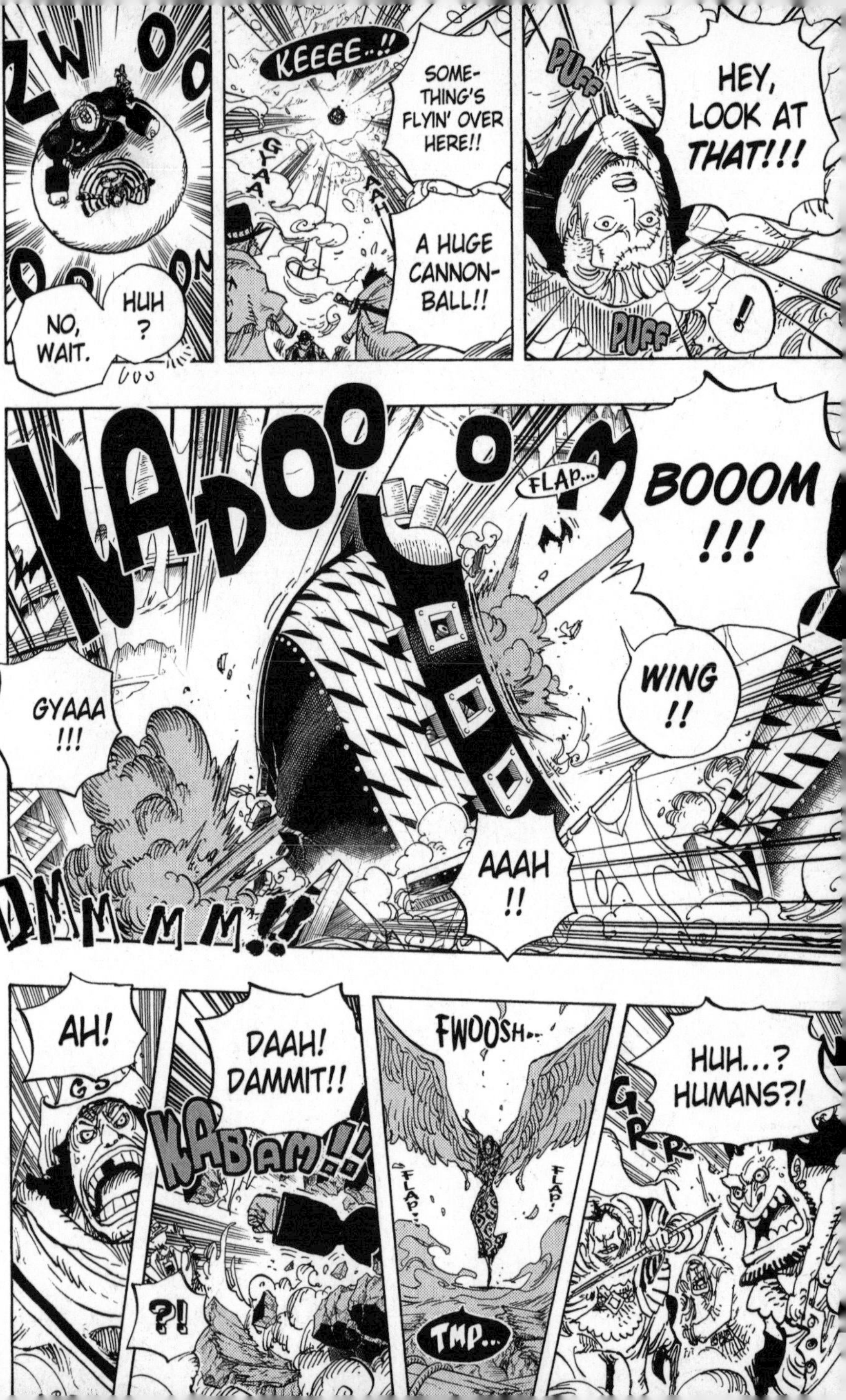
PUFF
HEY, LOOK AT THAT!!!
PUFF
!
KEEEE..!!
SOME-THING'S FLYIN' OVER HERE!!
GYAA
AAH
A HUGE CANNON-BALL!!
HUH ?
NO, WAIT.
BOOOM!!!
FLAP...
WING!!
AAAH!!
GYAAA!!!
HUH...? HUMANS?!
GRRR
FWOOSH..
FLAP
FLAP
TMP...
DAAH! DAMMIT!!
KABAM!!
?!
AH!

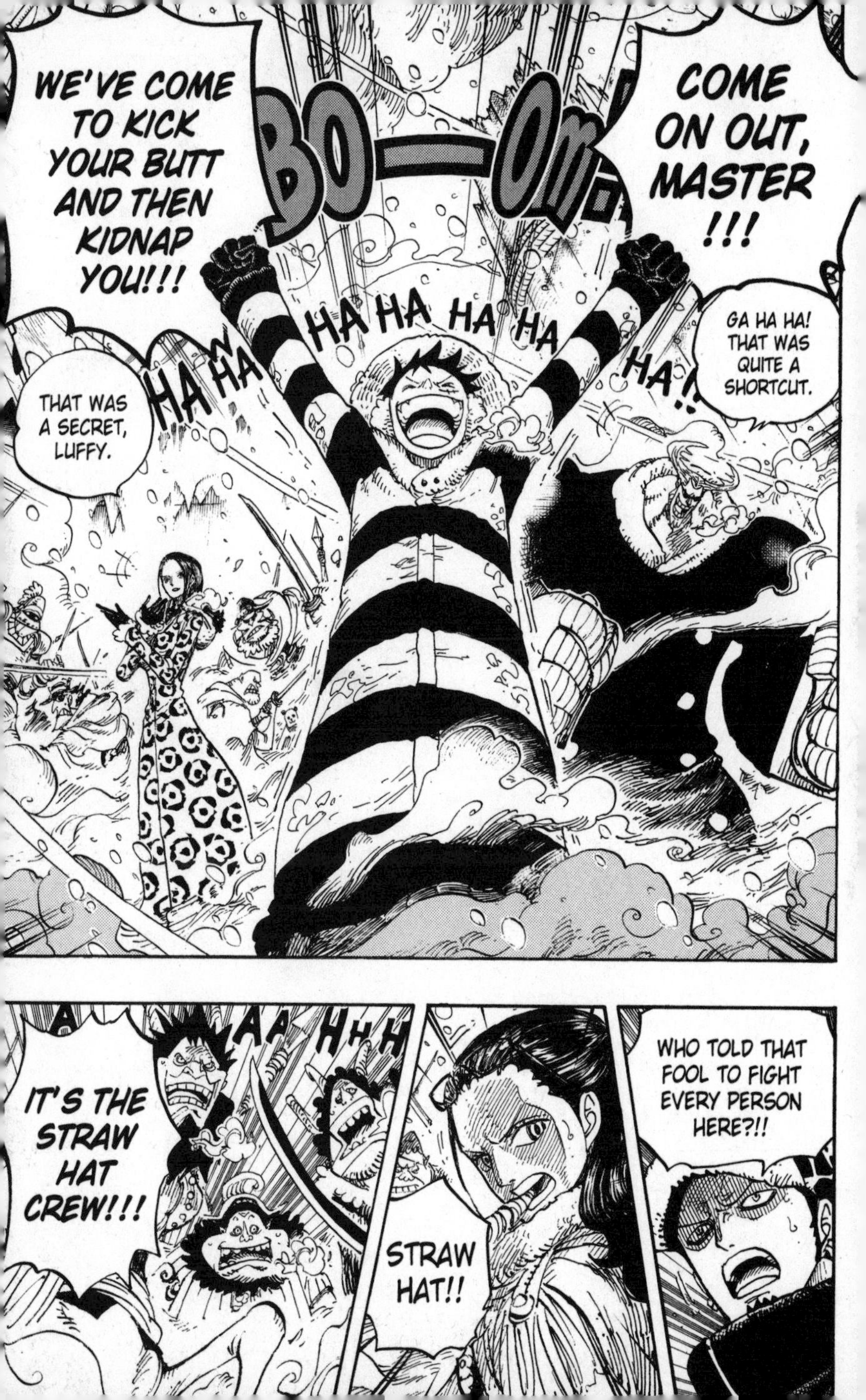
COME ON OUT, MASTER!!!
BO—OM
WE'VE COME TO KICK YOUR BUTT AND THEN KIDNAP YOU!!!
GA HA HA! THAT WAS QUITE A SHORTCUT.
HA HA HA HA HA HA HA!!
THAT WAS A SECRET, LUFFY.
WHO TOLD THAT FOOL TO FIGHT EVERY PERSON HERE?!!
STRAW HAT!!
AAAHHH
IT'S THE STRAW HAT CREW!!!

SBS Question Corner

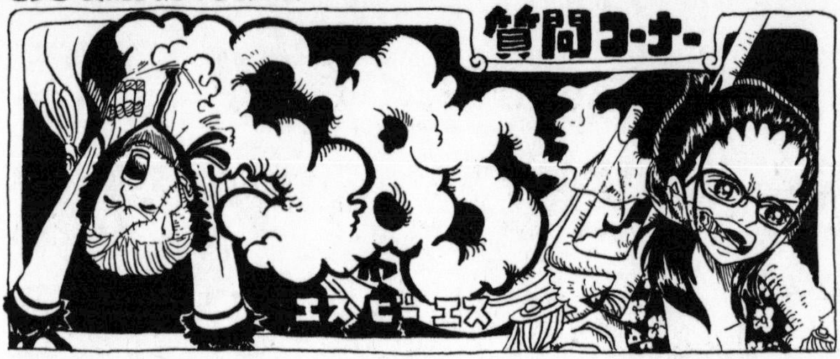

質問コーナー
エスビーエス

(Michi Nakahara, Tottori)

Q: Is it true that **he's** one of the Seven Warlords after the two-year time-skip?!

--I Heard It From My Brother

A: He's Back!!! Dang, it's Been a while!! Is that a Beard I see?! You look more grown-up! Now get lost!!

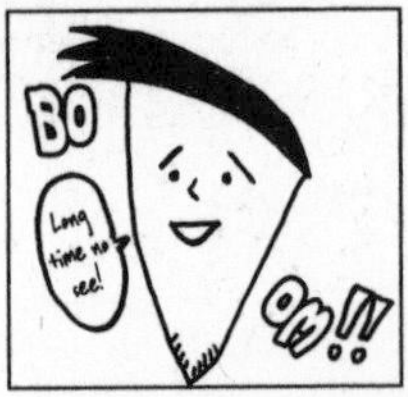

BO
Long time no see!
OM!!

Q: Mr. Oda!! This is my first-ever postcard. Now here's my question: Franky's hair in the New World seems to alter its form at will. How many different hairstyles can he make? I'm very curious.

--Ryusei

A: An unlimited amount!!! Look forward to more.

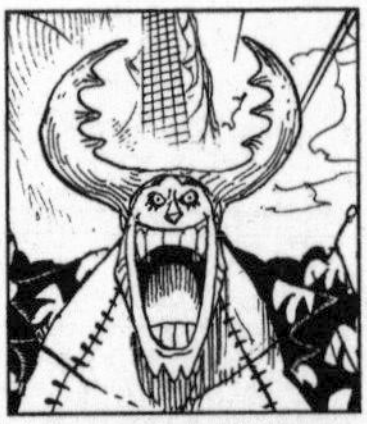

Q: Hey, hey, hey, hey, heyyy, what's up! Usopp's got his new Pop Greens now, but what happens if he runs out?

--Short-Haired Girls Are the Best ♡

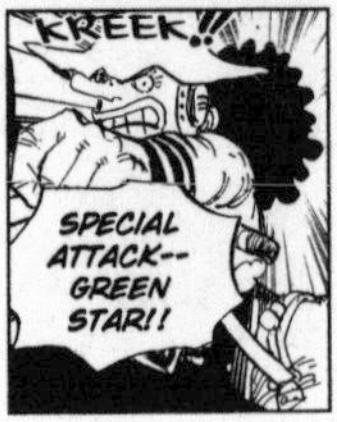

KREEK!!
SPECIAL ATTACK-- GREEN STAR!!

A: Hmm. I've been getting this question quite a bit. I was hoping to show this within the manga, but I just haven't been able to squeeze it in. However, I was able to work it into the script for the upcoming One Piece Film Z movie. It seems everyone was concerned that Usopp might run out because it's the seeds he shoots at enemies. Well, not to worry. There's a new "Usopp Garden" on the deck of the Thousand Sunny, which is where Usopp cultivates a steady supply of Pop Green seeds. There's a scene in the movie in which he removes harmful insects, so watch out for that. I'll get to it within the manga eventually too.

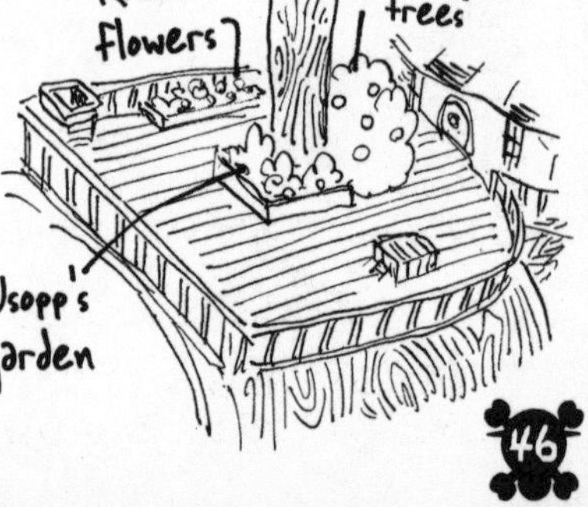

Robin's flowers
Nami's tangerine trees
Usopp's garden

Chapter 670:

BLIZZARD WITH A CHANCE OF SLIME

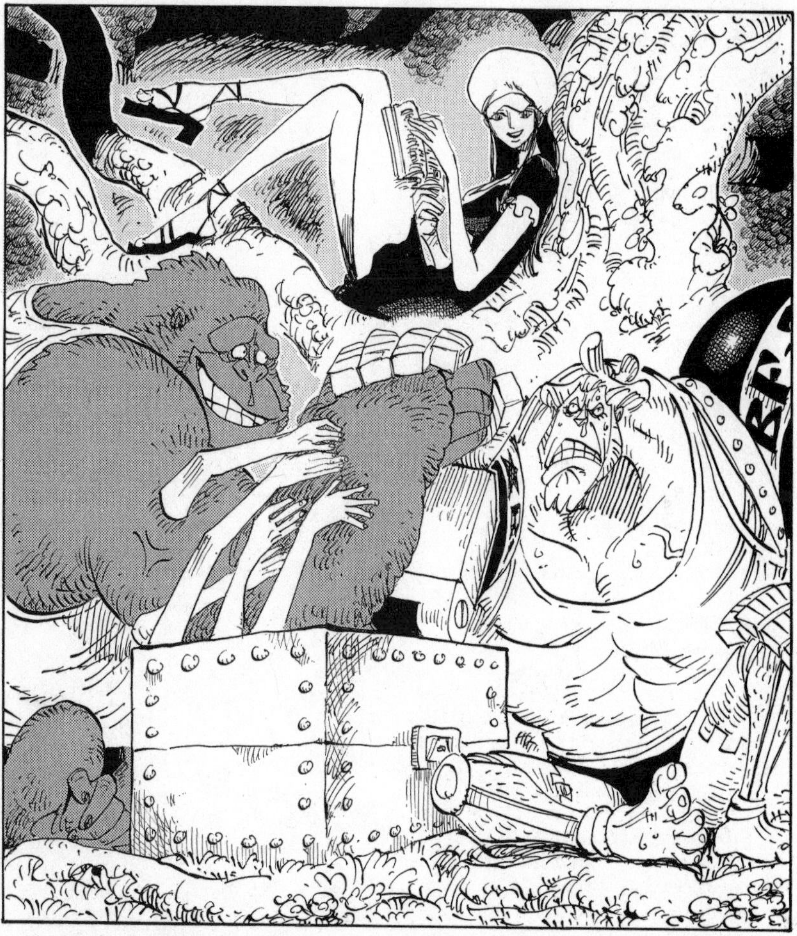

REQUEST: "ROBIN INTERFERES WITH AN ARM-WRESTLING MATCH BETWEEN FRANKY AND A GORILLA" BY TAKAHITO OGURA FROM CANADA

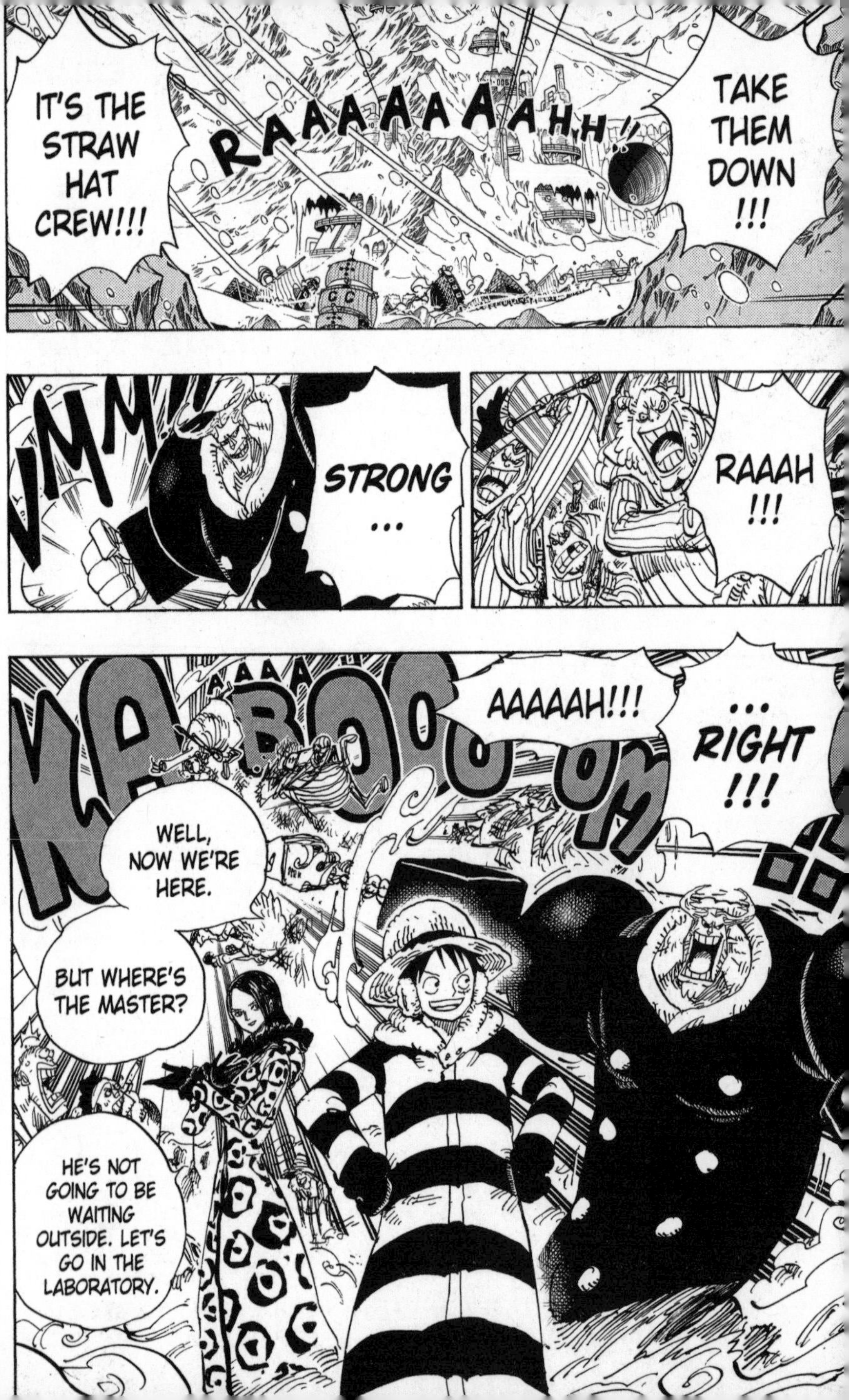
TAKE THEM DOWN!!!
RAAAAAAAAHH!!
IT'S THE STRAW HAT CREW!!!
RAAAH!!!
STRONG...
...RIGHT!!!
AAAAAH!!!
KABOOOM
WELL, NOW WE'RE HERE.
BUT WHERE'S THE MASTER?
HE'S NOT GOING TO BE WAITING OUTSIDE. LET'S GO IN THE LABORATORY.

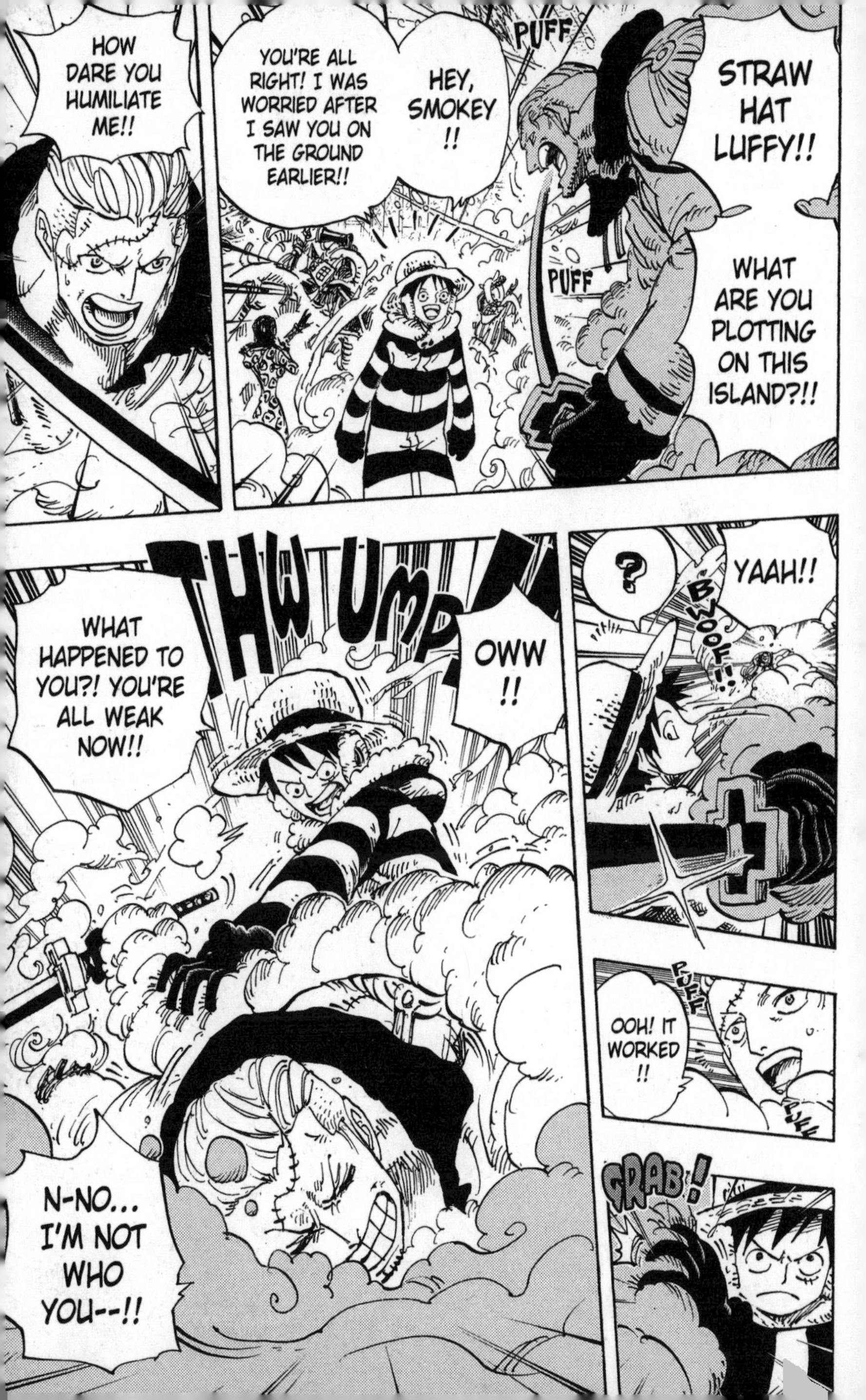
STRAW HAT LUFFY!!
WHAT ARE YOU PLOTTING ON THIS ISLAND?!!
PUFF
PUFF
HEY, SMOKEY !!
YOU'RE ALL RIGHT! I WAS WORRIED AFTER I SAW YOU ON THE GROUND EARLIER!!
HOW DARE YOU HUMILIATE ME!!
YAAH!!
BWOOF!!
?
PUFF
OOH! IT WORKED !!
GRAB!
THWUMP
OWW !!
WHAT HAPPENED TO YOU?! YOU'RE ALL WEAK NOW!!
N-NO... I'M NOT WHO YOU--!!

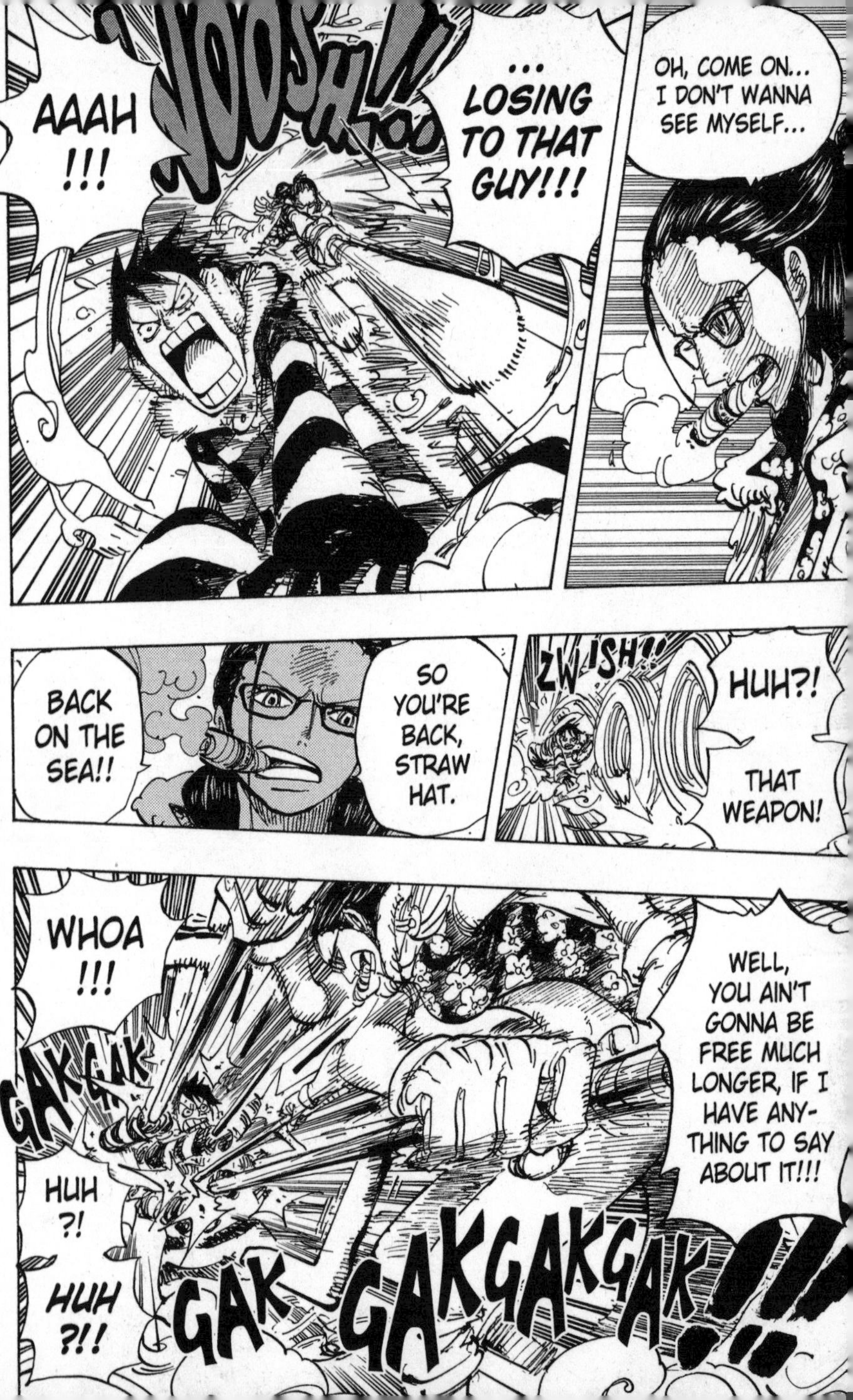
OH, COME ON... I DON'T WANNA SEE MYSELF...
... LOSING TO THAT GUY!!!
WOOSH!!
AAAH!!!
HUH?!
ZWISH!!
THAT WEAPON!
SO YOU'RE BACK, STRAW HAT.
BACK ON THE SEA!!
WELL, YOU AIN'T GONNA BE FREE MUCH LONGER, IF I HAVE ANY-THING TO SAY ABOUT IT!!!
WHOA!!!
GAK GAK
HUH?!
HUH?!!
GAK GAKGAKGAK!!!

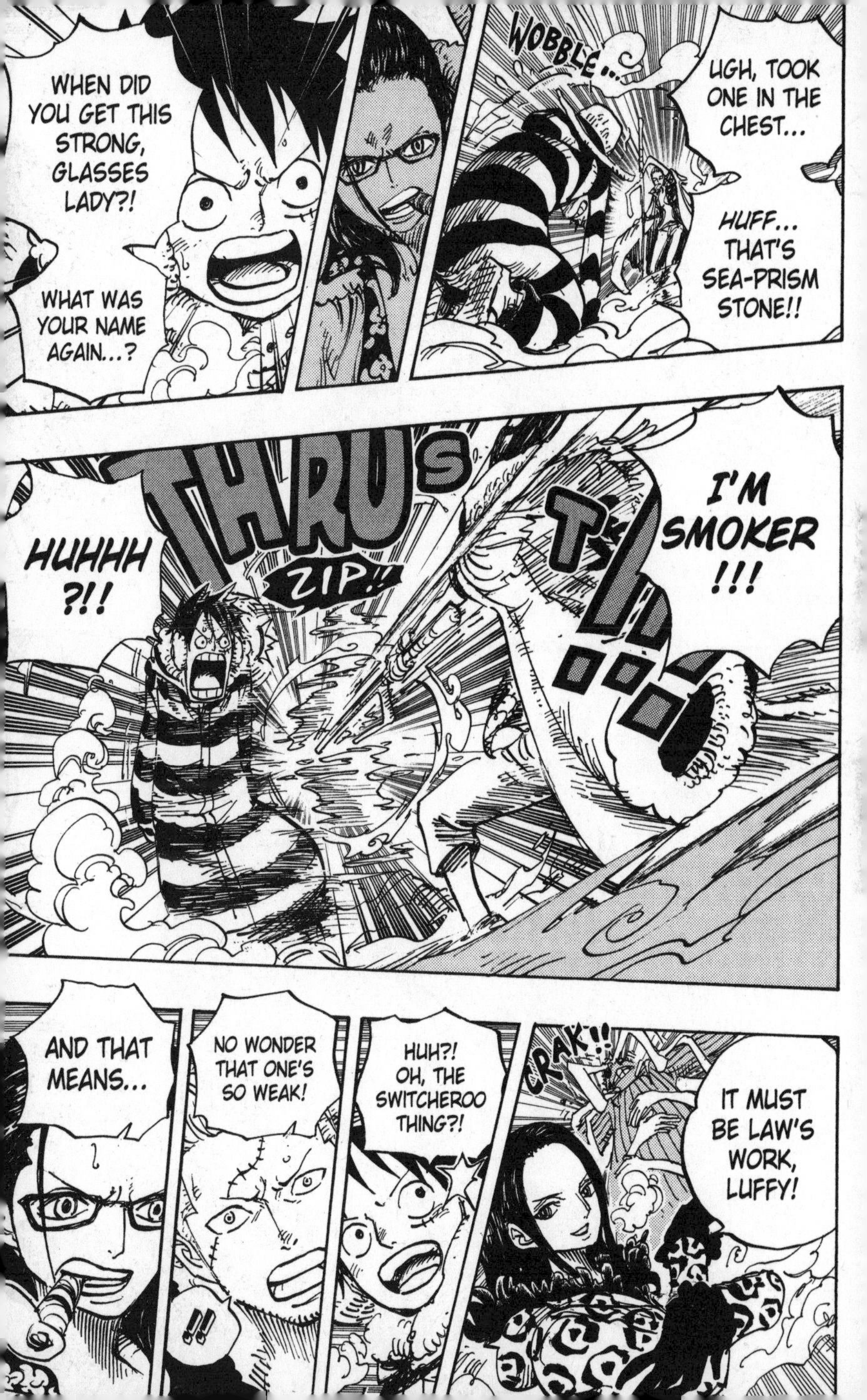
WOBBLE...
UGH, TOOK ONE IN THE CHEST...
HUFF... THAT'S SEA-PRISM STONE!!
WHEN DID YOU GET THIS STRONG, GLASSES LADY?!
WHAT WAS YOUR NAME AGAIN...?
I'M SMOKER!!!
THRUST!!
ZIP!!
HUHHH ?!!
CRAK!!
IT MUST BE LAW'S WORK, LUFFY!
HUH?! OH, THE SWITCHEROO THING?!
NO WONDER THAT ONE'S SO WEAK!
!!
AND THAT MEANS...

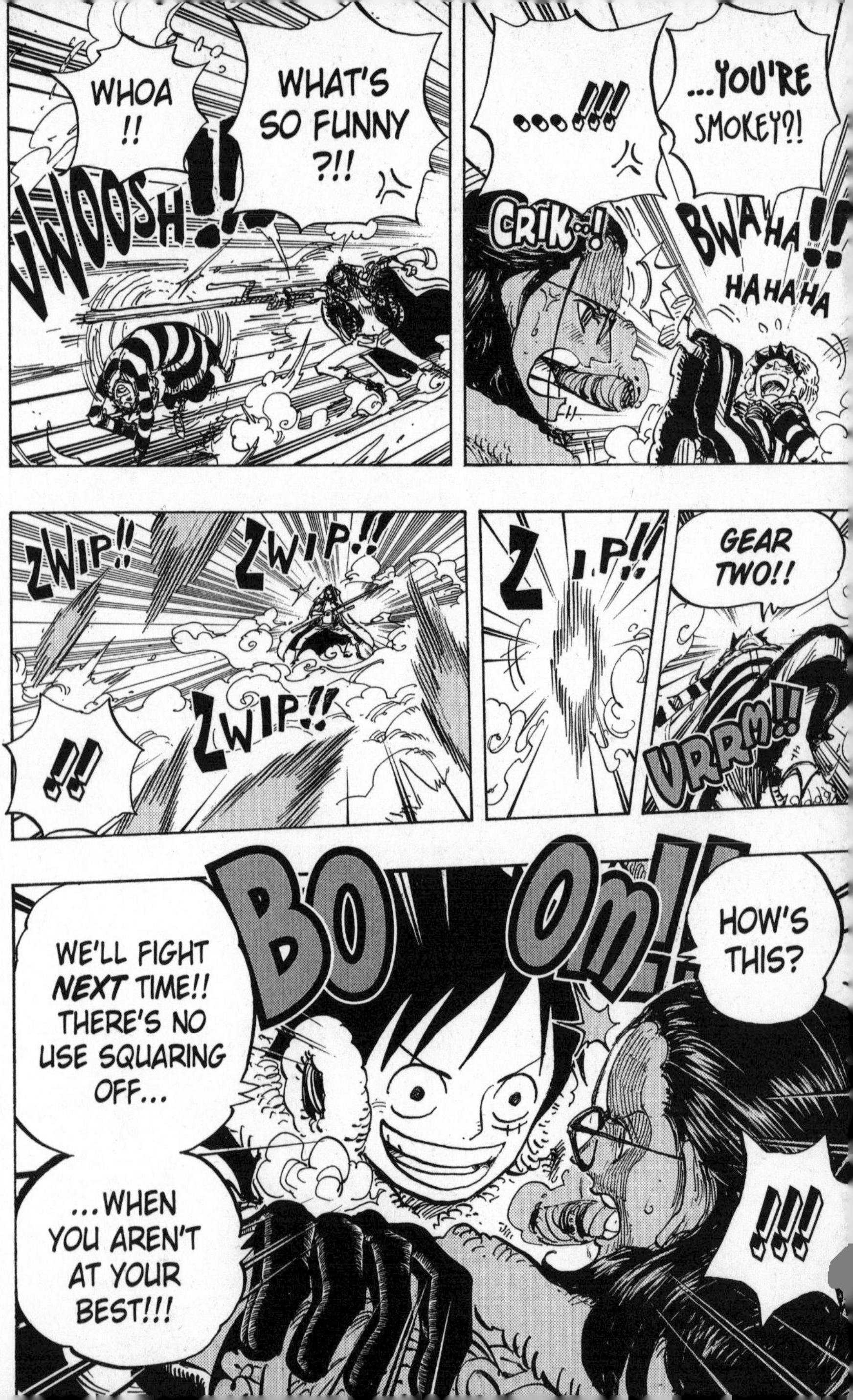

...YOU'RE SMOKEY?!
...!!!
BWAHA!! HAHAHA
CRIK..!
WHAT'S SO FUNNY ?!!
WHOA !!
WHOOSH!!
GEAR TWO!!
VRRM!!
ZIP!!
ZWIP!!
ZWIP!!
ZWIP!!
!!
HOW'S THIS?
BOOM!!
!!!
WE'LL FIGHT *NEXT* TIME!! THERE'S NO USE SQUARING OFF...
...WHEN YOU AREN'T AT YOUR BEST!!!

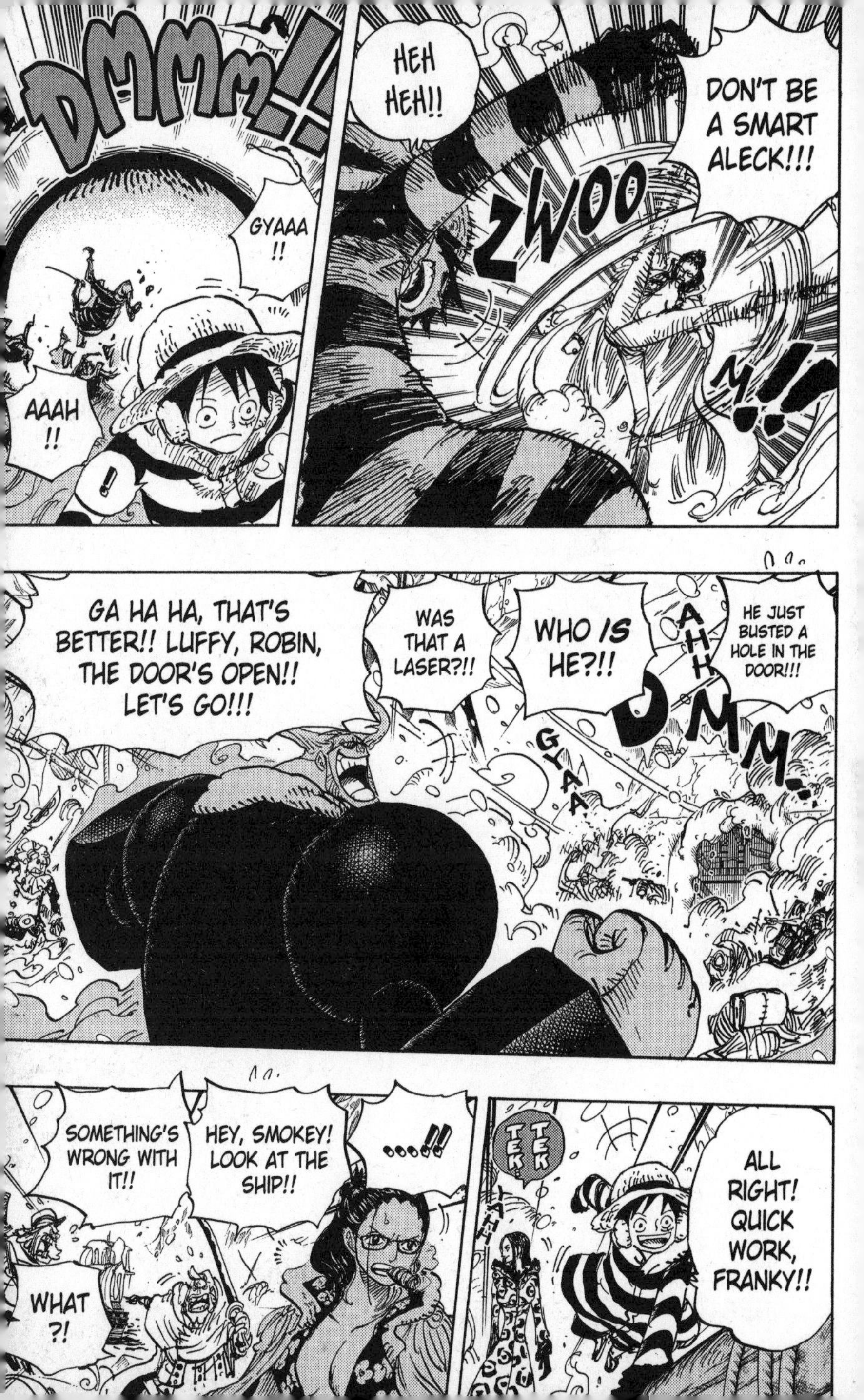

DON'T BE A SMART ALECK!!!
HEH HEH!!
ZWOO
M!!
DMMM!!
GYAAA !!
AAAH !!
!
HE JUST BUSTED A HOLE IN THE DOOR!!!
AHH
DMMM..
WHO *IS* HE?!!
WAS THAT A LASER?!!
GYAA
GA HA HA, THAT'S BETTER!! LUFFY, ROBIN, THE DOOR'S OPEN!! LET'S GO!!!
ALL RIGHT! QUICK WORK, FRANKY!!
TEK TEK
...!!
HEY, SMOKEY! LOOK AT THE SHIP!!
SOMETHING'S WRONG WITH IT!!
WHAT ?!

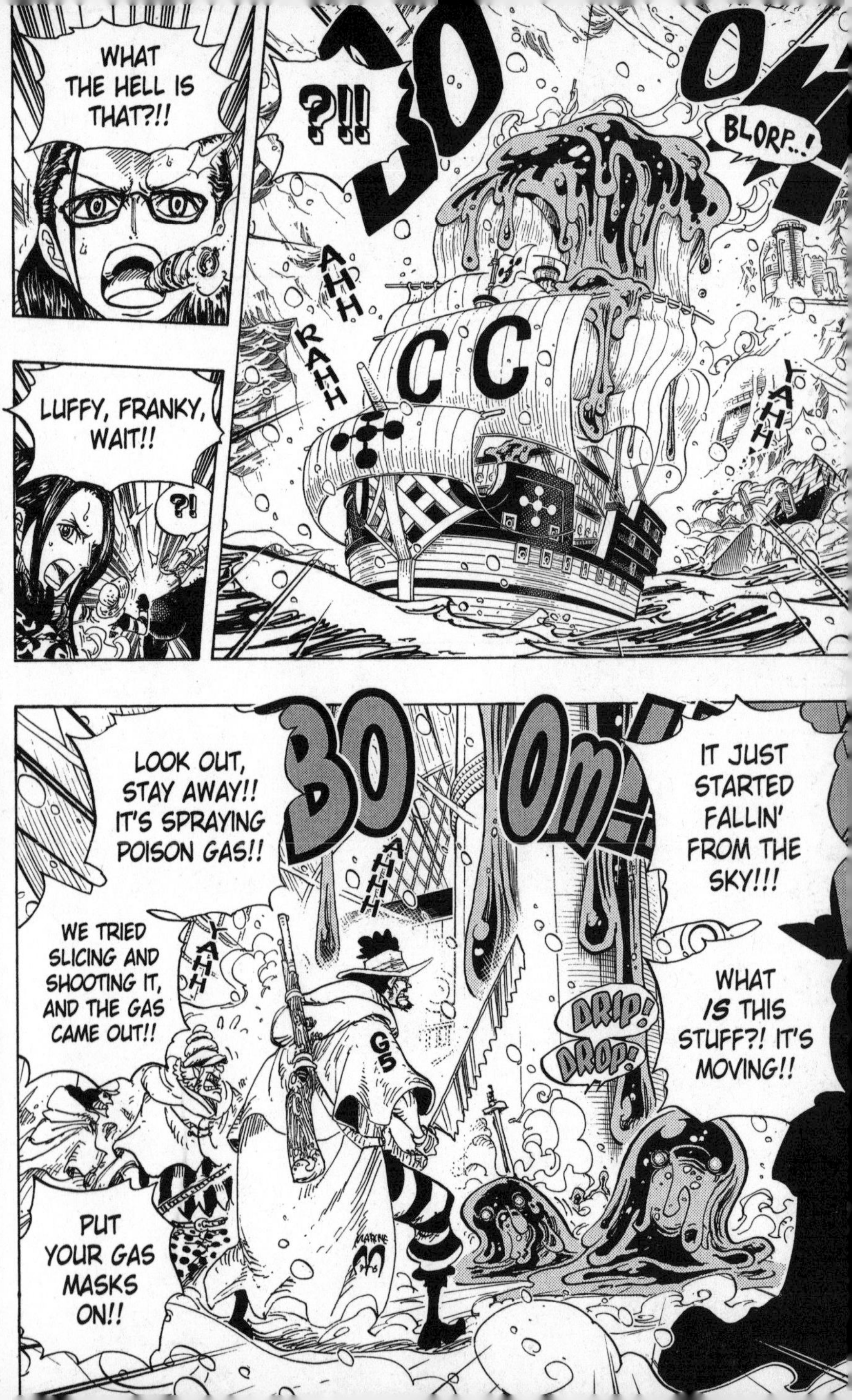
BOOM
?!!
BLORP..!
AHHH
RAHHH
YAHH
WHAT THE HELL IS THAT?!!
LUFFY, FRANKY, WAIT!!
?!
BOOM
IT JUST STARTED FALLIN' FROM THE SKY!!!!
WHAT IS THIS STUFF?! IT'S MOVING!!
DRIP! DROP!
AHHHH
LOOK OUT, STAY AWAY!! IT'S SPRAYING POISON GAS!!
WE TRIED SLICING AND SHOOTING IT, AND THE GAS CAME OUT!!
YAHH
PUT YOUR GAS MASKS ON!!

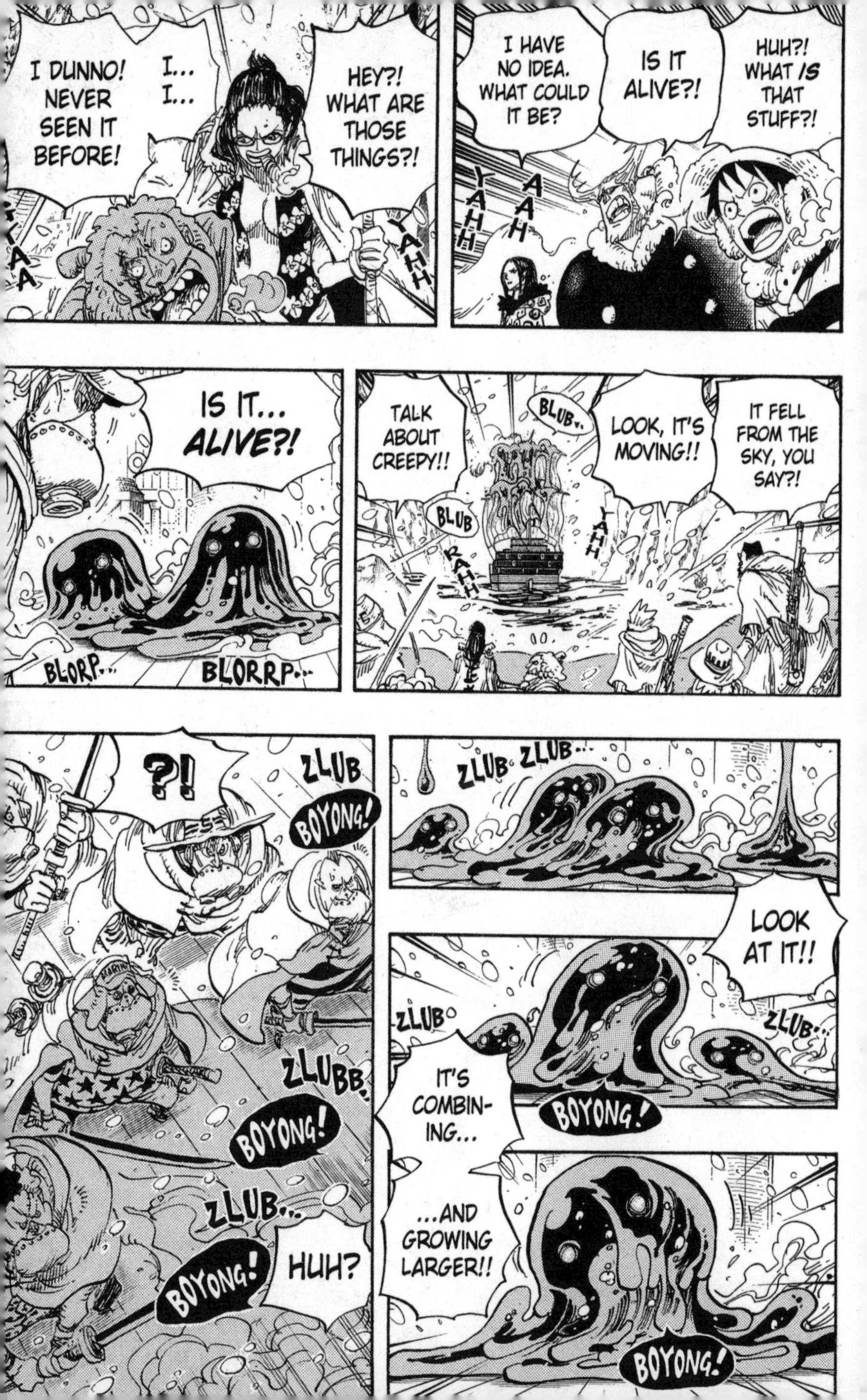
HUH?! WHAT IS THAT STUFF?!
IS IT ALIVE?!
I HAVE NO IDEA. WHAT COULD IT BE?
AAH
YAHH
HEY?! WHAT ARE THOSE THINGS?!
I... I...
I DUNNO! NEVER SEEN IT BEFORE!
YAHH
IT FELL FROM THE SKY, YOU SAY?!
LOOK, IT'S MOVING!!
BLUB..
TALK ABOUT CREEPY!!
YAHH
BLUB
RAHH
IS IT... ALIVE?!
BLORP...
BLORRP...
ZLUB ZLUB...
LOOK AT IT!!
ZLUB...
ZLUB
BOYONG!
IT'S COMBINING...
...AND GROWING LARGER!!
BOYONG!
?!
ZLUB
BOYONG!
ZLUBB...
BOYONG!
ZLUB...
BOYONG!
HUH?

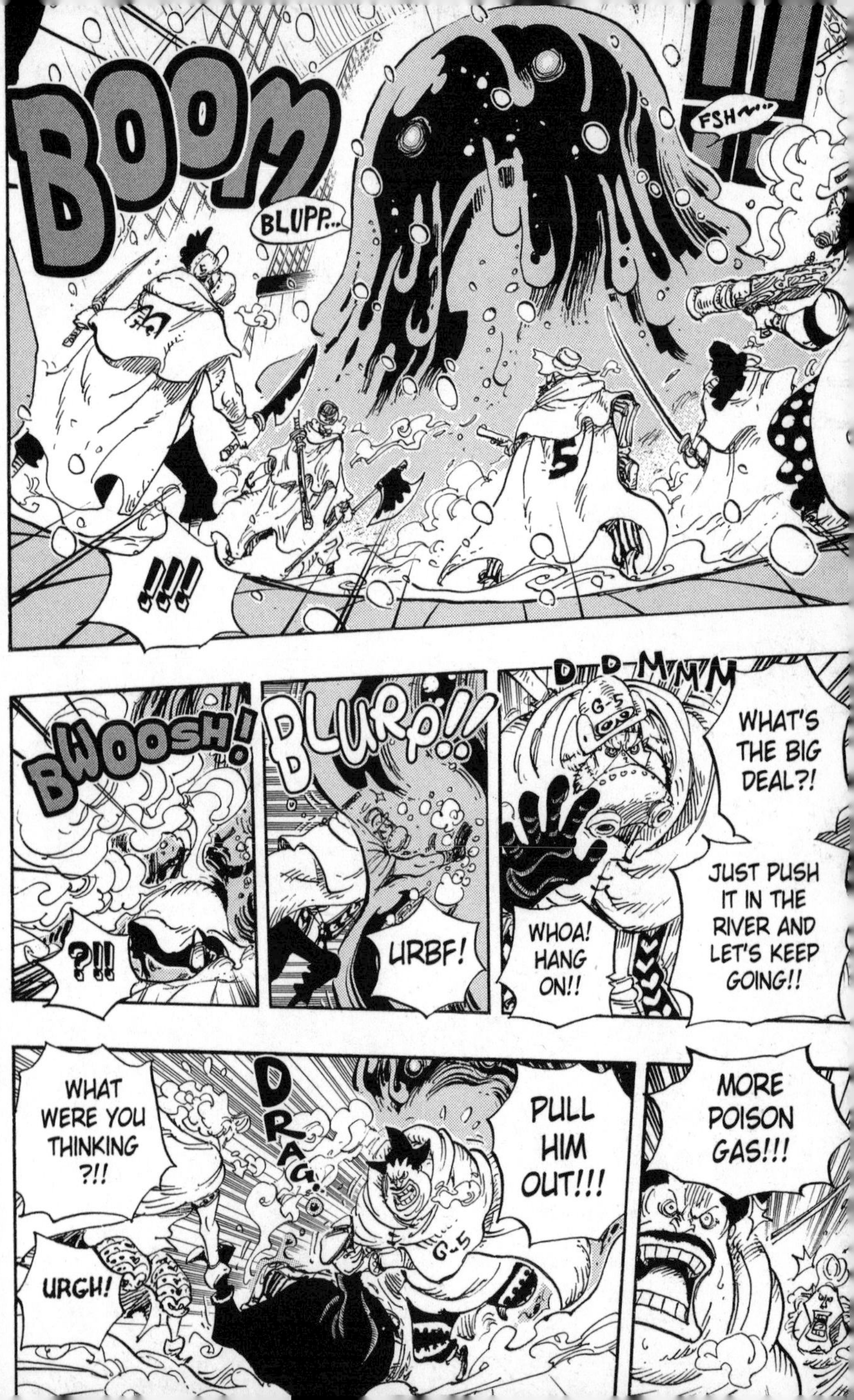
FSH~...
BOOM
BLUPP...
!!!
DDMMN
WHAT'S THE BIG DEAL?!
JUST PUSH IT IN THE RIVER AND LET'S KEEP GOING!!
WHOA! HANG ON!!
BLURP!!
URBF!
BWOOSH!
?!!
MORE POISON GAS!!!
PULL HIM OUT!!!
DRAG!
WHAT WERE YOU THINKING?!!
URGH!

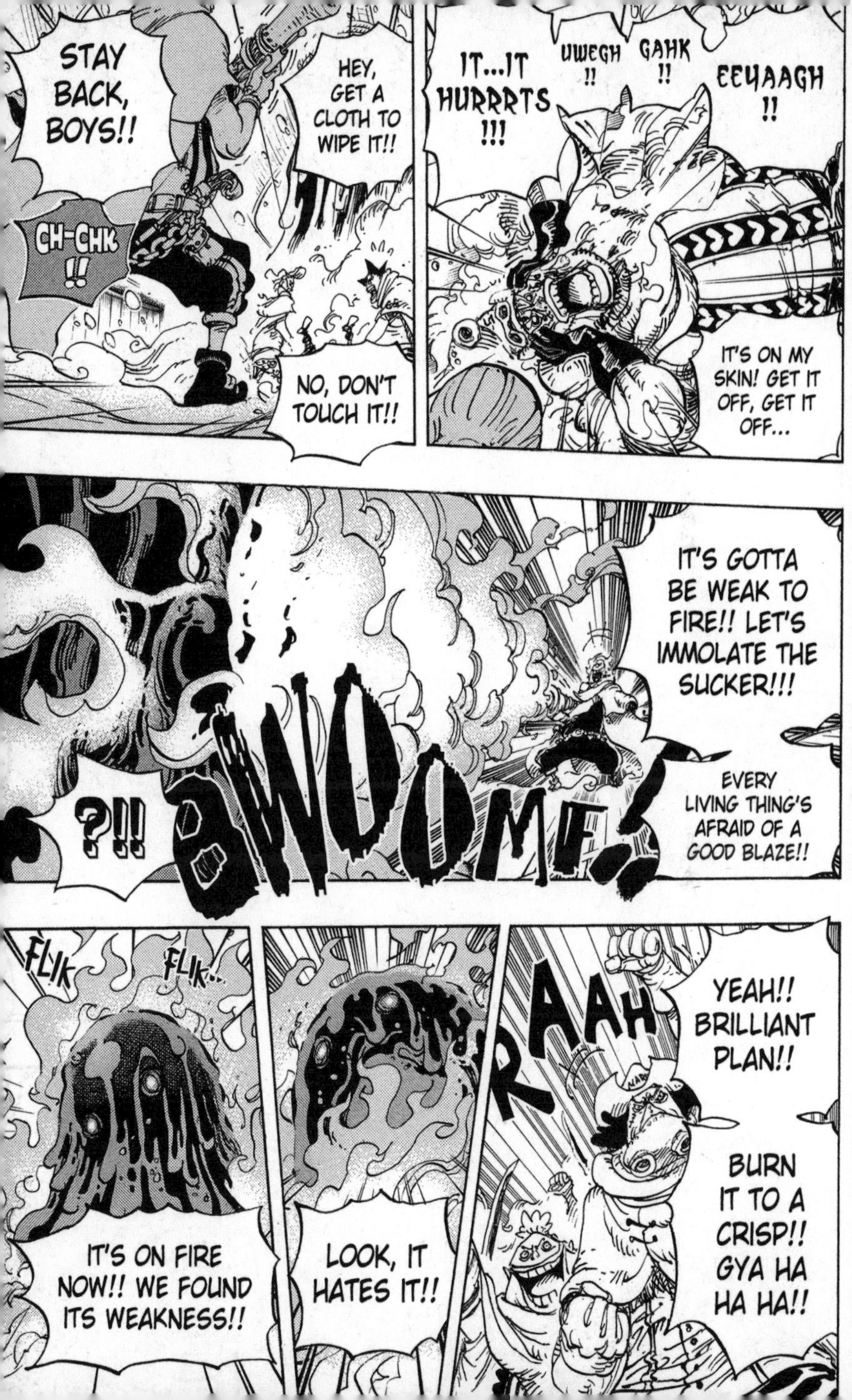
EEYAAGH!!
GAHK!!
UWEGH!!
IT...IT HURRRTS!!!
IT'S ON MY SKIN! GET IT OFF, GET IT OFF...
HEY, GET A CLOTH TO WIPE IT!!
STAY BACK, BOYS!!
CH-CHK!!
NO, DON'T TOUCH IT!!
IT'S GOTTA BE WEAK TO FIRE!! LET'S IMMOLATE THE SUCKER!!!
EVERY LIVING THING'S AFRAID OF A GOOD BLAZE!!
WOOMF
?!!
YEAH!! BRILLIANT PLAN!!
RAAH
BURN IT TO A CRISP!! GYA HA HA HA!!
LOOK, IT HATES IT!!
FLIK
FLIK
IT'S ON FIRE NOW!! WE FOUND ITS WEAKNESS!!

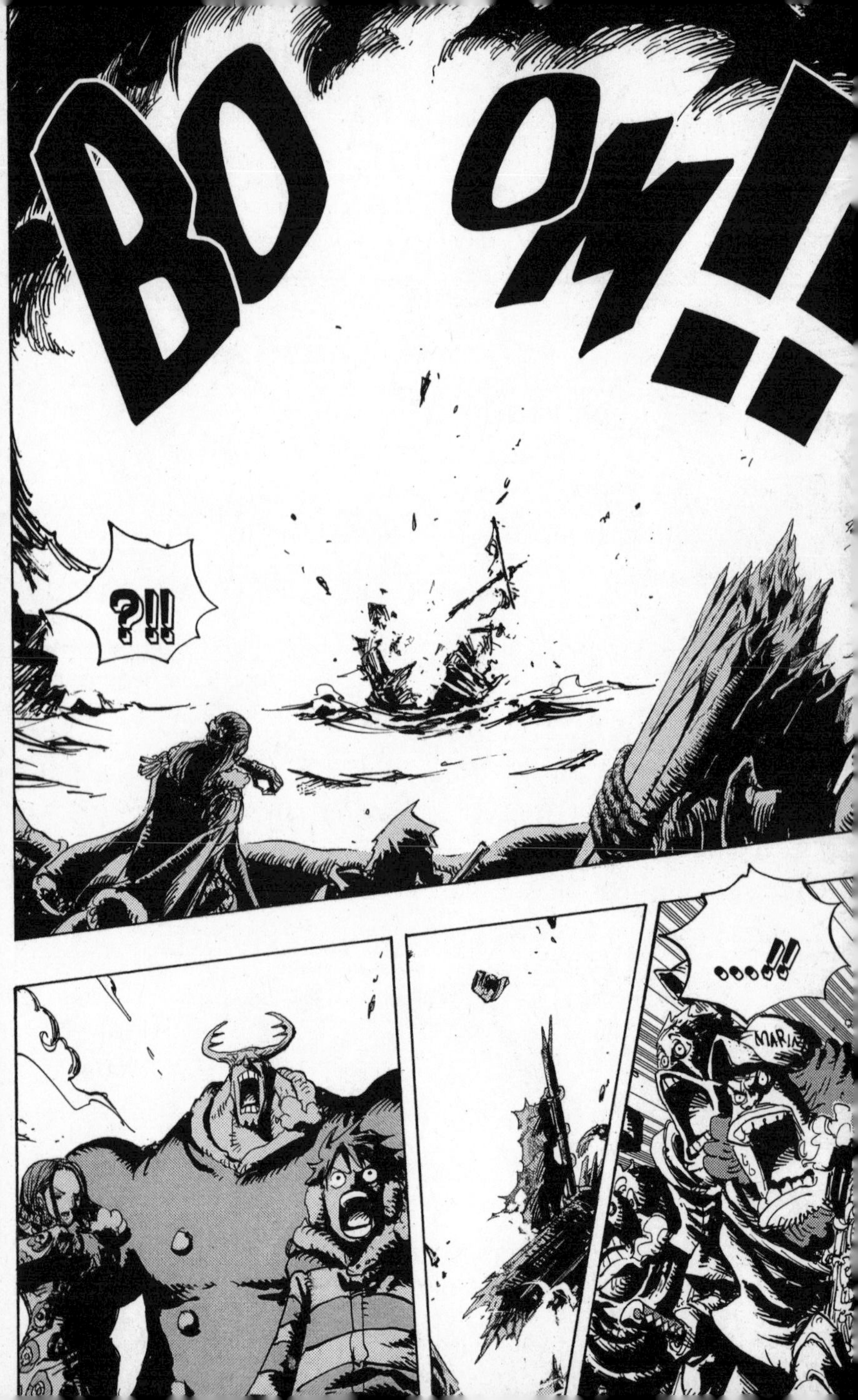

BOOM!!
?!!
.....!!
MARIN

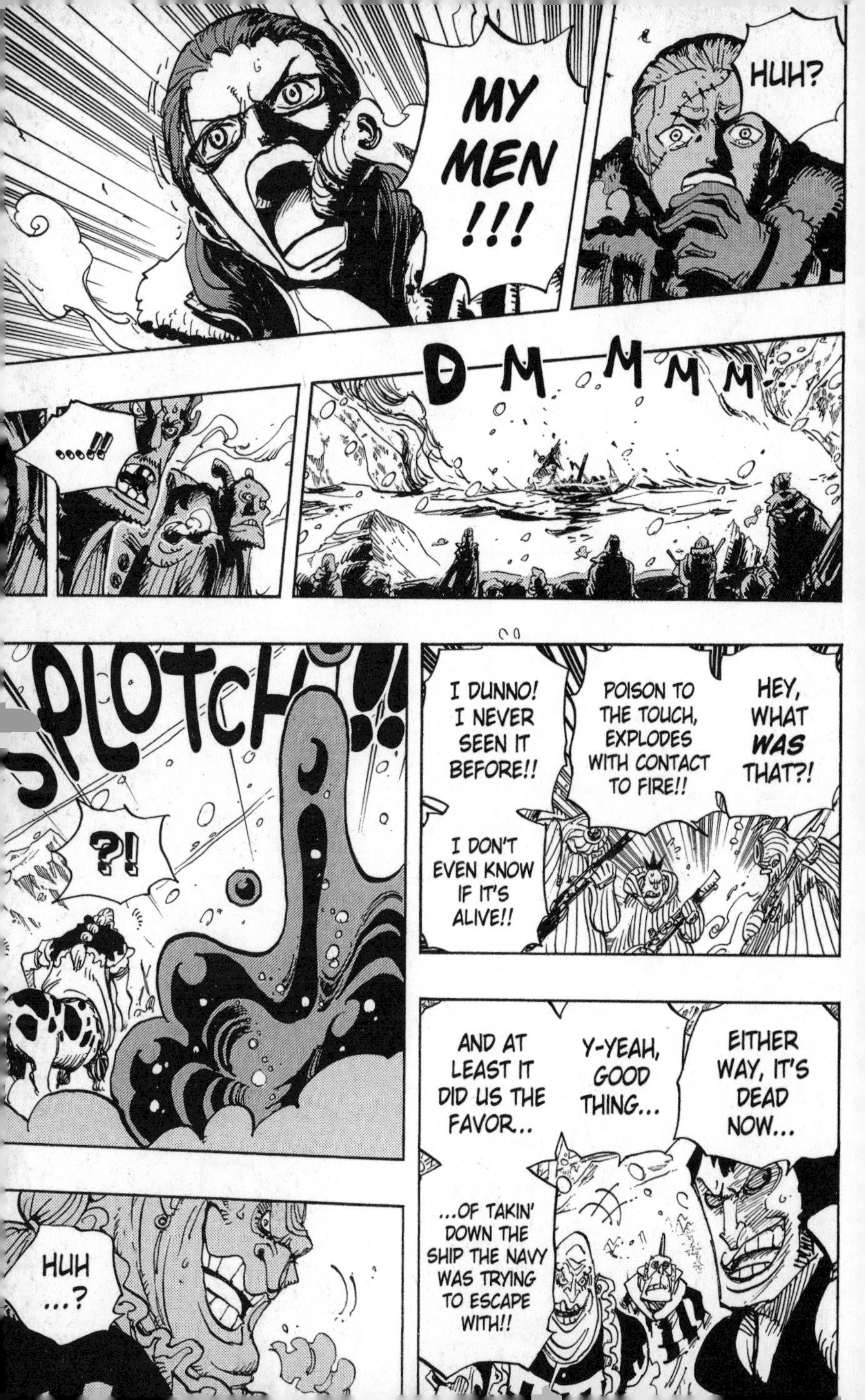
HUH?
MY MEN !!!
D M M M M M
...!!
SPLOTCH!!
HEY, WHAT WAS THAT?!
POISON TO THE TOUCH, EXPLODES WITH CONTACT TO FIRE!!
I DUNNO! I NEVER SEEN IT BEFORE!!
I DON'T EVEN KNOW IF IT'S ALIVE!!
?!
EITHER WAY, IT'S DEAD NOW...
Y-YEAH, GOOD THING...
AND AT LEAST IT DID US THE FAVOR...
...OF TAKIN' DOWN THE SHIP THE NAVY WAS TRYING TO ESCAPE WITH!!
HUH ...?

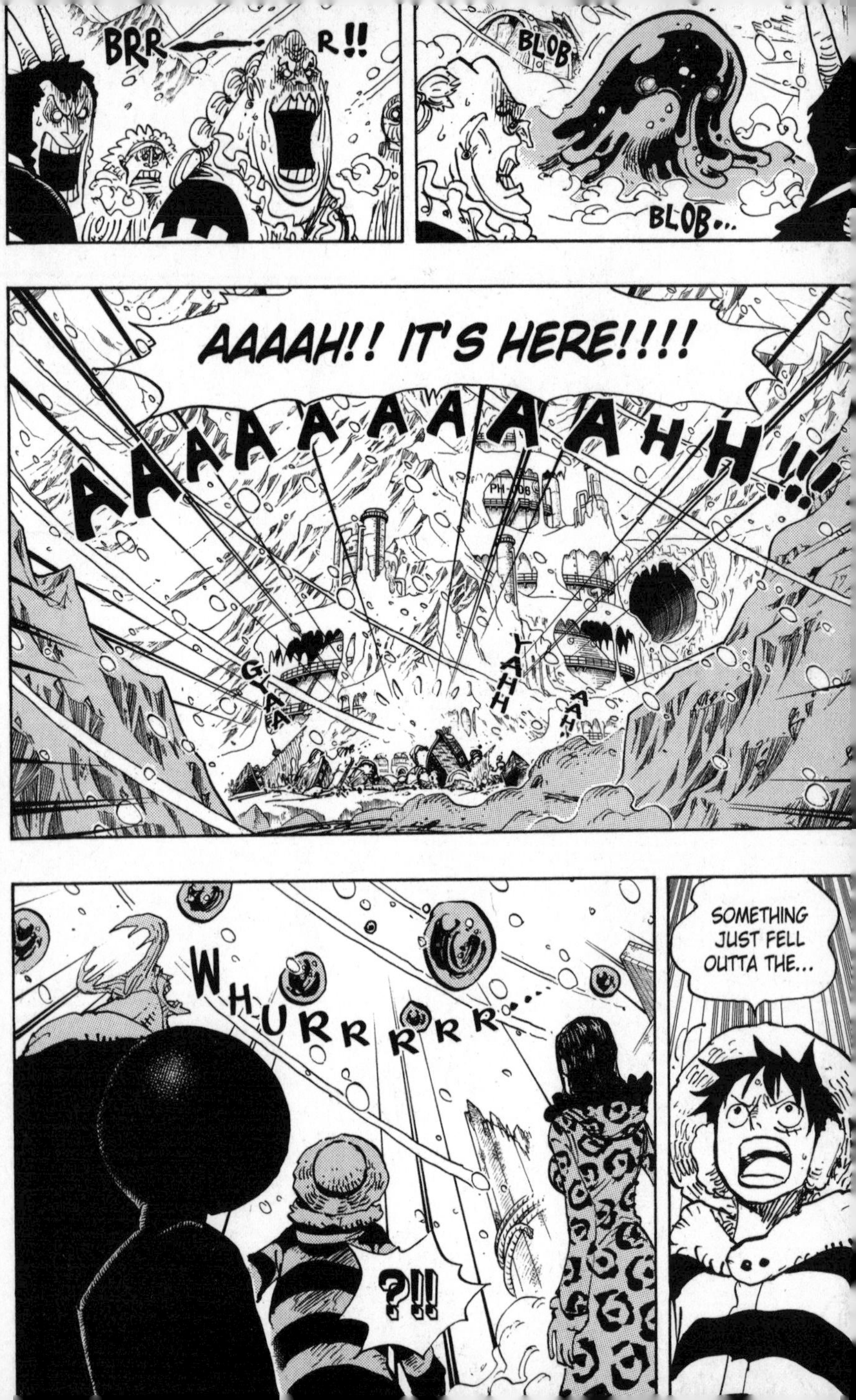
BLOB
BLOB...
BRR——R!!
AAAAH!! IT'S HERE!!!!
AAAAAAAAAAH!!!
GYAA
YAHH
AAH!
SOMETHING JUST FELL OUTTA THE...
WHURRRRRR...
?!!

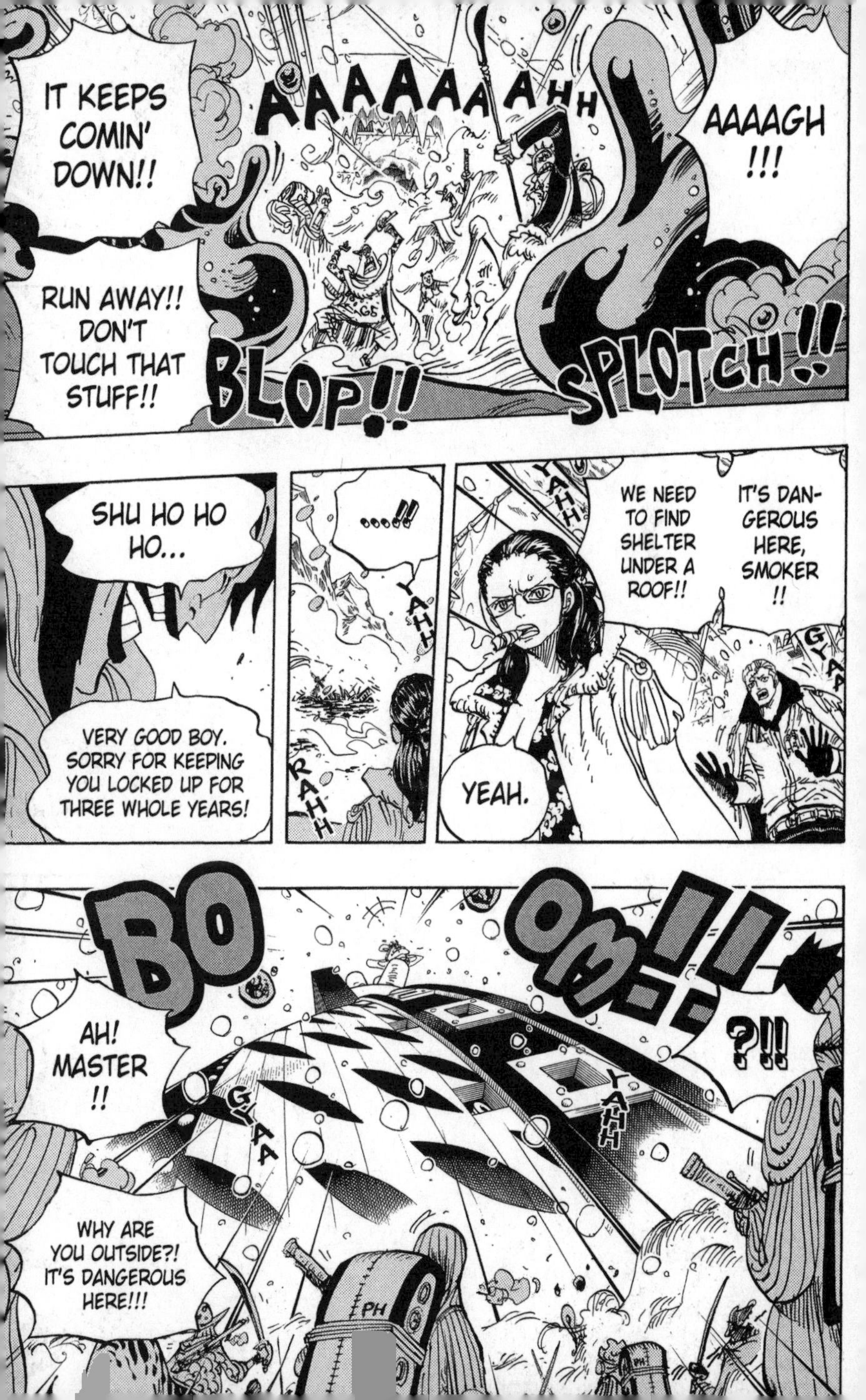
AAAAGH!!!
AAAAAAAHH
IT KEEPS COMIN' DOWN!!
SPLOTCH!!
BLOP!!
RUN AWAY!! DON'T TOUCH THAT STUFF!!
IT'S DAN-GEROUS HERE, SMOKER!!
WE NEED TO FIND SHELTER UNDER A ROOF!!
YAHH
GYAA
YEAH.
....!!
YAHH
RAHH
SHU HO HO HO...
VERY GOOD BOY. SORRY FOR KEEPING YOU LOCKED UP FOR THREE WHOLE YEARS!
BOOM!!
?!!
YAHH
AH! MASTER!!
GYAA
WHY ARE YOU OUTSIDE?! IT'S DANGEROUS HERE!!!

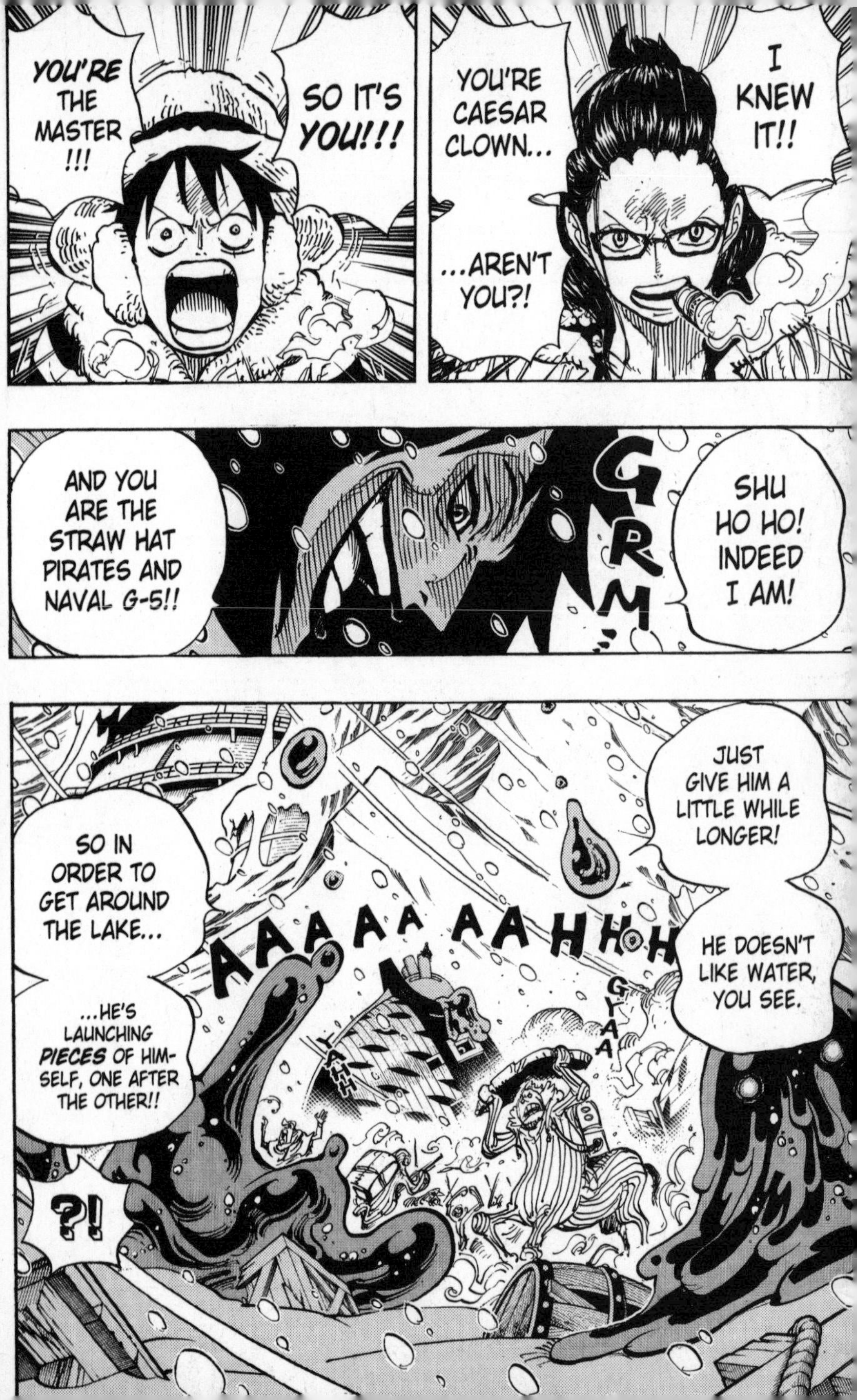
I KNEW IT!!
YOU'RE CAESAR CLOWN...
...AREN'T YOU?!
SO IT'S *YOU!!!*
YOU'RE THE MASTER !!!
SHU HO HO! INDEED I AM!
GRRM
AND YOU ARE THE STRAW HAT PIRATES AND NAVAL G-5!!
JUST GIVE HIM A LITTLE WHILE LONGER!
HE DOESN'T LIKE WATER, YOU SEE.
AAAAA AAHHH
GYAA
SO IN ORDER TO GET AROUND THE LAKE...
...HE'S LAUNCHING *PIECES* OF HIM-SELF, ONE AFTER THE OTHER!!
?!

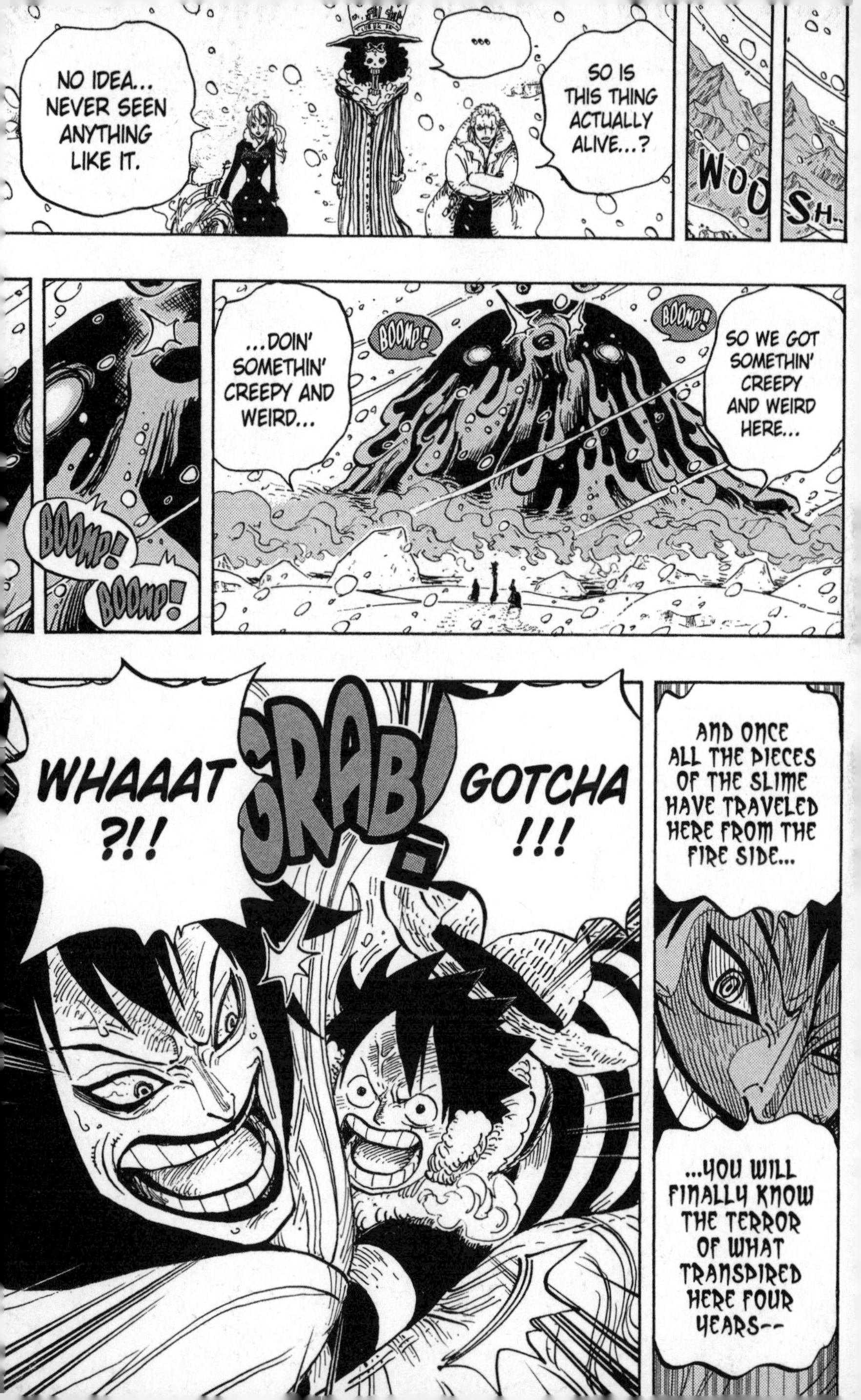
WOOSH..
SO IS THIS THING ACTUALLY ALIVE...?
...
NO IDEA... NEVER SEEN ANYTHING LIKE IT.
BOOMP!
SO WE GOT SOMETHIN' CREEPY AND WEIRD HERE...
BOOMP!
...DOIN' SOMETHIN' CREEPY AND WEIRD...
BOOMP!
BOOMP!
AND ONCE ALL THE PIECES OF THE SLIME HAVE TRAVELED HERE FROM THE FIRE SIDE...
...YOU WILL FINALLY KNOW THE TERROR OF WHAT TRANSPIRED HERE FOUR YEARS--
GOTCHA!!!
GRAB!
WHAAAT?!!

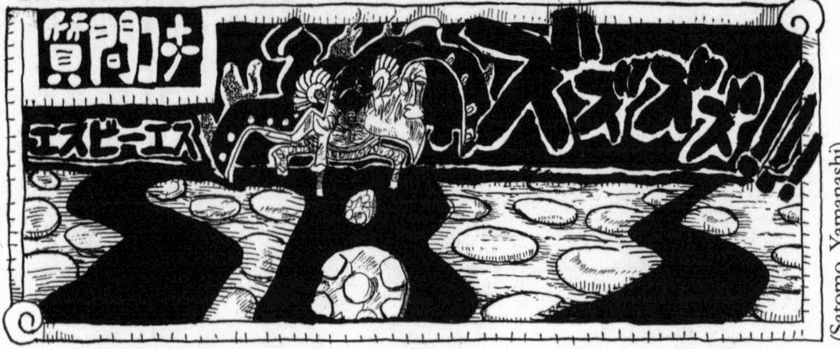
質問コーナー
エスビーエス

(Satomo, Yamanashi)

Q: Yo, Odacchi! You drawing manga right now? You'll be surprised to know that I examined every page of *One Piece* and counted up each and every **exclamation point!!** Isn't that amazing? Including the sound effects and combined marks like "?!" I found that through Chapter 636, there are a grand total of **150,096 exclamation points.** That's an average of 236 exclamation points per chapter…☆ That's amazing, Odacchi!♡

A: ...!! ...I can't believe you counted them... What for? What a stupid question! Yeah! Exclamation points! Thanks so much!!!!!!!!!!

Q: Thanks for your super-answer to my super-question, Odacchi! I super-don't get the meaning of Franky's Black Rhino FR-U4. I'd super-like to know what it stands for.

--Match & Takeshi

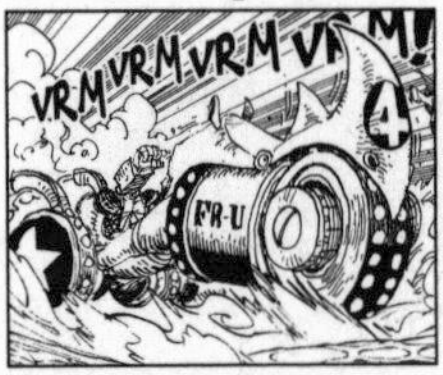
VRM VRM VRM VR M!
4
FR-U

A: Ah, yes. FR-U. It stands for Franky-Ude (arms). When Franky transforms into General Franky, Black Rhino FR-U4 makes up the robot's arms.

Q: Hello, Mr. Oda. I've always thought that when he was first introduced, Sanji looked a lot like Leonardo DiCaprio in the movie *Romeo + Juliet*. My friend says no way. Did you model him after anyone??

--Noel

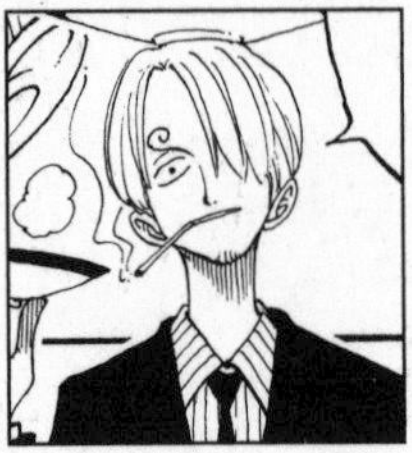

A: Many people would ask about DiCaprio way back then. But as a matter of fact, Sanji's model has a much more obscure background. I didn't model him to the point of wanting an obvious physical resemblance; it was more like I hoped to get his attitude and mannerisms across. Sanji was based on the actor Steve Buscemi, especially his role in Reservoir Dogs. He's really super cool. The only person who's ever guessed it correctly was an employee at Bandai, years ago.

Chapter 671:

GAS-GAS FRUIT

*CAT BURGLARS

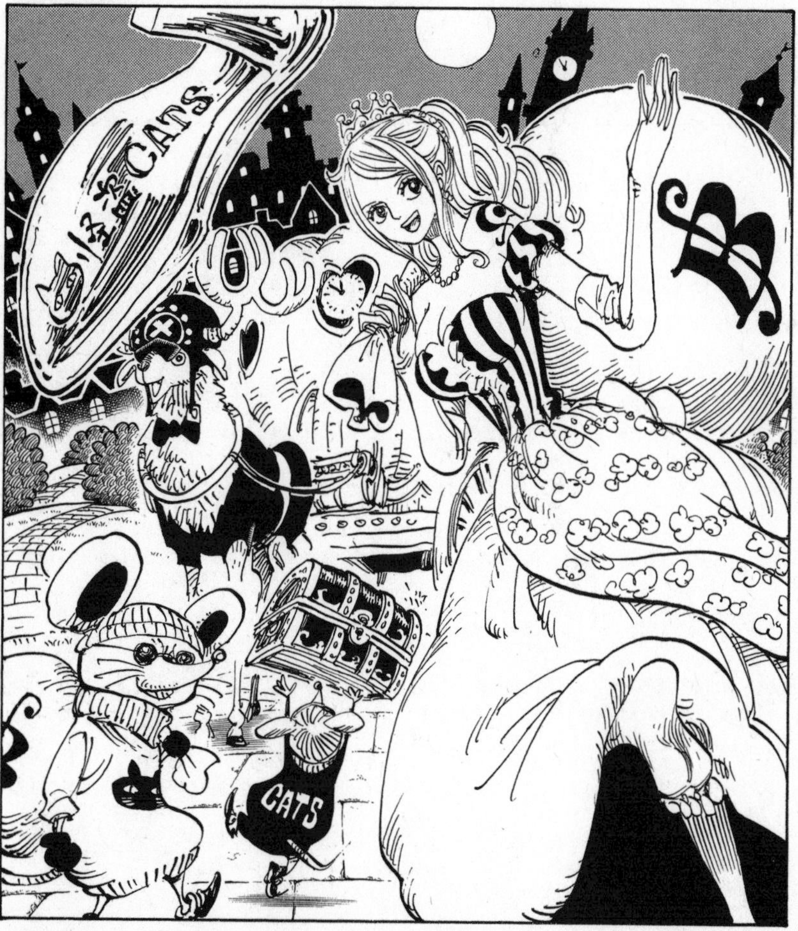
CATS
CATS

REQUEST: "NAMIRELLA & HER MICE TAKE A RIDE ON CHOPPER'S PUMPKIN CARRIAGE" BY AKEMI ISAKA FROM IBARAKI

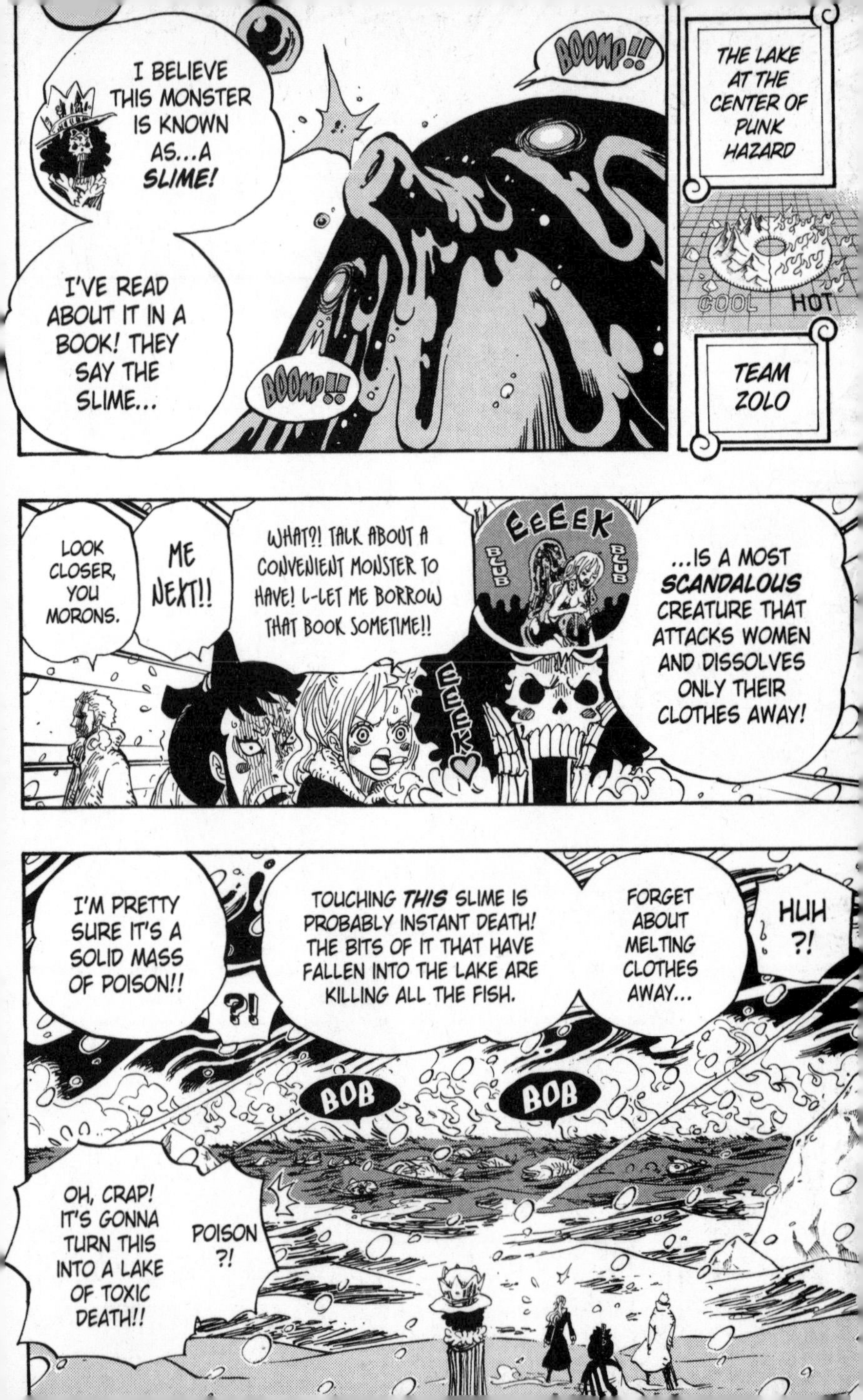
THE LAKE AT THE CENTER OF PUNK HAZARD
COOL
HOT
TEAM ZOLO
BOOMP!!
I BELIEVE THIS MONSTER IS KNOWN AS...A SLIME!
I'VE READ ABOUT IT IN A BOOK! THEY SAY THE SLIME...
BOOMP!!
...IS A MOST SCANDALOUS CREATURE THAT ATTACKS WOMEN AND DISSOLVES ONLY THEIR CLOTHES AWAY!
EEEEK
BLUB
BLUB
EEEEK
WHAT?! TALK ABOUT A CONVENIENT MONSTER TO HAVE! L-LET ME BORROW THAT BOOK SOMETIME!!
ME NEXT!!
LOOK CLOSER, YOU MORONS.
HUH ?!
FORGET ABOUT MELTING CLOTHES AWAY...
TOUCHING THIS SLIME IS PROBABLY INSTANT DEATH! THE BITS OF IT THAT HAVE FALLEN INTO THE LAKE ARE KILLING ALL THE FISH.
?!
I'M PRETTY SURE IT'S A SOLID MASS OF POISON!!
BOB
BOB
POISON ?!
OH, CRAP! IT'S GONNA TURN THIS INTO A LAKE OF TOXIC DEATH!!

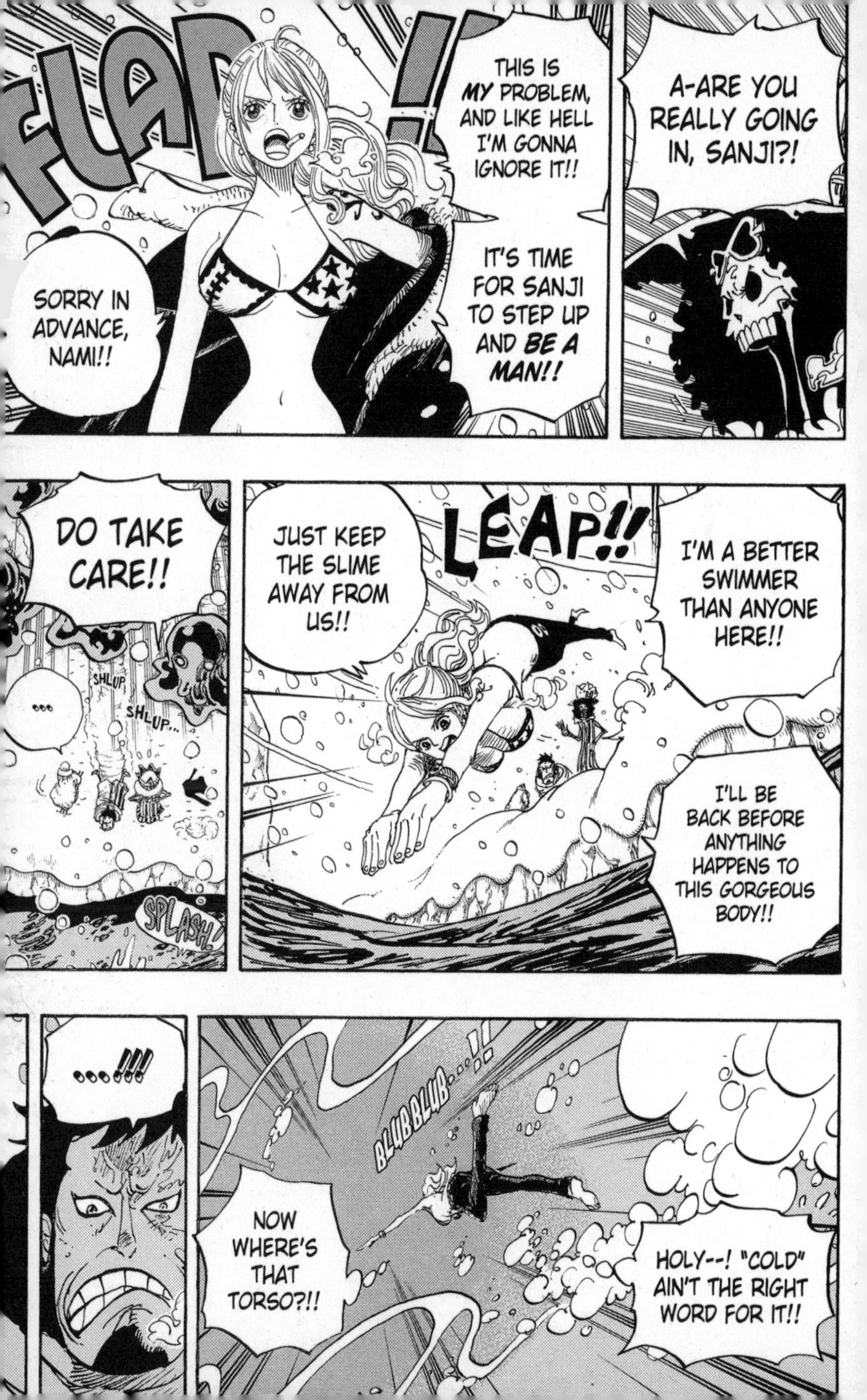
A-ARE YOU REALLY GOING IN, SANJI?!
FLAP!!
THIS IS MY PROBLEM, AND LIKE HELL I'M GONNA IGNORE IT!!
IT'S TIME FOR SANJI TO STEP UP AND BE A MAN!!
SORRY IN ADVANCE, NAMI!!
I'M A BETTER SWIMMER THAN ANYONE HERE!!
LEAP!!
JUST KEEP THE SLIME AWAY FROM US!!
I'LL BE BACK BEFORE ANYTHING HAPPENS TO THIS GORGEOUS BODY!!
DO TAKE CARE!!
SHLUP
SHLUP...
...
SPLASH!
BLUB BLUB...
HOLY--! "COLD" AIN'T THE RIGHT WORD FOR IT!!
NOW WHERE'S THAT TORSO?!!
...!!!

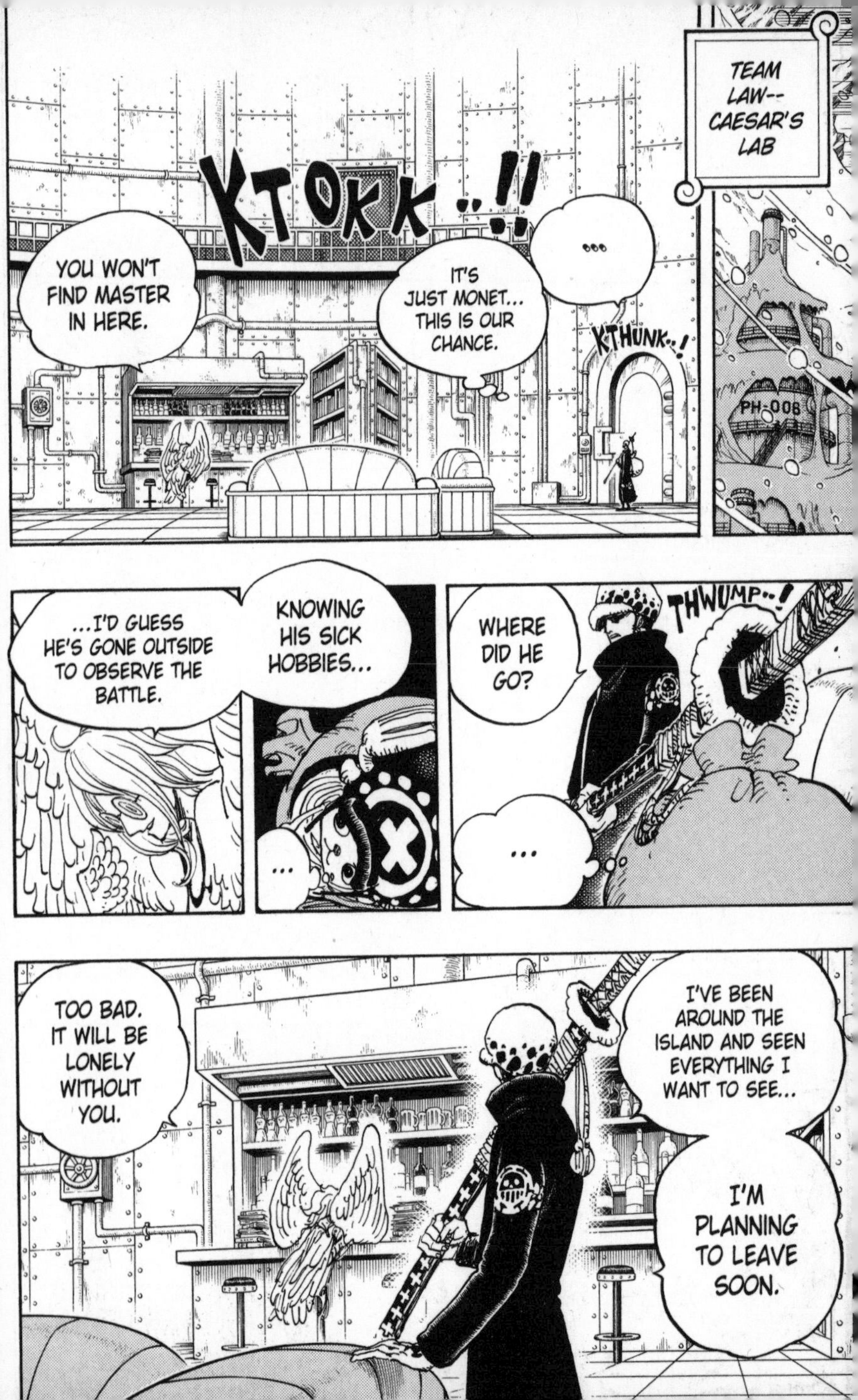
TEAM LAW-- CAESAR'S LAB
...
KTOKK..!!
IT'S JUST MONET... THIS IS OUR CHANCE.
KTHUNK..!
YOU WON'T FIND MASTER IN HERE.
THWUMP..!
WHERE DID HE GO?
...
KNOWING HIS SICK HOBBIES...
...
...I'D GUESS HE'S GONE OUTSIDE TO OBSERVE THE BATTLE.
I'VE BEEN AROUND THE ISLAND AND SEEN EVERYTHING I WANT TO SEE...
I'M PLANNING TO LEAVE SOON.
TOO BAD. IT WILL BE LONELY WITHOUT YOU.

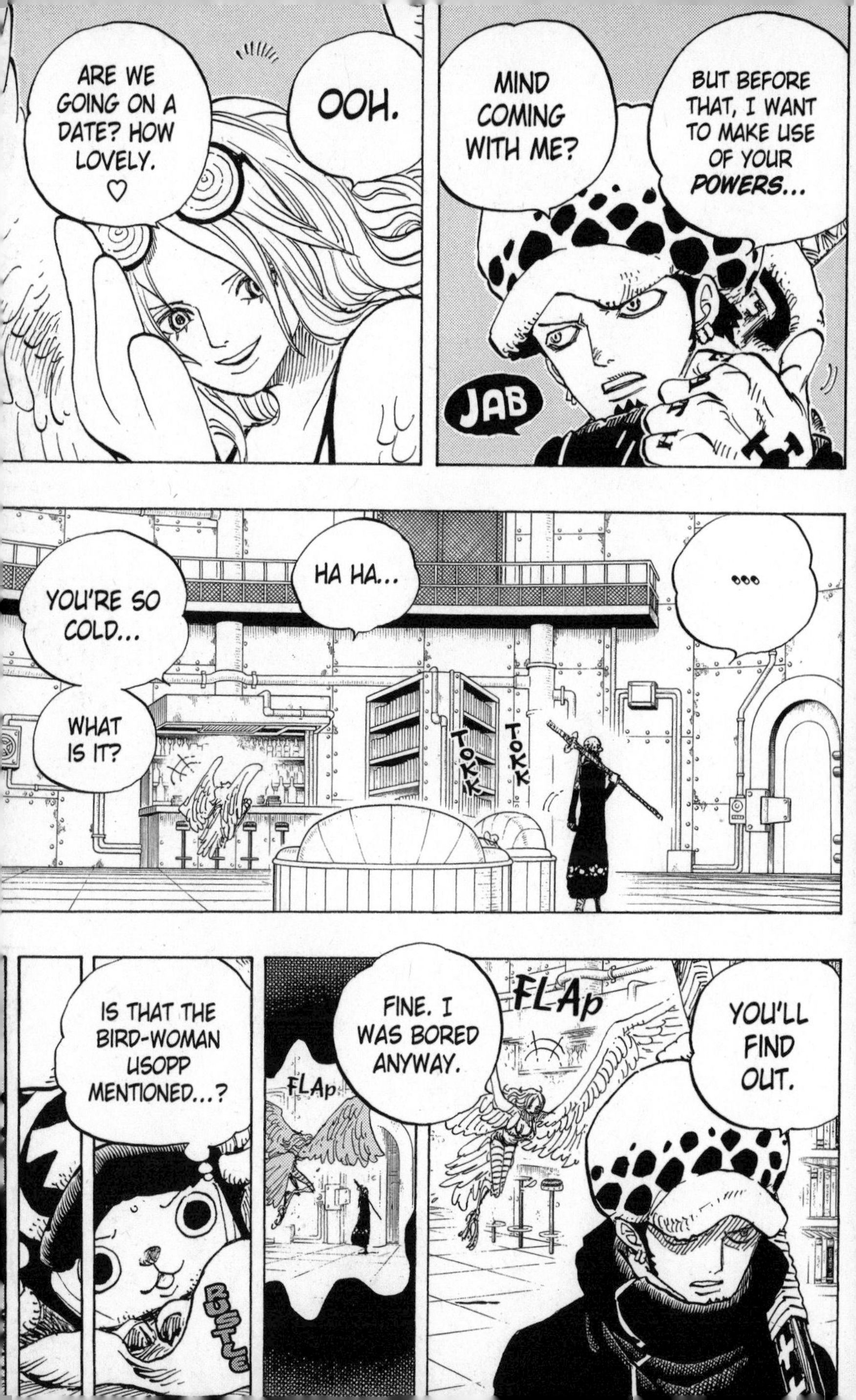
BUT BEFORE THAT, I WANT TO MAKE USE OF YOUR *POWERS*...
MIND COMING WITH ME?
JAB
OOH.
ARE WE GOING ON A DATE? HOW LOVELY. ♡
...
HA HA...
YOU'RE SO COLD...
WHAT IS IT?
TOKK
TOKK
YOU'LL FIND OUT.
FLAp
FINE. I WAS BORED ANYWAY.
FLAp
IS THAT THE BIRD-WOMAN USOPP MENTIONED...?
RUSTLE

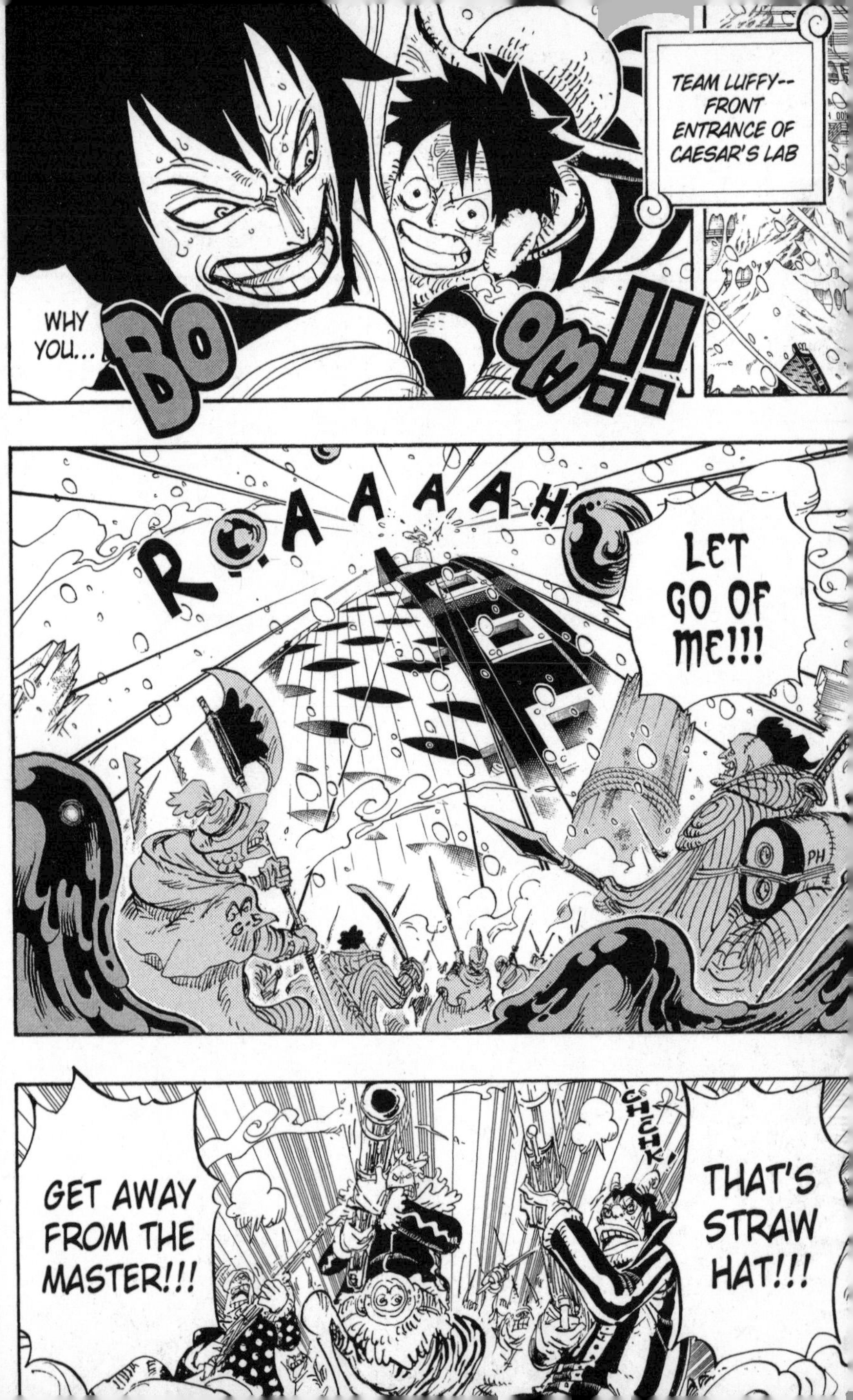
TEAM LUFFY-- FRONT ENTRANCE OF CAESAR'S LAB
WHY YOU...
BOOM!!
LET GO OF ME!!!
RAAAAAH
THAT'S STRAW HAT!!!
CHCHK
GET AWAY FROM THE MASTER!!!

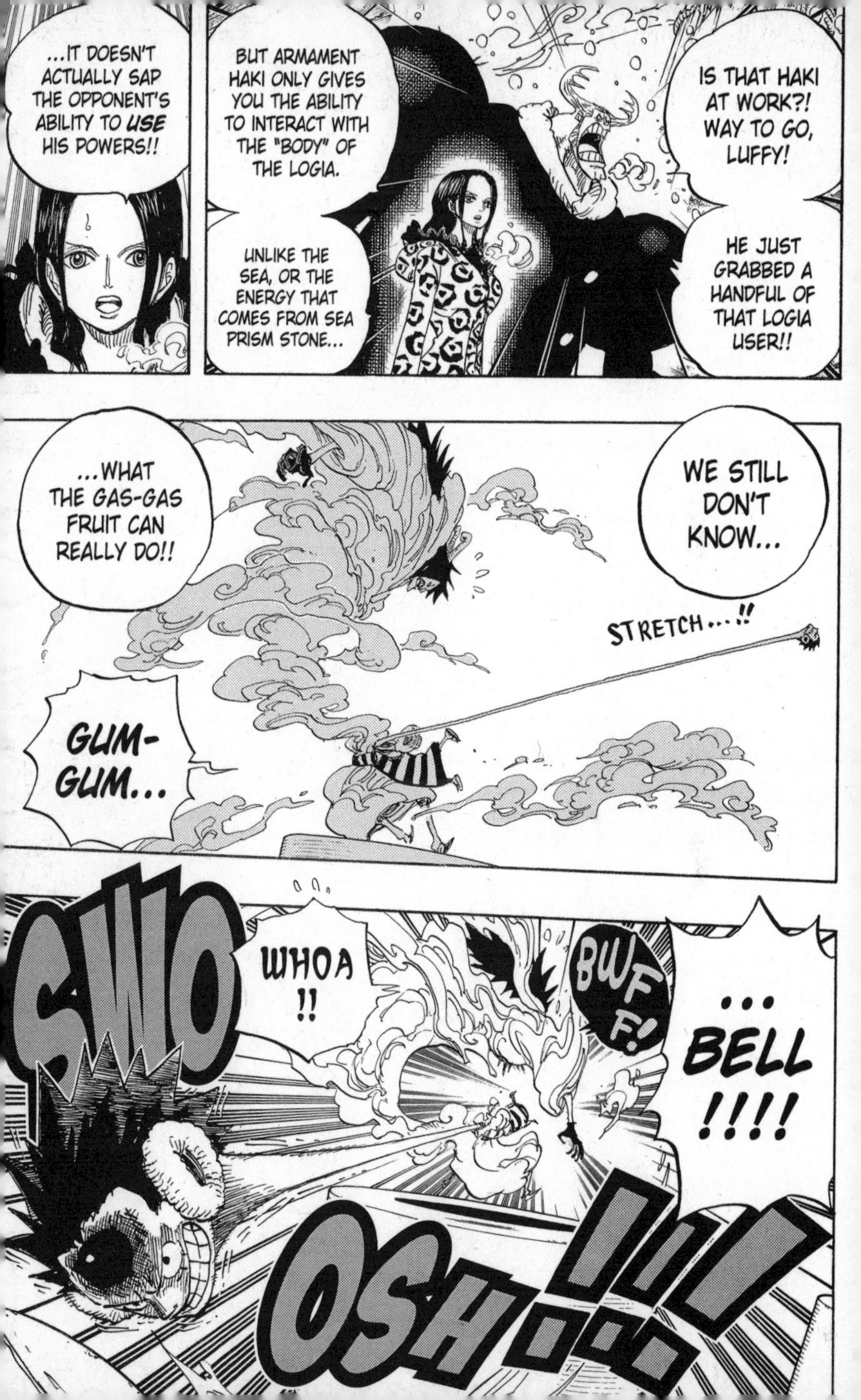
IS THAT HAKI AT WORK?! WAY TO GO, LUFFY!
HE JUST GRABBED A HANDFUL OF THAT LOGIA USER!!
BUT ARMAMENT HAKI ONLY GIVES YOU THE ABILITY TO INTERACT WITH THE "BODY" OF THE LOGIA.
UNLIKE THE SEA, OR THE ENERGY THAT COMES FROM SEA PRISM STONE...
...IT DOESN'T ACTUALLY SAP THE OPPONENT'S ABILITY TO USE HIS POWERS!!
WE STILL DON'T KNOW...
...WHAT THE GAS-GAS FRUIT CAN REALLY DO!!
STRETCH...!!
GUM-GUM...
...BELL!!!!
BWFF!
WHOA!!
SWO
OSH...!!!!

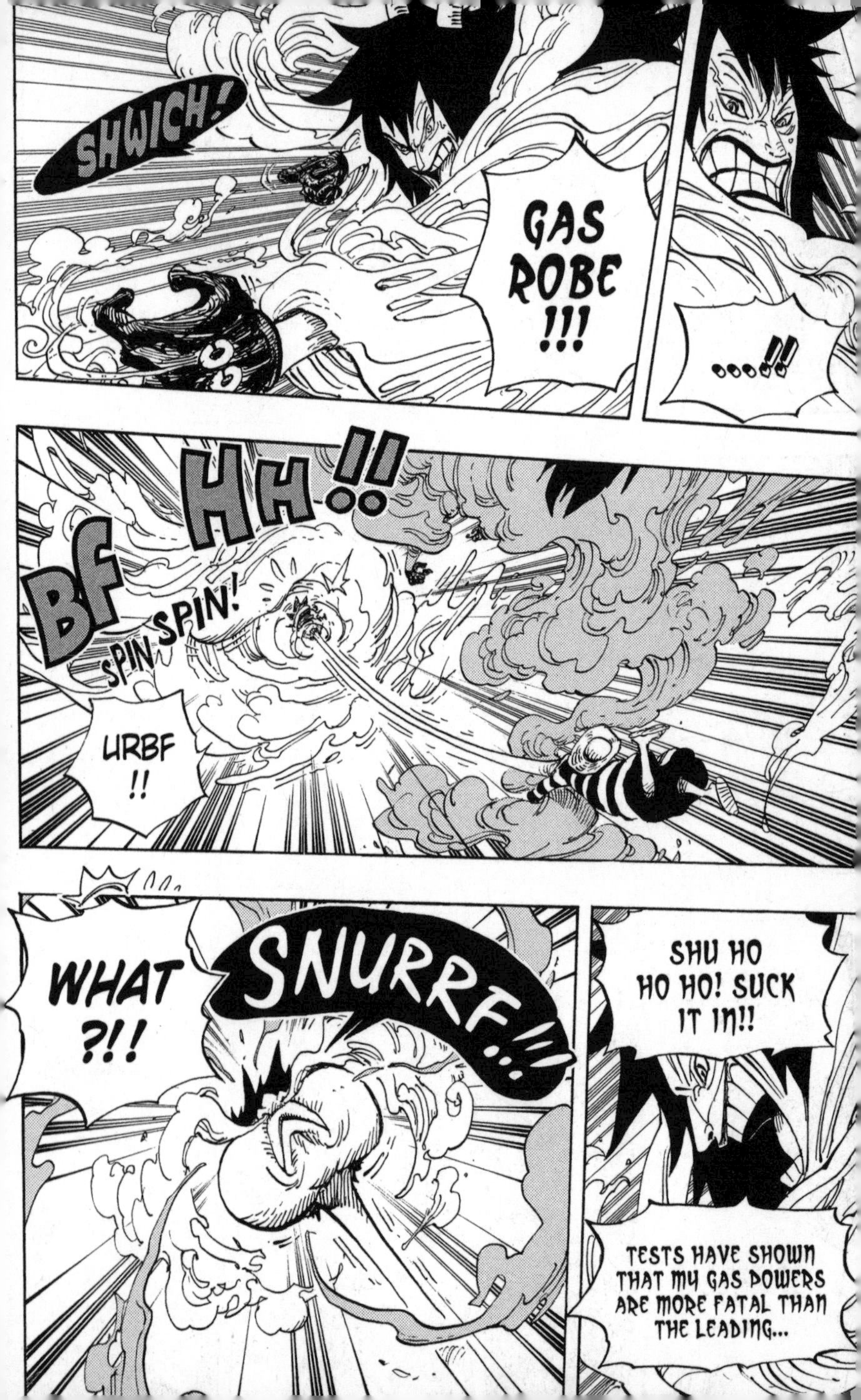
....!!
GAS ROBE !!!
SHWICH!
BFHH!!
SPIN SPIN!
URBF !!
SHU HO HO HO! SUCK IT IN!!
TESTS HAVE SHOWN THAT MY GAS POWERS ARE MORE FATAL THAN THE LEADING...
SNURRF!!!
WHAT ?!!

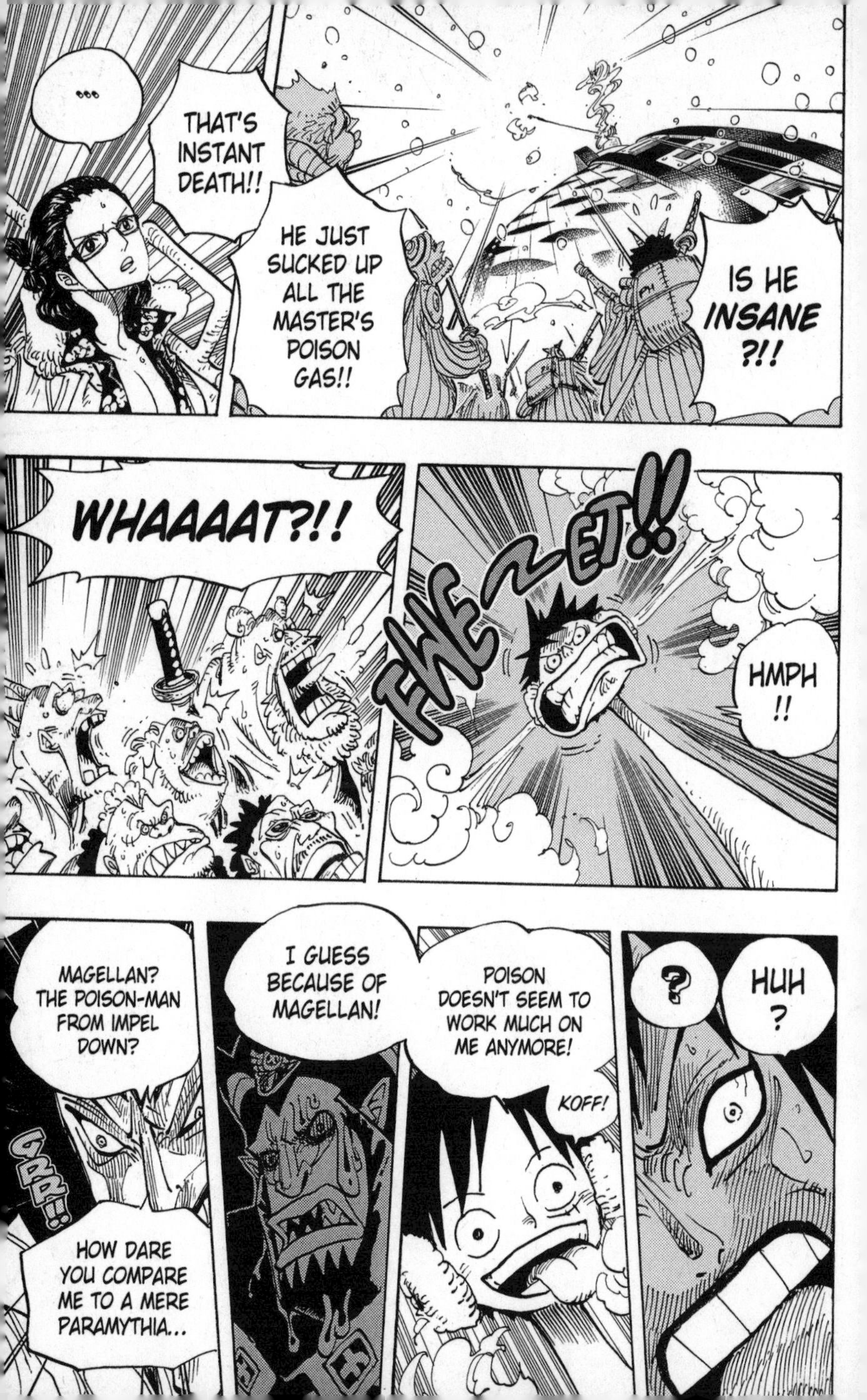
IS HE INSANE ?!!
HE JUST SUCKED UP ALL THE MASTER'S POISON GAS!!
THAT'S INSTANT DEATH!!
...
HMPH !!
FWE~ET!!
WHAAAAT?!!
?
HUH ?
POISON DOESN'T SEEM TO WORK MUCH ON ME ANYMORE!
KOFF!
I GUESS BECAUSE OF MAGELLAN!
MAGELLAN? THE POISON-MAN FROM IMPEL DOWN?
HOW DARE YOU COMPARE ME TO A MERE PARAMYTHIA...

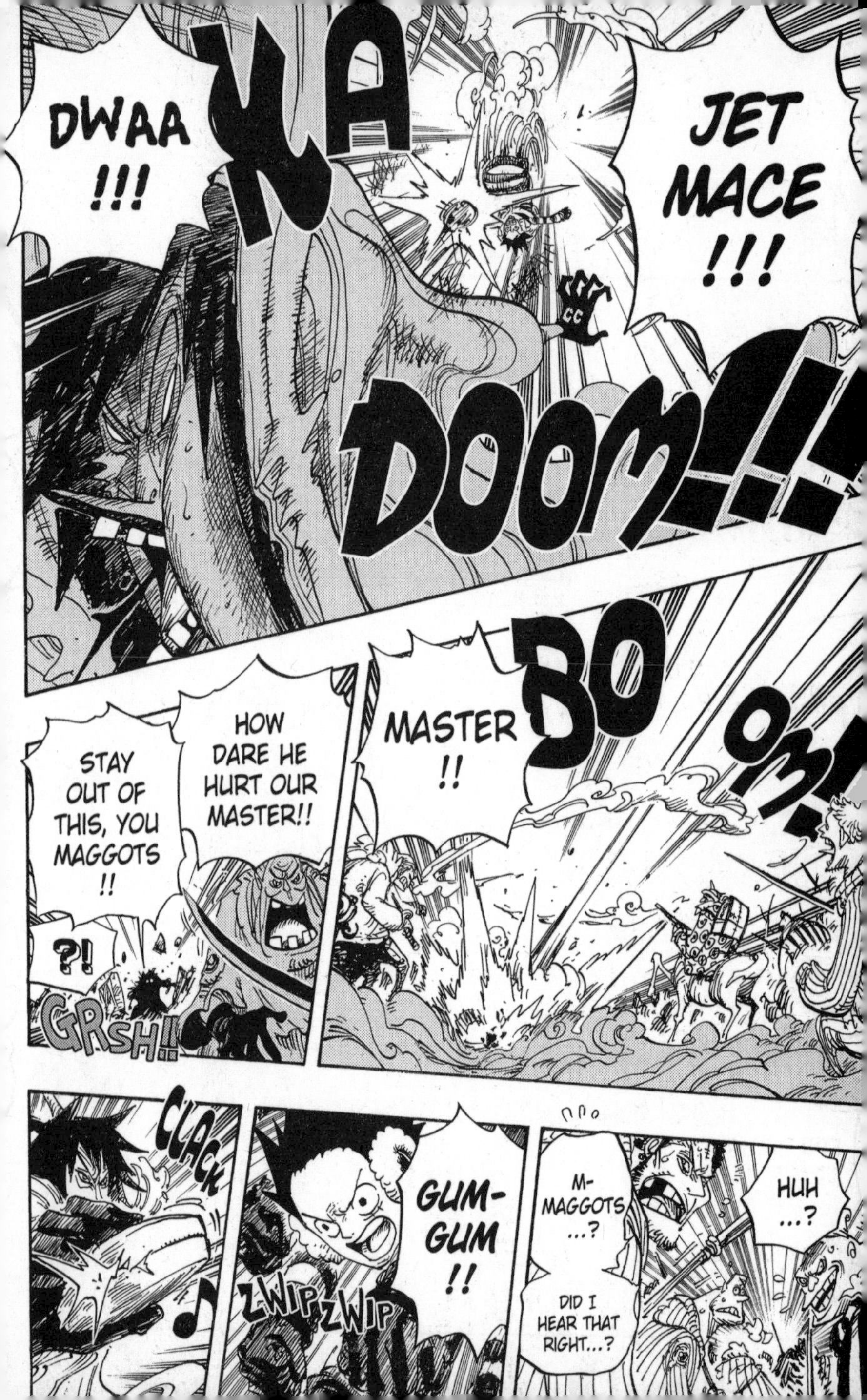
JET MACE!!!
KA
DWAA!!!
DOOM!!!
BOOM!
MASTER!!
HOW DARE HE HURT OUR MASTER!!
STAY OUT OF THIS, YOU MAGGOTS!!
?!
GRSH!!
HUH...?
M-MAGGOTS...?
DID I HEAR THAT RIGHT...?
GUM-GUM!!
ZWIPZWIP
CLACK

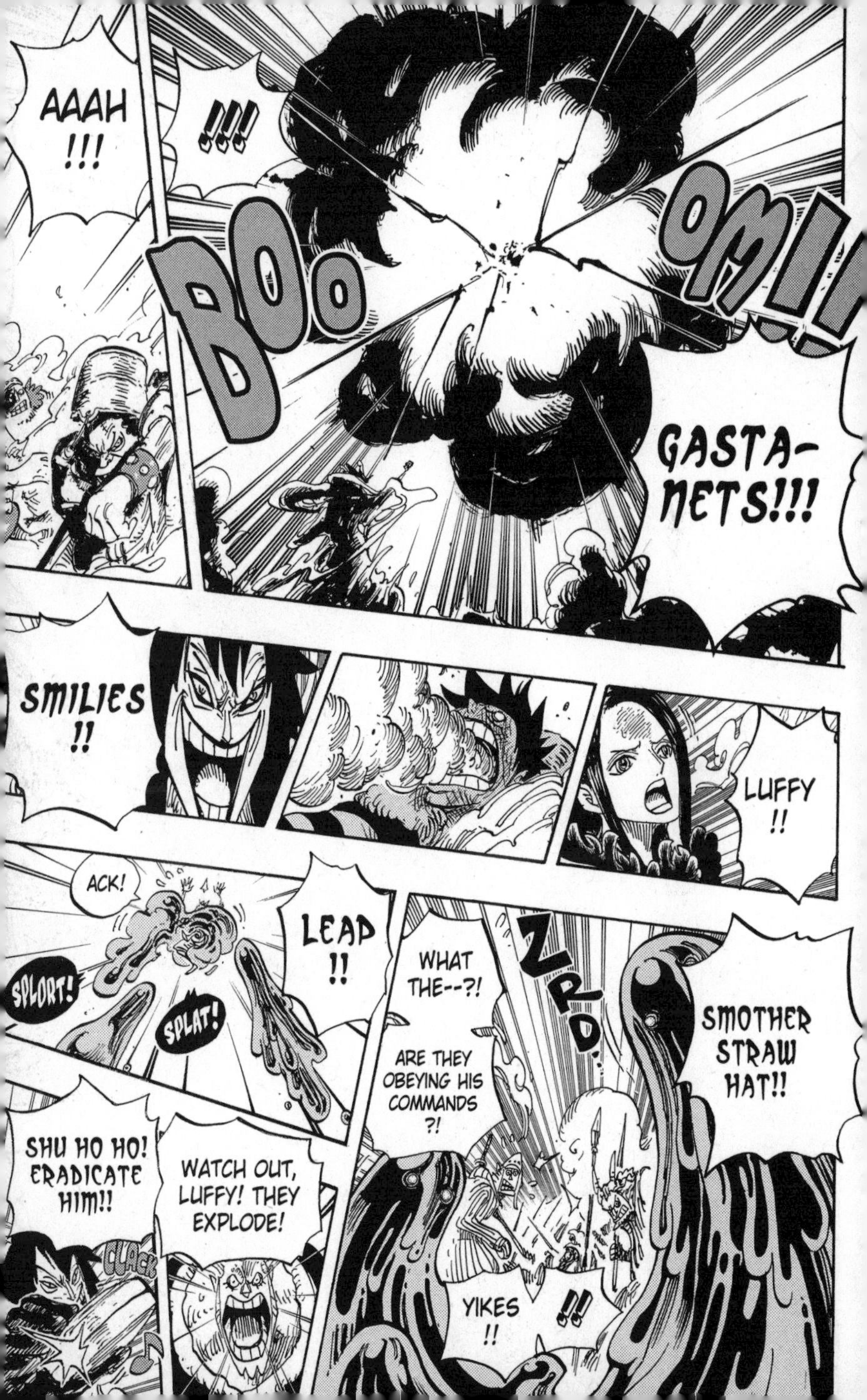
BOOOM!!
GASTA-NETS!!!
!!!
AAAH !!!
LUFFY !!
SMILIES !!
SMOTHER STRAW HAT!!
ZRD
WHAT THE--?!
ARE THEY OBEYING HIS COMMANDS ?!
YIKES !!
!!
LEAP !!
ACK!
SPLORT!
SPLAT!
WATCH OUT, LUFFY! THEY EXPLODE!
SHU HO HO! ERADICATE HIM!!
CLACK

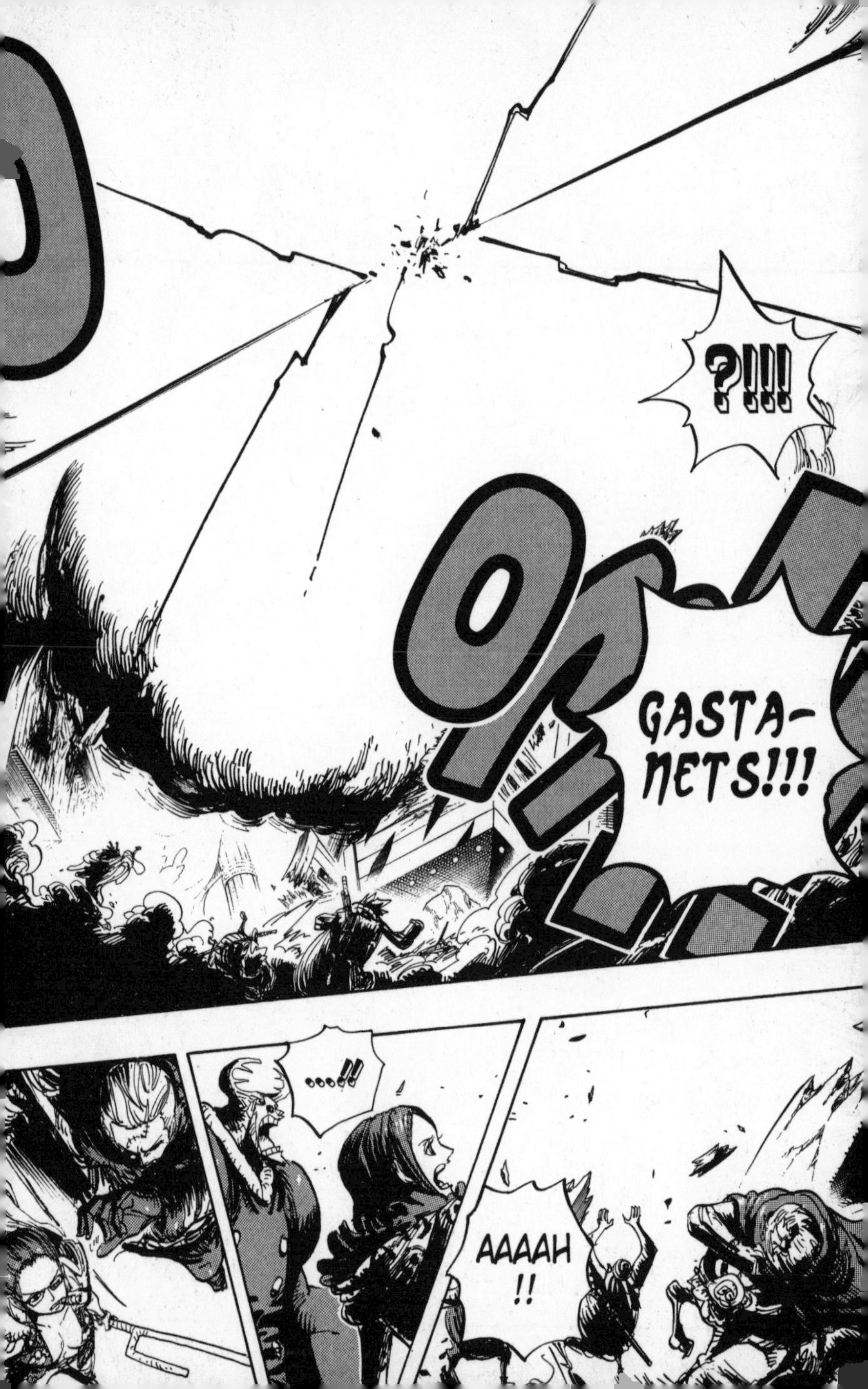
?!!!
GASTA-
NETS!!!
AAAAH
!!
...!!

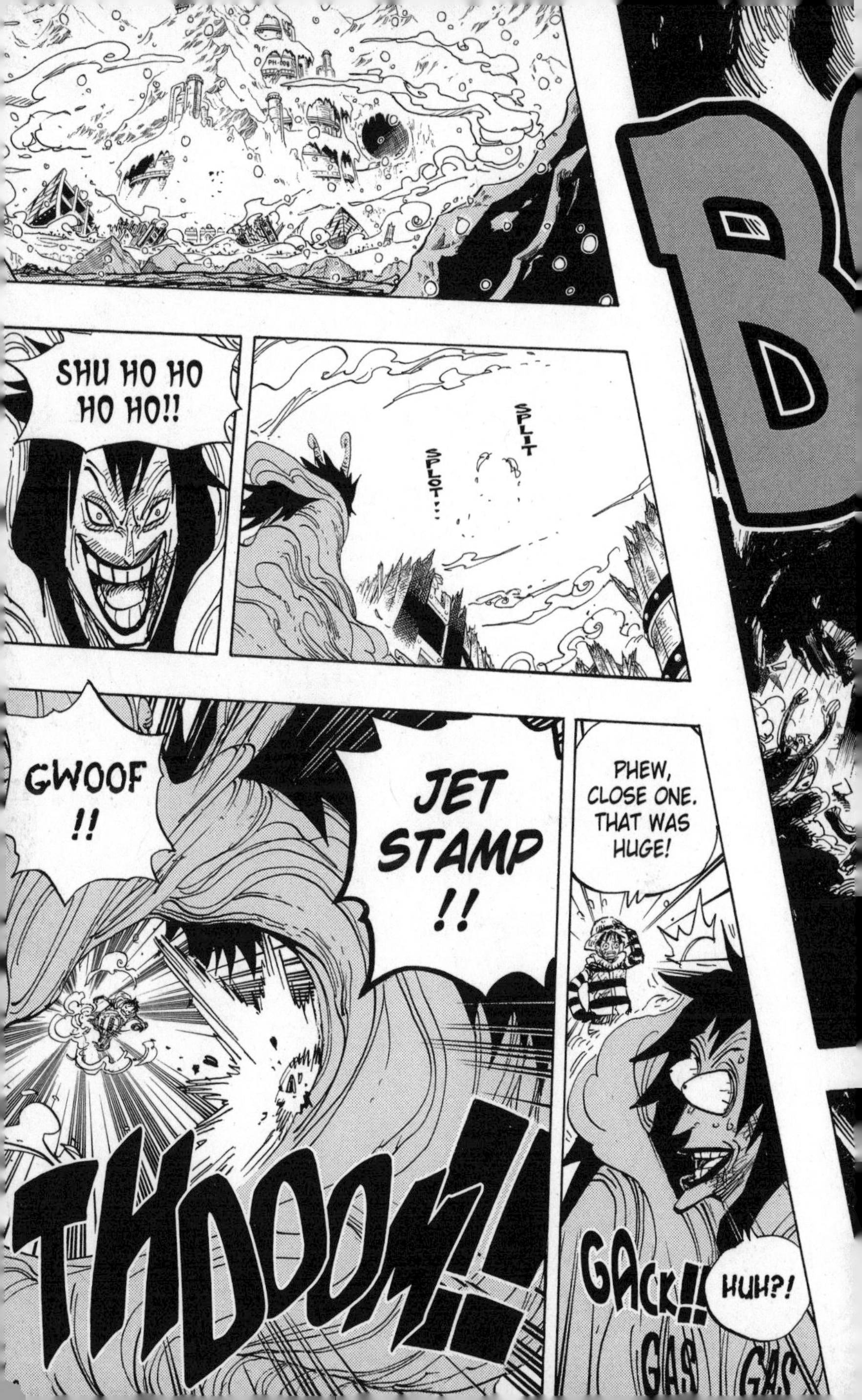
SPLIT
SPLOT...
SHU HO HO HO HO!!
PHEW, CLOSE ONE. THAT WAS HUGE!
HUH?!
GACK!!
GAS GAS
JET STAMP!!
GWOOF!!
THDOOM!!

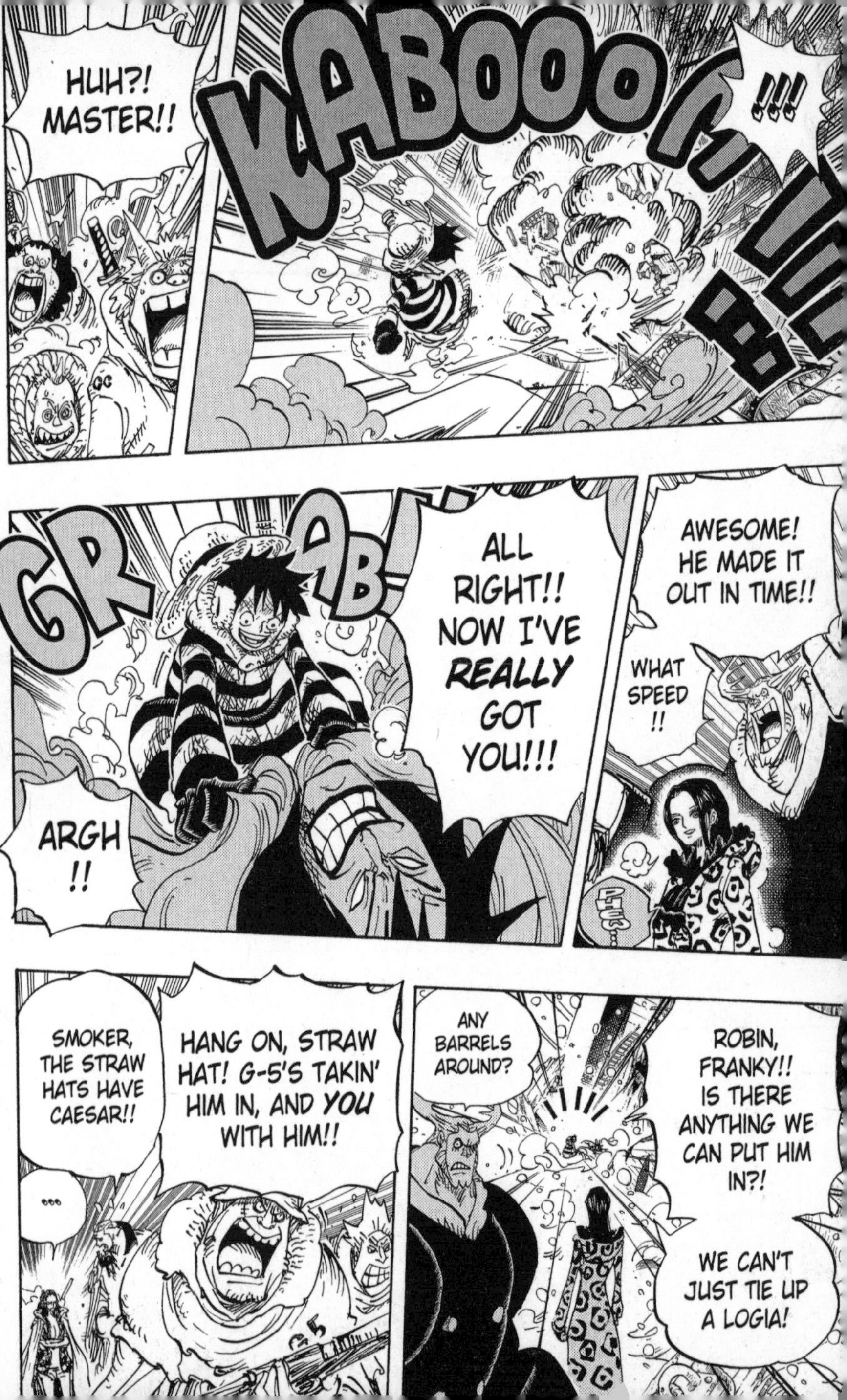
KABOOOM!!!
HUH?! MASTER!!
AWESOME! HE MADE IT OUT IN TIME!!
WHAT SPEED !!
GRAB!
ALL RIGHT!! NOW I'VE *REALLY* GOT YOU!!!
ARGH !!
ROBIN, FRANKY!! IS THERE ANYTHING WE CAN PUT HIM IN?!
ANY BARRELS AROUND?
WE CAN'T JUST TIE UP A LOGIA!
HANG ON, STRAW HAT! G-5'S TAKIN' HIM IN, AND *YOU* WITH HIM!!
SMOKER, THE STRAW HATS HAVE CAESAR!!
...

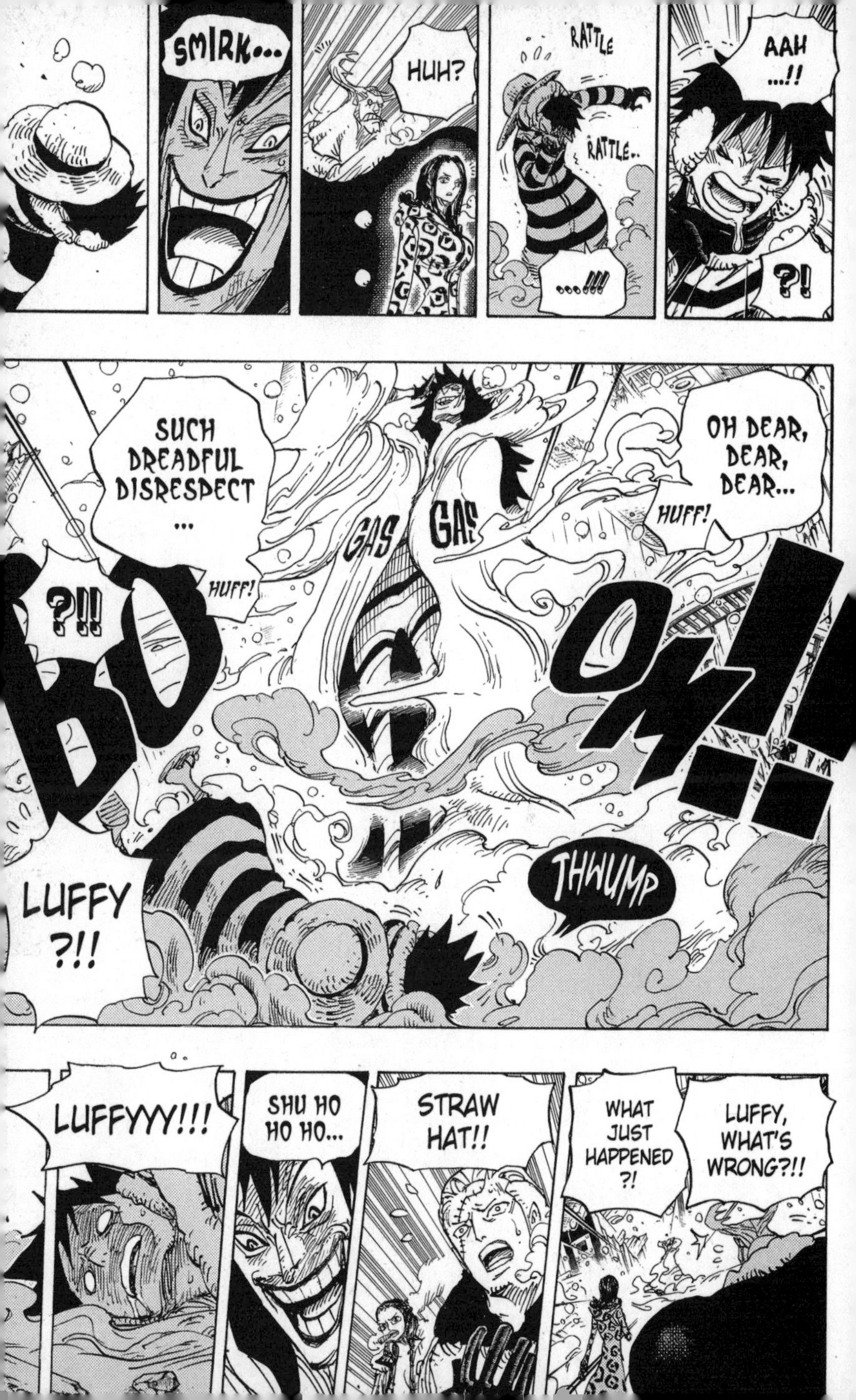
AAH ...!!
?!
RATTLE
RATTLE..
...!!!
HUH?
SMIRK...
OH DEAR, DEAR, DEAR...
HUFF!
GAS
GAS
SUCH DREADFUL DISRESPECT ...
HUFF!
?!!
BOOM!!
THWUMP
LUFFY ?!!
LUFFY, WHAT'S WRONG?!!
WHAT JUST HAPPENED ?!
STRAW HAT!!
SHU HO HO HO...
LUFFYYY!!!

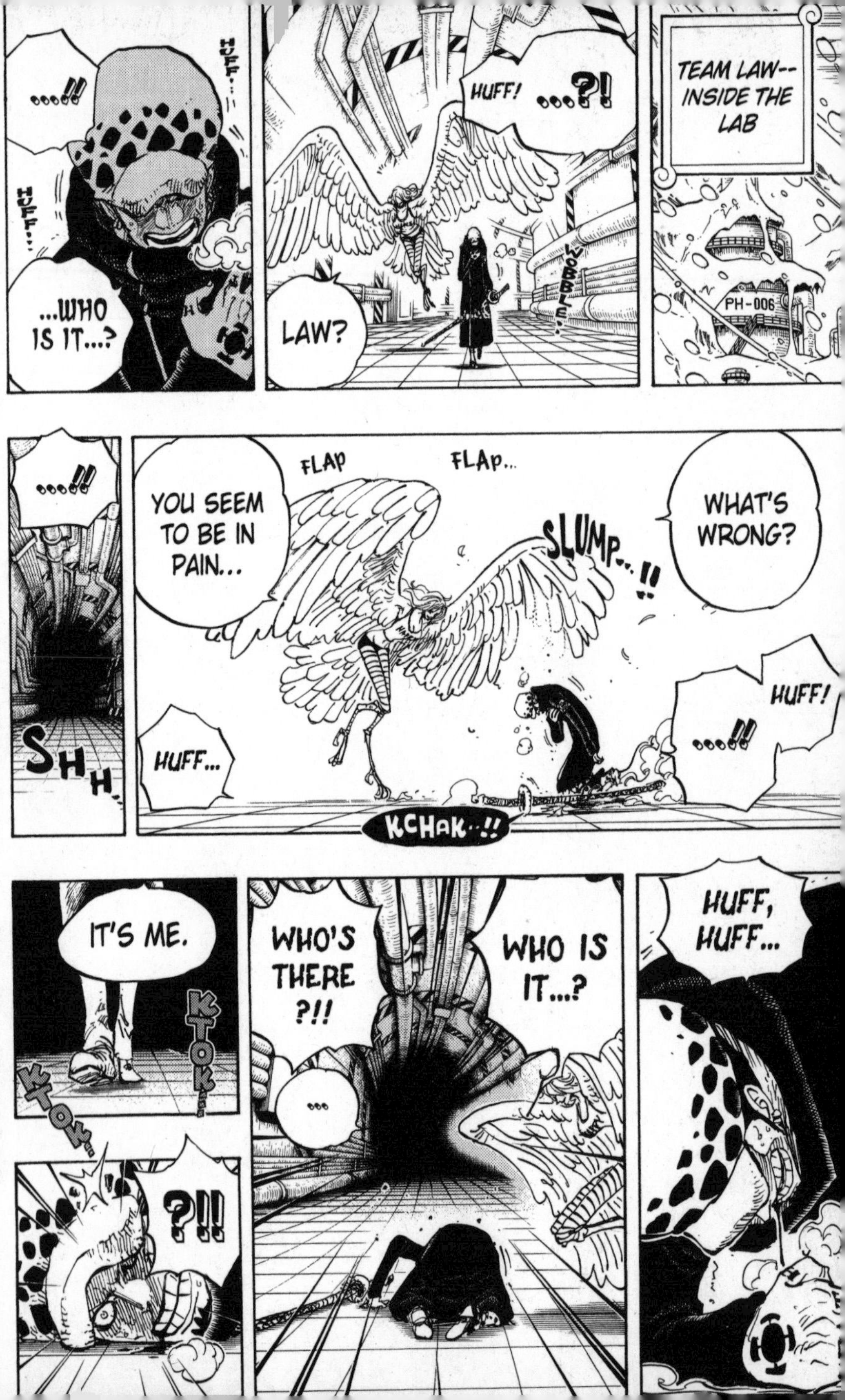
TEAM LAW-- INSIDE THE LAB
PH-006
HUFF!
...?!
WOBBLE...
LAW?
HUFF...
...!!
HUFF...
...WHO IS IT...?
WHAT'S WRONG?
FLAP...
FLAP
SLUMP...!!
YOU SEEM TO BE IN PAIN...
HUFF!
...!!
HUFF...
KCHAK..!!
...!!
SHH
HUFF, HUFF...
WHO IS IT...?
WHO'S THERE?!!
...
IT'S ME.
KTOK
KTOK
?!!

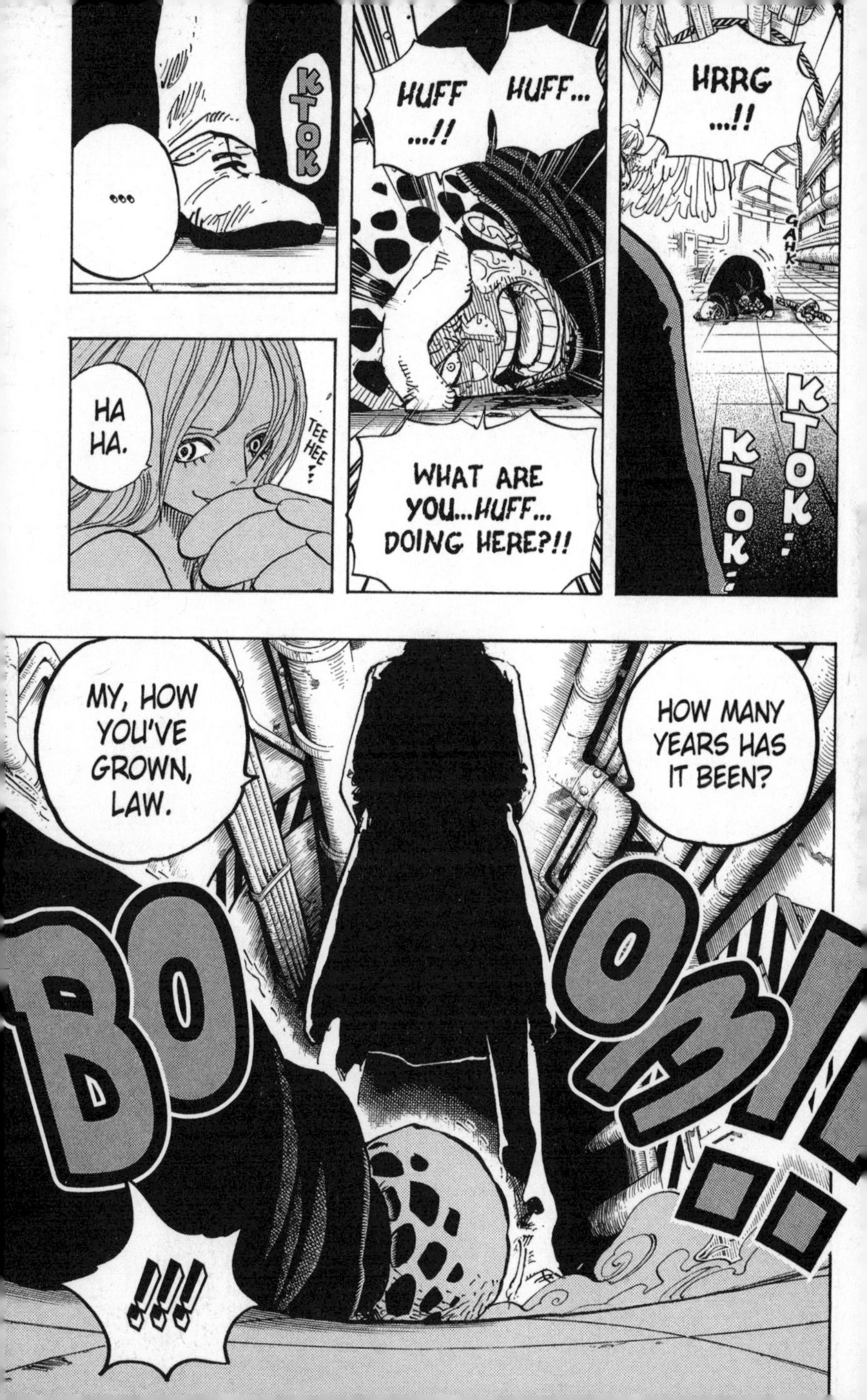

HRRG ...!!
GAHK
KTOK
KTOK...
HUFF...
HUFF ...!!
WHAT ARE YOU...HUFF... DOING HERE?!!
KTOK
...
HA HA.
TEE HEE
HOW MANY YEARS HAS IT BEEN?
MY, HOW YOU'VE GROWN, LAW.
BOOM!!
!!!

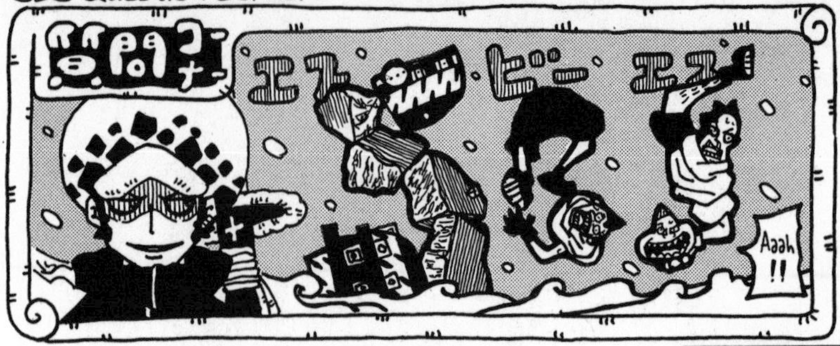
Aaah !!

(Haru, Nagano)

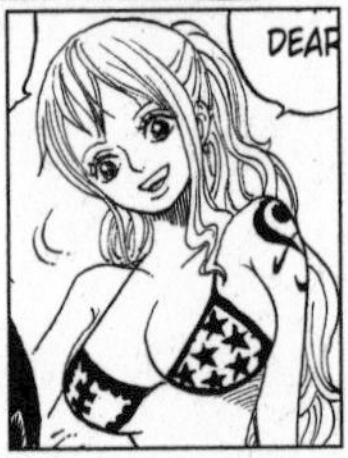
DEAR

Q: Can I touch Nami's boobs, Oda?

--Fake Tamori

A: What are you saying?! Are you insane?!

Q: Huh?!! What?!!! Say that again!!!!

--Haribo III

A: Okay, uh... What are you saying?! Are you insane?!

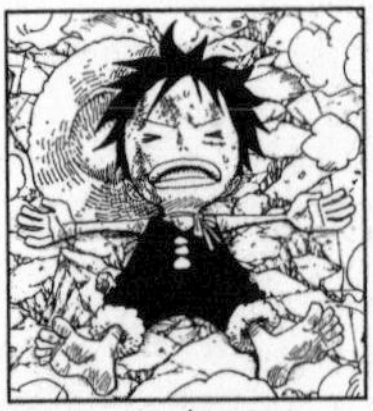

Q: Did Luffy stop shrinking after using Gear Three because you're a pervert, or because he's strengthened his powers?! Explain yourself!!

--I'm Legend

A: The answer is because Luffy's strengthened his powers. I don't understand what the first option means. Basically, after his lengthy training, Luffy's gotten much better at using Gear Two and Gear Three. When I told the anime staff that Luffy wouldn't be shrinking anymore, they said, "Thanks a bunch." It helps me too, since that usually takes extra panels to depict. Thanks, Luffy!!

Q: Nice to meet you, Odacchi!♡ It's like a dream getting to submit a question to the SBS.☆ Now, I have a whole ton of questions to ask, but the most pressing one is--! What are the ages and heights of all the rookies?♡ I'll wait until the ends of time for your answer!

--Louie

A: Okay, okay. These are all based on the point before the time skip. So for every character who's reappeared, add two years, and you can assume that their heights haven't changed. Because of Bonney's powers, her age is an estimate.

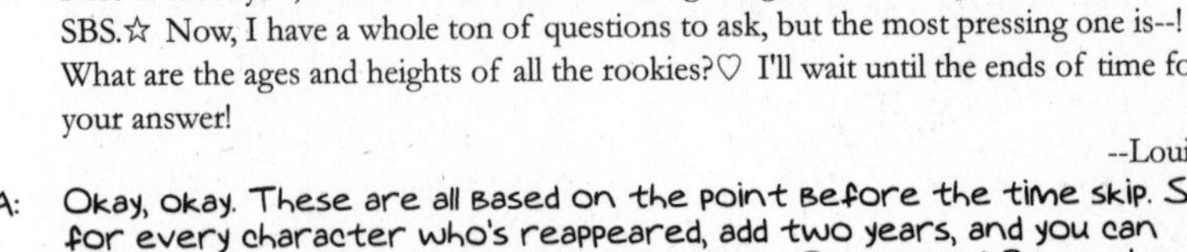

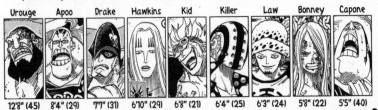

Urouge	Apoo	Drake	Hawkins	Kid	Killer	Law	Bonney	Capone
12'8" (45)	8'4" (29)	7'7" (31)	6'10" (29)	6'8" (21)	6'4" (25)	6'3" (24)	5'8" (22)	5'5" (40)

Chapter 672:

MY NAME IS KIN'EMON!!

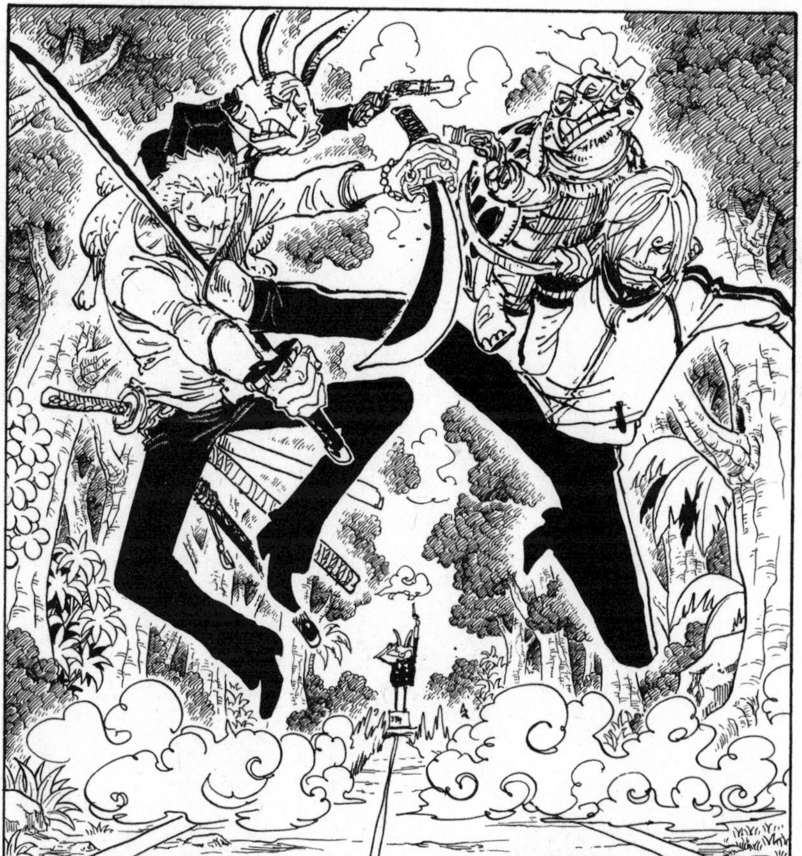

REQUEST: "ZOLO AND SANJI RACE CARRYING THE TORTOISE AND THE HARE" BY MEGANE-DANUKI FROM AKITA

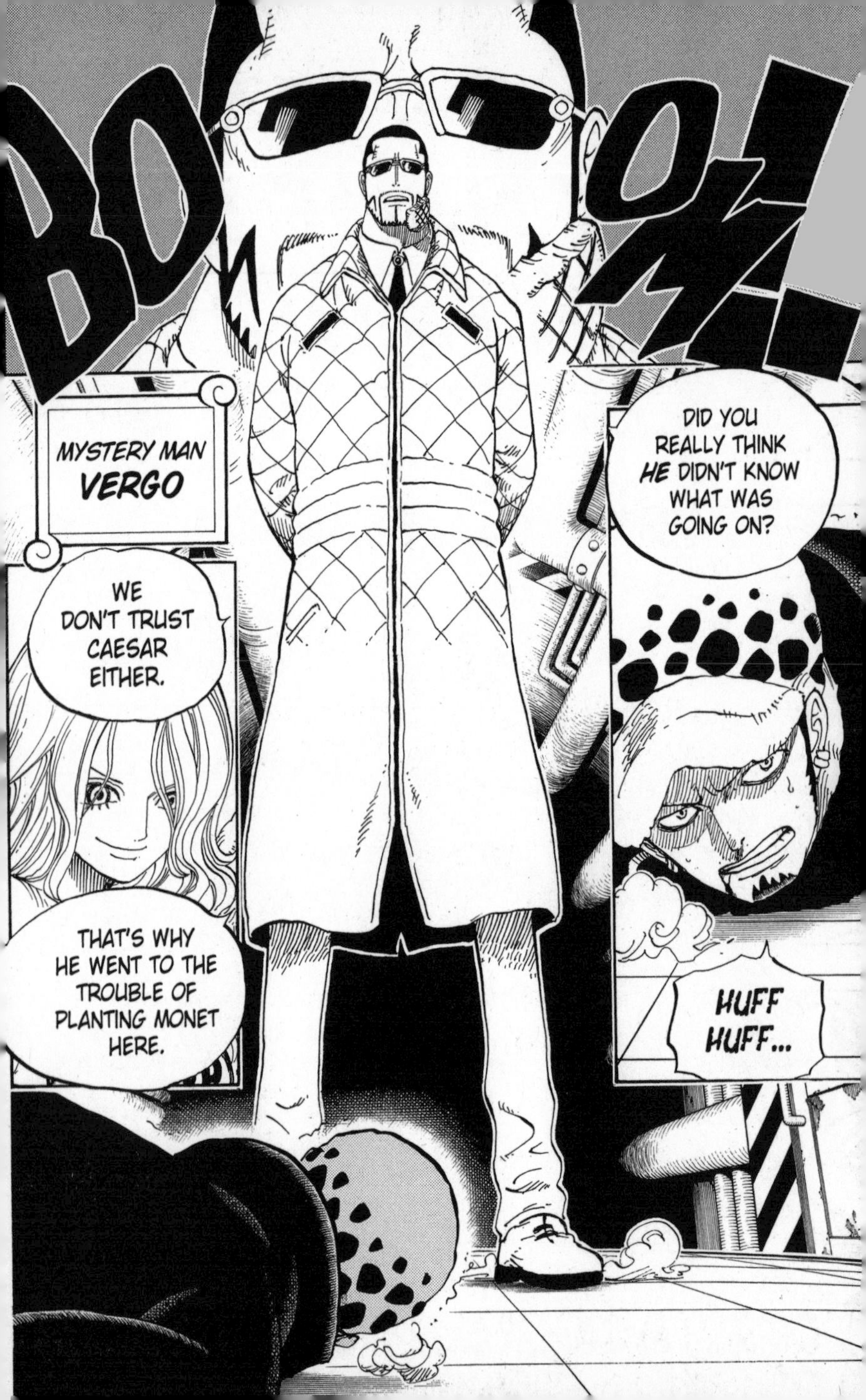
BOOM!!
DID YOU REALLY THINK **HE** DIDN'T KNOW WHAT WAS GOING ON?
HUFF HUFF...
MYSTERY MAN
VERGO
WE DON'T TRUST CAESAR EITHER.
THAT'S WHY HE WENT TO THE TROUBLE OF PLANTING MONET HERE.

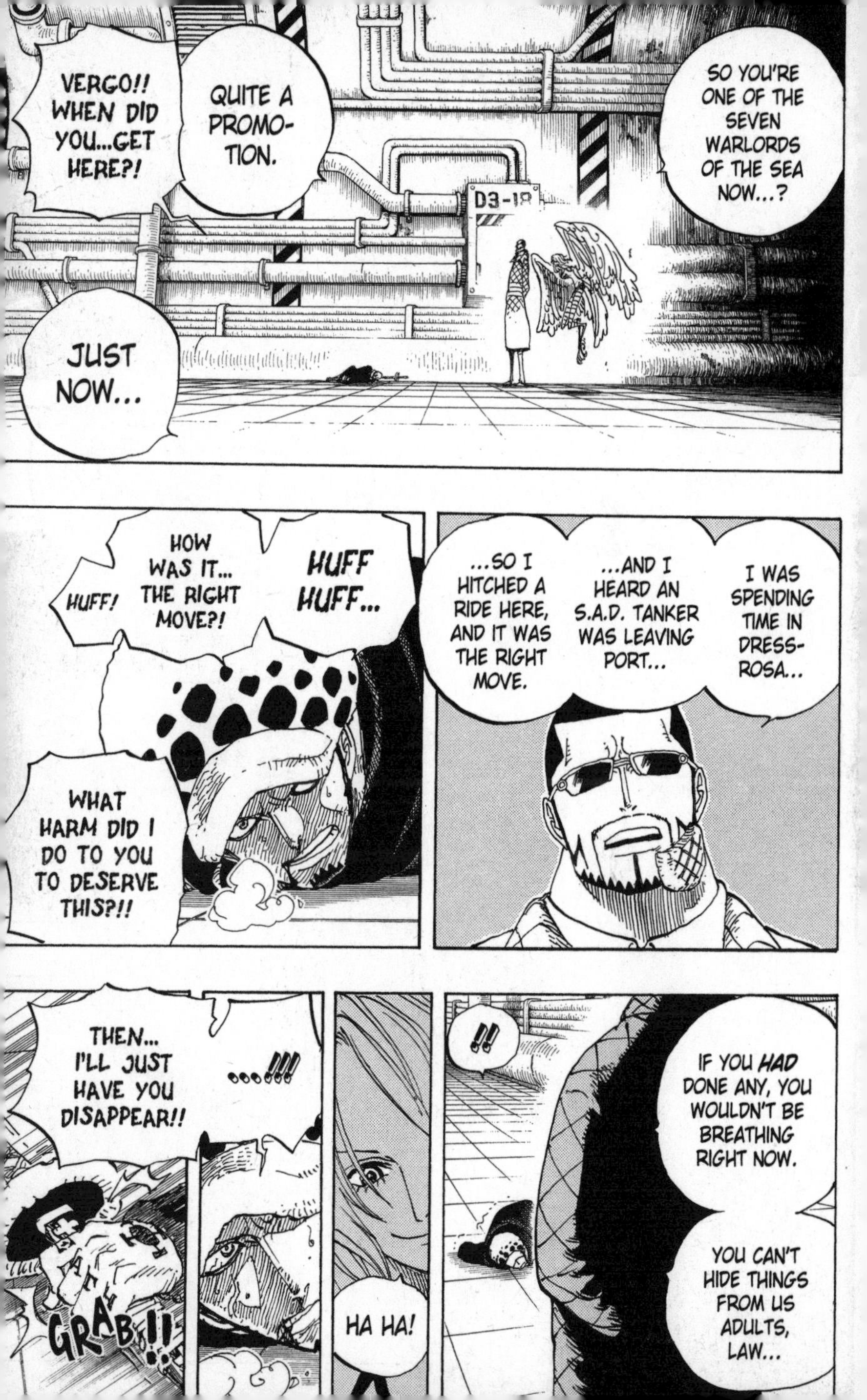
SO YOU'RE ONE OF THE SEVEN WARLORDS OF THE SEA NOW...?
D3-18
QUITE A PROMO- TION.
VERGO!! WHEN DID YOU...GET HERE?!
JUST NOW...
I WAS SPENDING TIME IN DRESS- ROSA...
...AND I HEARD AN S.A.D. TANKER WAS LEAVING PORT...
...SO I HITCHED A RIDE HERE, AND IT WAS THE RIGHT MOVE.
HUFF HUFF...
HOW WAS IT... THE RIGHT MOVE?!
HUFF!
WHAT HARM DID I DO TO YOU TO DESERVE THIS?!!
IF YOU *HAD* DONE ANY, YOU WOULDN'T BE BREATHING RIGHT NOW.
!!
YOU CAN'T HIDE THINGS FROM US ADULTS, LAW...
HA HA!
...!!!
THEN... I'LL JUST HAVE YOU DISAPPEAR!!
GRAB!!

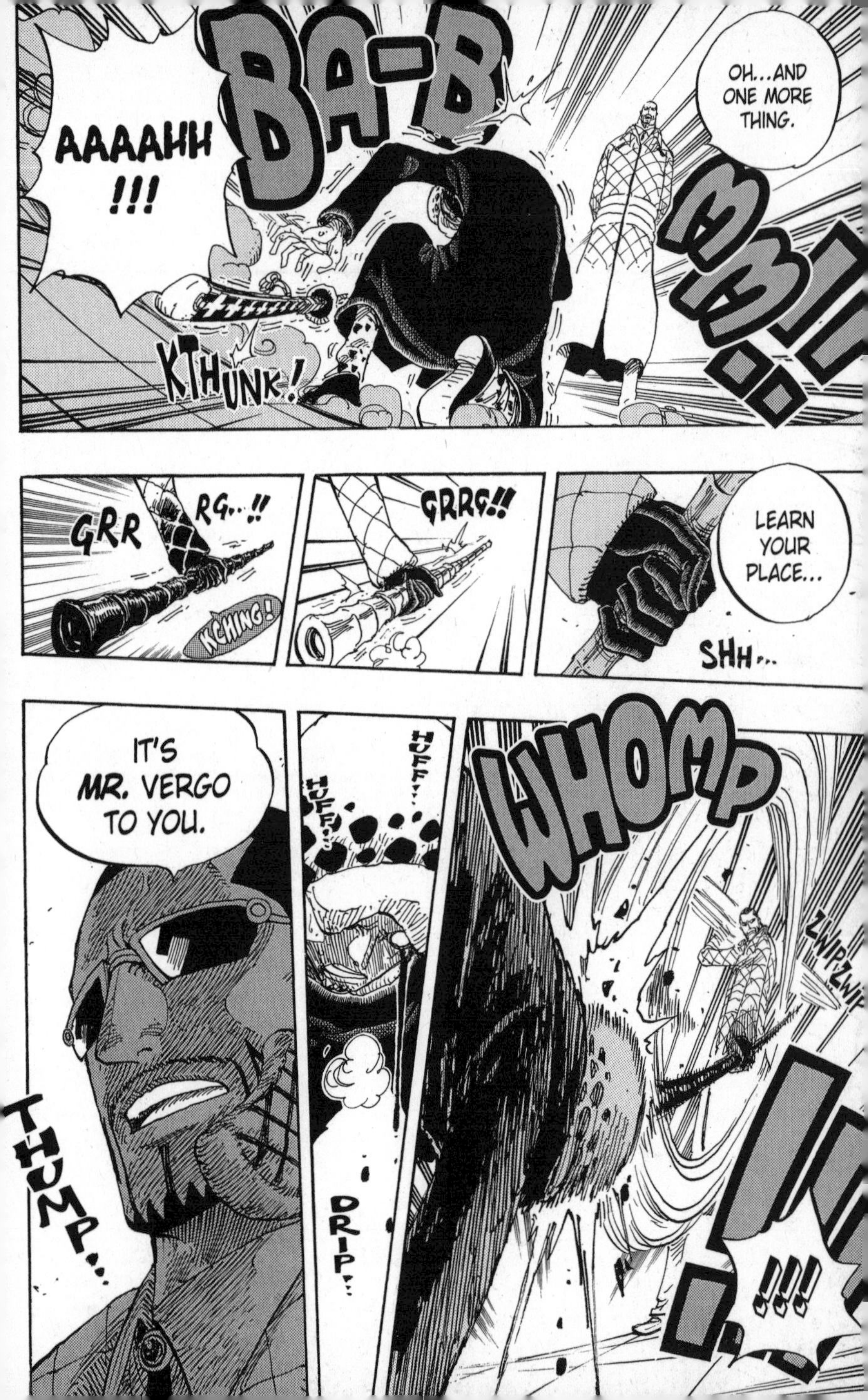
OH...AND ONE MORE THING.
BA-BAM!!
AAAAHH!!!
KTHUNK!
LEARN YOUR PLACE...
SHH...
GRRG!!
GRRRG...!!
KCHING!
WHOMP
ZWIP ZWIP
!!!
HUFF...
HUFF...
DRIP...
IT'S MR. VERGO TO YOU.
THUMP...

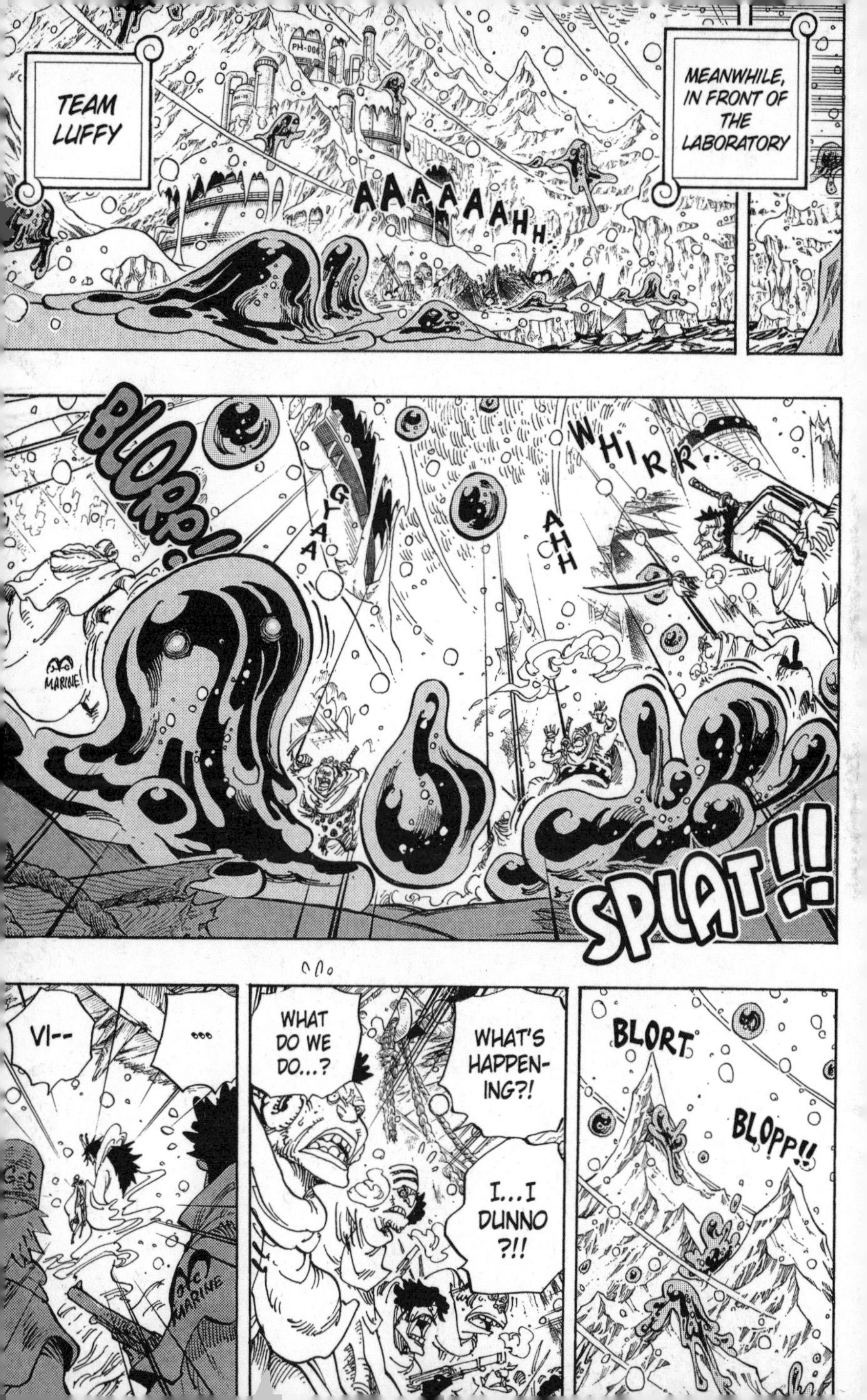

MEANWHILE, IN FRONT OF THE LABORATORY
AAAAAAAHH
TEAM LUFFY
WHIRRR
AHH
GYAAA
BLORP!
MARINE
SPLAT!!
BLORT
BLOPP!!
WHAT'S HAPPEN-ING?!
WHAT DO WE DO...?
I...I DUNNO ?!!
...
VI--
MARINE

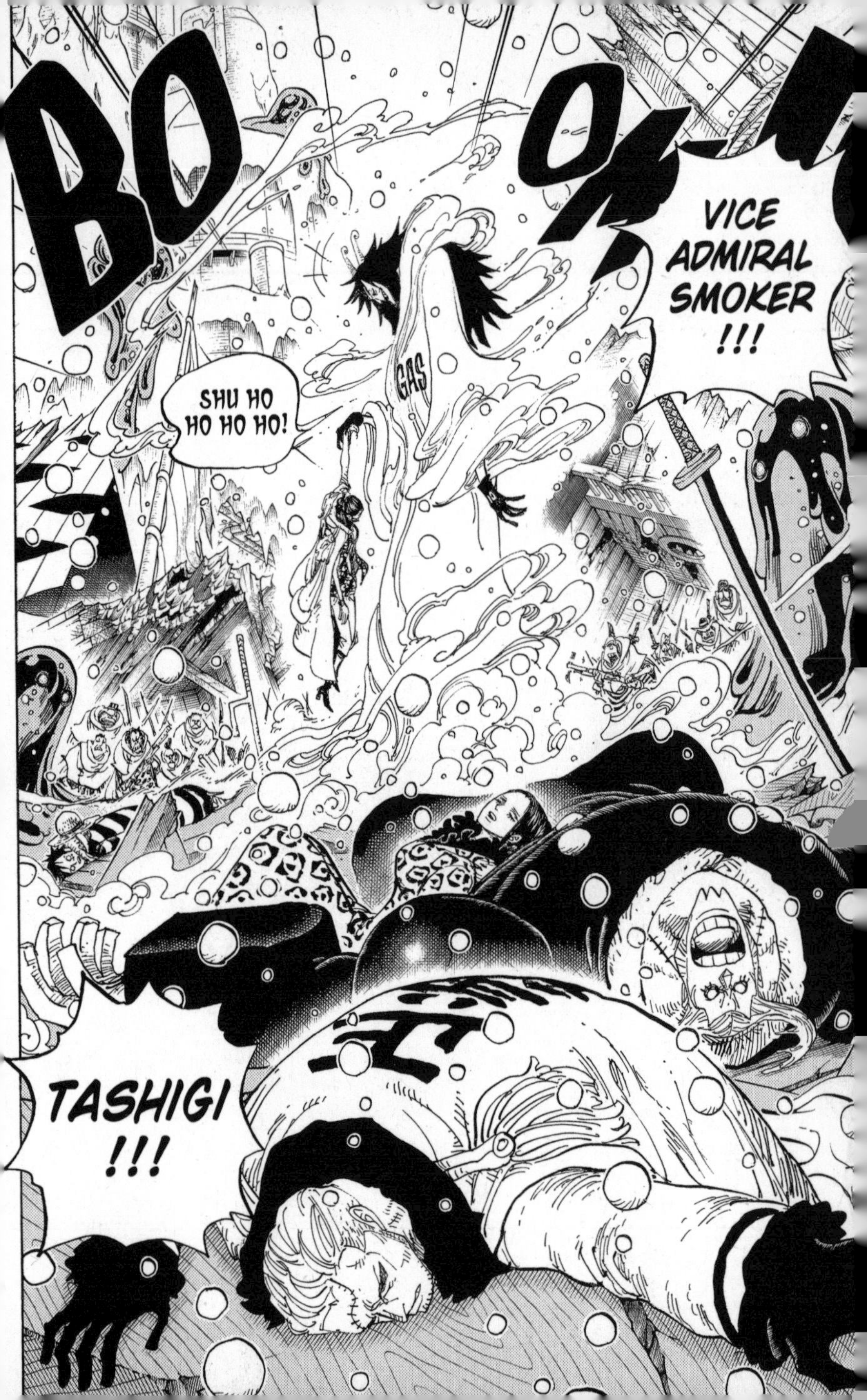
VICE ADMIRAL SMOKER !!!
SHU HO HO HO HO!
TASHIGI !!!

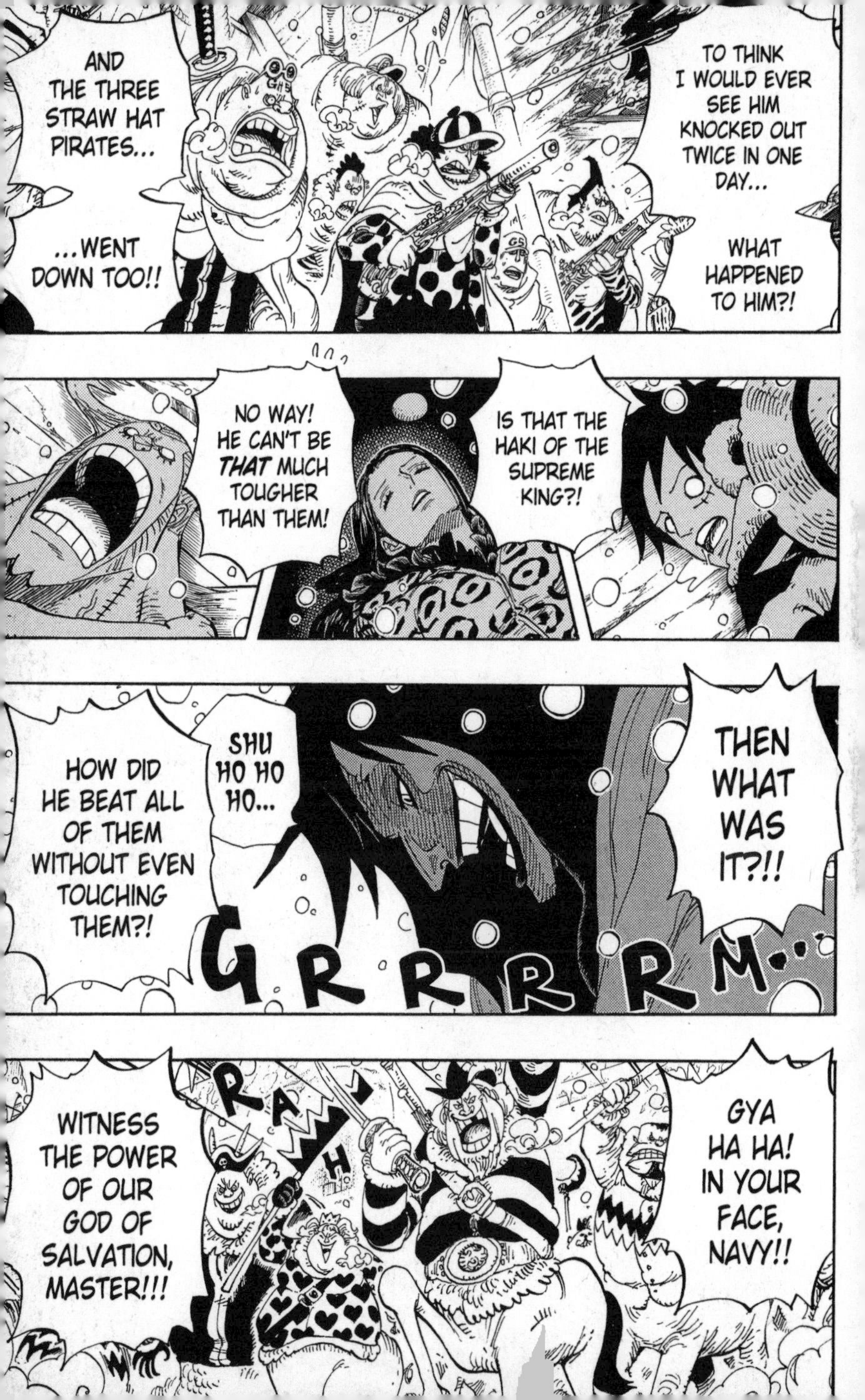
TO THINK I WOULD EVER SEE HIM KNOCKED OUT TWICE IN ONE DAY...
WHAT HAPPENED TO HIM?!
AND THE THREE STRAW HAT PIRATES...
...WENT DOWN TOO!!
IS THAT THE HAKI OF THE SUPREME KING?!
NO WAY! HE CAN'T BE *THAT* MUCH TOUGHER THAN THEM!
THEN WHAT WAS IT?!!
SHU HO HO HO...
HOW DID HE BEAT ALL OF THEM WITHOUT EVEN TOUCHING THEM?!
GRRRRRM...
GYA HA HA! IN YOUR FACE, NAVY!!
RAWH
WITNESS THE POWER OF OUR GOD OF SALVATION, MASTER!!!

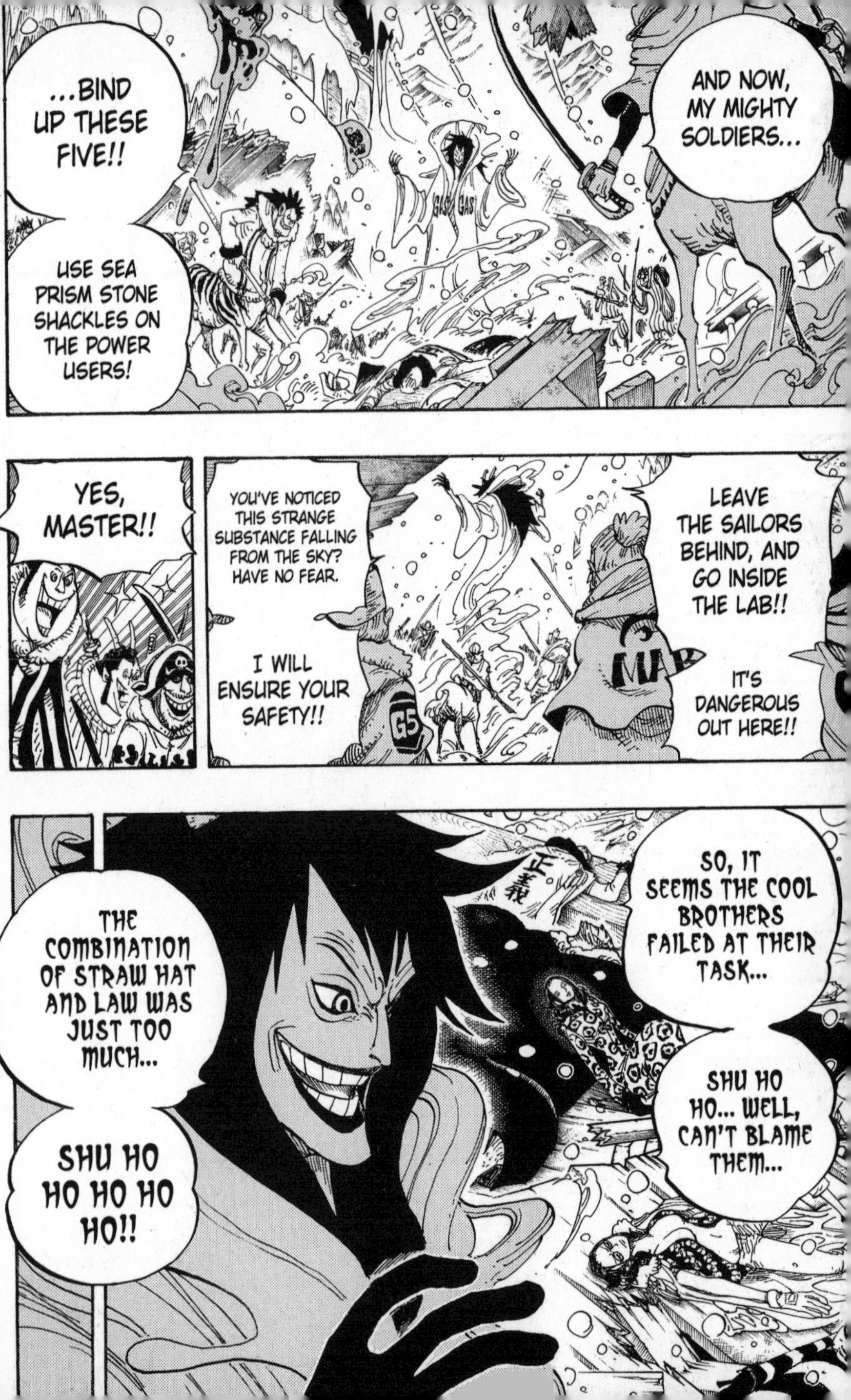
AND NOW, MY MIGHTY SOLDIERS...
...BIND UP THESE FIVE!!
USE SEA PRISM STONE SHACKLES ON THE POWER USERS!
LEAVE THE SAILORS BEHIND, AND GO INSIDE THE LAB!!
IT'S DANGEROUS OUT HERE!!
YOU'VE NOTICED THIS STRANGE SUBSTANCE FALLING FROM THE SKY? HAVE NO FEAR.
I WILL ENSURE YOUR SAFETY!!
YES, MASTER!!
SO, IT SEEMS THE COOL BROTHERS FAILED AT THEIR TASK...
SHU HO HO... WELL, CAN'T BLAME THEM...
THE COMBINATION OF STRAW HAT AND LAW WAS JUST TOO MUCH...
SHU HO HO HO HO HO!!

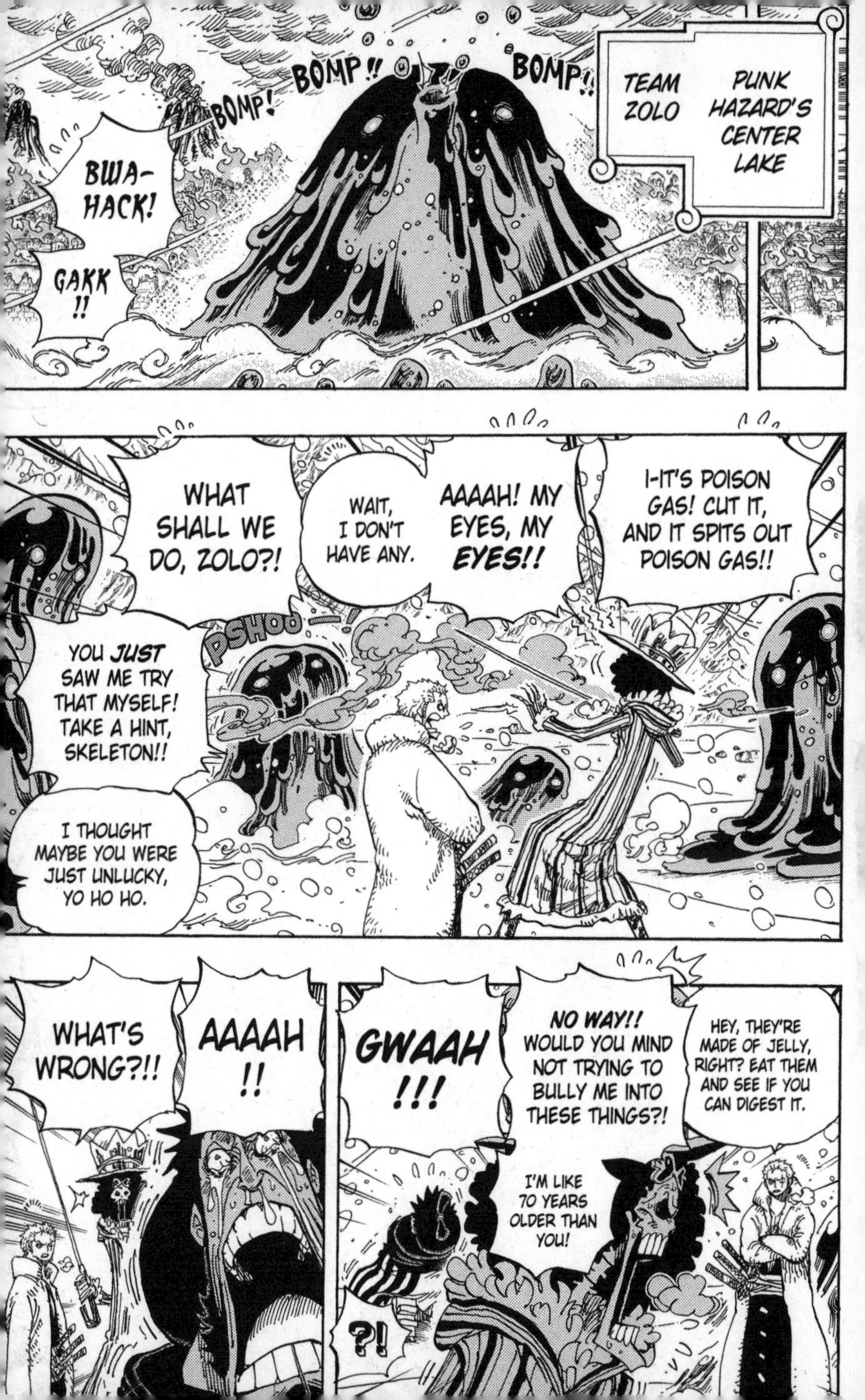
TEAM ZOLO
PUNK HAZARD'S CENTER LAKE
BOMP!!
BOMP!!
BOMP!
BWA-HACK!
GAKK!!
I-IT'S POISON GAS! CUT IT, AND IT SPITS OUT POISON GAS!!
AAAAH! MY EYES, MY EYES!!
WAIT, I DON'T HAVE ANY.
WHAT SHALL WE DO, ZOLO?!
PSHOO—!
YOU JUST SAW ME TRY THAT MYSELF! TAKE A HINT, SKELETON!!
I THOUGHT MAYBE YOU WERE JUST UNLUCKY, YO HO HO.
HEY, THEY'RE MADE OF JELLY, RIGHT? EAT THEM AND SEE IF YOU CAN DIGEST IT.
NO WAY!! WOULD YOU MIND NOT TRYING TO BULLY ME INTO THESE THINGS?!
GWAAH!!!
I'M LIKE 70 YEARS OLDER THAN YOU!
?!
AAAAH!!
WHAT'S WRONG?!!

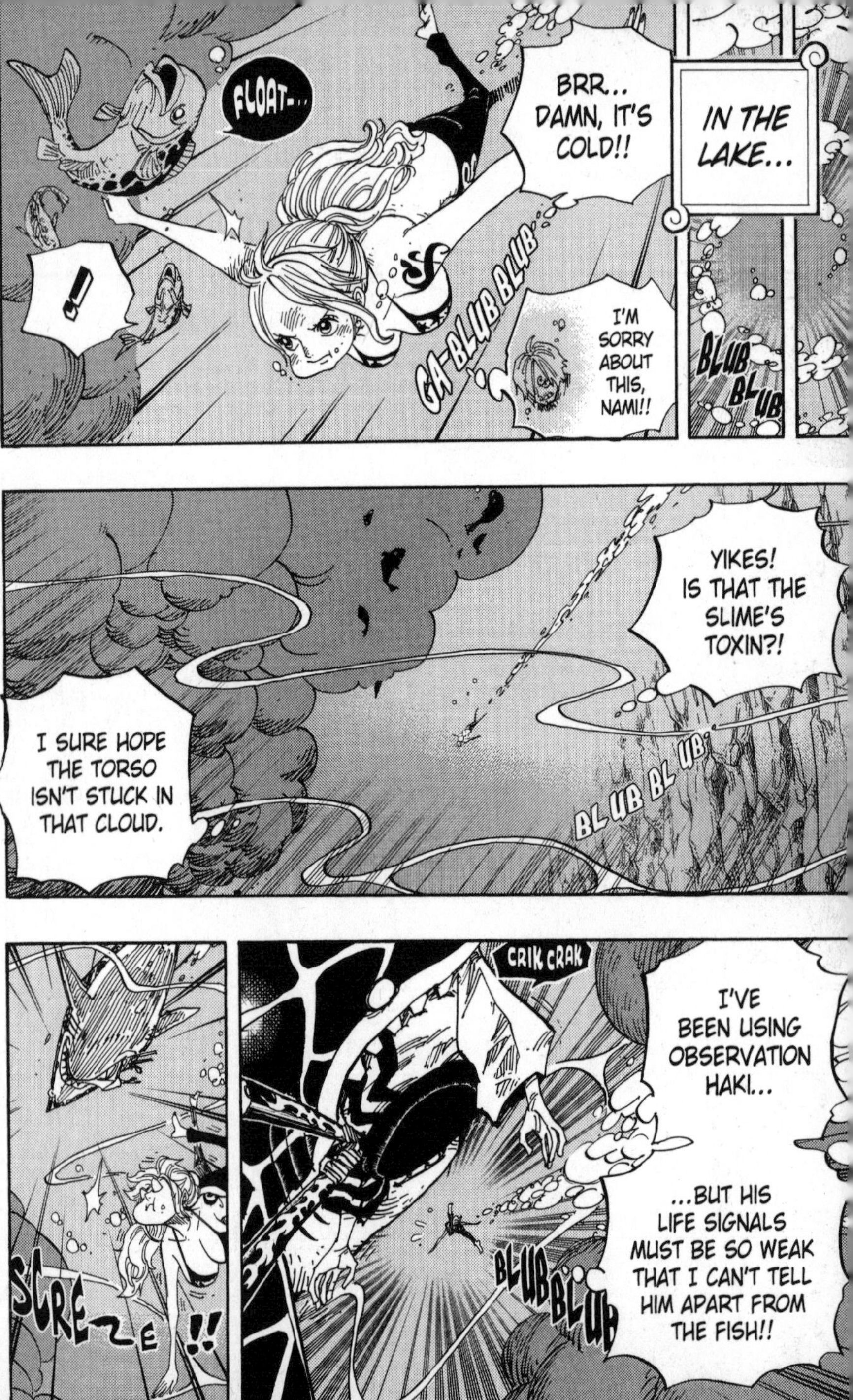
IN THE LAKE...
BLUB BLUB
BRR... DAMN, IT'S COLD!!
FLOAT-...
GA-BLUB BLUB
I'M SORRY ABOUT THIS, NAMI!!
!
YIKES! IS THAT THE SLIME'S TOXIN?!
BLUB BL UB
I SURE HOPE THE TORSO ISN'T STUCK IN THAT CLOUD.
CRIK CRAK
I'VE BEEN USING OBSERVATION HAKI...
...BUT HIS LIFE SIGNALS MUST BE SO WEAK THAT I CAN'T TELL HIM APART FROM THE FISH!!
BLUB BLUB
SCREEZE!!

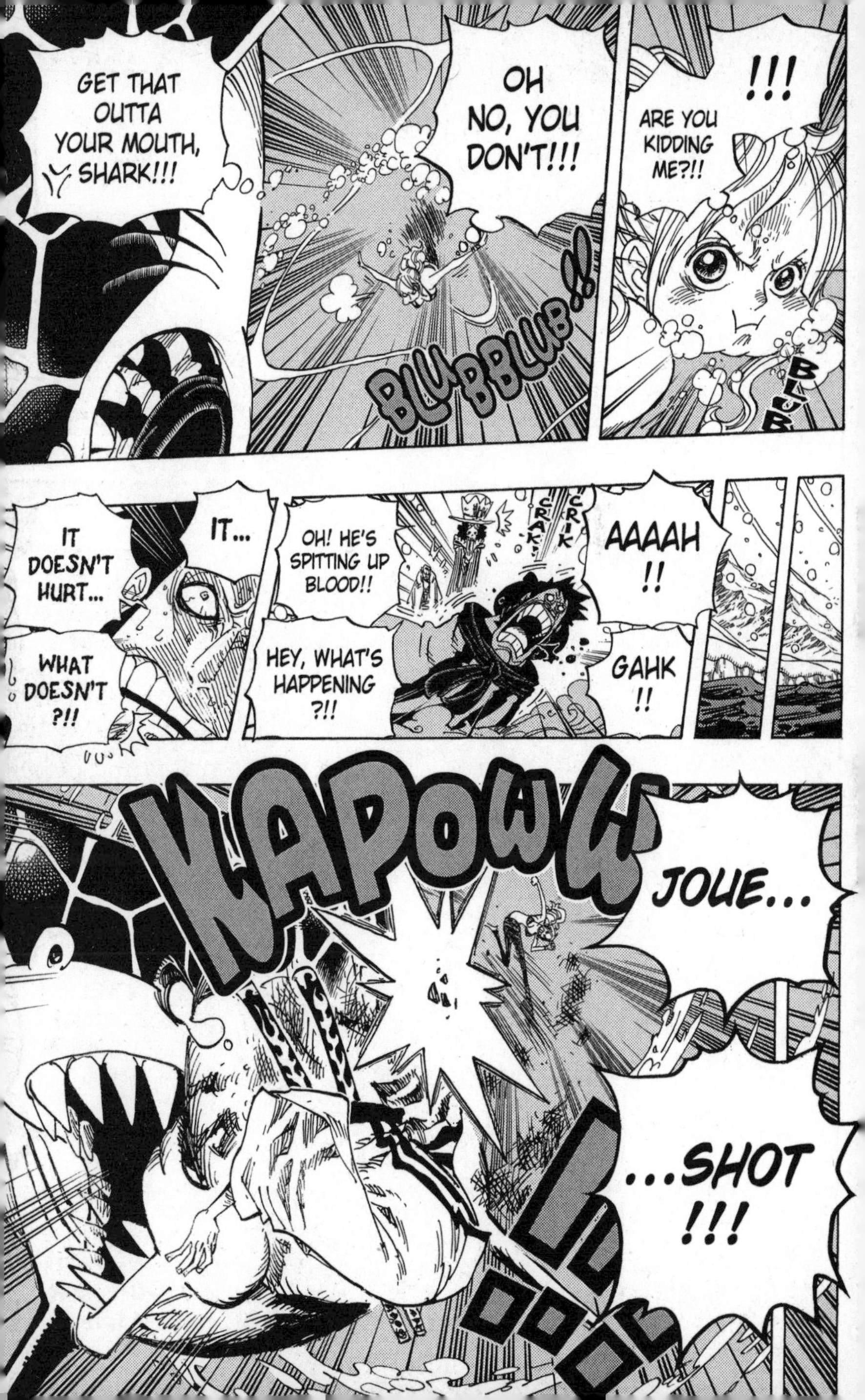
!!!
ARE YOU KIDDING ME?!!
BLUB
OH NO, YOU DON'T!!!
BLUBBLUB!!
GET THAT OUTTA YOUR MOUTH, SHARK!!!
AAAAH!!
GAHK!!
CRIK
CRAK
OH! HE'S SPITTING UP BLOOD!!
HEY, WHAT'S HAPPENING?!!
IT...
IT DOESN'T HURT...
WHAT DOESN'T?!!
KAPOW!!
JOUE...
...SHOT!!!

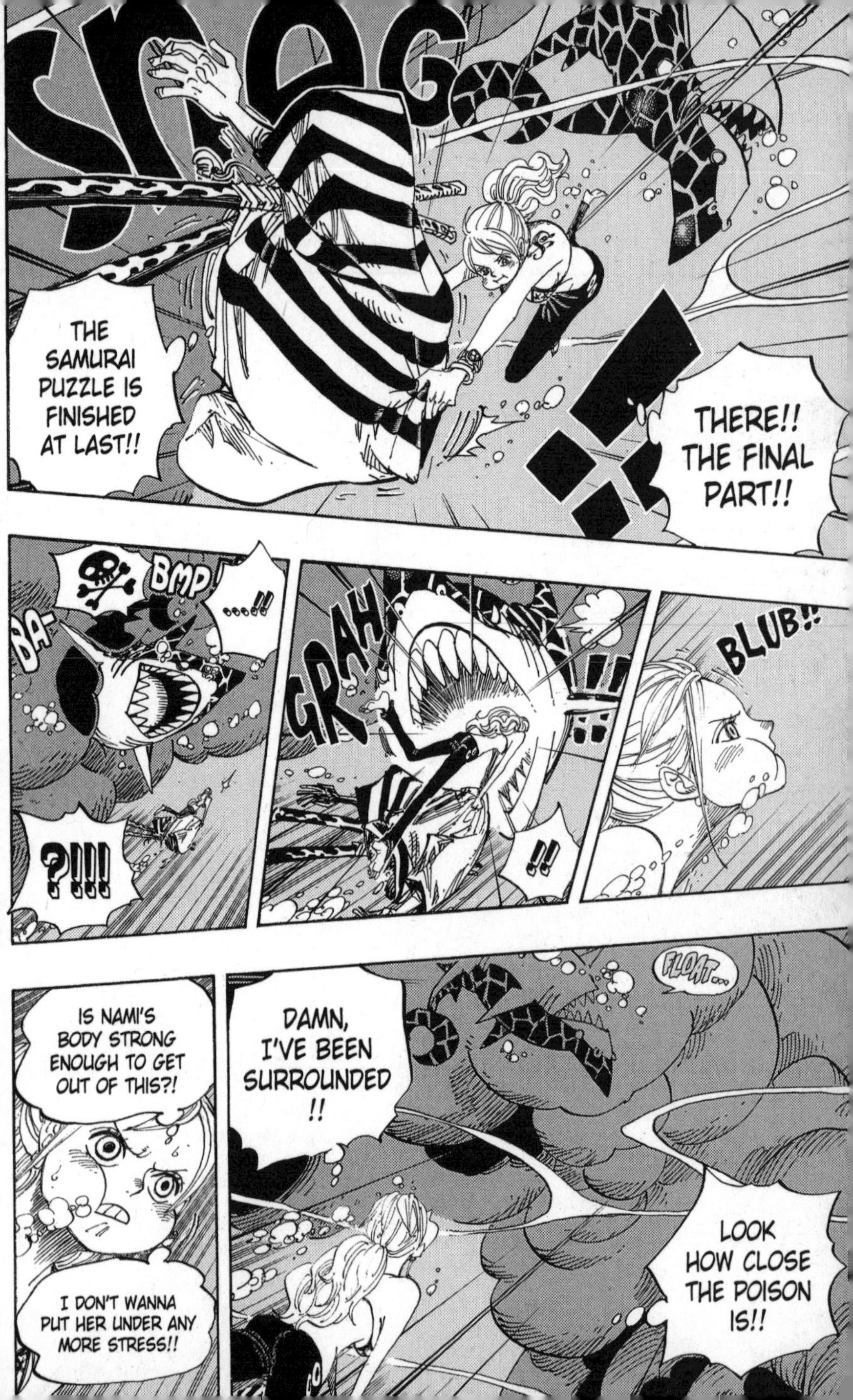
THERE!! THE FINAL PART!!
THE SAMURAI PUZZLE IS FINISHED AT LAST!!
BLUB!!
GRAH
!!
!!
BMP
...!!
BA-
?!!!
FLOAT...
LOOK HOW CLOSE THE POISON IS!!
DAMN, I'VE BEEN SURROUNDED !!
IS NAMI'S BODY STRONG ENOUGH TO GET OUT OF THIS?!
I DON'T WANNA PUT HER UNDER ANY MORE STRESS!!

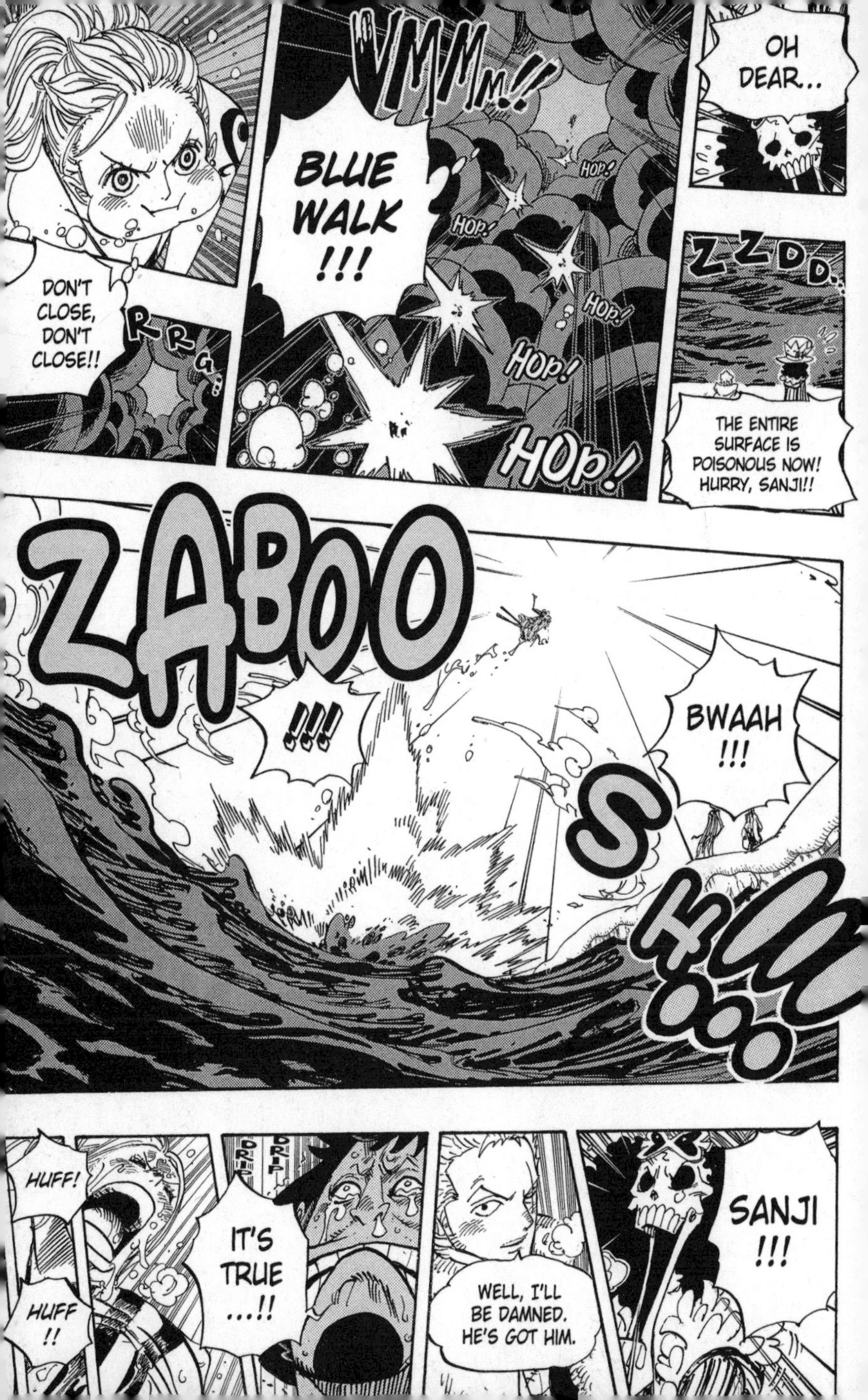
OH DEAR...
ZZDD..
THE ENTIRE SURFACE IS POISONOUS NOW! HURRY, SANJI!!
VMMM!!
BLUE WALK!!!
HOP!
HOP!
HOP!
HOP!
HOP!
DON'T CLOSE, DON'T CLOSE!!
RRG!
BWAAH!!!
ZABOO!!!
SSH...
SANJI!!!
WELL, I'LL BE DAMNED. HE'S GOT HIM.
DRIP
DRIP
IT'S TRUE...!!
HUFF!
HUFF!!

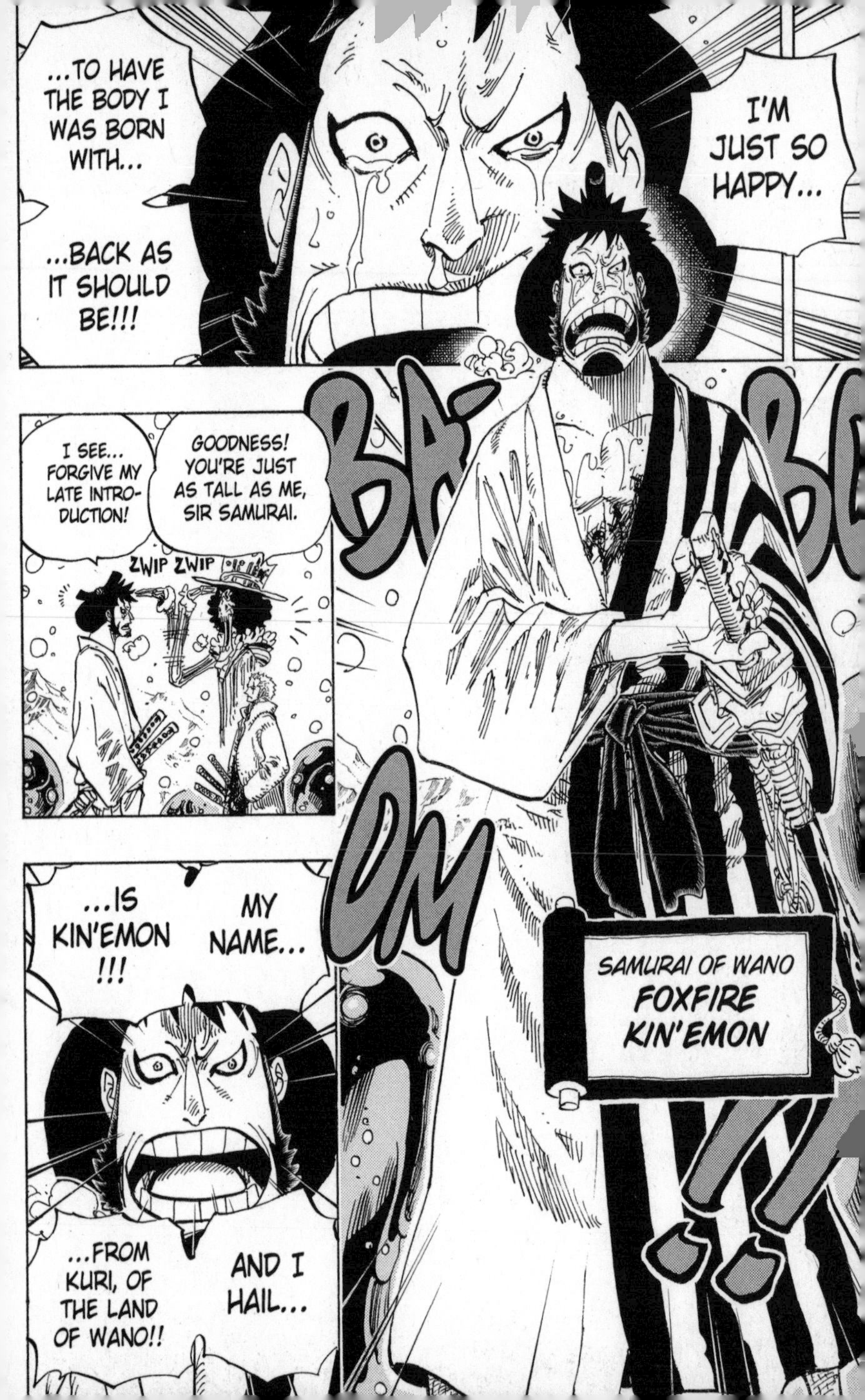
I'M JUST SO HAPPY...
...TO HAVE THE BODY I WAS BORN WITH...
...BACK AS IT SHOULD BE!!!
BA-BOOM
SAMURAI OF WANO FOXFIRE KIN'EMON
GOODNESS! YOU'RE JUST AS TALL AS ME, SIR SAMURAI.
I SEE... FORGIVE MY LATE INTRODUCTION!
ZWIP ZWIP
MY NAME...
...IS KIN'EMON!!!
AND I HAIL...
...FROM KURI, OF THE LAND OF WANO!!

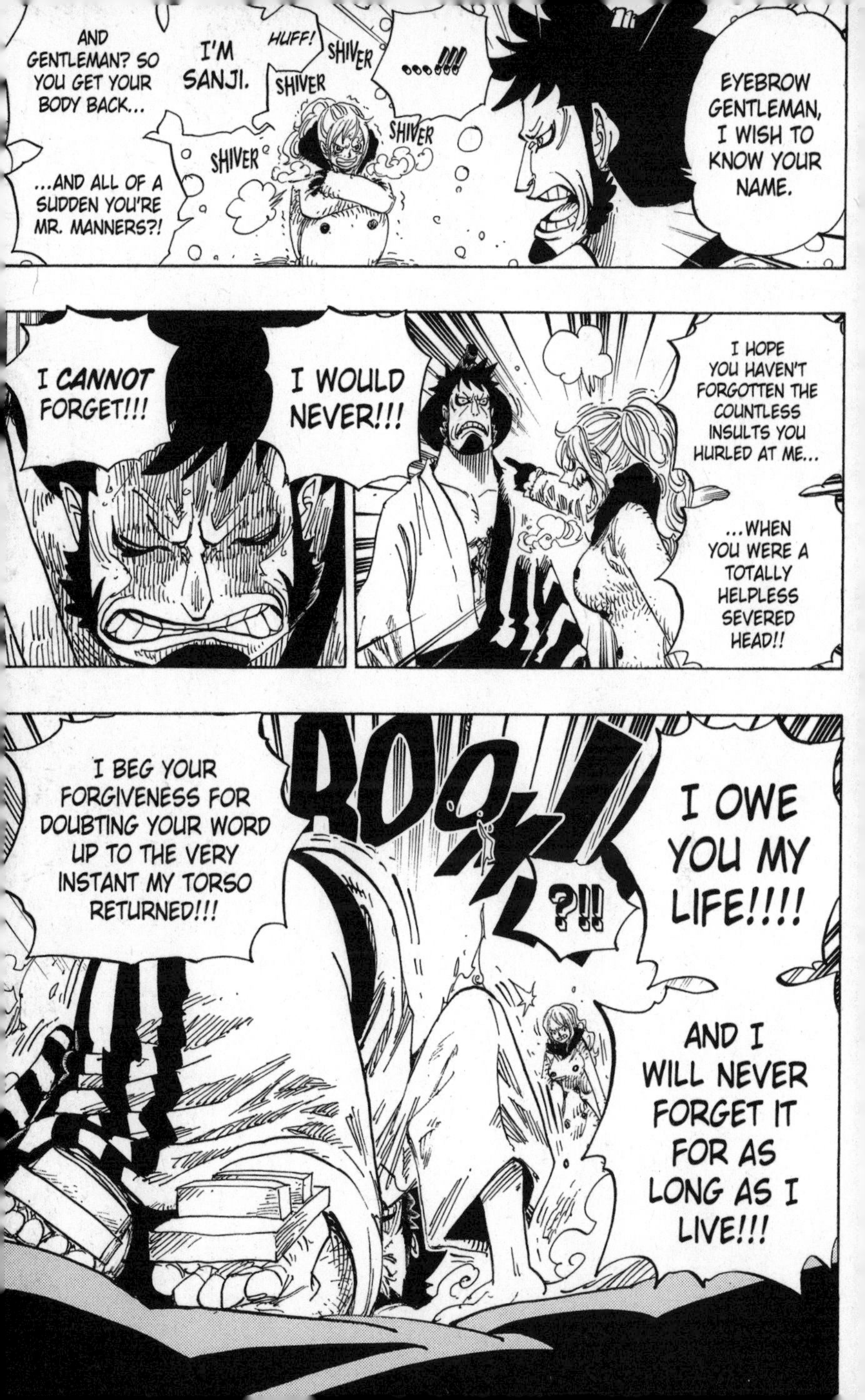
EYEBROW GENTLEMAN, I WISH TO KNOW YOUR NAME.
...!!!
SHIVER
SHIVER
HUFF!
I'M SANJI.
AND GENTLEMAN? SO YOU GET YOUR BODY BACK...
...AND ALL OF A SUDDEN YOU'RE MR. MANNERS?!
SHIVER
SHIVER
I HOPE YOU HAVEN'T FORGOTTEN THE COUNTLESS INSULTS YOU HURLED AT ME...
...WHEN YOU WERE A TOTALLY HELPLESS SEVERED HEAD!!
I WOULD NEVER!!!
I CANNOT FORGET!!!
I OWE YOU MY LIFE!!!!
?!!
I BEG YOUR FORGIVENESS FOR DOUBTING YOUR WORD UP TO THE VERY INSTANT MY TORSO RETURNED!!!
AND I WILL NEVER FORGET IT FOR AS LONG AS I LIVE!!!

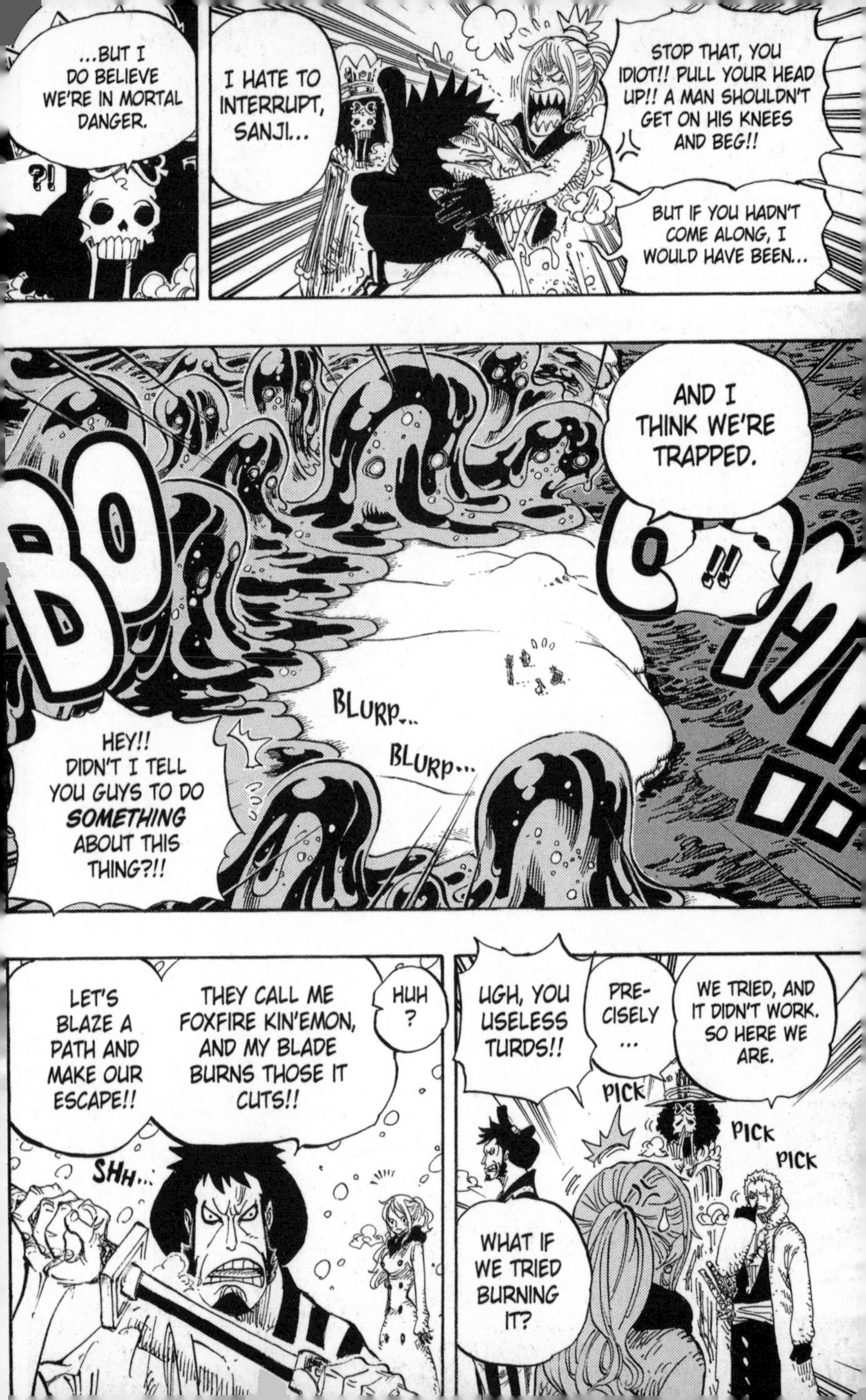
STOP THAT, YOU IDIOT!! PULL YOUR HEAD UP!! A MAN SHOULDN'T GET ON HIS KNEES AND BEG!!
BUT IF YOU HADN'T COME ALONG, I WOULD HAVE BEEN...
I HATE TO INTERRUPT, SANJI...
...BUT I DO BELIEVE WE'RE IN MORTAL DANGER.
?!
AND I THINK WE'RE TRAPPED.
!!
BLURP...
BLURP...
HEY!! DIDN'T I TELL YOU GUYS TO DO *SOMETHING* ABOUT THIS THING?!!
WE TRIED, AND IT DIDN'T WORK. SO HERE WE ARE.
PRE-CISELY...
UGH, YOU USELESS TURDS!!
PICK
PICK
PICK
WHAT IF WE TRIED BURNING IT?
HUH?
THEY CALL ME FOXFIRE KIN'EMON, AND MY BLADE BURNS THOSE IT CUTS!!
LET'S BLAZE A PATH AND MAKE OUR ESCAPE!!
SHH...

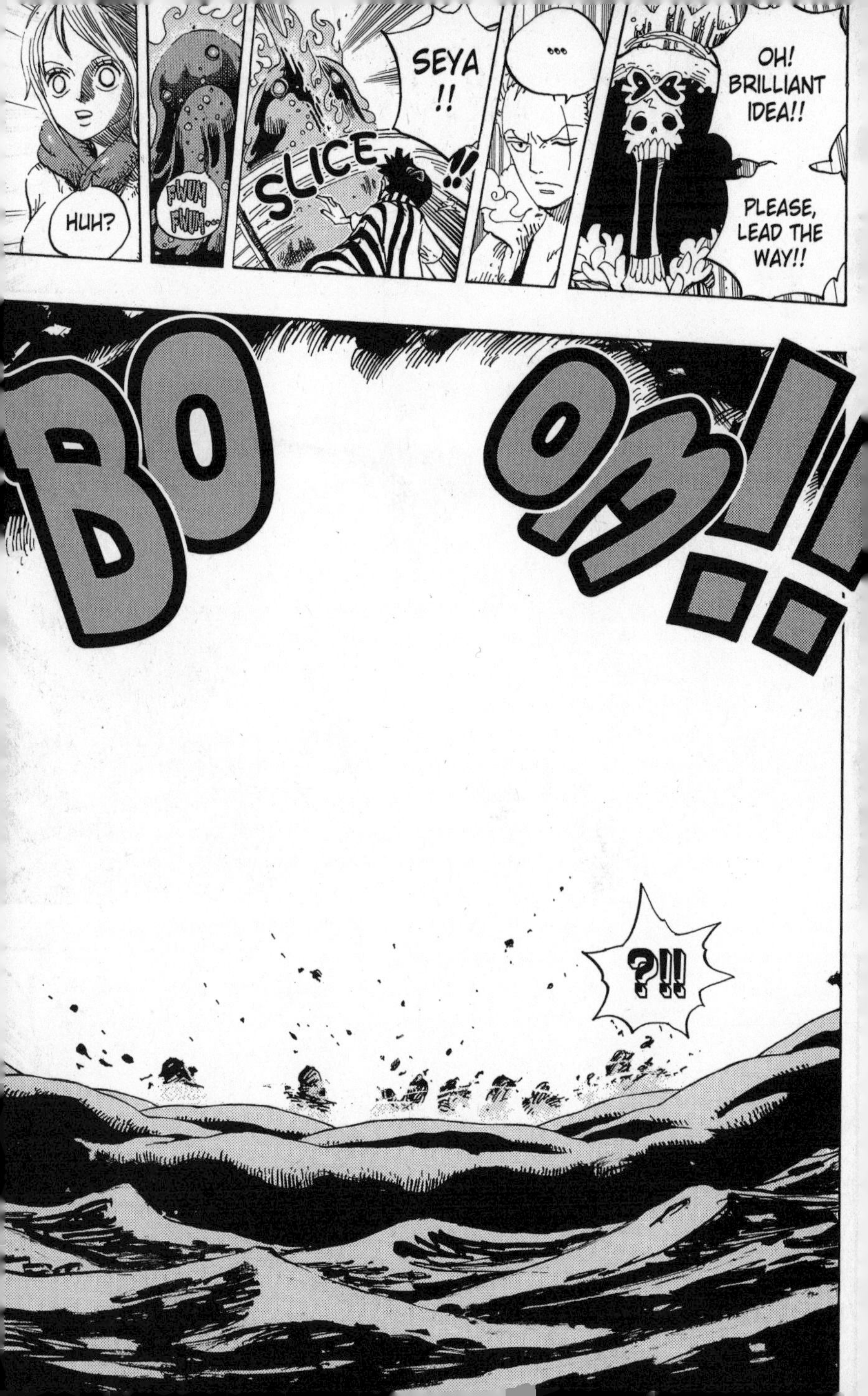
OH! BRILLIANT IDEA!!
PLEASE, LEAD THE WAY!!
...
SEYA !!
SLICE!!
FWUM FWUM...
HUH?
BOOOM!!
?!!

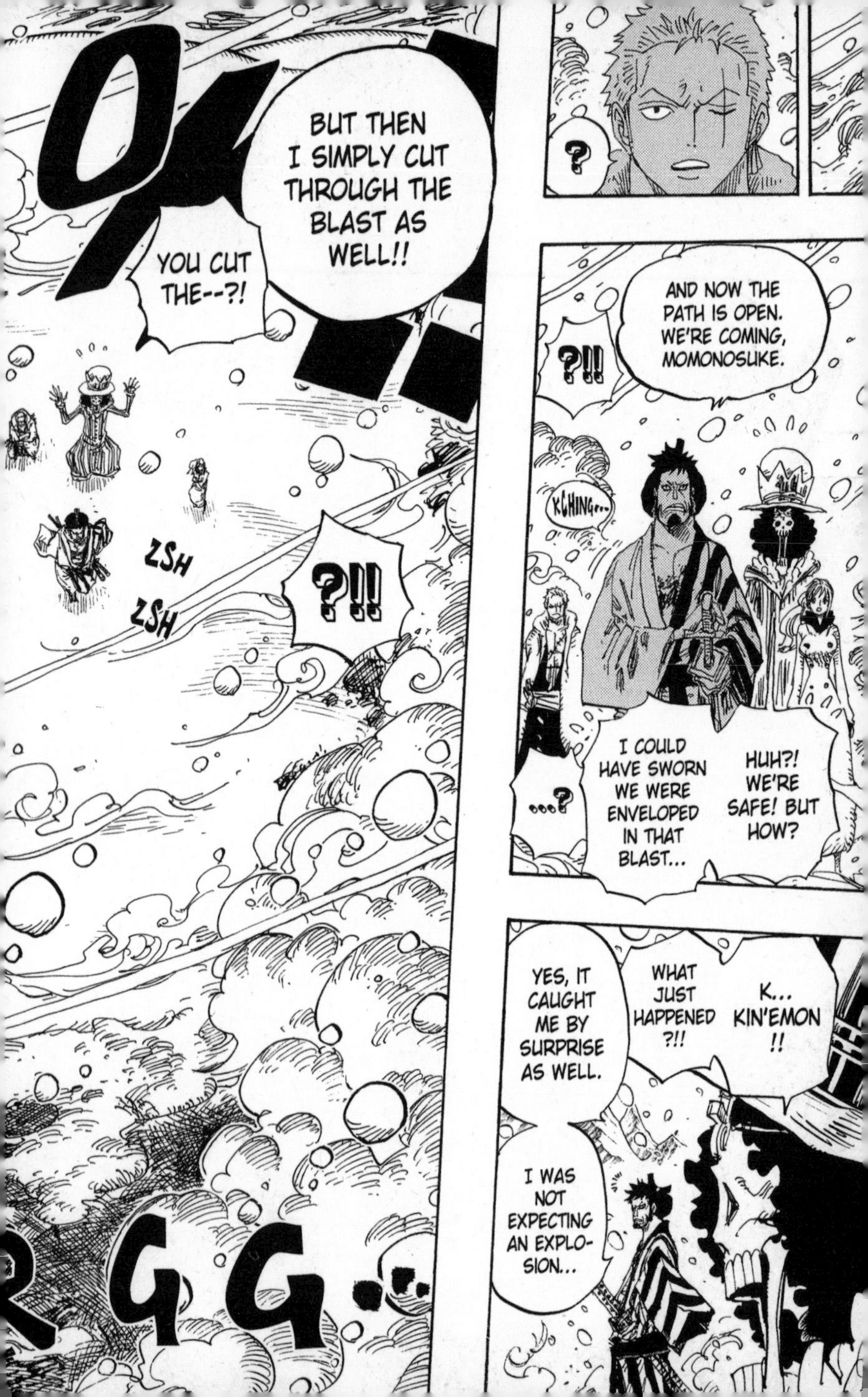
?
AND NOW THE PATH IS OPEN. WE'RE COMING, MOMONOSUKE.
?!!
KCHING...
HUH?! WE'RE SAFE! BUT HOW?
I COULD HAVE SWORN WE WERE ENVELOPED IN THAT BLAST...
...?
K... KIN'EMON !!
WHAT JUST HAPPENED ?!!
YES, IT CAUGHT ME BY SURPRISE AS WELL.
I WAS NOT EXPECTING AN EXPLO-SION...
BUT THEN I SIMPLY CUT THROUGH THE BLAST AS WELL!!
YOU CUT THE--?!
?!!
ZSH
ZSH
RGG...

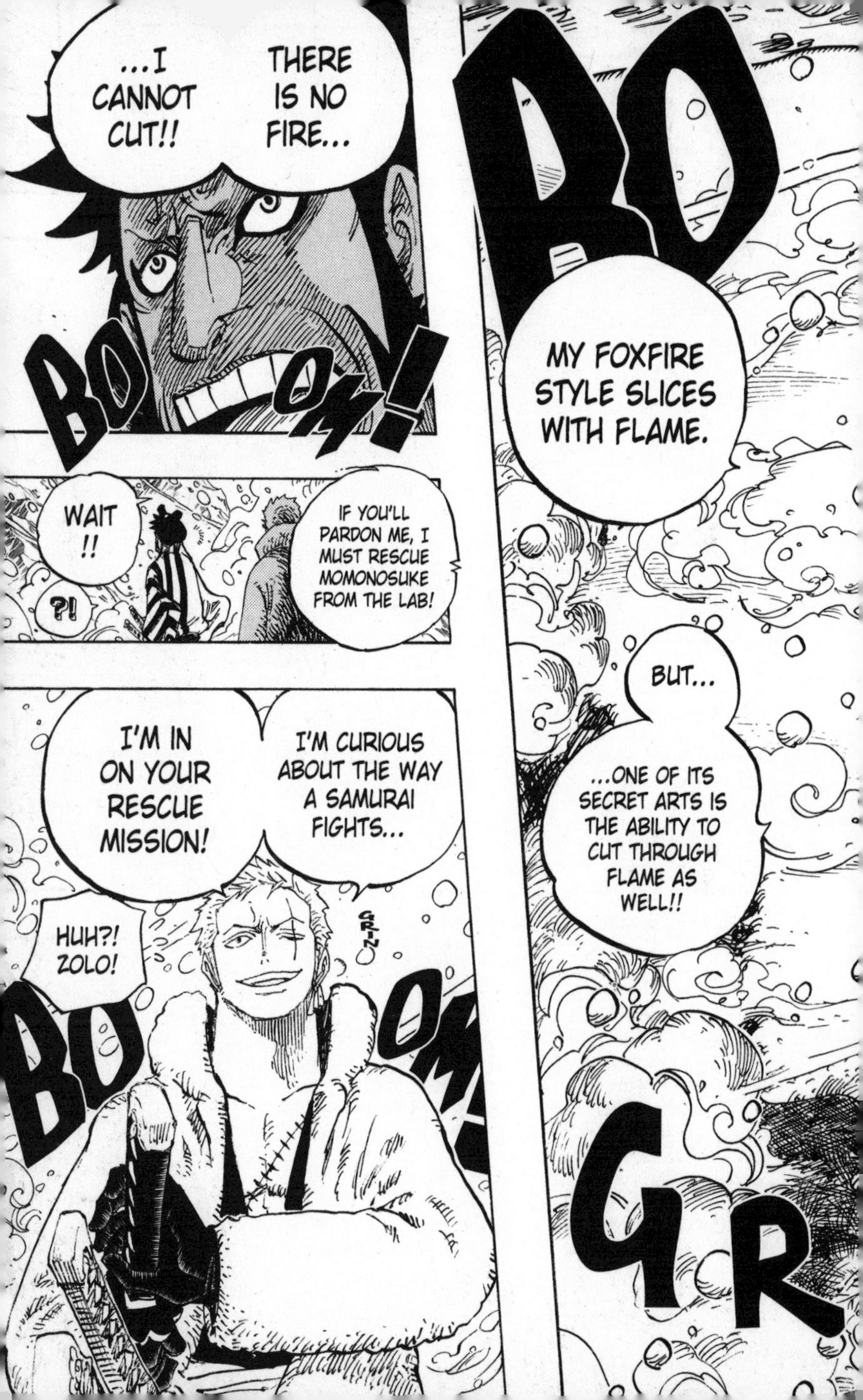
BO
MY FOXFIRE STYLE SLICES WITH FLAME.
BUT...
...ONE OF ITS SECRET ARTS IS THE ABILITY TO CUT THROUGH FLAME AS WELL!!
GR
THERE IS NO FIRE...
...I CANNOT CUT!!
BOOM!
IF YOU'LL PARDON ME, I MUST RESCUE MOMONOSUKE FROM THE LAB!
WAIT!!
?!
I'M CURIOUS ABOUT THE WAY A SAMURAI FIGHTS...
I'M IN ON YOUR RESCUE MISSION!
GRIN
HUH?! ZOLO!
BOOM

SBS Question Corner

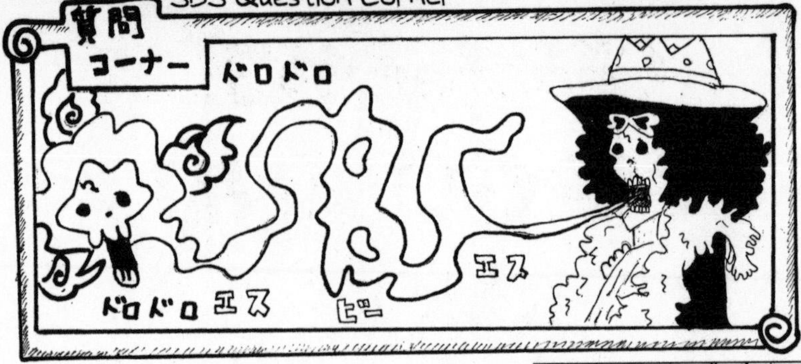
質問
コーナー
ドロドロ
ドロドロ エス
ビー
エス
(Soyoka Mori, Aichi)

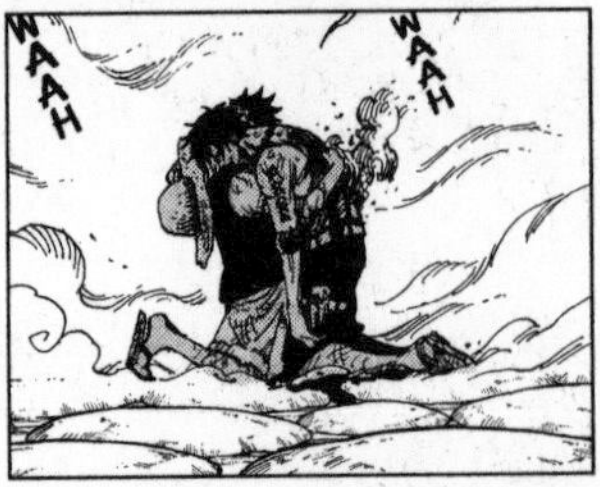
WAAH
WAAH

Q: Right before Ace dies, he leaves a message for Luffy to pass on, since he can barely speak anymore. Did Luffy actually relay, "Thank you for loving me" to the others?

--Otohimememe

A: I see. He did make a promise, didn't he? The way the action flows after that, it's hard to imagine that Luffy met any of the Whitebeard Pirates. But you know what? That's okay. The Whitebeard Pirates loved Ace--the Paramount War was the result of that--and not a single one of them needed to hear those words from his own lips to know his gratitude. In fact, Ace's message held another unspoken request. What does it mean that he ordered Luffy to tell his words to the others **later?** That he needed to survive that war, and live to see another day. I think the last words Ace spoke reached the hearts of more people than we can possibly imagine.

Q: Odacchi! I went to "One Piece Ten," the art exhibit. When I went, the original art for chapter 668, "Pirate Alliance," was on display!!! And on the cover page for "Decks of the World," there were three cups before Ace's grave!!! Should I assume that you-know-who visited Ace's grave?? Because only Luffy and you-know-who would understand what that means…

--Gonke Barber

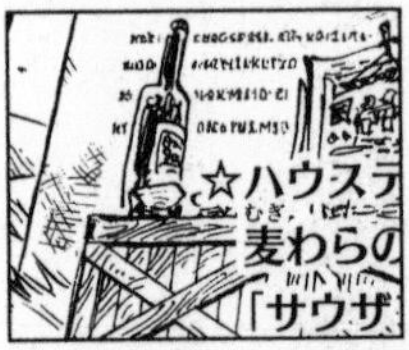
☆ハウステ
麦わらの
「サウザ

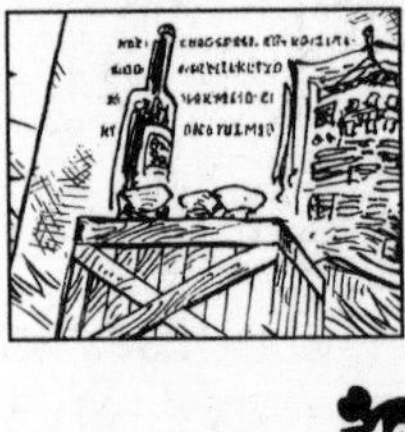

A: Yes. This illustration is from the cover page of Chapter 668, but unfortunately, the original printing in Weekly Shonen Jump in Japan had some promotional text covering that part up. However, since the art exhibit was running in Tokyo at the time, I know some readers went down to see the original illustration without the text. You can see it for yourself here in this book. As for what it means, I leave that to your imagination.

Chapter 673: VERGO AND JOKER

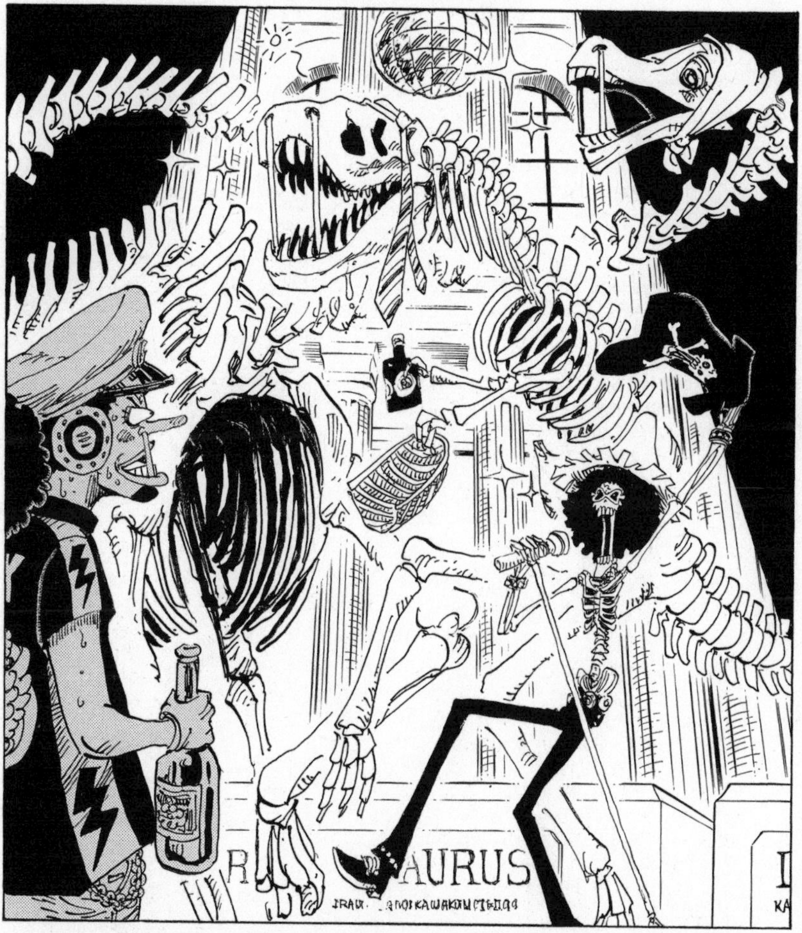
AURUS

REQUEST: "MUSEUM SECURITY GUARD USOPP FINDS BROOK DANCING WITH THE DINO SKELETON LATE AT NIGHT" BY SEAN FROM AOMORI

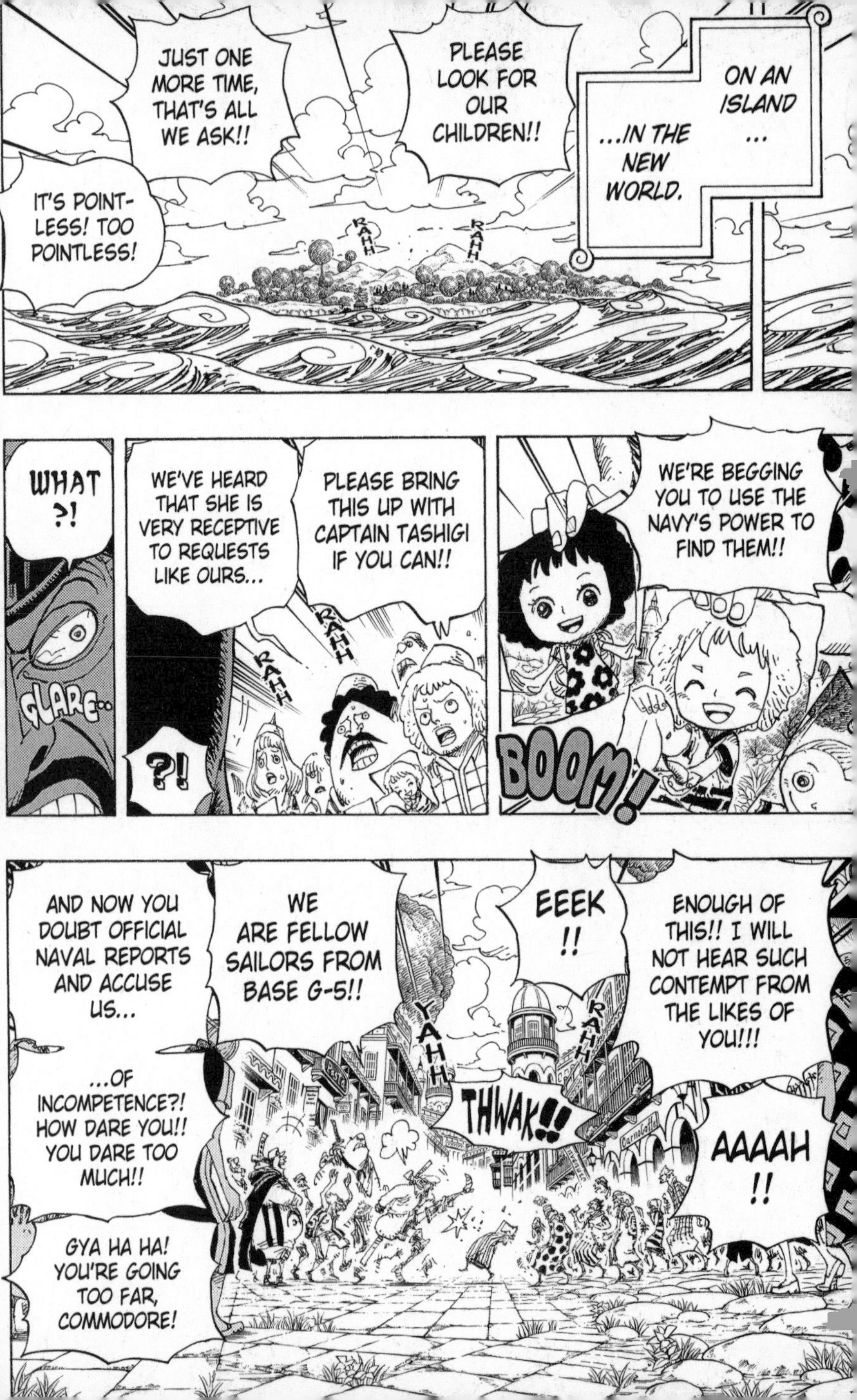
ON AN ISLAND ...
...IN THE NEW WORLD.
PLEASE LOOK FOR OUR CHILDREN!!
JUST ONE MORE TIME, THAT'S ALL WE ASK!!
RAHH
RAHH
IT'S POINTLESS! TOO POINTLESS!
WE'RE BEGGING YOU TO USE THE NAVY'S POWER TO FIND THEM!!
BOOM!
PLEASE BRING THIS UP WITH CAPTAIN TASHIGI IF YOU CAN!!
WE'VE HEARD THAT SHE IS VERY RECEPTIVE TO REQUESTS LIKE OURS...
RAHH
RAHH
?!
WHAT ?!
GLARE..
ENOUGH OF THIS!! I WILL NOT HEAR SUCH CONTEMPT FROM THE LIKES OF YOU!!!
EEEK !!
RAHH
WE ARE FELLOW SAILORS FROM BASE G-5!!
YAHH
AND NOW YOU DOUBT OFFICIAL NAVAL REPORTS AND ACCUSE US...
THWAK!!
AAAAH !!
...OF INCOMPETENCE?! HOW DARE YOU!! YOU DARE TOO MUCH!!
GYA HA HA! YOU'RE GOING TOO FAR, COMMODORE!

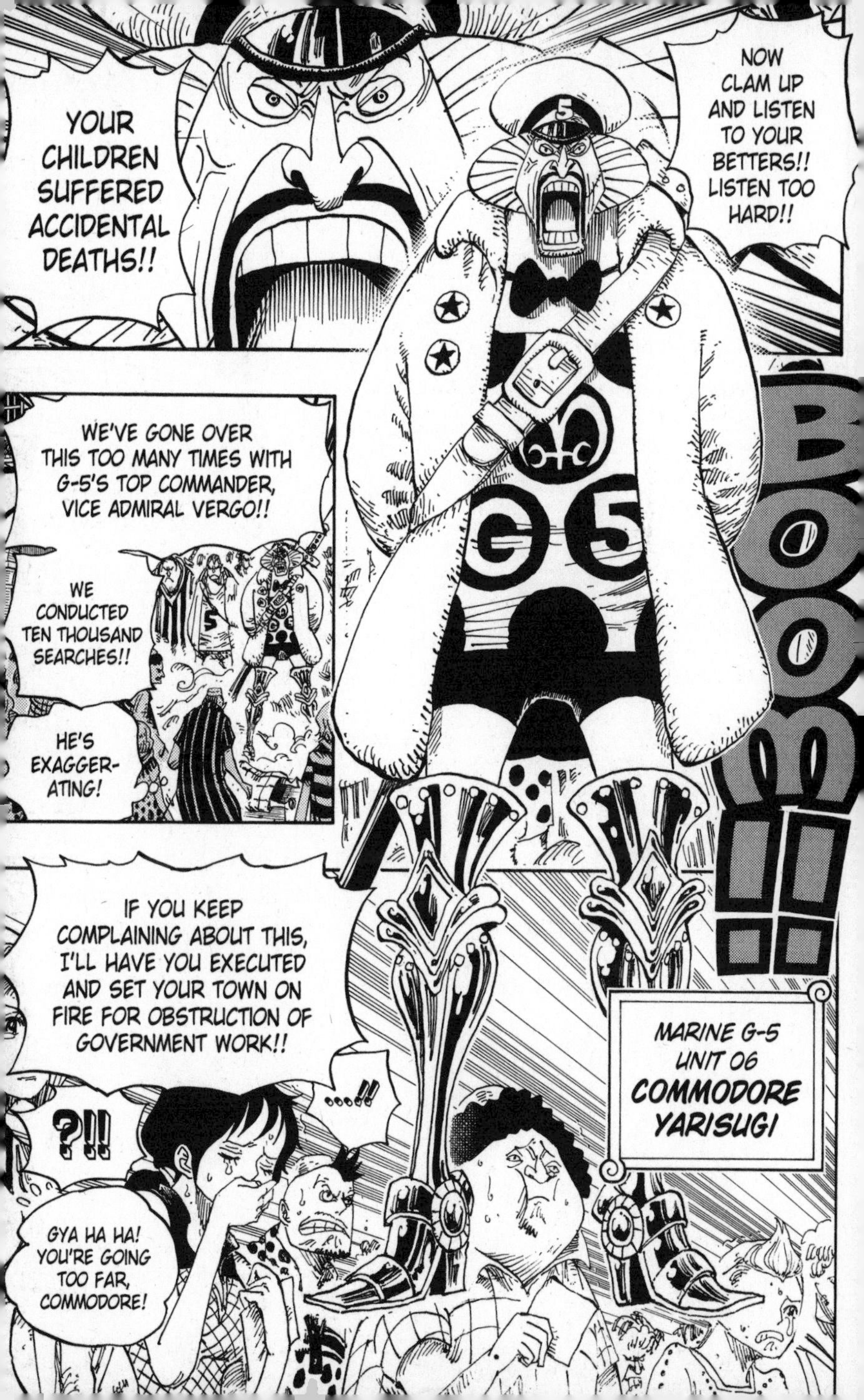

NOW CLAM UP AND LISTEN TO YOUR BETTERS!! LISTEN TOO HARD!!
YOUR CHILDREN SUFFERED ACCIDENTAL DEATHS!!
BOOM!!
WE'VE GONE OVER THIS TOO MANY TIMES WITH G-5'S TOP COMMANDER, VICE ADMIRAL VERGO!!
WE CONDUCTED TEN THOUSAND SEARCHES!!
HE'S EXAGGER-ATING!
MARINE G-5 UNIT 06 COMMODORE YARISUGI
IF YOU KEEP COMPLAINING ABOUT THIS, I'LL HAVE YOU EXECUTED AND SET YOUR TOWN ON FIRE FOR OBSTRUCTION OF GOVERNMENT WORK!!
...!!
?!!
GYA HA HA! YOU'RE GOING TOO FAR, COMMODORE!

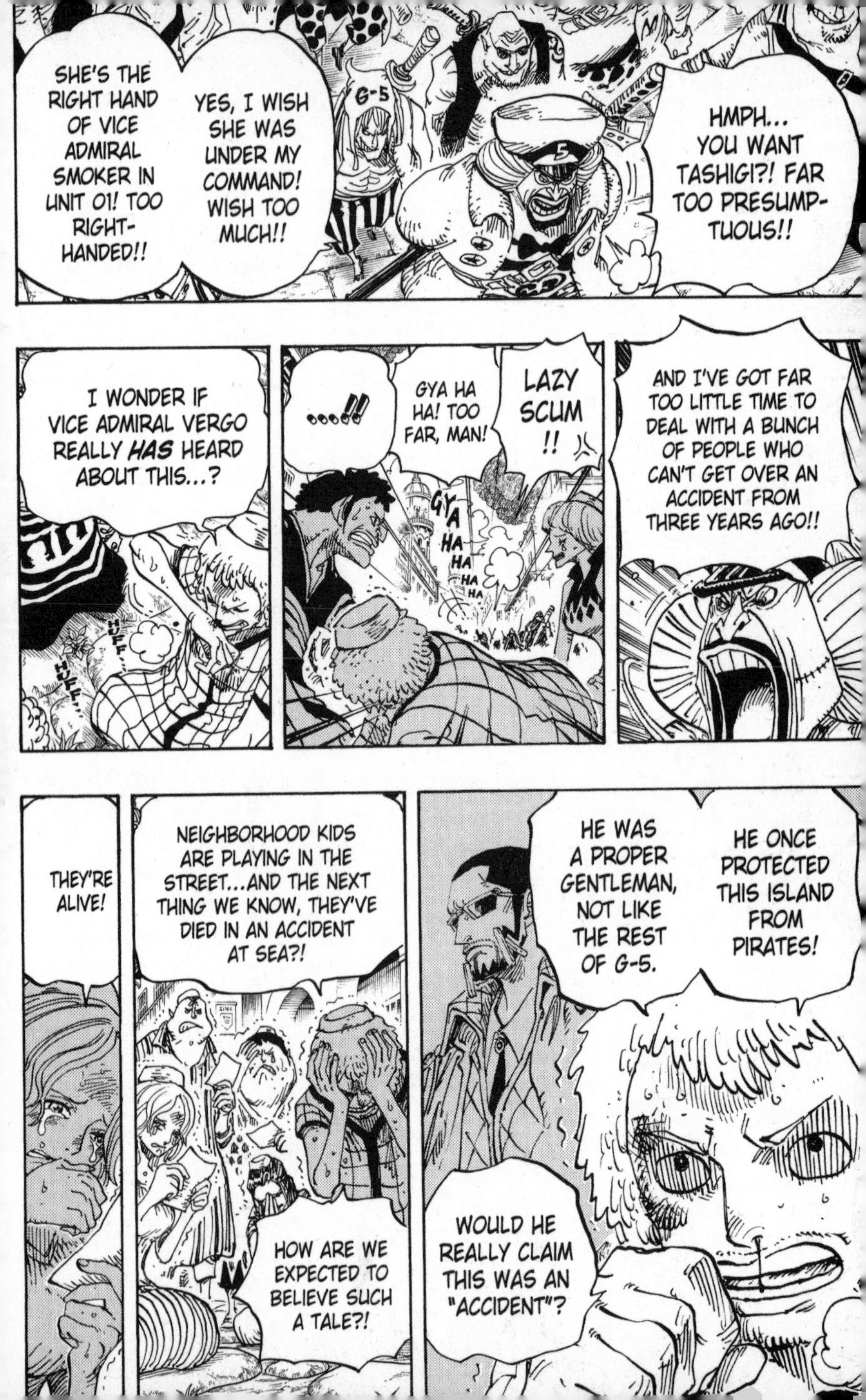
HMPH... YOU WANT TASHIGI?! FAR TOO PRESUMPTUOUS!!
YES, I WISH SHE WAS UNDER MY COMMAND! WISH TOO MUCH!!
SHE'S THE RIGHT HAND OF VICE ADMIRAL SMOKER IN UNIT 01! TOO RIGHT-HANDED!!
AND I'VE GOT FAR TOO LITTLE TIME TO DEAL WITH A BUNCH OF PEOPLE WHO CAN'T GET OVER AN ACCIDENT FROM THREE YEARS AGO!!
LAZY SCUM!!
GYA HA HA! TOO FAR, MAN!
...!!
GYAHA HA HA HA HA
I WONDER IF VICE ADMIRAL VERGO REALLY HAS HEARD ABOUT THIS...?
HUFF... HUFF...
HE ONCE PROTECTED THIS ISLAND FROM PIRATES!
HE WAS A PROPER GENTLEMAN, NOT LIKE THE REST OF G-5.
WOULD HE REALLY CLAIM THIS WAS AN "ACCIDENT"?
NEIGHBORHOOD KIDS ARE PLAYING IN THE STREET...AND THE NEXT THING WE KNOW, THEY'VE DIED IN AN ACCIDENT AT SEA?!
HOW ARE WE EXPECTED TO BELIEVE SUCH A TALE?!
THEY'RE ALIVE!

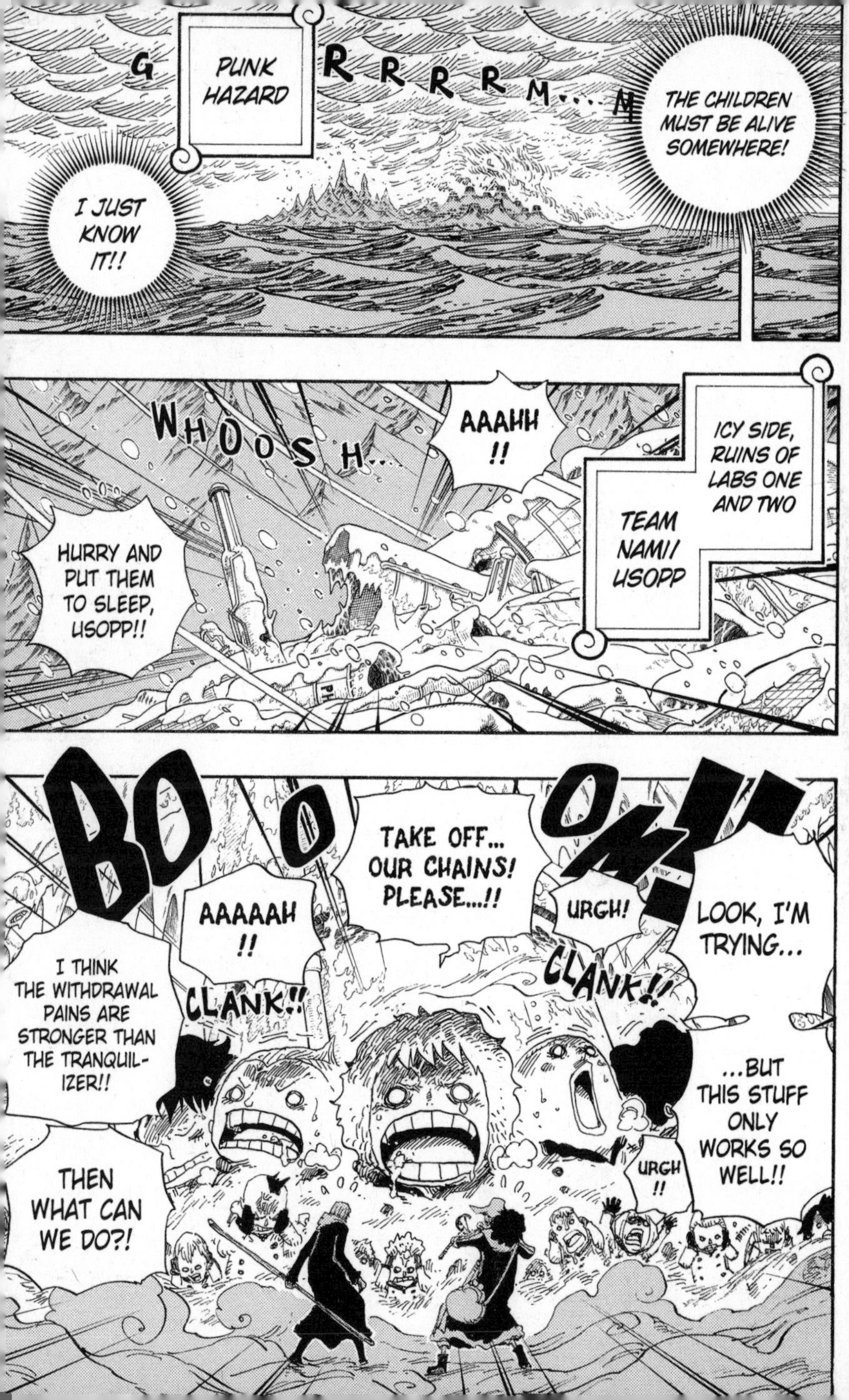
PUNK HAZARD
GRRRRRM...M
THE CHILDREN MUST BE ALIVE SOMEWHERE!
I JUST KNOW IT!!
ICY SIDE, RUINS OF LABS ONE AND TWO
TEAM NAMI/USOPP
AAAHH!!
WHOOSH...
HURRY AND PUT THEM TO SLEEP, USOPP!!
BOOOM
LOOK, I'M TRYING...
URGH!
CLANK!!
TAKE OFF... OUR CHAINS! PLEASE...!!
AAAAAH!!
CLANK!!
...BUT THIS STUFF ONLY WORKS SO WELL!!
URGH!!
I THINK THE WITHDRAWAL PAINS ARE STRONGER THAN THE TRANQUIL-IZER!!
THEN WHAT CAN WE DO?!

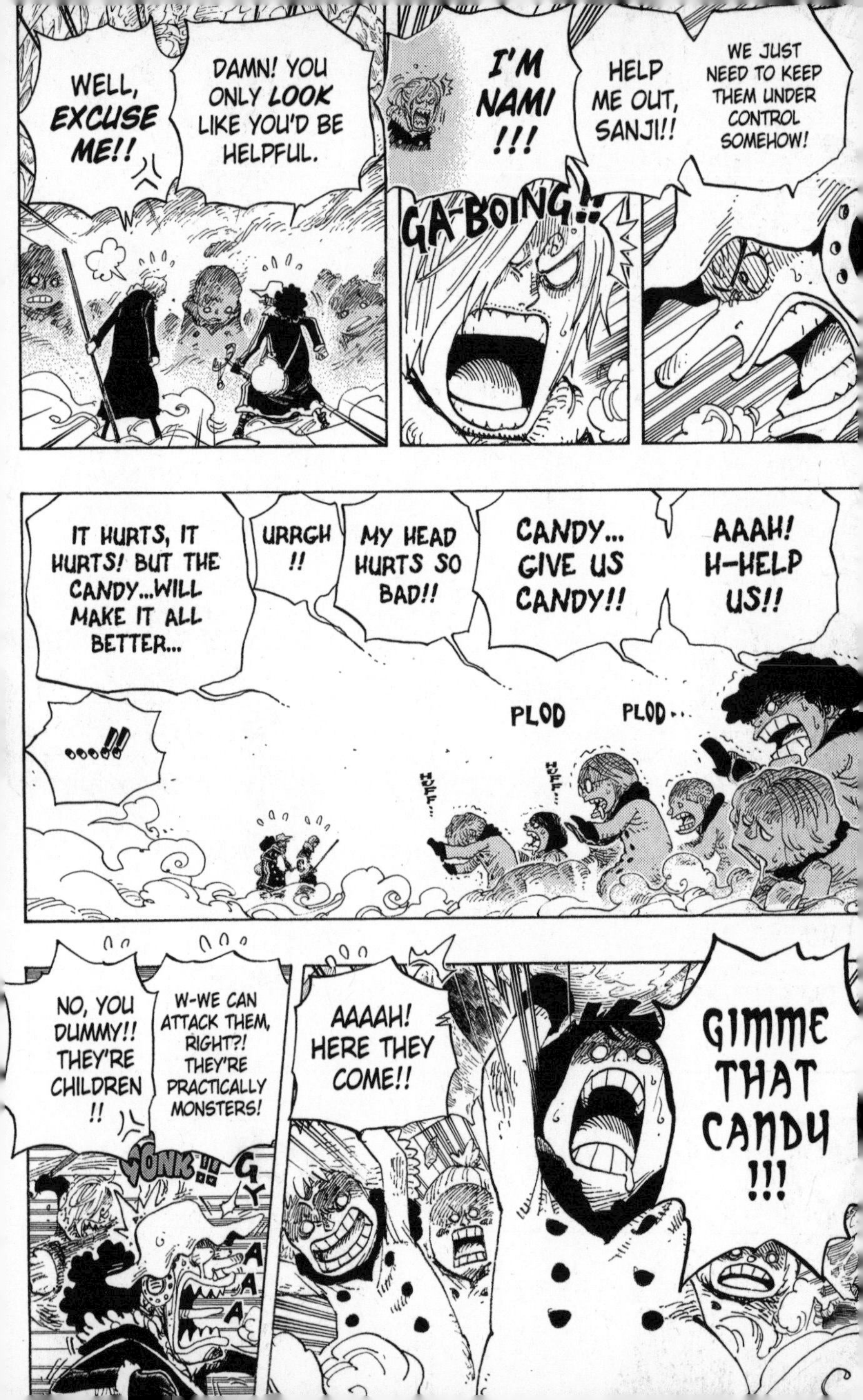
WE JUST NEED TO KEEP THEM UNDER CONTROL SOMEHOW!
HELP ME OUT, SANJI!!
I'M NAMI!!!
GA-BOING!!
DAMN! YOU ONLY LOOK LIKE YOU'D BE HELPFUL.
WELL, EXCUSE ME!!
AAAH! H-HELP US!!
CANDY... GIVE US CANDY!!
MY HEAD HURTS SO BAD!!
URRGH!!
IT HURTS, IT HURTS! BUT THE CANDY...WILL MAKE IT ALL BETTER...
PLOD PLOD...
HUFF...
HUFF...
....!!
GIMME THAT CANDY!!!
AAAAH! HERE THEY COME!!
W-WE CAN ATTACK THEM, RIGHT?! THEY'RE PRACTICALLY MONSTERS!
NO, YOU DUMMY!! THEY'RE CHILDREN!!
WONK!!
GYAAA

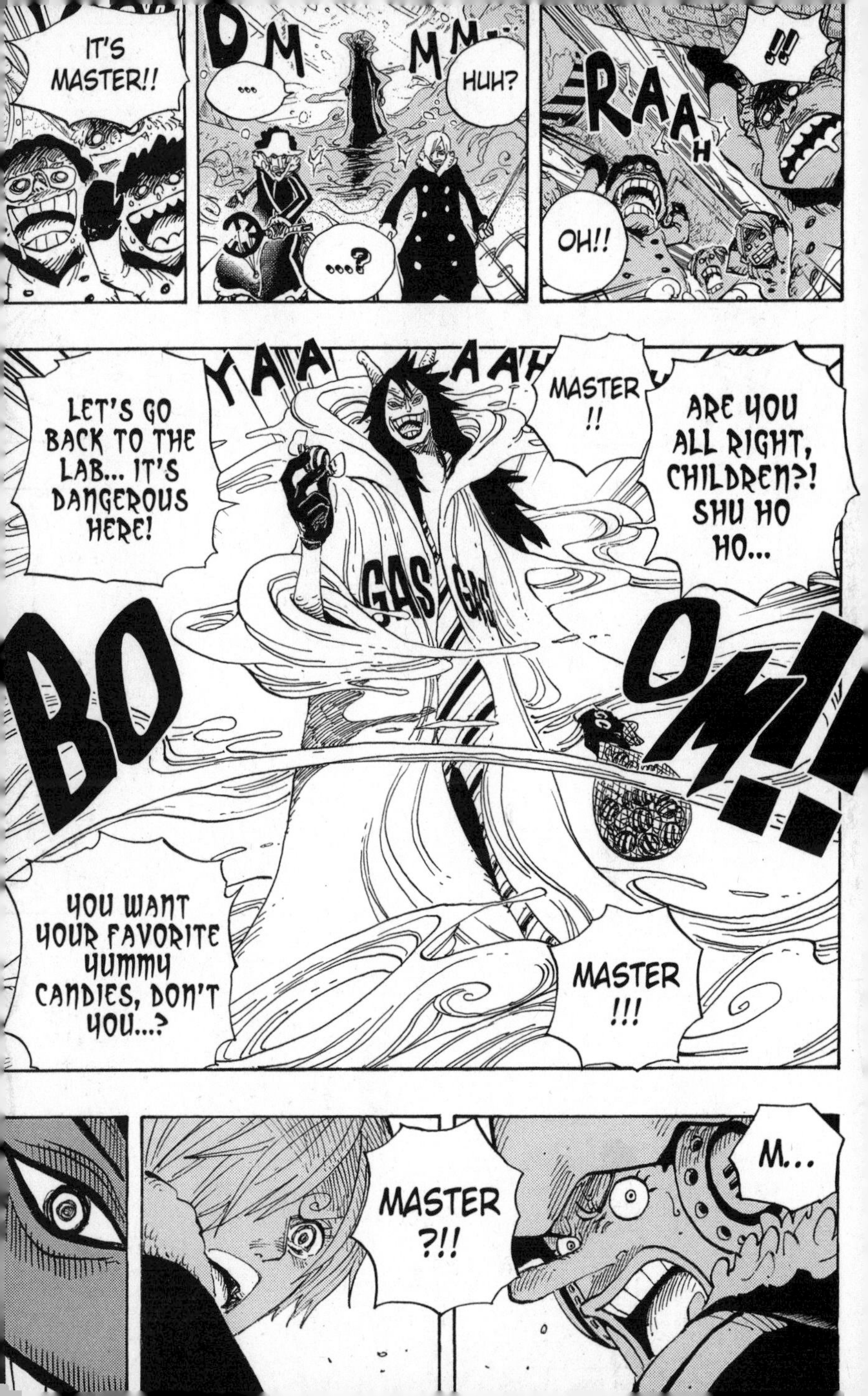
!!
RAAAH
OH!!
HUH?
DM MN...
...
...?
IT'S MASTER!!
ARE YOU ALL RIGHT, CHILDREN?! SHU HO HO...
MASTER !!
YAAAAH
LET'S GO BACK TO THE LAB... IT'S DANGEROUS HERE!
BOOM!!
MASTER !!!
YOU WANT YOUR FAVORITE YUMMY CANDIES, DON'T YOU...?
M...
MASTER ?!!

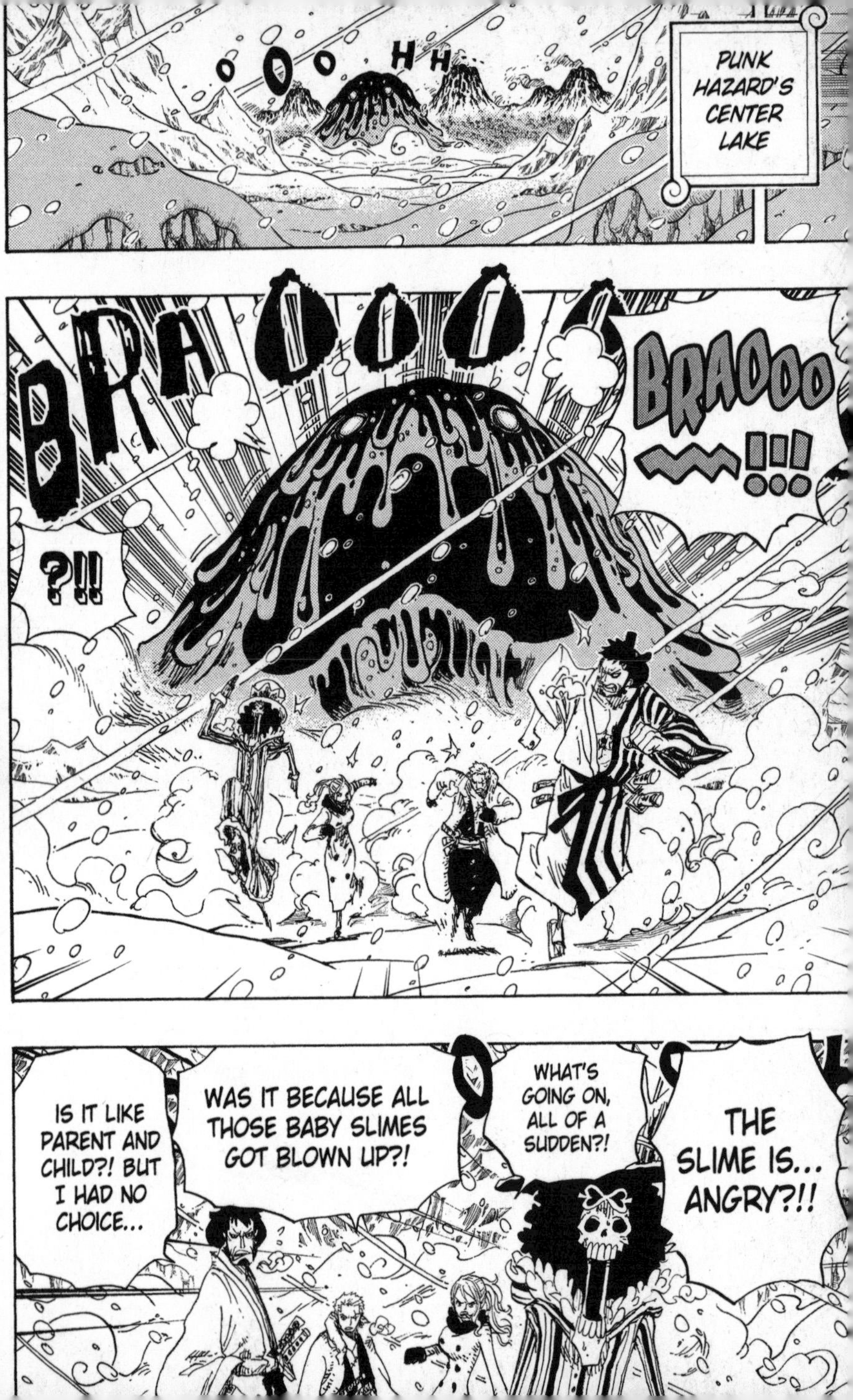
PUNK HAZARD'S CENTER LAKE
OOOHH
BRAOOO ~~!!!
BRAOOOO
?!!
THE SLIME IS... ANGRY?!!
WHAT'S GOING ON, ALL OF A SUDDEN?!
WAS IT BECAUSE ALL THOSE BABY SLIMES GOT BLOWN UP?!
IS IT LIKE PARENT AND CHILD?! BUT I HAD NO CHOICE...

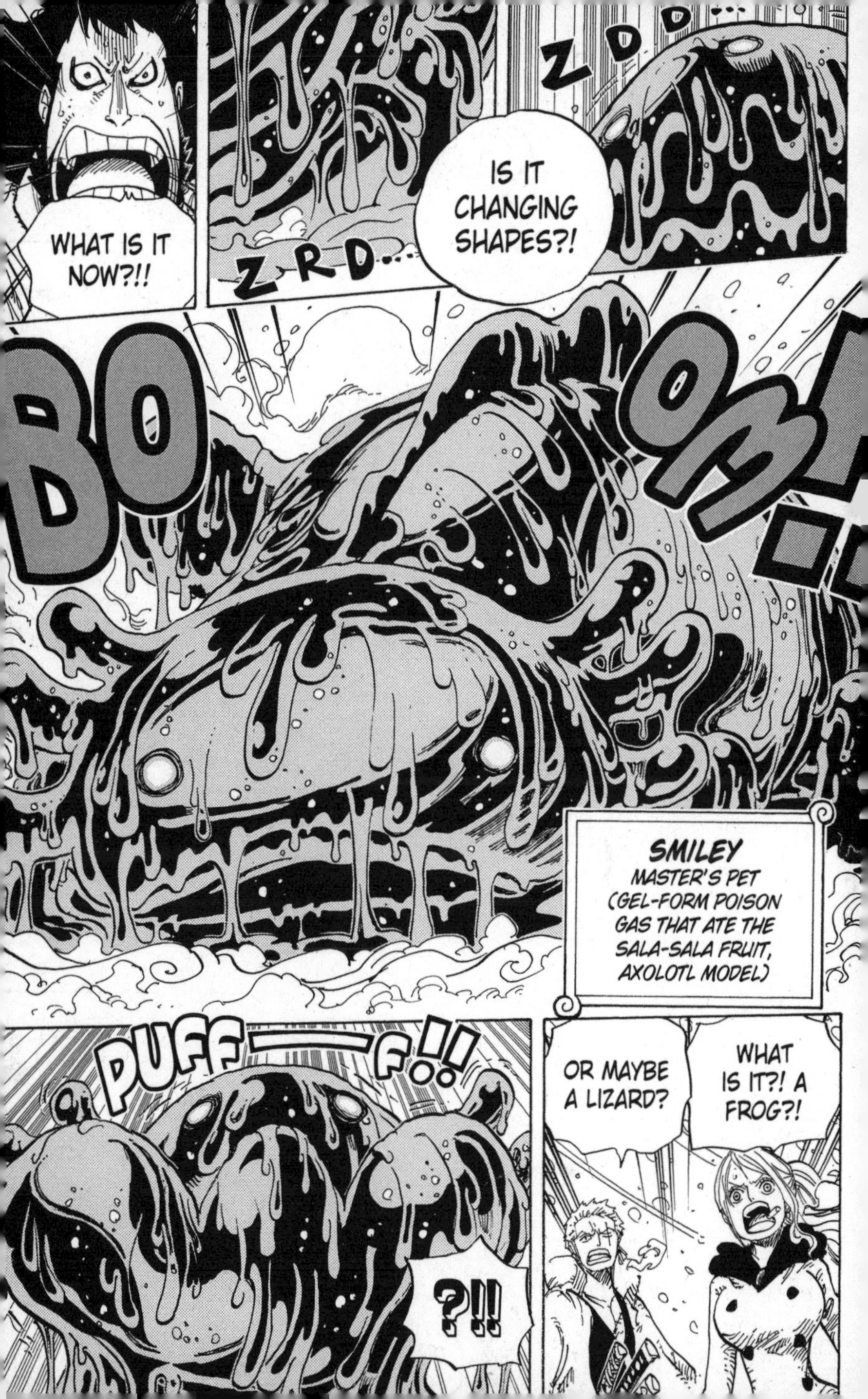
ZDD...
IS IT CHANGING SHAPES?!
ZRD...
WHAT IS IT NOW?!!
BOOM!!
SMILEY
MASTER'S PET
(GEL-FORM POISON GAS THAT ATE THE SALA-SALA FRUIT, AXOLOTL MODEL)
WHAT IS IT?! A FROG?!
OR MAYBE A LIZARD?
PUFF—F!!
?!!

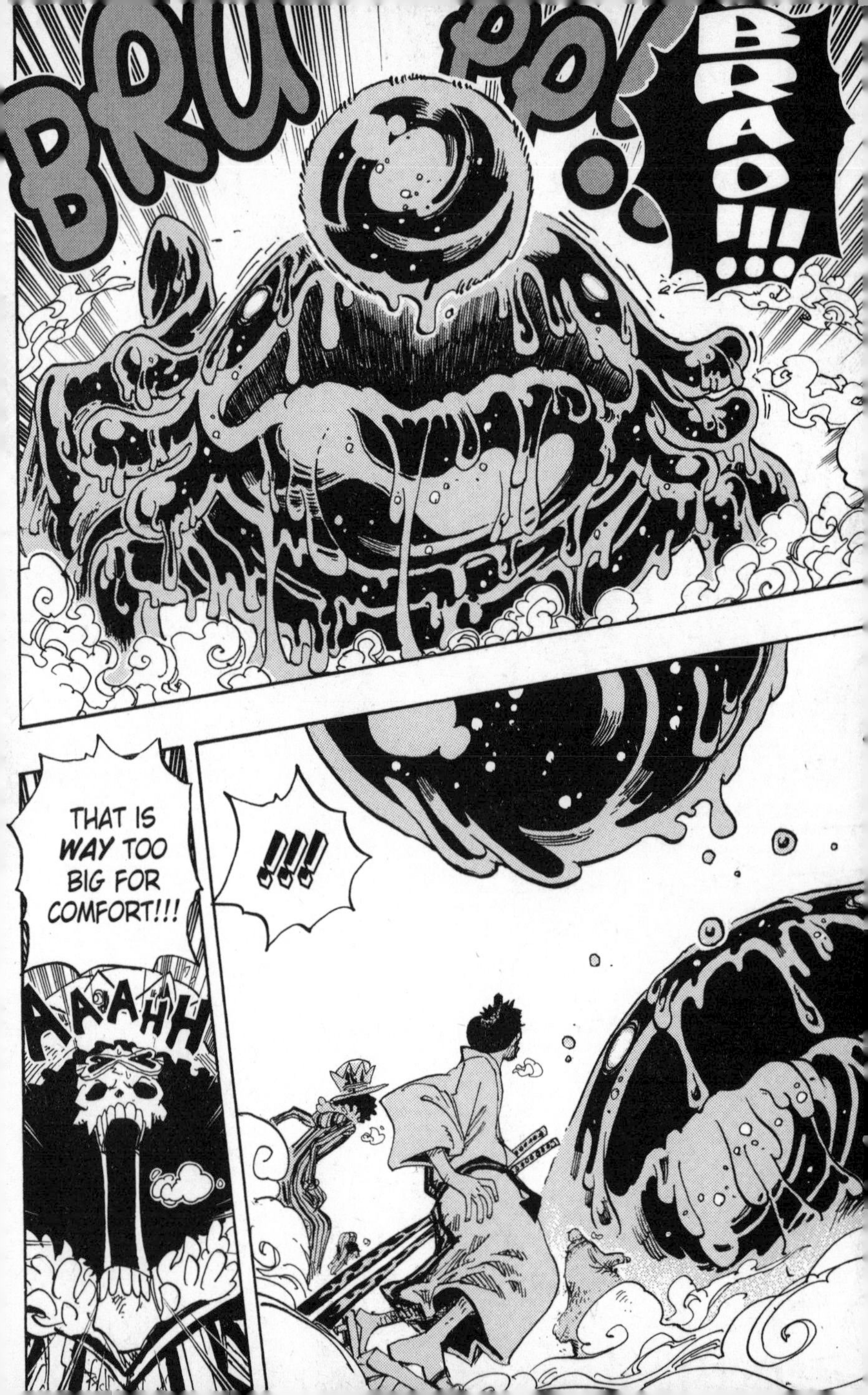
BRAO!!!
BRUPP!
!!!
THAT IS WAY TOO BIG FOR COMFORT!!!
AAHH

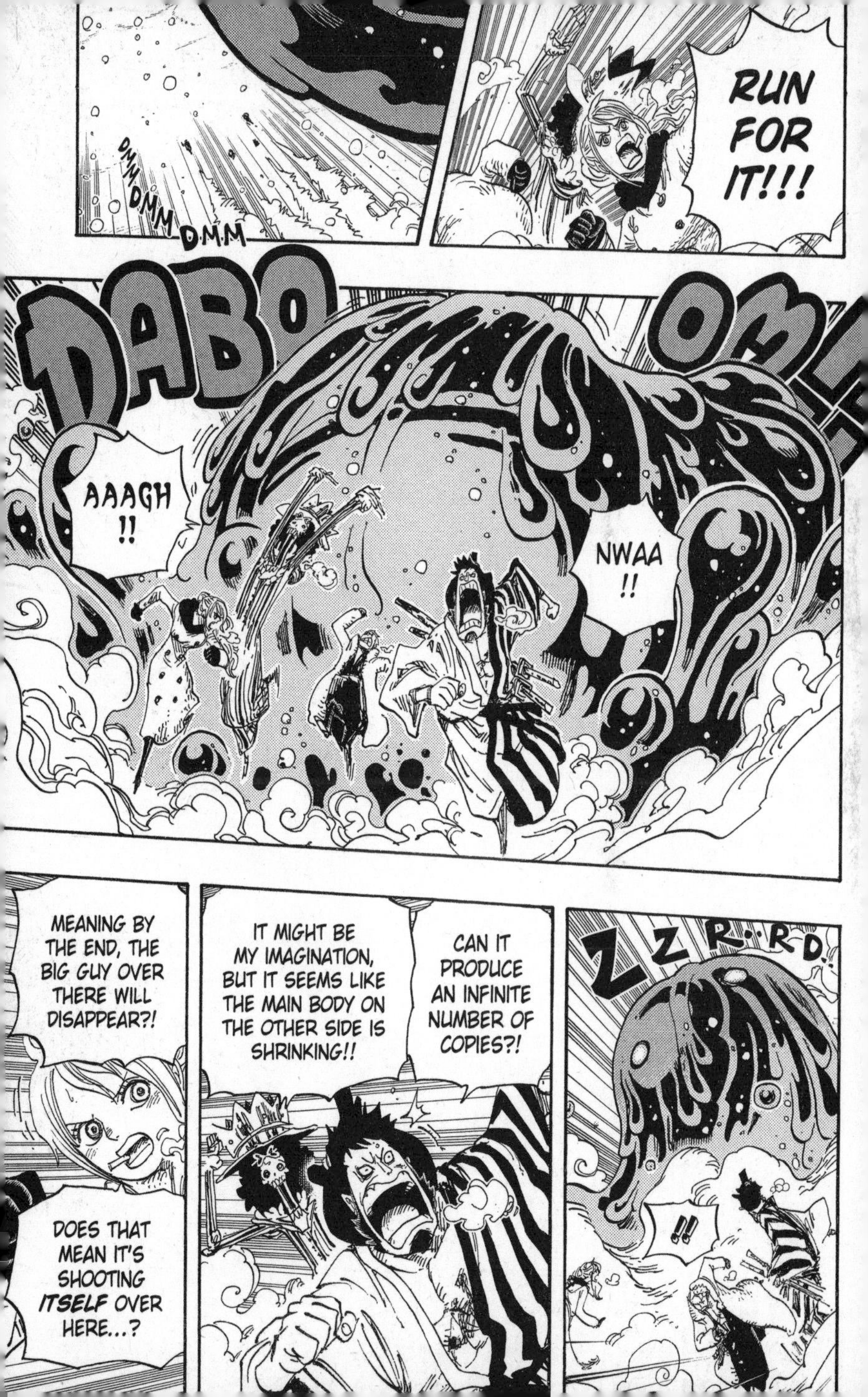

RUN FOR IT!!!
D·M·M D·M·M D·M·M
DABO
OOM!
NWAA!!
AAAGH!!
ZZR·R·D
!!
CAN IT PRODUCE AN INFINITE NUMBER OF COPIES?!
IT MIGHT BE MY IMAGINATION, BUT IT SEEMS LIKE THE MAIN BODY ON THE OTHER SIDE IS SHRINKING!!
MEANING BY THE END, THE BIG GUY OVER THERE WILL DISAPPEAR?!
DOES THAT MEAN IT'S SHOOTING *ITSELF* OVER HERE...?

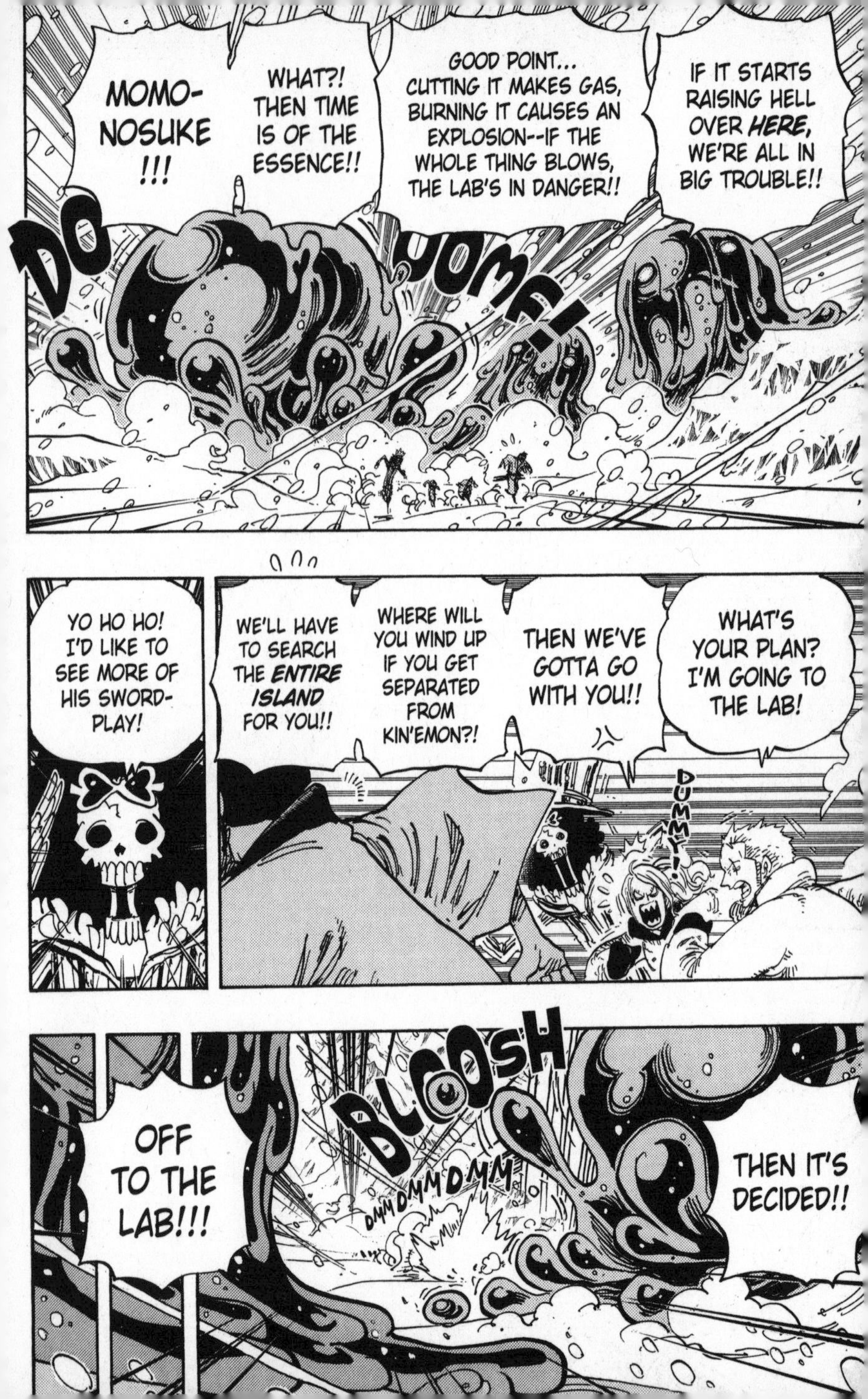

IF IT STARTS RAISING HELL OVER HERE, WE'RE ALL IN BIG TROUBLE!!
GOOD POINT... CUTTING IT MAKES GAS, BURNING IT CAUSES AN EXPLOSION--IF THE WHOLE THING BLOWS, THE LAB'S IN DANGER!!
WHAT?! THEN TIME IS OF THE ESSENCE!!
MOMO-NOSUKE!!!
DOOOMF!!
WHAT'S YOUR PLAN? I'M GOING TO THE LAB!
THEN WE'VE GOTTA GO WITH YOU!!
WHERE WILL YOU WIND UP IF YOU GET SEPARATED FROM KIN'EMON?!
WE'LL HAVE TO SEARCH THE ENTIRE ISLAND FOR YOU!!
DUMMY!!
YO HO HO! I'D LIKE TO SEE MORE OF HIS SWORD-PLAY!
THEN IT'S DECIDED!!
BLOOOSH
DMM DMM DMM DMM
OFF TO THE LAB!!!

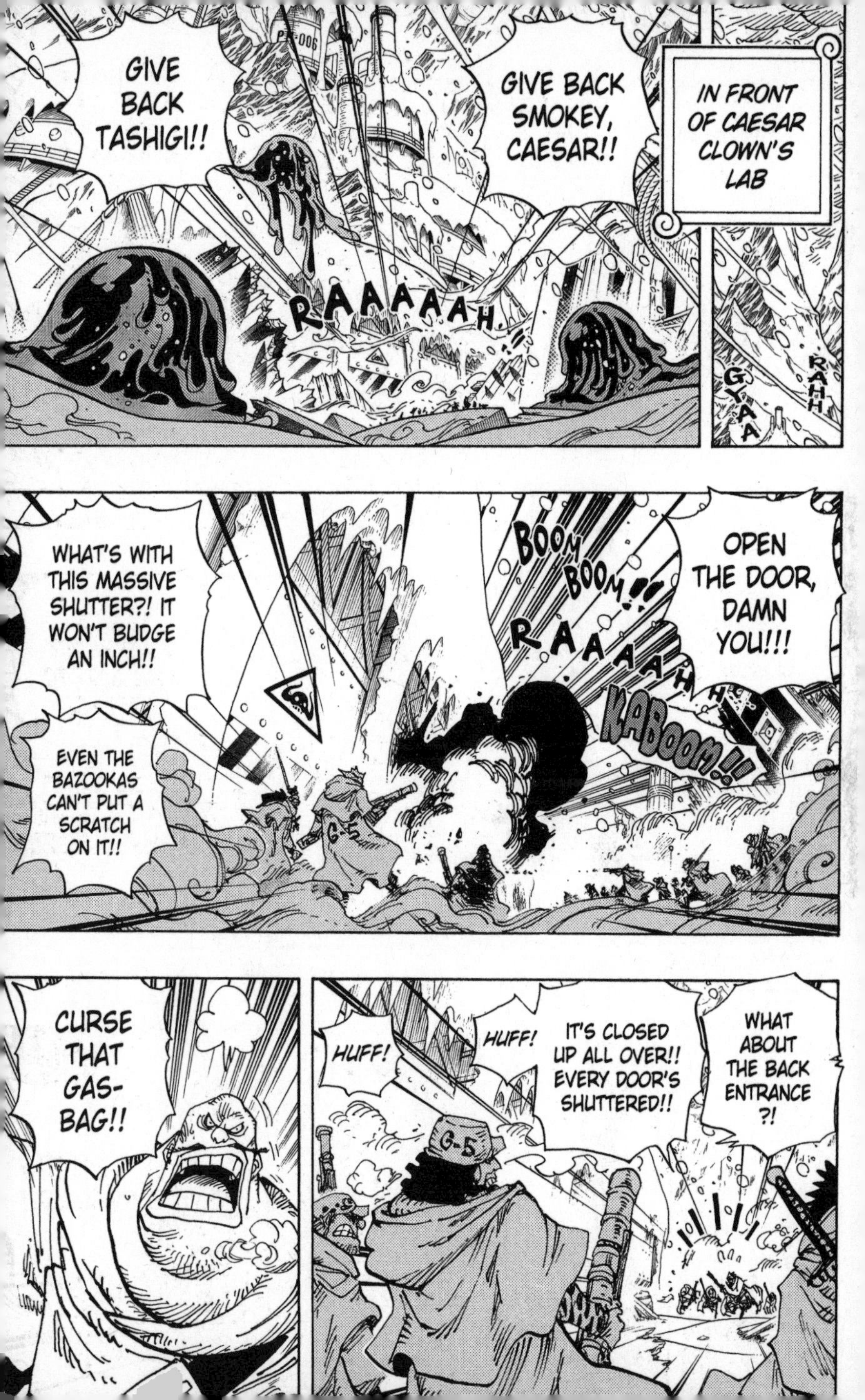
IN FRONT OF CAESAR CLOWN'S LAB
GYAA
RAHH
GIVE BACK SMOKEY, CAESAR!!
GIVE BACK TASHIGI!!
RAAAAAH
OPEN THE DOOR, DAMN YOU!!!
BOOM BOOM!!
RAAAAH
KABOOM!!
WHAT'S WITH THIS MASSIVE SHUTTER?! IT WON'T BUDGE AN INCH!!
EVEN THE BAZOOKAS CAN'T PUT A SCRATCH ON IT!!
WHAT ABOUT THE BACK ENTRANCE?!
IT'S CLOSED UP ALL OVER!! EVERY DOOR'S SHUTTERED!!
HUFF!
HUFF!
CURSE THAT GAS-BAG!!

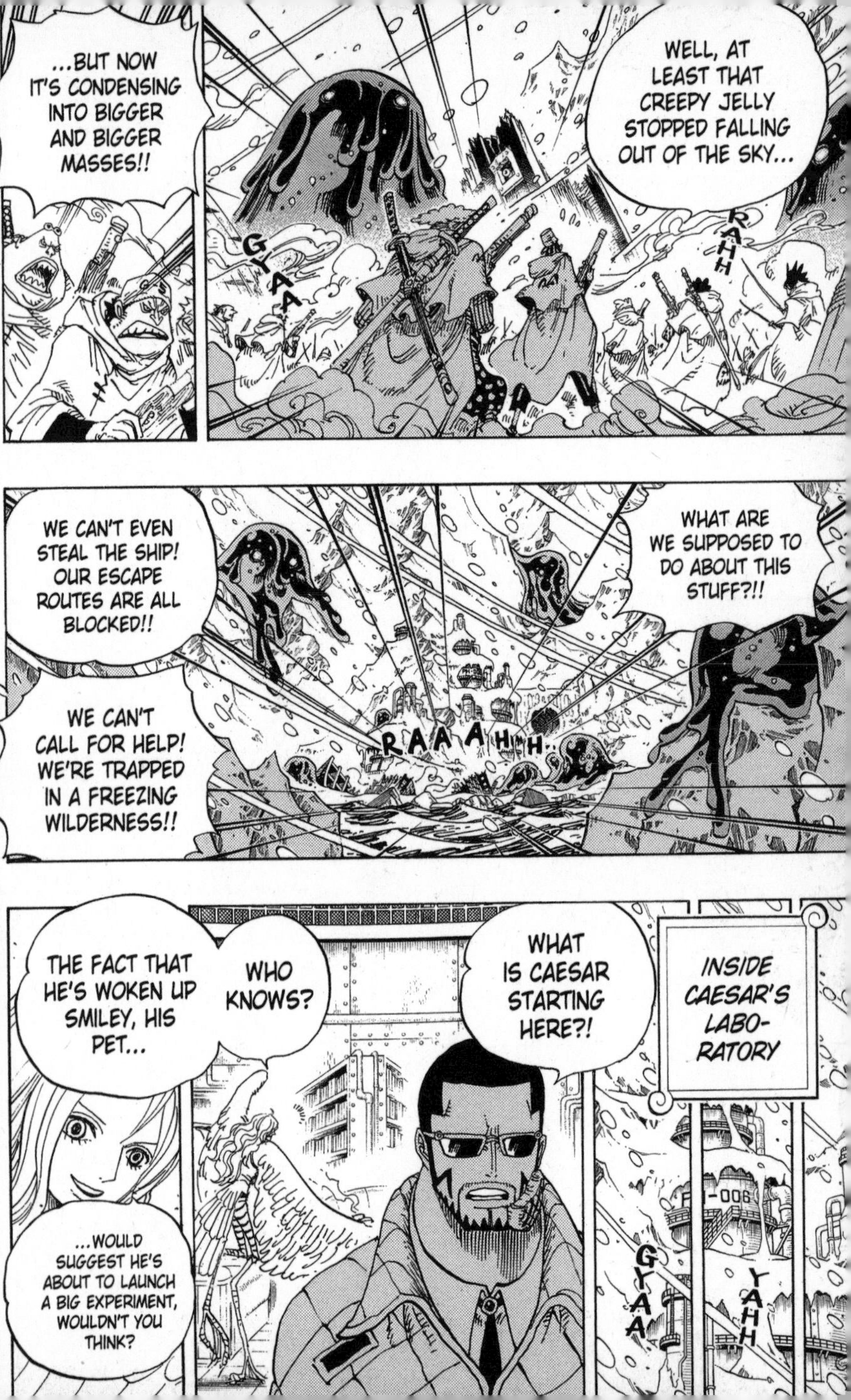
WELL, AT LEAST THAT CREEPY JELLY STOPPED FALLING OUT OF THE SKY...
RAHH
GYAA
...BUT NOW IT'S CONDENSING INTO BIGGER AND BIGGER MASSES!!
WHAT ARE WE SUPPOSED TO DO ABOUT THIS STUFF?!!
WE CAN'T EVEN STEAL THE SHIP! OUR ESCAPE ROUTES ARE ALL BLOCKED!!
RAAAHH
WE CAN'T CALL FOR HELP! WE'RE TRAPPED IN A FREEZING WILDERNESS!!
INSIDE CAESAR'S LABORATORY
YAHH
GYAA
WHAT IS CAESAR STARTING HERE?!
WHO KNOWS?
THE FACT THAT HE'S WOKEN UP SMILEY, HIS PET...
...WOULD SUGGEST HE'S ABOUT TO LAUNCH A BIG EXPERIMENT, WOULDN'T YOU THINK?

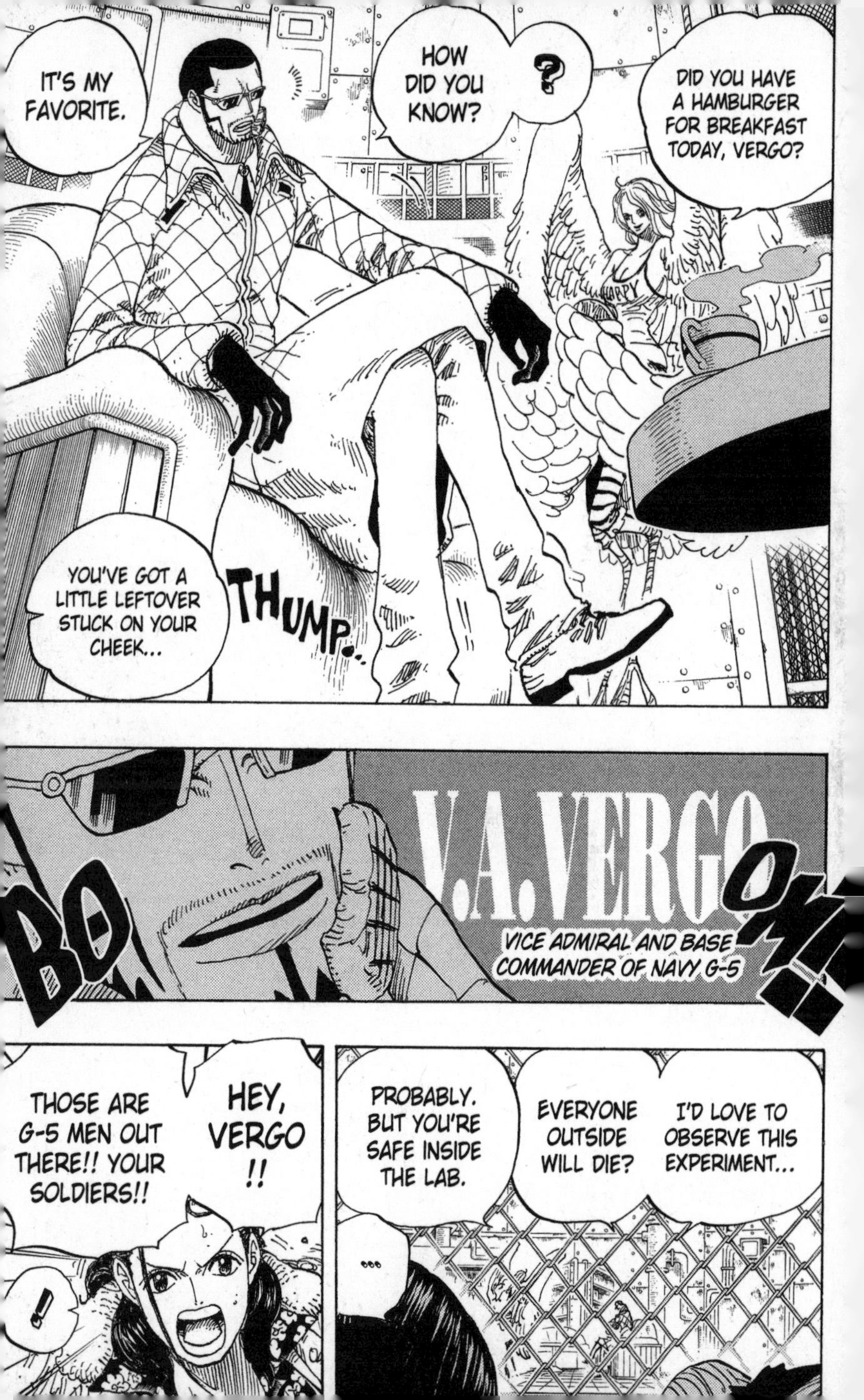
DID YOU HAVE A HAMBURGER FOR BREAKFAST TODAY, VERGO?
?
HOW DID YOU KNOW?
IT'S MY FAVORITE.
YOU'VE GOT A LITTLE LEFTOVER STUCK ON YOUR CHEEK...
THUMP...
V.A. VERGO
VICE ADMIRAL AND BASE COMMANDER OF NAVY G-5
BOOM!!
I'D LOVE TO OBSERVE THIS EXPERIMENT...
EVERYONE OUTSIDE WILL DIE?
PROBABLY. BUT YOU'RE SAFE INSIDE THE LAB.
...
HEY, VERGO!!
THOSE ARE G-5 MEN OUT THERE!! YOUR SOLDIERS!!
!

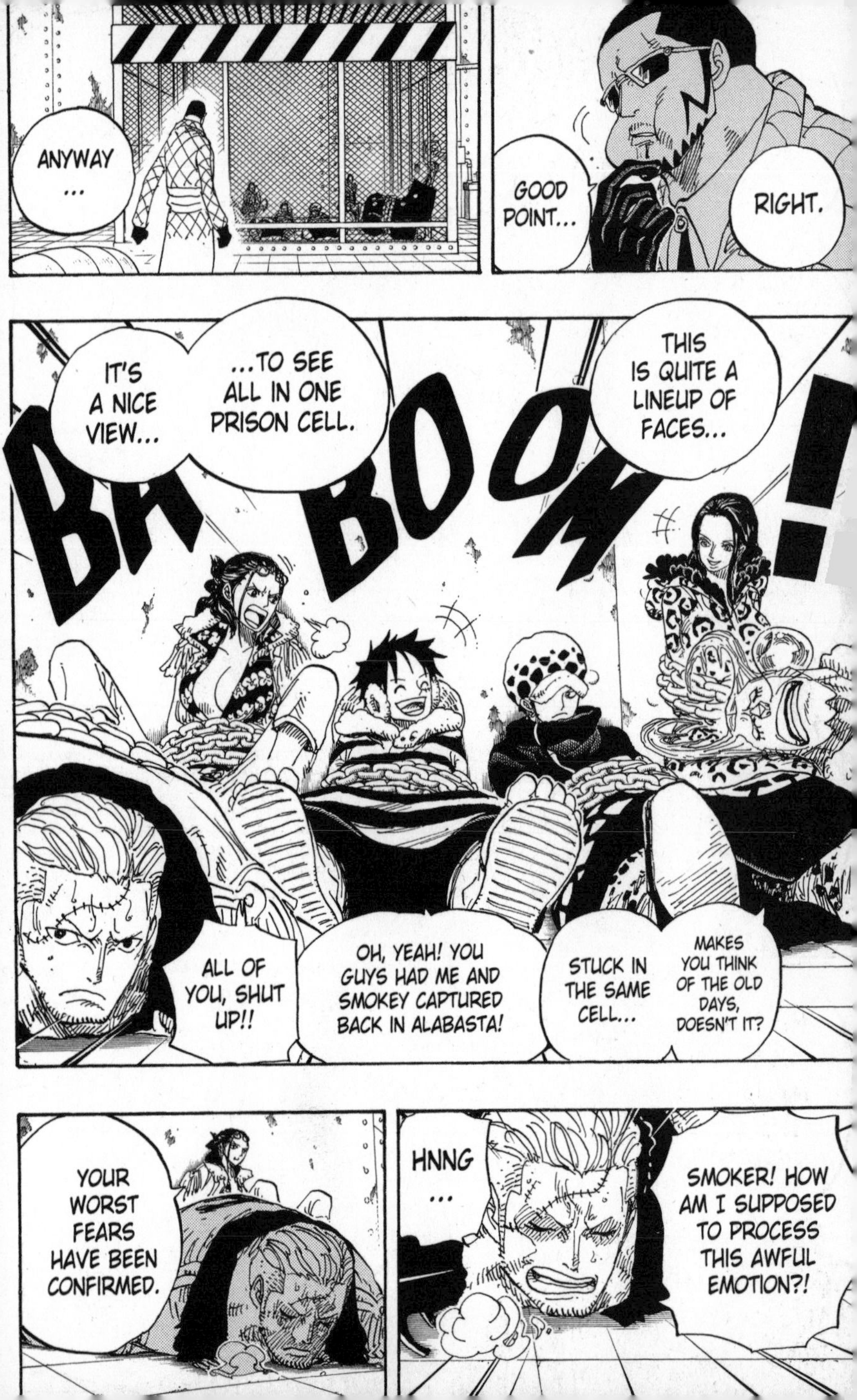

RIGHT.
GOOD POINT...
ANYWAY ...
THIS IS QUITE A LINEUP OF FACES...
IT'S A NICE VIEW...
...TO SEE ALL IN ONE PRISON CELL.
BA BOOM!
STUCK IN THE SAME CELL...
MAKES YOU THINK OF THE OLD DAYS, DOESN'T IT?
OH, YEAH! YOU GUYS HAD ME AND SMOKEY CAPTURED BACK IN ALABASTA!
ALL OF YOU, SHUT UP!!
SMOKER! HOW AM I SUPPOSED TO PROCESS THIS AWFUL EMOTION?!
HNNG ...
YOUR WORST FEARS HAVE BEEN CONFIRMED.

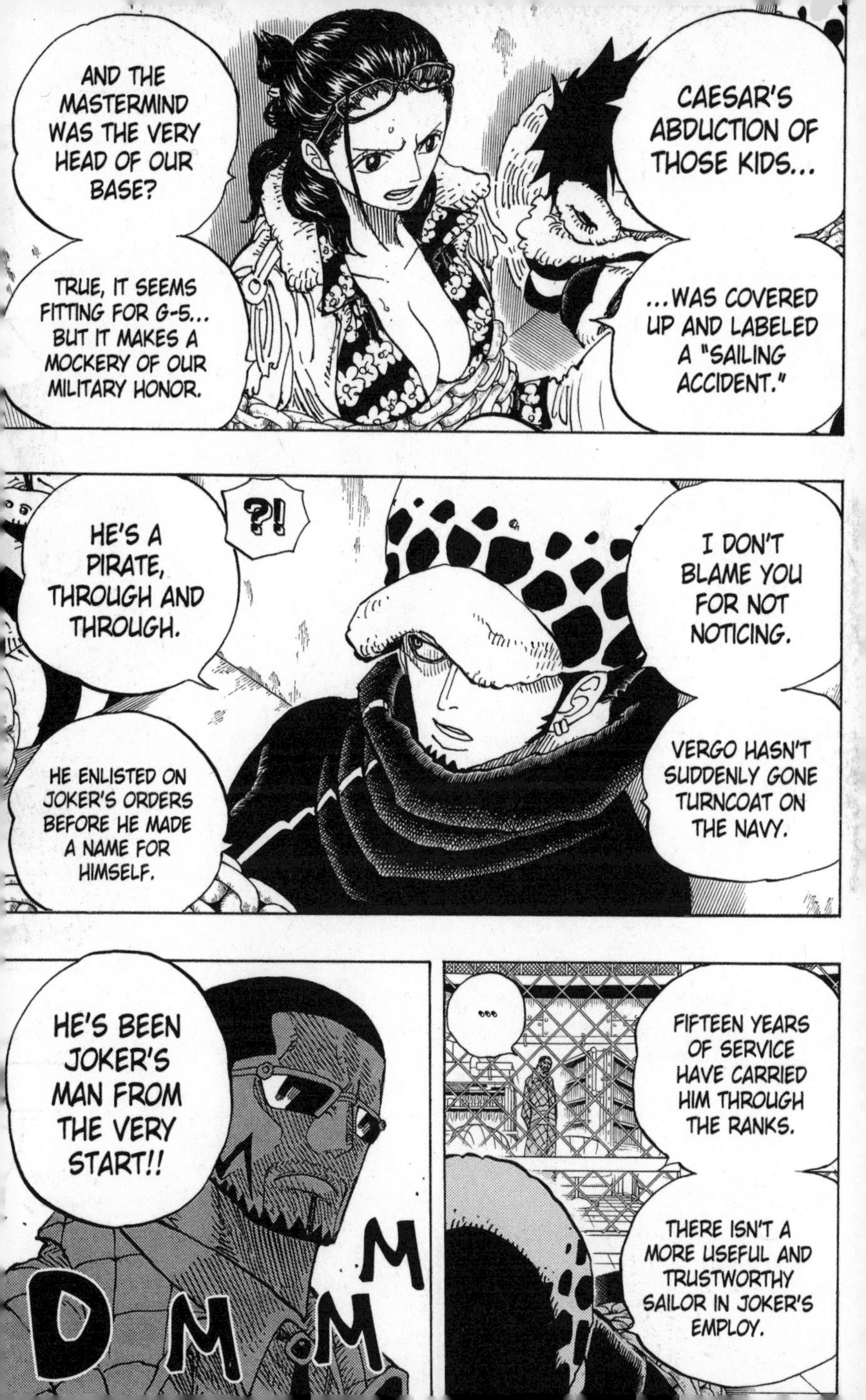
CAESAR'S ABDUCTION OF THOSE KIDS...
...WAS COVERED UP AND LABELED A "SAILING ACCIDENT."
AND THE MASTERMIND WAS THE VERY HEAD OF OUR BASE?
TRUE, IT SEEMS FITTING FOR G-5... BUT IT MAKES A MOCKERY OF OUR MILITARY HONOR.
I DON'T BLAME YOU FOR NOT NOTICING.
VERGO HASN'T SUDDENLY GONE TURNCOAT ON THE NAVY.
?!
HE'S A PIRATE, THROUGH AND THROUGH.
HE ENLISTED ON JOKER'S ORDERS BEFORE HE MADE A NAME FOR HIMSELF.
FIFTEEN YEARS OF SERVICE HAVE CARRIED HIM THROUGH THE RANKS.
...
THERE ISN'T A MORE USEFUL AND TRUSTWORTHY SAILOR IN JOKER'S EMPLOY.
HE'S BEEN JOKER'S MAN FROM THE VERY START!!
DMMM

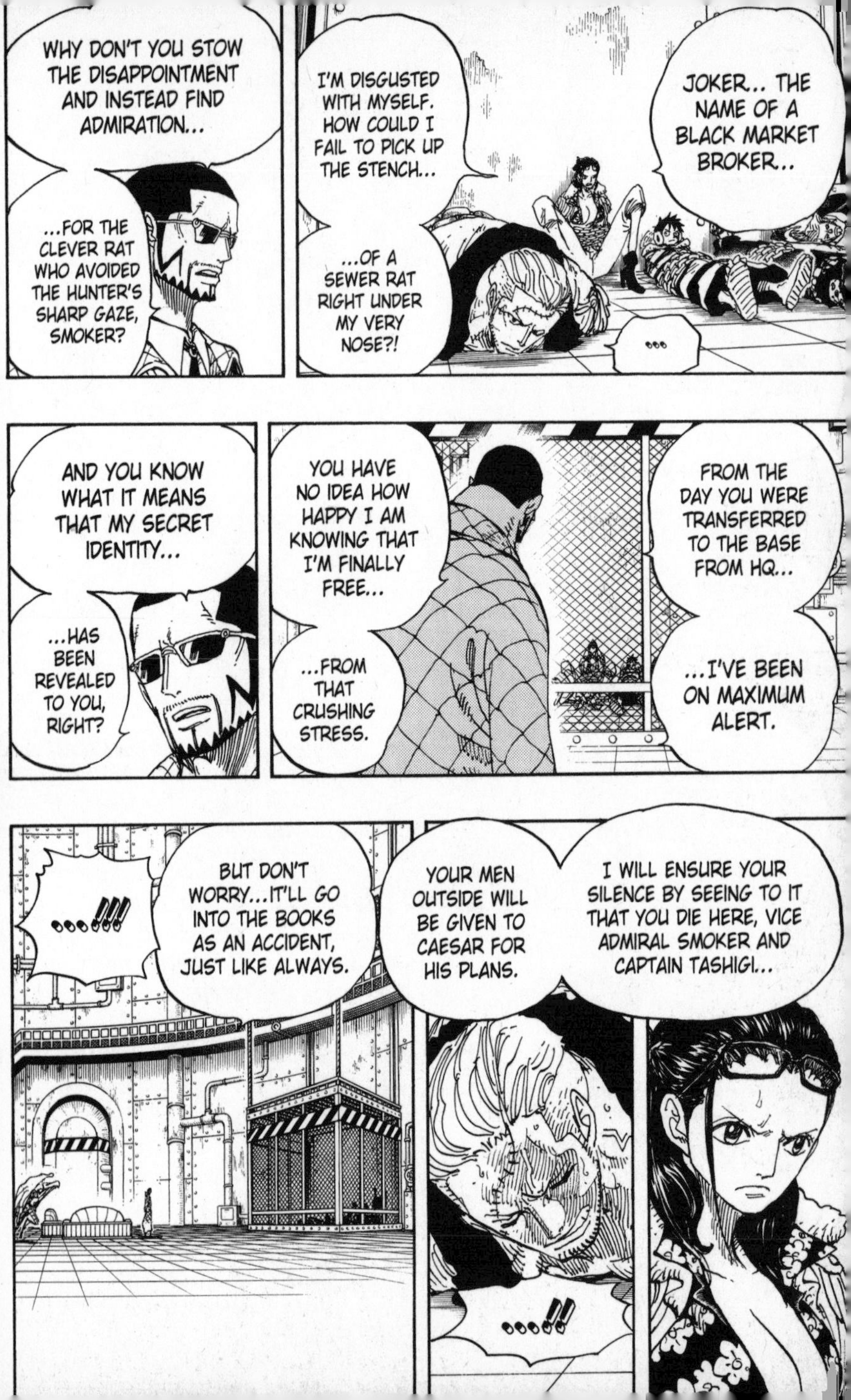

JOKER... THE NAME OF A BLACK MARKET BROKER...
...
I'M DISGUSTED WITH MYSELF. HOW COULD I FAIL TO PICK UP THE STENCH...
...OF A SEWER RAT RIGHT UNDER MY VERY NOSE?!
WHY DON'T YOU STOW THE DISAPPOINTMENT AND INSTEAD FIND ADMIRATION...
...FOR THE CLEVER RAT WHO AVOIDED THE HUNTER'S SHARP GAZE, SMOKER?
FROM THE DAY YOU WERE TRANSFERRED TO THE BASE FROM HQ...
...I'VE BEEN ON MAXIMUM ALERT.
YOU HAVE NO IDEA HOW HAPPY I AM KNOWING THAT I'M FINALLY FREE...
...FROM THAT CRUSHING STRESS.
AND YOU KNOW WHAT IT MEANS THAT MY SECRET IDENTITY...
...HAS BEEN REVEALED TO YOU, RIGHT?
I WILL ENSURE YOUR SILENCE BY SEEING TO IT THAT YOU DIE HERE, VICE ADMIRAL SMOKER AND CAPTAIN TASHIGI...
YOUR MEN OUTSIDE WILL BE GIVEN TO CAESAR FOR HIS PLANS.
....!!
BUT DON'T WORRY...IT'LL GO INTO THE BOOKS AS AN ACCIDENT, JUST LIKE ALWAYS.
....!!!

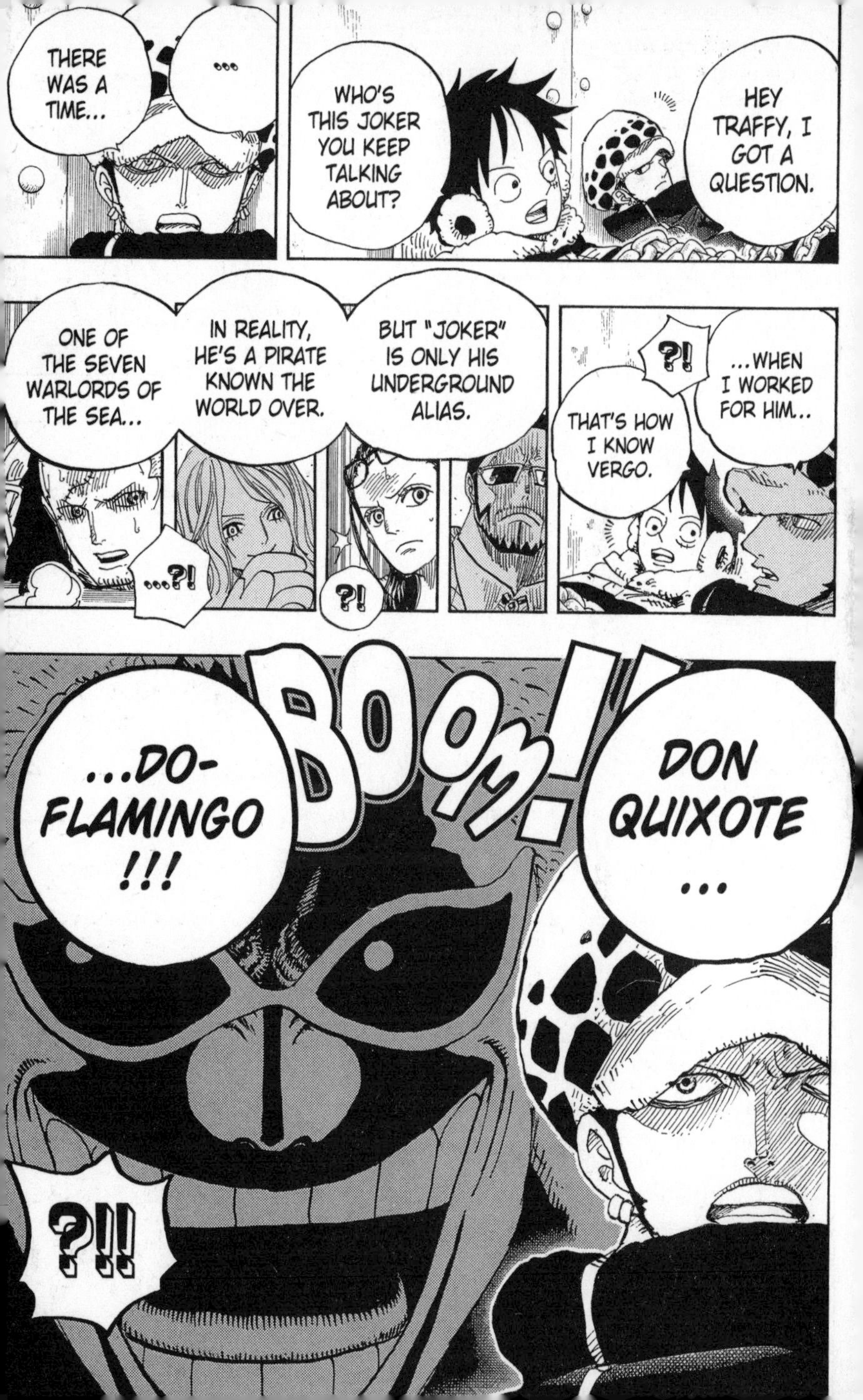
HEY TRAFFY, I GOT A QUESTION.
WHO'S THIS JOKER YOU KEEP TALKING ABOUT?
...
THERE WAS A TIME...
...WHEN I WORKED FOR HIM...
?!
THAT'S HOW I KNOW VERGO.
BUT "JOKER" IS ONLY HIS UNDERGROUND ALIAS.
IN REALITY, HE'S A PIRATE KNOWN THE WORLD OVER.
ONE OF THE SEVEN WARLORDS OF THE SEA...
?!
...?!
DON QUIXOTE ...
BOOM!!
...DO-FLAMINGO !!!
?!!

質問コーナー
スー…
エスビーエス
SBS
見えなくしてどうする!!!
あんたも一緒に見えなくなればいい…

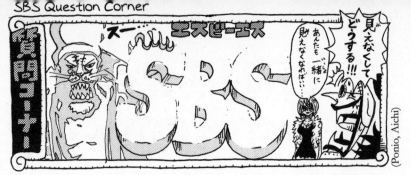

(Ponio, Aichi)

Q: Since there seems to be an ongoing series of childhood portraits, do Hina, Smoker and Tashigi next!!
--Kumakoro

A: Here we GO.

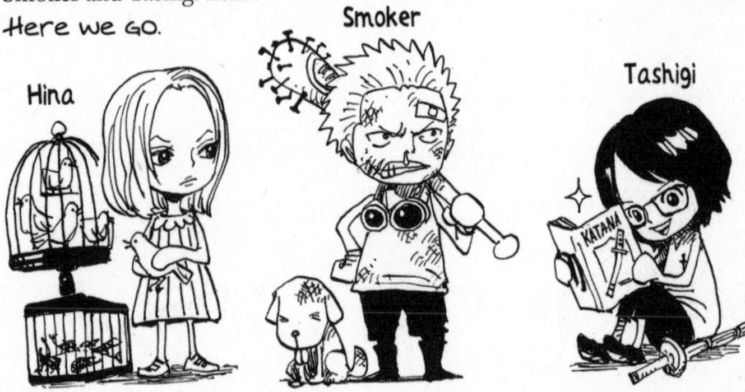

Smoker
Hina
Tashigi
KATANA

Q: Nice to meet you!! I wanted to be in the SBS corner so bad, I did something insane! I tallied up every piece of art printed in the Usopp Gallery Pirates fan art sections and ranked the prefectures of Japan by most pieces!! Here's the Top 5☆

1	2)	3)	4)	5)
Tokyo (219)	Osaka (143)	Kanagawa (142)	Saitama (139)	Chiba (120)

No surprise, Tokyo takes the top spot! (•∀•) It took forever to count them all!
--Nao

All the rest

6)	Aichi	(115)
7)	Hyogo	(100)
8)	Hokkaido	(90)
9)	Miyagi	(84)
10)	Fukuoka	(78)
11)	Hiroshima	(72)
12)	Ibaraki	(59)
13)	Shizuoka	(54)
14)	Niigata	(48)
15)	Gunma	(40)
16)	Gifu	(37)
17)	Okayama	
	Fukushima	(35)
19)	Aomori	
	Iwate	
	Nagano	
	Nara	(34)
23)	Tochigi	
	Nagasaki	(33)
25)	Ishikawa	(32)
26)	Kumamoto	
	Kagoshima	(28)
28)	Mie	
	Shiga	
	Kyoto	
	Toyama	(27)
32)	Akita	
	Tokushima	(26)
34)	Oita	(23)
35)	Fukui	(21)
35)	Yamaguchi	(21)
37)	Shimane	
	Miyazaki	(20)
39)	Yamagata	
	Ehime	(19)
41)	Wakayama	(18)
42)	Yamanashi	(16)
43)	Saga	(15)
44)	Okinawa	(13)
45)	Tottori	(11)
46)	Kagawa	(8)
47)	Kochi	(7)
Also		
	America	(4)
	Italy	(3)
	Taiwan	(2)
	Russia	(1)

A: Wow, thank you so much!! But what the heck is going on?! The number of exclamation points, the number of fan drawings... Is counting the new big thing?! Maybe I should count the number of things I've lost!! One, two, three, four...f-five...sniff... The SBS is...hic...over!! Sob sob... There's stuff about the movie at the end of the...hic...book.

Chapter 674:
THE OBSERVERS

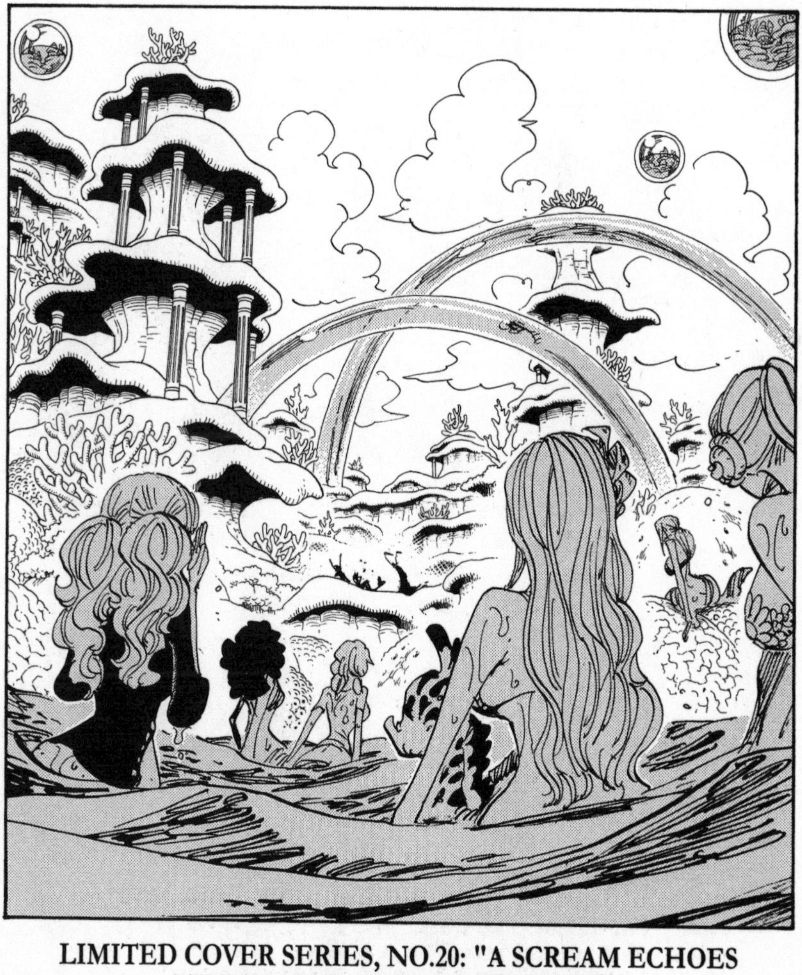

LIMITED COVER SERIES, NO.20: "A SCREAM ECHOES THROUGH THE MERMAID INLET"

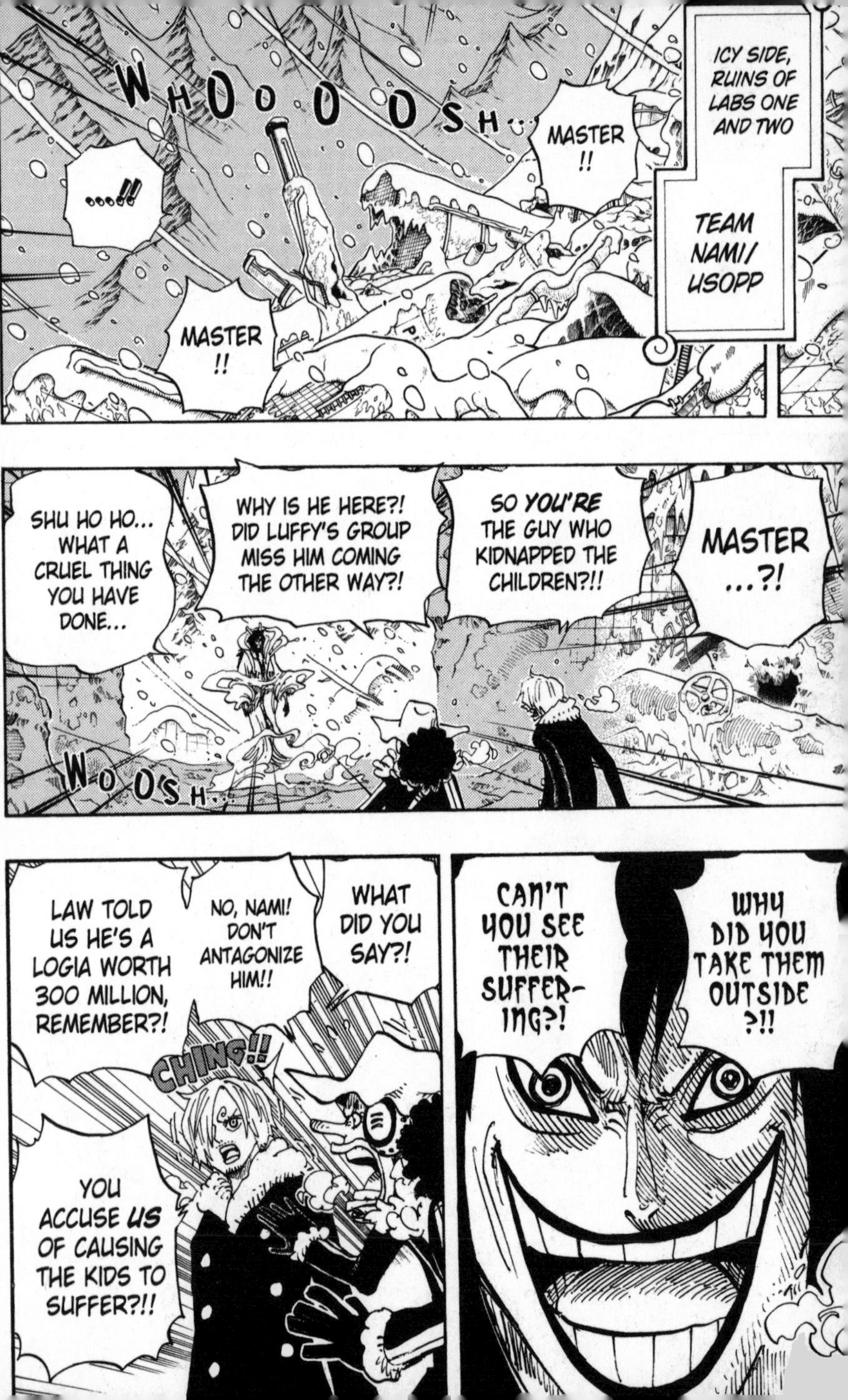
ICY SIDE, RUINS OF LABS ONE AND TWO
TEAM NAMI/USOPP
MASTER !!
WHOOOOSH...
...!!
MASTER !!
MASTER ...?!
SO *YOU'RE* THE GUY WHO KIDNAPPED THE CHILDREN?!!
WHY IS HE HERE?! DID LUFFY'S GROUP MISS HIM COMING THE OTHER WAY?!
SHU HO HO... WHAT A CRUEL THING YOU HAVE DONE...
WOOSH...
WHY DID YOU TAKE THEM OUTSIDE ?!!
CAN'T YOU SEE THEIR SUFFER-ING?!
WHAT DID YOU SAY?!
NO, NAMI! DON'T ANTAGONIZE HIM!!
LAW TOLD US HE'S A LOGIA WORTH 300 MILLION, REMEMBER?!
CHING!!
YOU ACCUSE *US* OF CAUSING THE KIDS TO SUFFER?!!

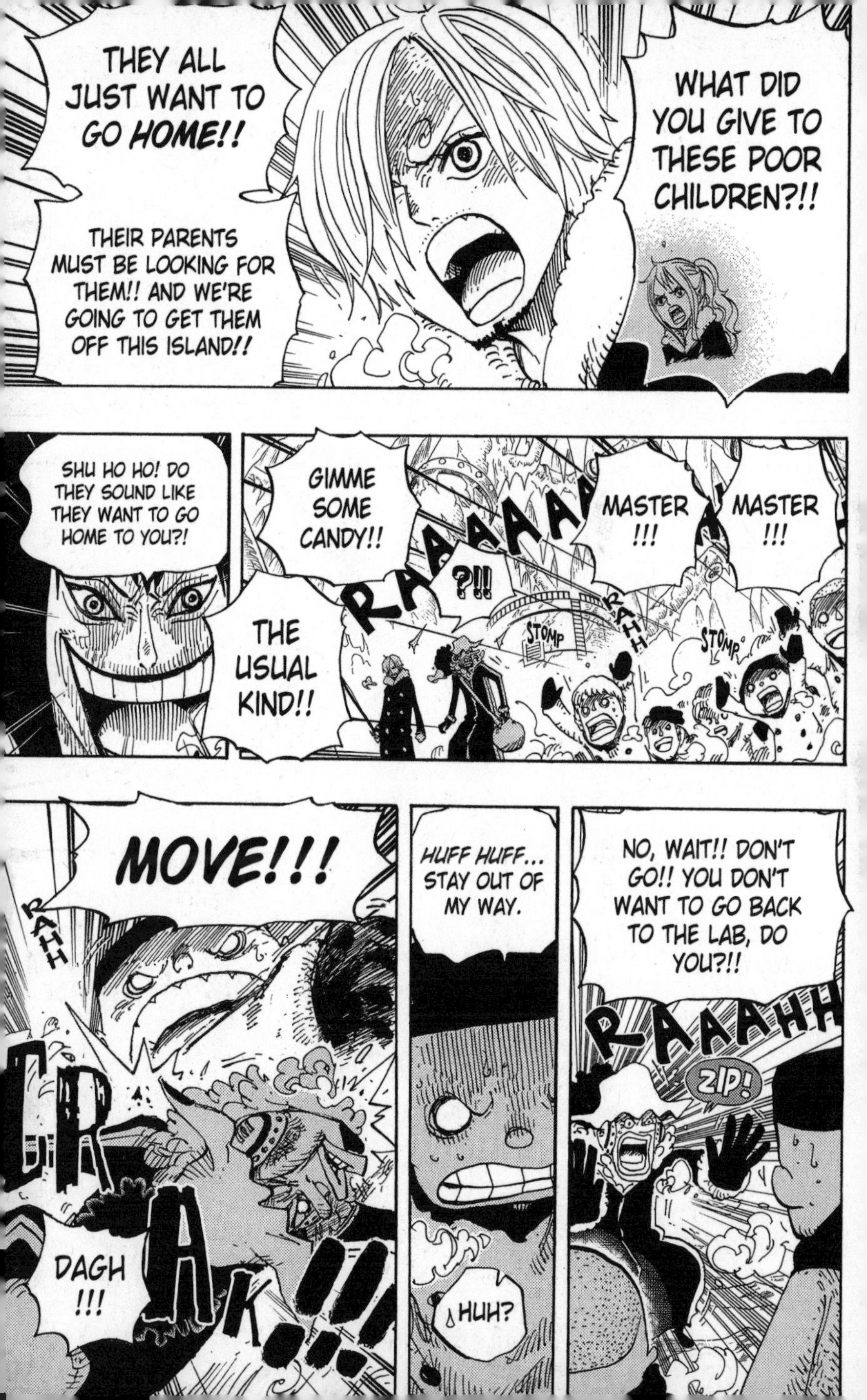
WHAT DID YOU GIVE TO THESE POOR CHILDREN?!!
THEY ALL JUST WANT TO GO *HOME!!*
THEIR PARENTS MUST BE LOOKING FOR THEM!! AND WE'RE GOING TO GET THEM OFF THIS ISLAND!!
MASTER !!!
MASTER !!!
RAAAAAAA
GIMME SOME CANDY!!
?!!
RAHH
STOMP
STOMP
THE USUAL KIND!!
SHU HO HO! DO THEY SOUND LIKE THEY WANT TO GO HOME TO YOU?!
NO, WAIT!! DON'T GO!! YOU DON'T WANT TO GO BACK TO THE LAB, DO YOU?!!
RAAAHH
ZIP!
HUFF HUFF... STAY OUT OF MY WAY.
HUH?
MOVE!!!
RAHH
CRAK!!!
DAGH !!!

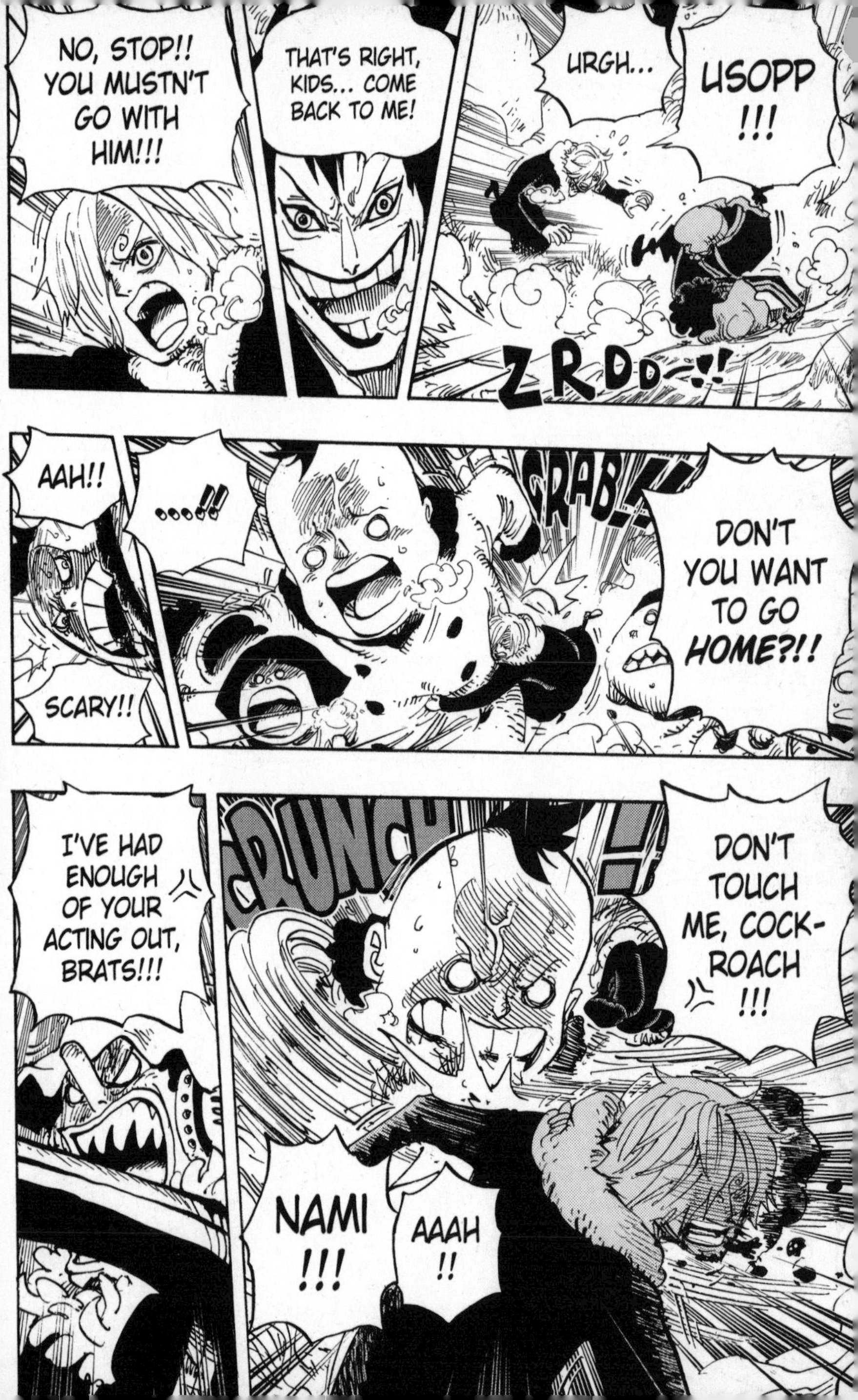
USOPP !!!
URGH...
ZRDD!!
THAT'S RIGHT, KIDS... COME BACK TO ME!
NO, STOP!! YOU MUSTN'T GO WITH HIM!!!
GRAB!!
DON'T YOU WANT TO GO HOME?!!
...!!
AAH!!
SCARY!!
CRUNCH!!
DON'T TOUCH ME, COCK-ROACH !!!
AAAH !!
NAMI !!!
I'VE HAD ENOUGH OF YOUR ACTING OUT, BRATS!!!

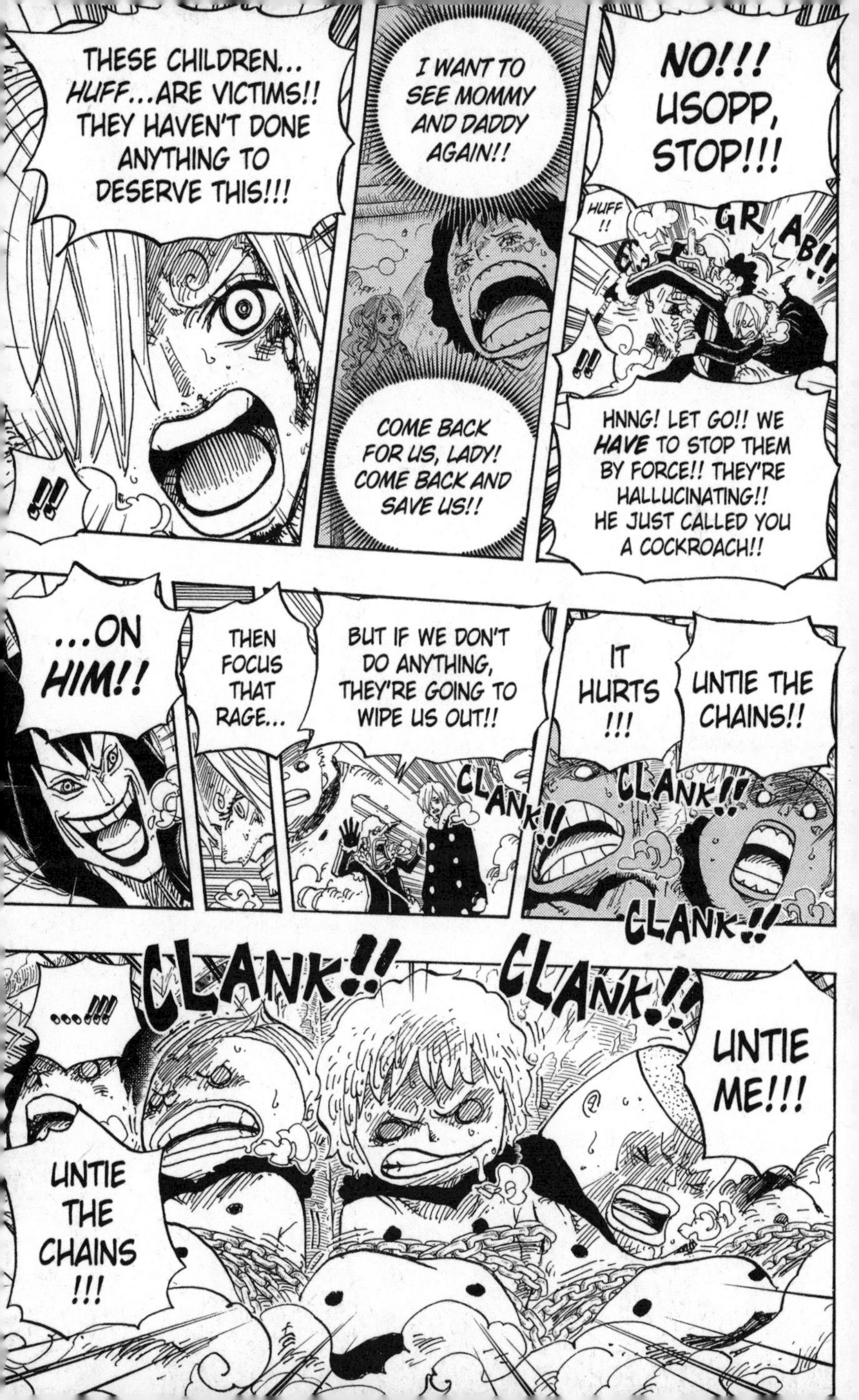
NO!!! USOPP, STOP!!!
HUFF !!
GRAB!!
!!
HNNG! LET GO!! WE *HAVE* TO STOP THEM BY FORCE!! THEY'RE HALLUCINATING!! HE JUST CALLED YOU A COCKROACH!!
I WANT TO SEE MOMMY AND DADDY AGAIN!!
COME BACK FOR US, LADY! COME BACK AND SAVE US!!
THESE CHILDREN... *HUFF*...ARE VICTIMS!! THEY HAVEN'T DONE ANYTHING TO DESERVE THIS!!!
!!
UNTIE THE CHAINS!!
IT HURTS!!!
CLANK!!
CLANK!!
BUT IF WE DON'T DO ANYTHING, THEY'RE GOING TO WIPE US OUT!!
CLANK!!
THEN FOCUS THAT RAGE...
...ON *HIM!!*
UNTIE ME!!!
CLANK!!
CLANK!!
...!!!
UNTIE THE CHAINS!!!

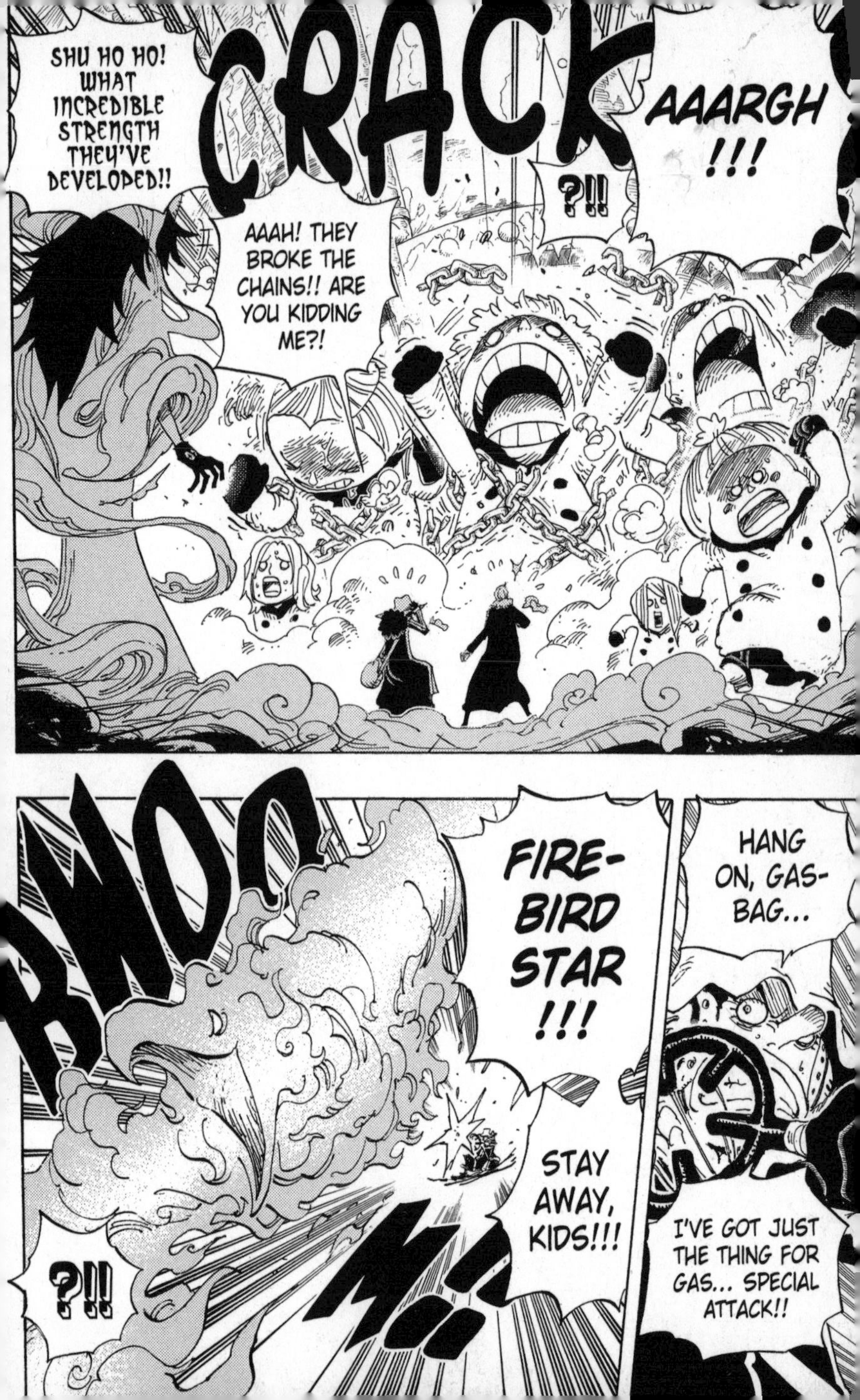
AAARGH!!!
?!!
CRACK
SHU HO HO! WHAT INCREDIBLE STRENGTH THEY'VE DEVELOPED!!
AAAH! THEY BROKE THE CHAINS!! ARE YOU KIDDING ME?!
HANG ON, GAS-BAG...
I'VE GOT JUST THE THING FOR GAS... SPECIAL ATTACK!!
FIRE-BIRD STAR!!!
STAY AWAY, KIDS!!!
?!!

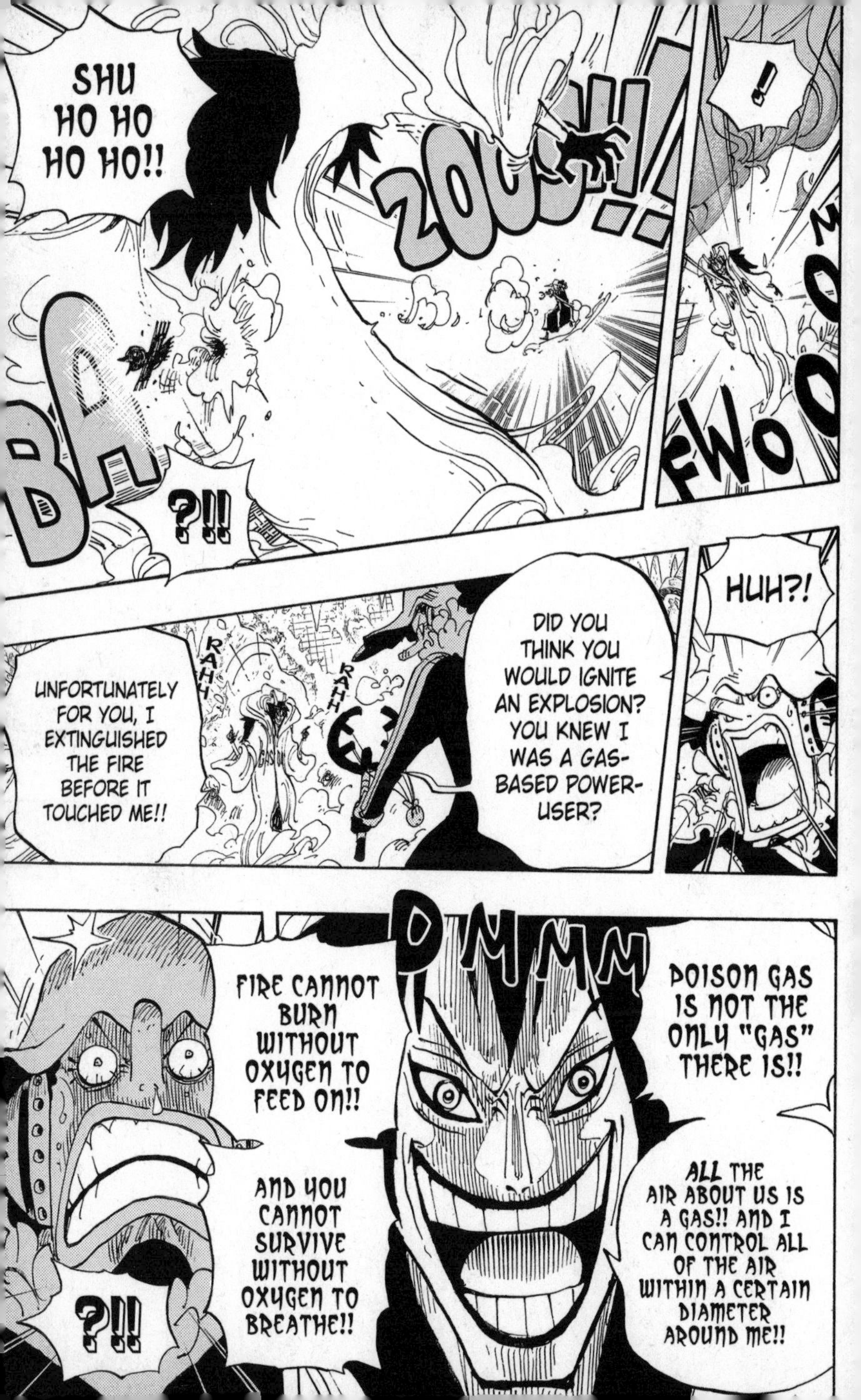
!
FWOOOM
ZOO H!!
SHU HO HO HO HO!!
BA
?!!
HUH?!
DID YOU THINK YOU WOULD IGNITE AN EXPLOSION? YOU KNEW I WAS A GAS-BASED POWER-USER?
RAHH
RAHH
UNFORTUNATELY FOR YOU, I EXTINGUISHED THE FIRE BEFORE IT TOUCHED ME!!
DMMM
POISON GAS IS NOT THE ONLY "GAS" THERE IS!!
FIRE CANNOT BURN WITHOUT OXYGEN TO FEED ON!!
ALL THE AIR ABOUT US IS A GAS!! AND I CAN CONTROL ALL OF THE AIR WITHIN A CERTAIN DIAMETER AROUND ME!!
AND YOU CANNOT SURVIVE WITHOUT OXYGEN TO BREATHE!!
?!!

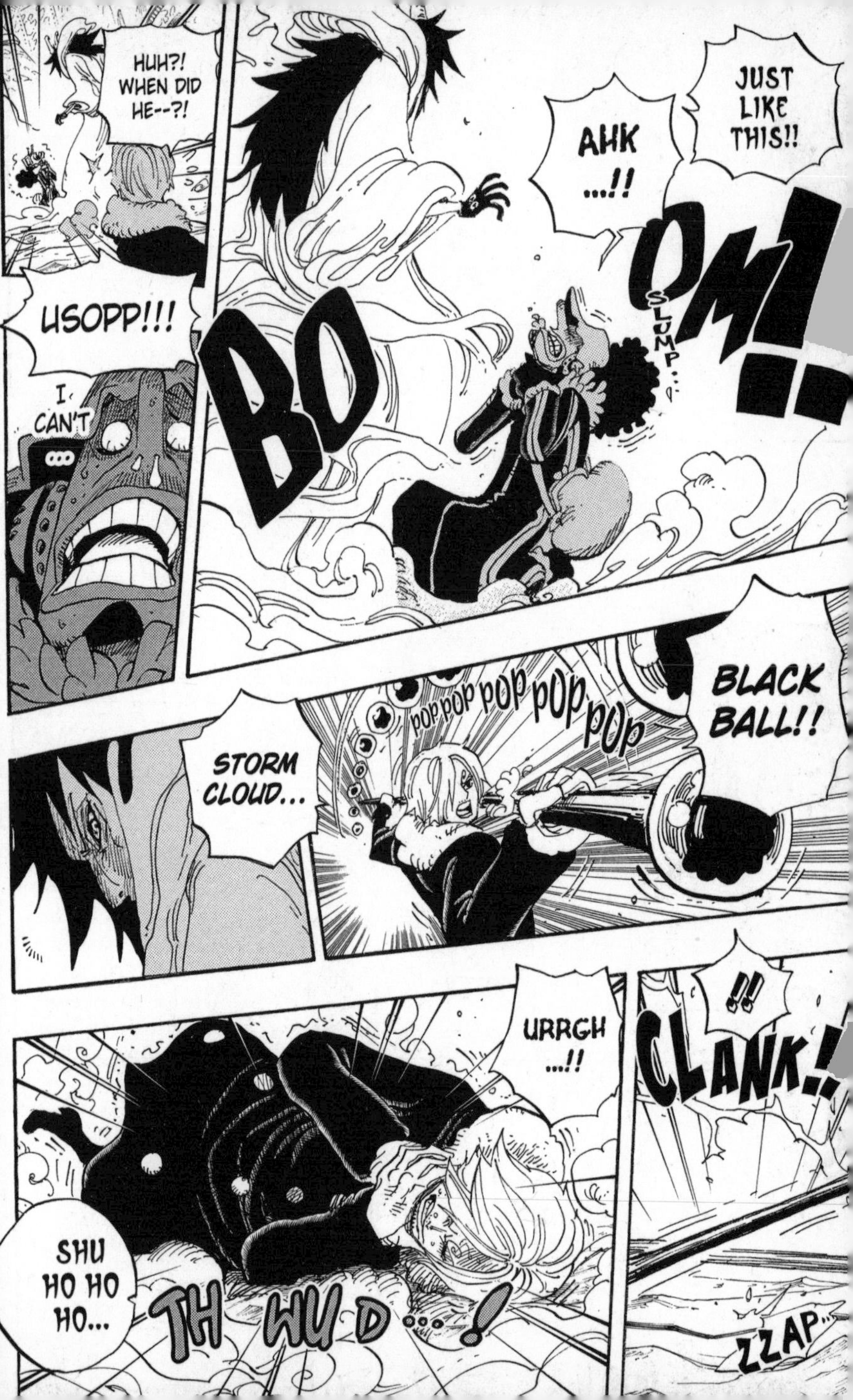
JUST LIKE THIS!!
AHK ...!!
BOOM!!
SLUMP...
HUH?! WHEN DID HE--?!
USOPP!!!
I CAN'T ...
BLACK BALL!!
POP POP POP POP POP
STORM CLOUD...
!!
CLANK!!
ZZAP...
URRGH ...!!
SHU HO HO HO...
THWUD...!

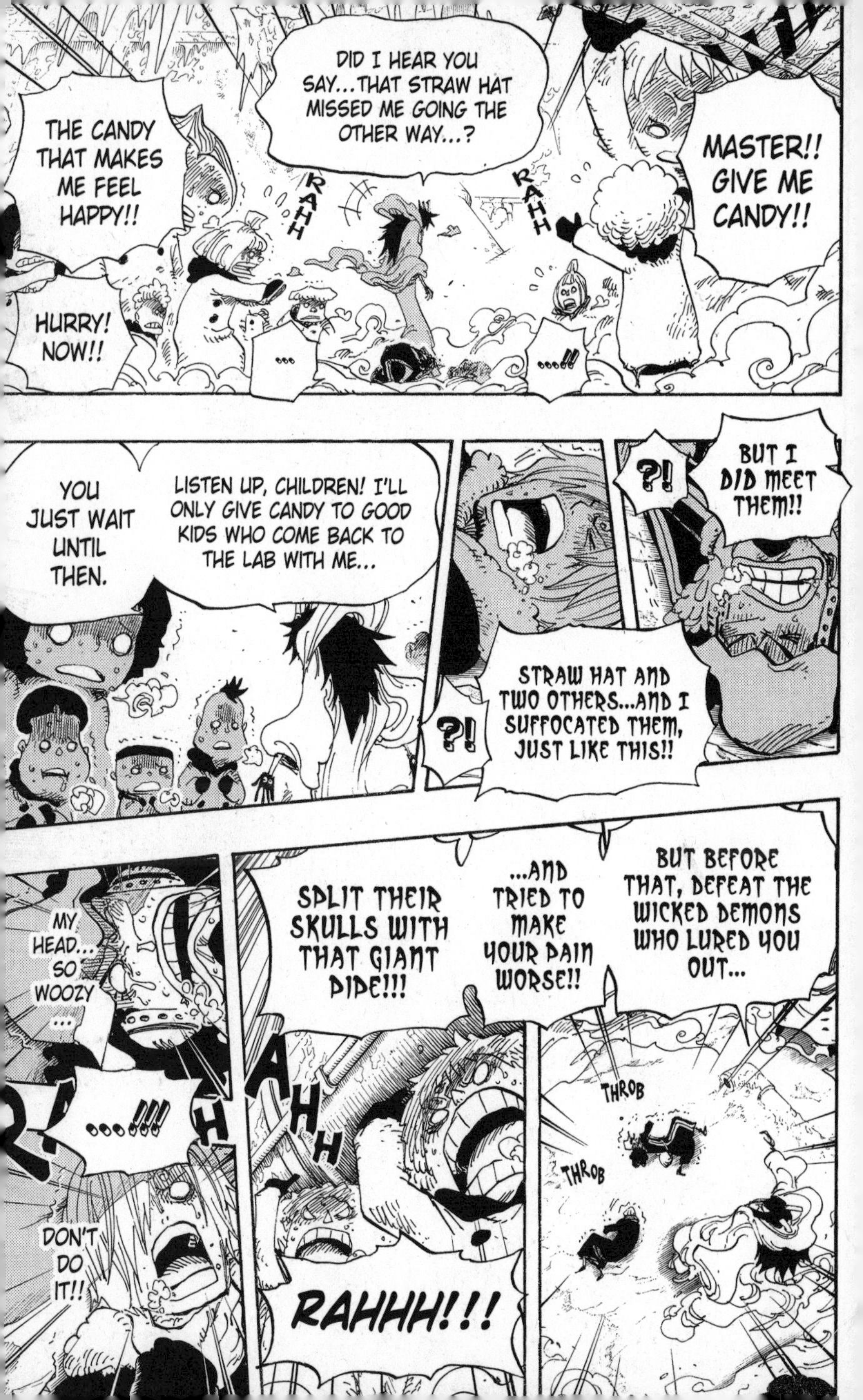
MASTER!! GIVE ME CANDY!!
RAHH
DID I HEAR YOU SAY...THAT STRAW HAT MISSED ME GOING THE OTHER WAY...?
RAHH
THE CANDY THAT MAKES ME FEEL HAPPY!!
HURRY! NOW!!
...!!
...
?!
BUT I DID MEET THEM!!
STRAW HAT AND TWO OTHERS...AND I SUFFOCATED THEM, JUST LIKE THIS!!
?!
LISTEN UP, CHILDREN! I'LL ONLY GIVE CANDY TO GOOD KIDS WHO COME BACK TO THE LAB WITH ME...
YOU JUST WAIT UNTIL THEN.
BUT BEFORE THAT, DEFEAT THE WICKED DEMONS WHO LURED YOU OUT...
THROB
THROB
...AND TRIED TO MAKE YOUR PAIN WORSE!!
SPLIT THEIR SKULLS WITH THAT GIANT PIPE!!!
AHH
RAHHH!!!
MY HEAD... SO WOOZY ...
...!!!
DON'T DO IT!!

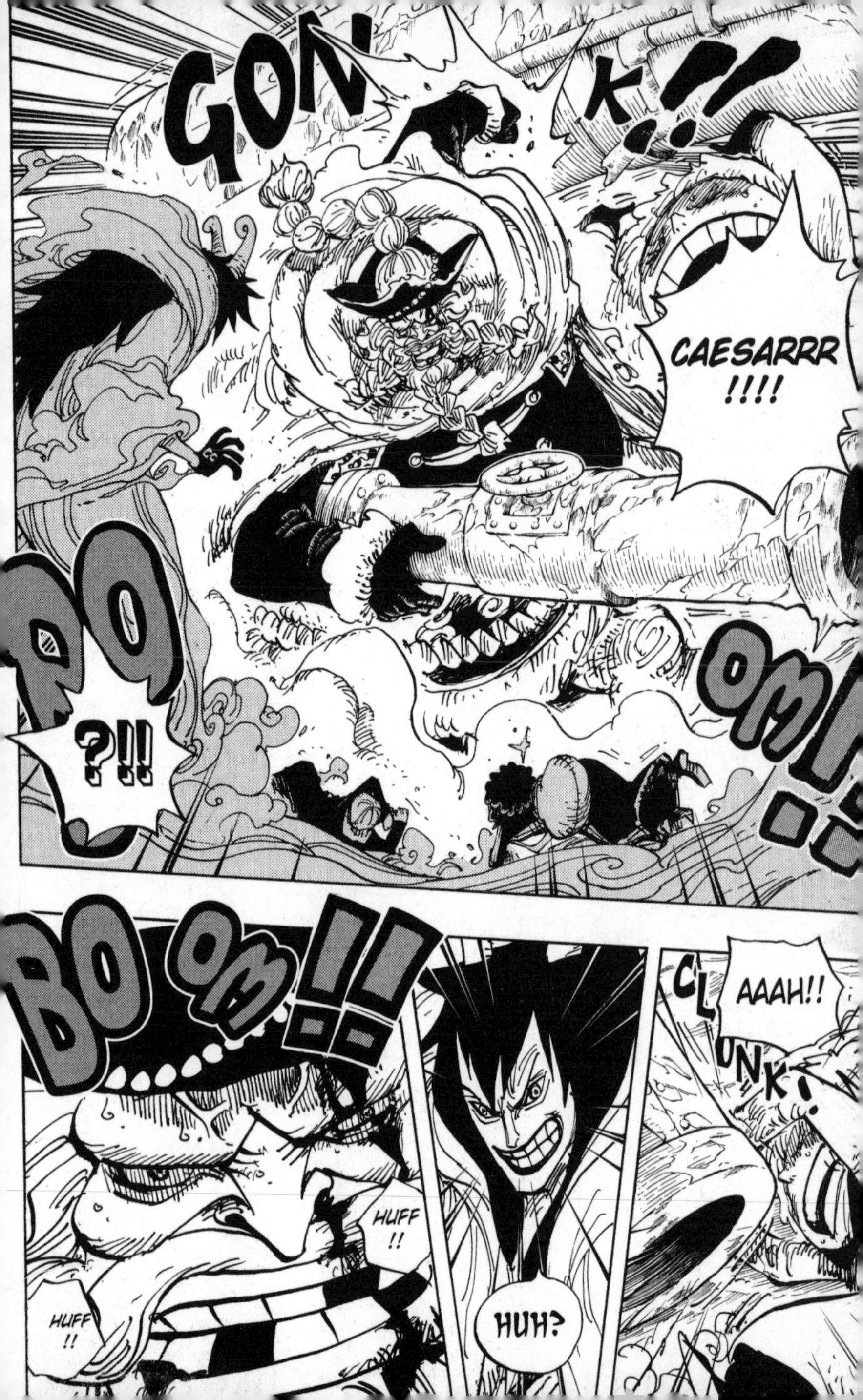
GONK!!
CAESARRR!!!!
BOOM!!
?!!
CLUNK!
AAAH!!
HUH?
BOOM!!
HUFF!!
HUFF!!

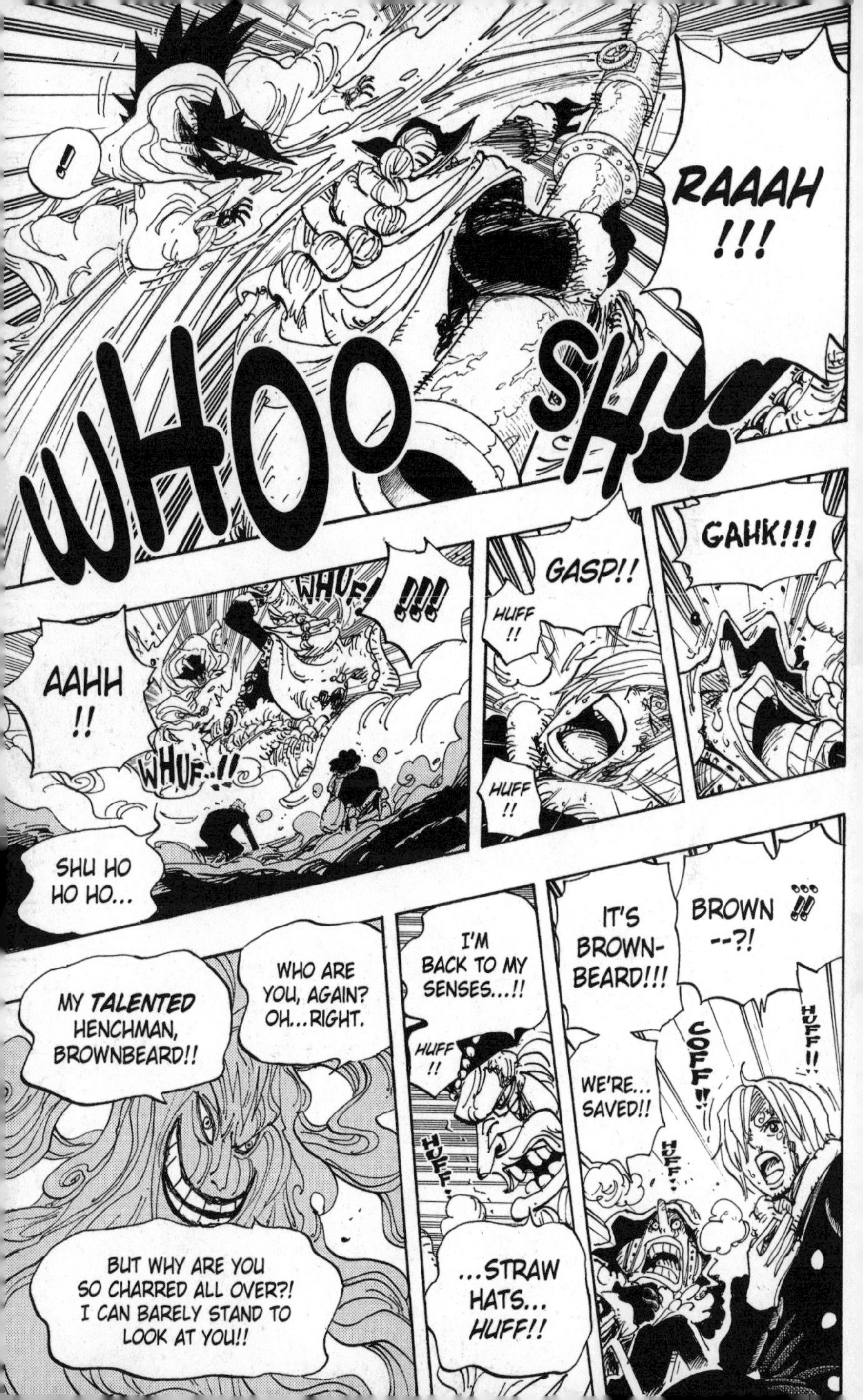
RAAAH !!!
!
WHOOSH...
GAHK!!!
GASP!!
HUFF !!
HUFF !!
WHUF!
!!!
AAHH !!
WHUF..!!
SHU HO HO HO...
BROWN --?!
...!!
HUFF !!
IT'S BROWNBEARD!!!
COFF!!
WE'RE... SAVED!!
HUFF...
I'M BACK TO MY SENSES...!!
HUFF !!
HUFF...
...STRAW HATS... HUFF!!
WHO ARE YOU, AGAIN? OH...RIGHT.
MY TALENTED HENCHMAN, BROWNBEARD!!
BUT WHY ARE YOU SO CHARRED ALL OVER?! I CAN BARELY STAND TO LOOK AT YOU!!

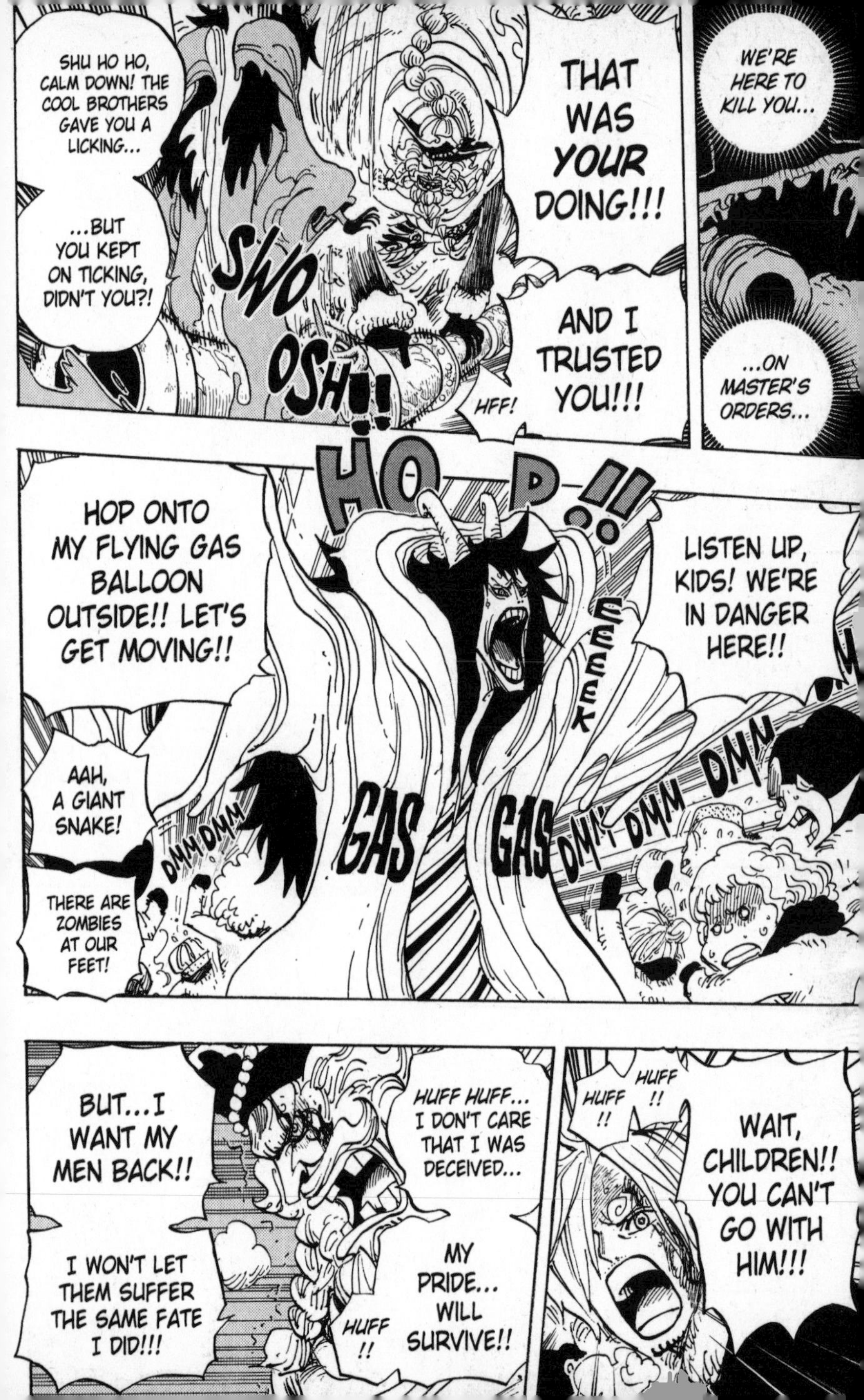
WE'RE HERE TO KILL YOU...
...ON MASTER'S ORDERS...
THAT WAS YOUR DOING!!!
AND I TRUSTED YOU!!!
HFF!
SHU HO HO, CALM DOWN! THE COOL BROTHERS GAVE YOU A LICKING...
...BUT YOU KEPT ON TICKING, DIDN'T YOU?!
SWOOSH!!
HOP!!
LISTEN UP, KIDS! WE'RE IN DANGER HERE!!
HOP ONTO MY FLYING GAS BALLOON OUTSIDE!! LET'S GET MOVING!!
EEEEK
DMM DMM DMM
GAS GAS
AAH, A GIANT SNAKE!
DMM DMM
THERE ARE ZOMBIES AT OUR FEET!
HUFF!!
HUFF!!
WAIT, CHILDREN!! YOU CAN'T GO WITH HIM!!!
HUFF HUFF... I DON'T CARE THAT I WAS DECEIVED...
BUT...I WANT MY MEN BACK!!
MY PRIDE... WILL SURVIVE!!
HUFF!!
I WON'T LET THEM SUFFER THE SAME FATE I DID!!!

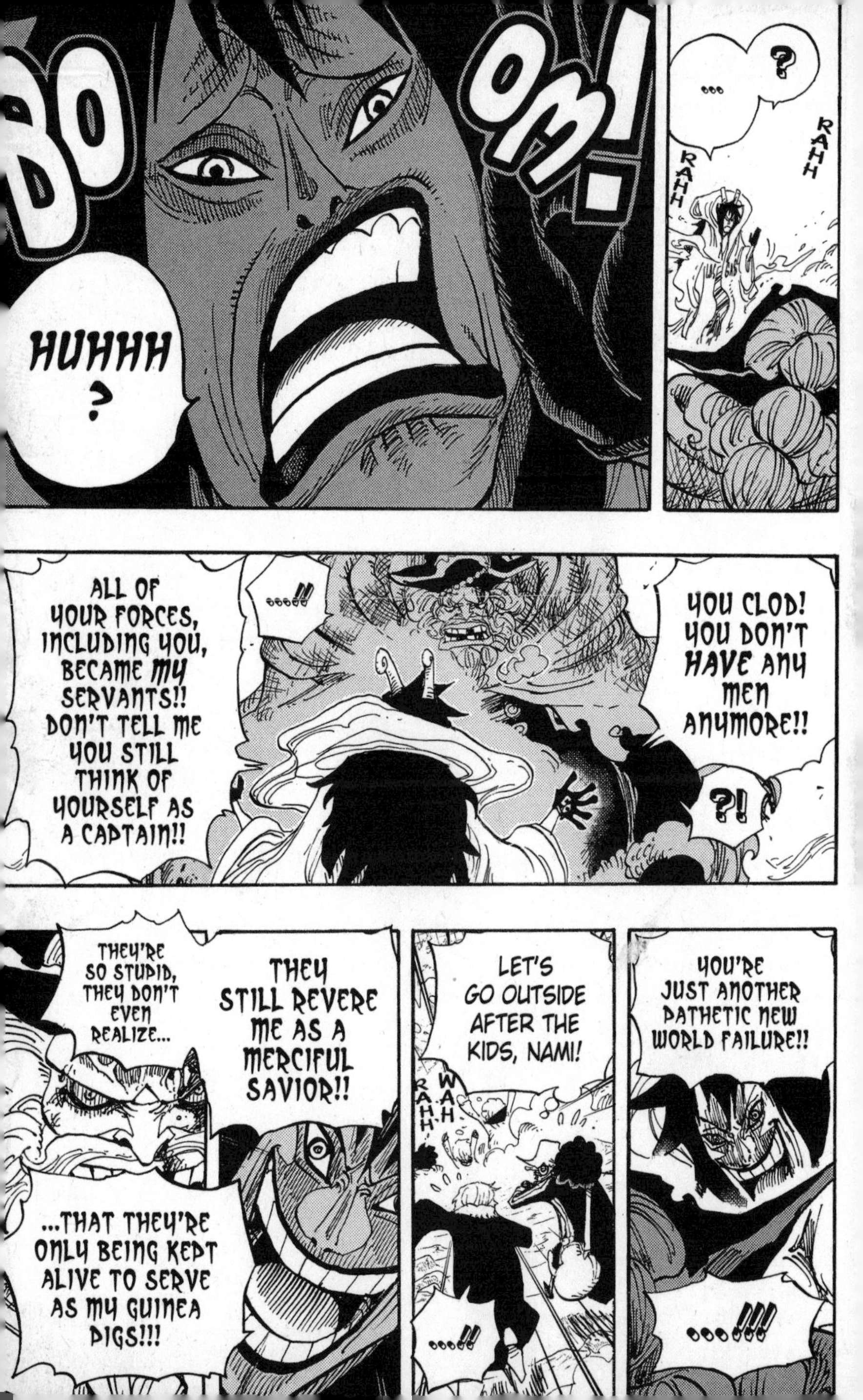
...
?
RAHH
RAHH
BOOM!
HUHHH ?
YOU CLOD! YOU DON'T HAVE ANY MEN ANYMORE!!
...!!
ALL OF YOUR FORCES, INCLUDING YOU, BECAME MY SERVANTS!! DON'T TELL ME YOU STILL THINK OF YOURSELF AS A CAPTAIN!!
?!
YOU'RE JUST ANOTHER PATHETIC NEW WORLD FAILURE!!
...!!!
LET'S GO OUTSIDE AFTER THE KIDS, NAMI!
WAH
RAHH
...!!
THEY STILL REVERE ME AS A MERCIFUL SAVIOR!!
THEY'RE SO STUPID, THEY DON'T EVEN REALIZE...
...THAT THEY'RE ONLY BEING KEPT ALIVE TO SERVE AS MY GUINEA PIGS!!!

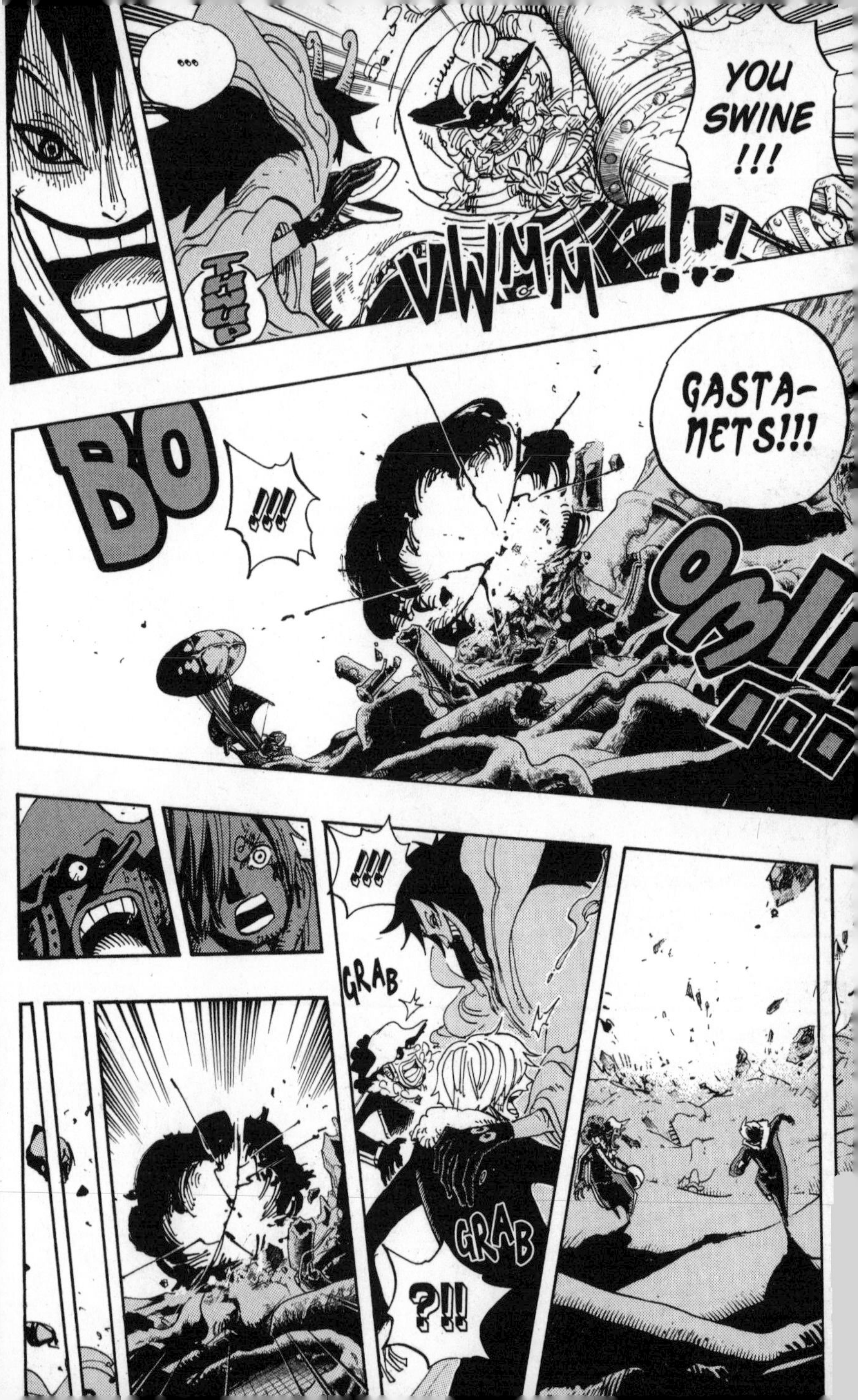

YOU SWINE!!!
VWMM!!!
...
GASTA-NETS!!!
BOOM!!!
!!!
!!!
GRAB
GRAB
?!!

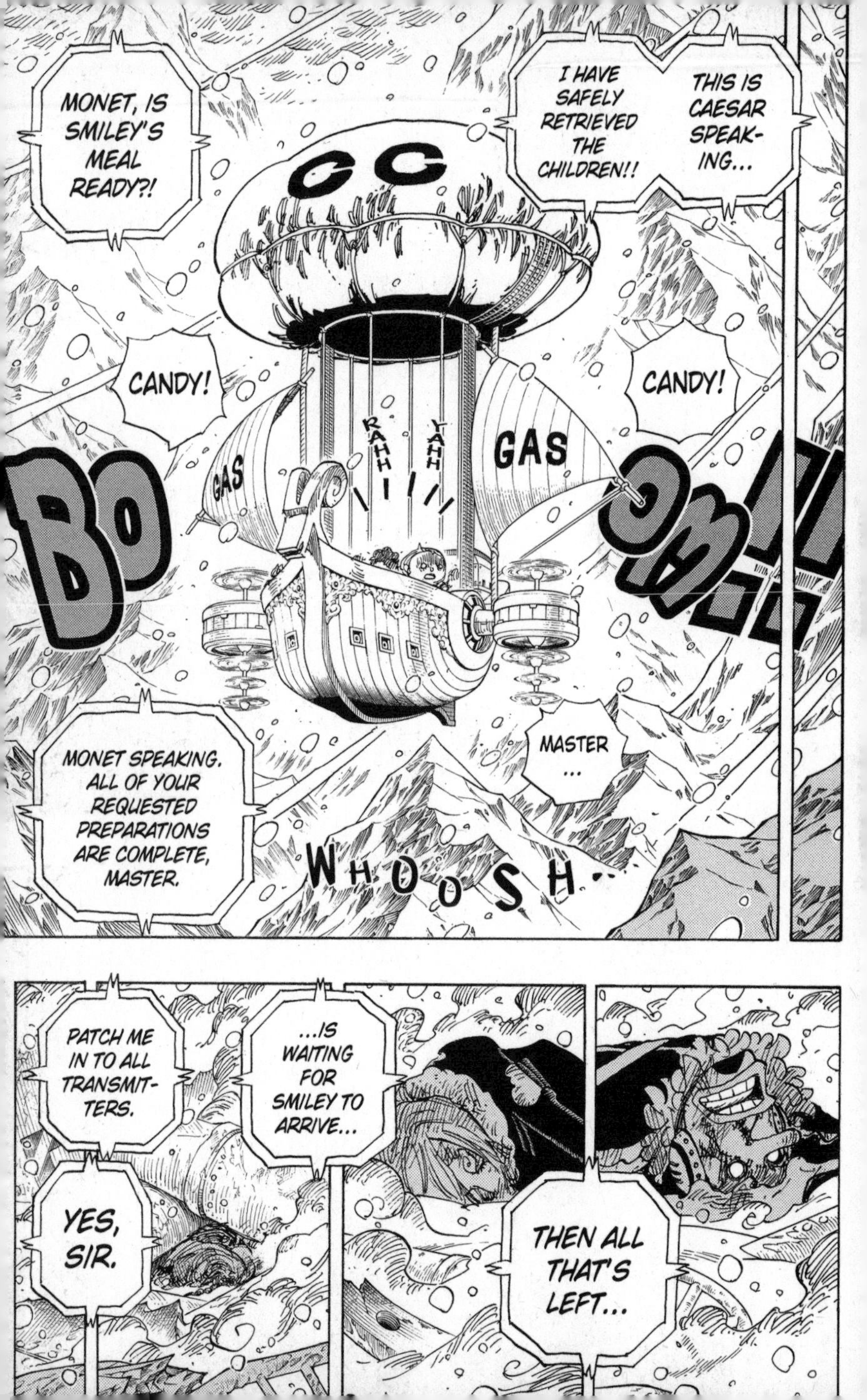
THIS IS CAESAR SPEAKING...
I HAVE SAFELY RETRIEVED THE CHILDREN!!
MONET, IS SMILEY'S MEAL READY?!
CANDY!
CANDY!
GAS
GAS
YAHH
RAHHH
BOOM!!
MASTER...
MONET SPEAKING. ALL OF YOUR REQUESTED PREPARATIONS ARE COMPLETE, MASTER.
WHOOSH...
THEN ALL THAT'S LEFT...
...IS WAITING FOR SMILEY TO ARRIVE...
PATCH ME IN TO ALL TRANSMITTERS.
YES, SIR.

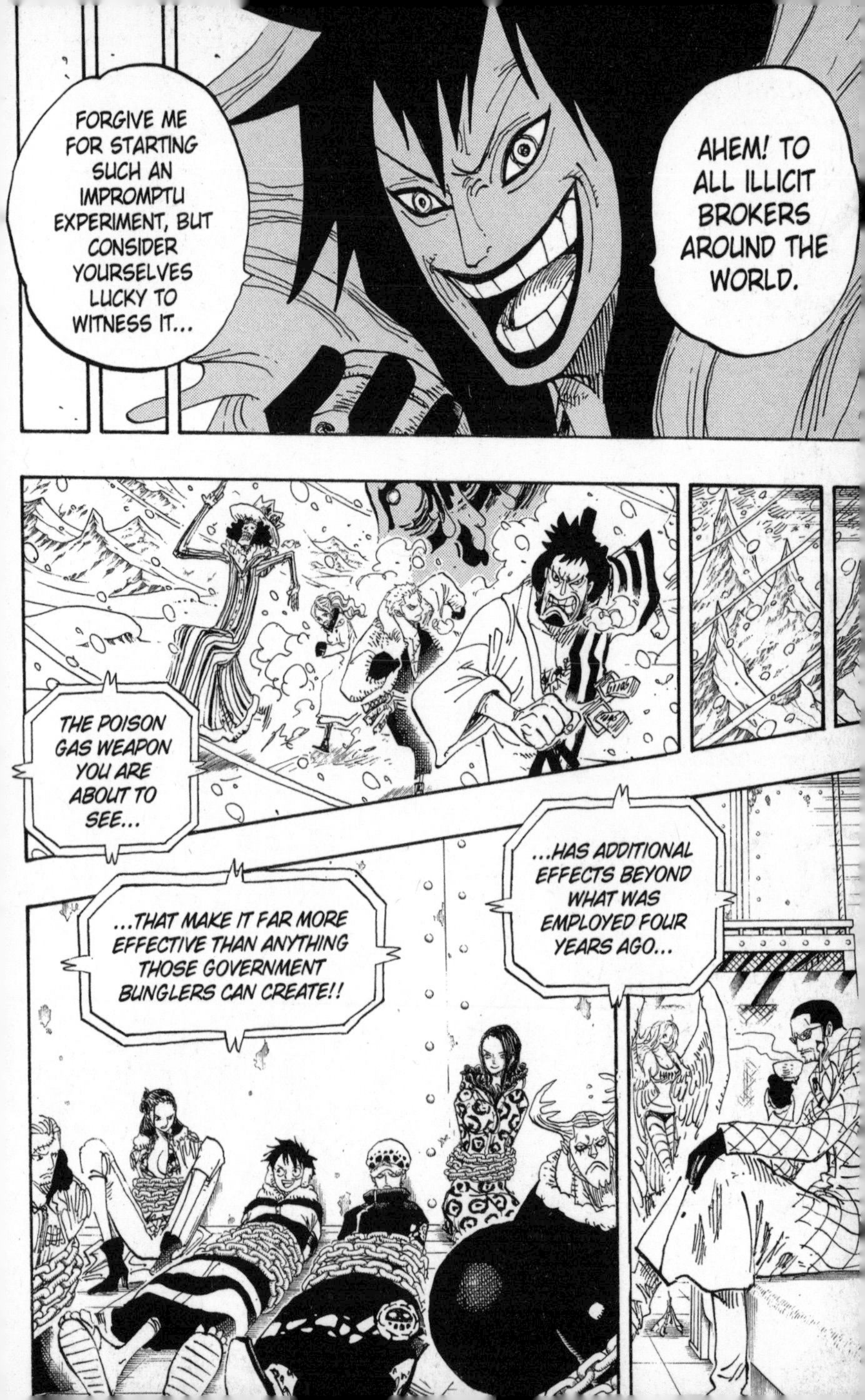
AHEM! TO ALL ILLICIT BROKERS AROUND THE WORLD.
FORGIVE ME FOR STARTING SUCH AN IMPROMPTU EXPERIMENT, BUT CONSIDER YOURSELVES LUCKY TO WITNESS IT...
THE POISON GAS WEAPON YOU ARE ABOUT TO SEE...
...HAS ADDITIONAL EFFECTS BEYOND WHAT WAS EMPLOYED FOUR YEARS AGO...
...THAT MAKE IT FAR MORE EFFECTIVE THAN ANYTHING THOSE GOVERNMENT BUNGLERS CAN CREATE!!

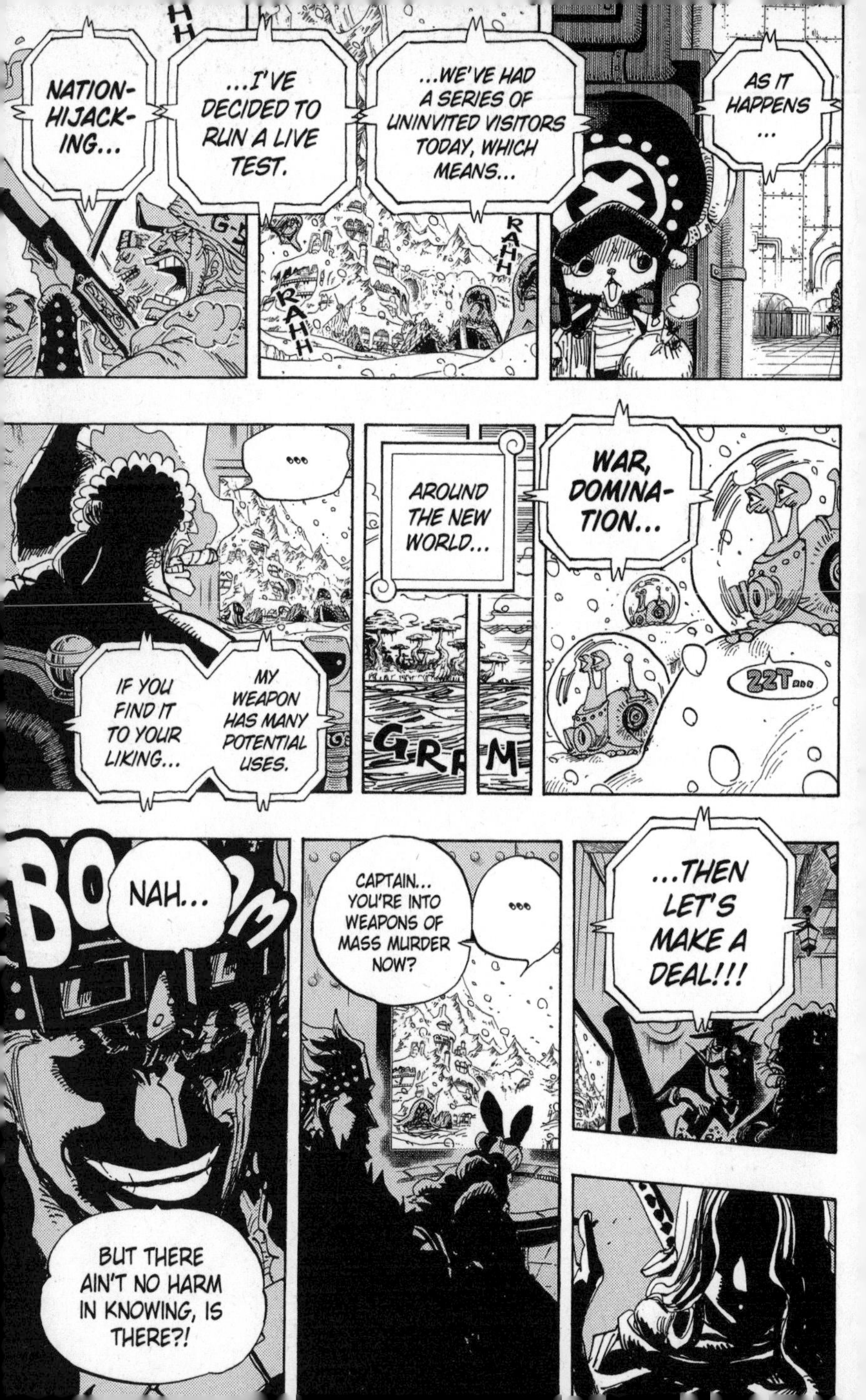
AS IT HAPPENS...
...WE'VE HAD A SERIES OF UNINVITED VISITORS TODAY, WHICH MEANS...
RAHH
RAHH
...I'VE DECIDED TO RUN A LIVE TEST.
NATION-HIJACKING...
WAR, DOMINATION...
ZZT...
AROUND THE NEW WORLD...
GRRM
...
MY WEAPON HAS MANY POTENTIAL USES.
IF YOU FIND IT TO YOUR LIKING...
...THEN LET'S MAKE A DEAL!!!
...
CAPTAIN... YOU'RE INTO WEAPONS OF MASS MURDER NOW?
BOOM
NAH...
BUT THERE AIN'T NO HARM IN KNOWING, IS THERE?!

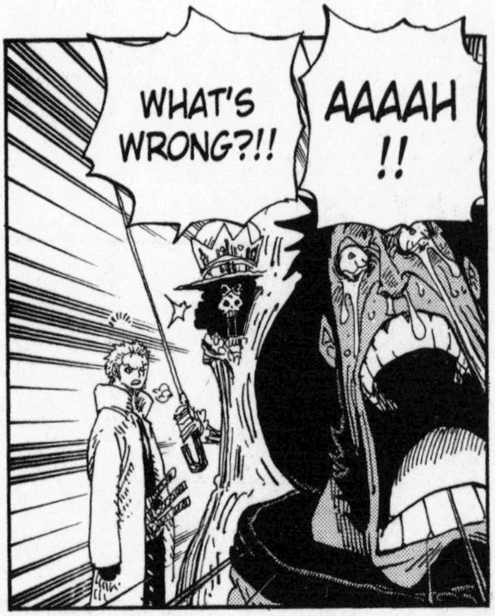
AAAAH !!
WHAT'S WRONG?!!

Chapter 675:
I CALL IT LAND OF THE DEAD

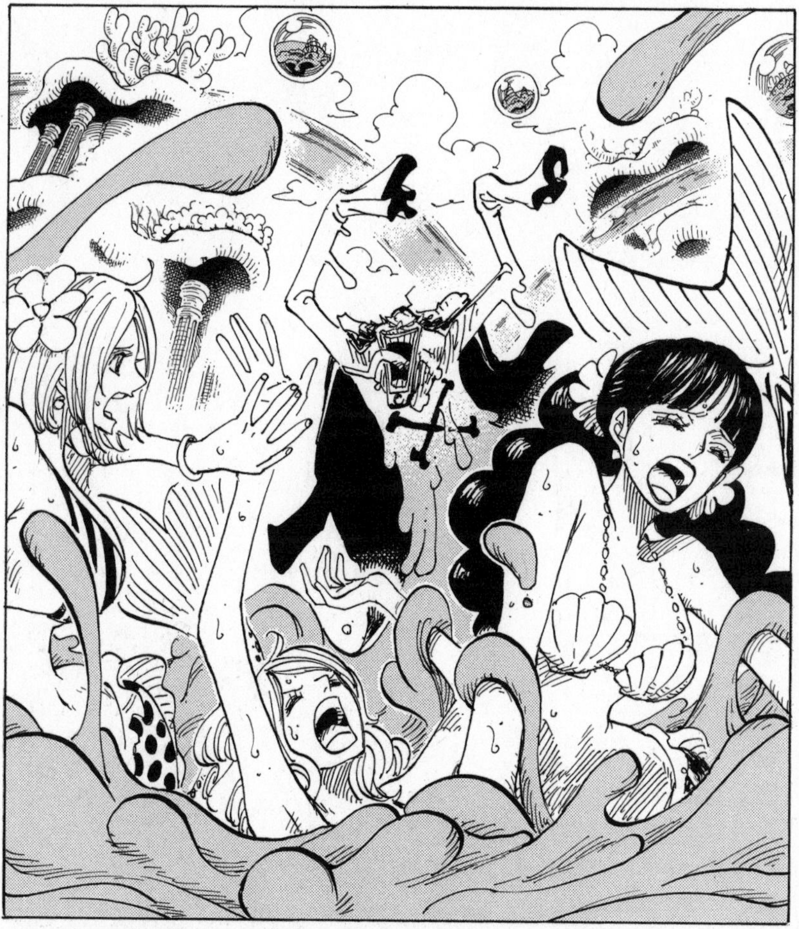

CARIBOU'S NEW WORLD KEE HEE HEE, VOL. 2:
"NO RUNNIN' AWAY NOW, MY SWEET LI'L MERMAIDS!!"

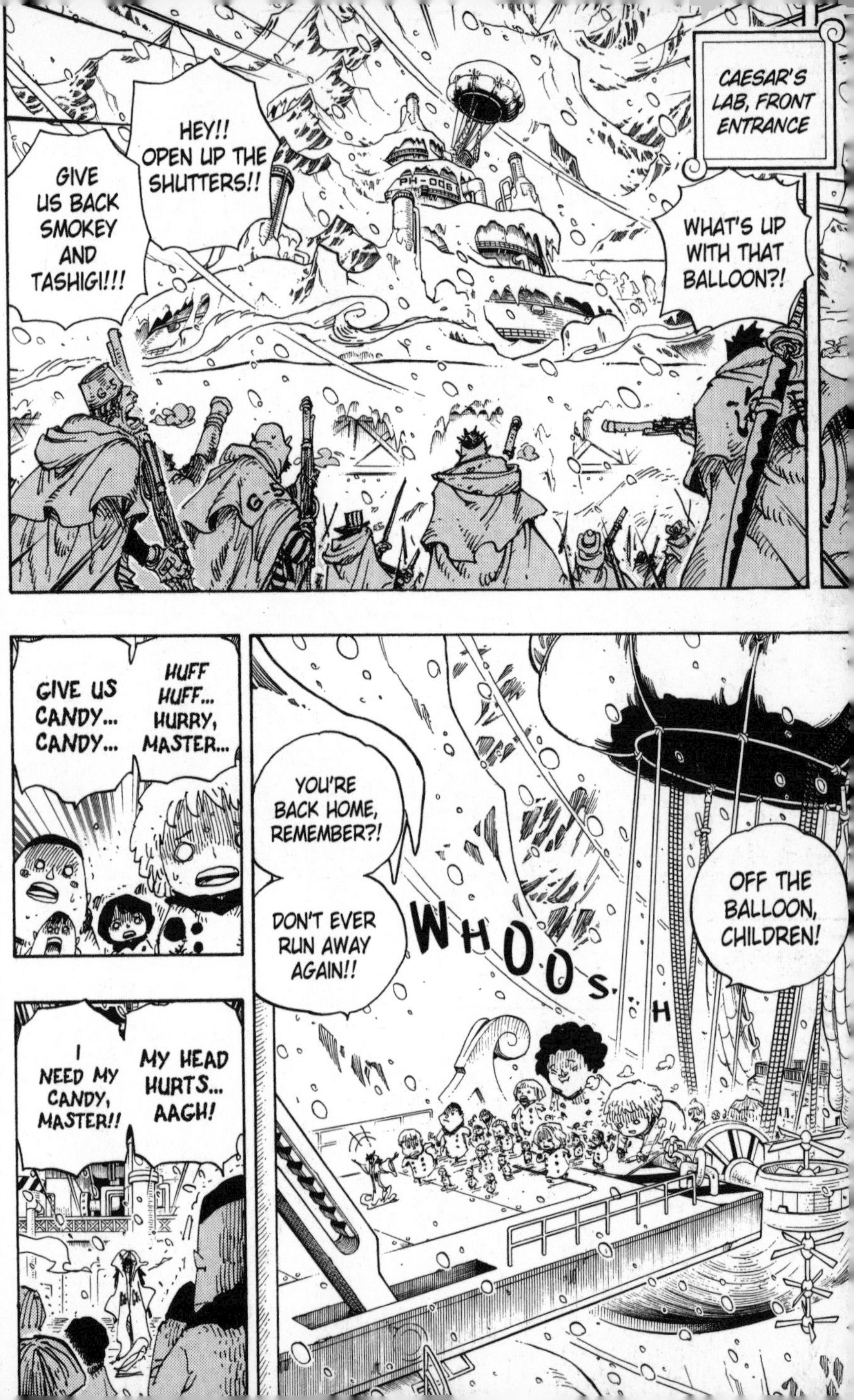
CAESAR'S LAB, FRONT ENTRANCE
WHAT'S UP WITH THAT BALLOON?!
HEY!! OPEN UP THE SHUTTERS!!
GIVE US BACK SMOKEY AND TASHIGI!!!
OFF THE BALLOON, CHILDREN!
YOU'RE BACK HOME, REMEMBER?!
DON'T EVER RUN AWAY AGAIN!!
WHOOSH
HUFF HUFF... HURRY, MASTER...
GIVE US CANDY... CANDY...
MY HEAD HURTS... AAGH!
I NEED MY CANDY, MASTER!!

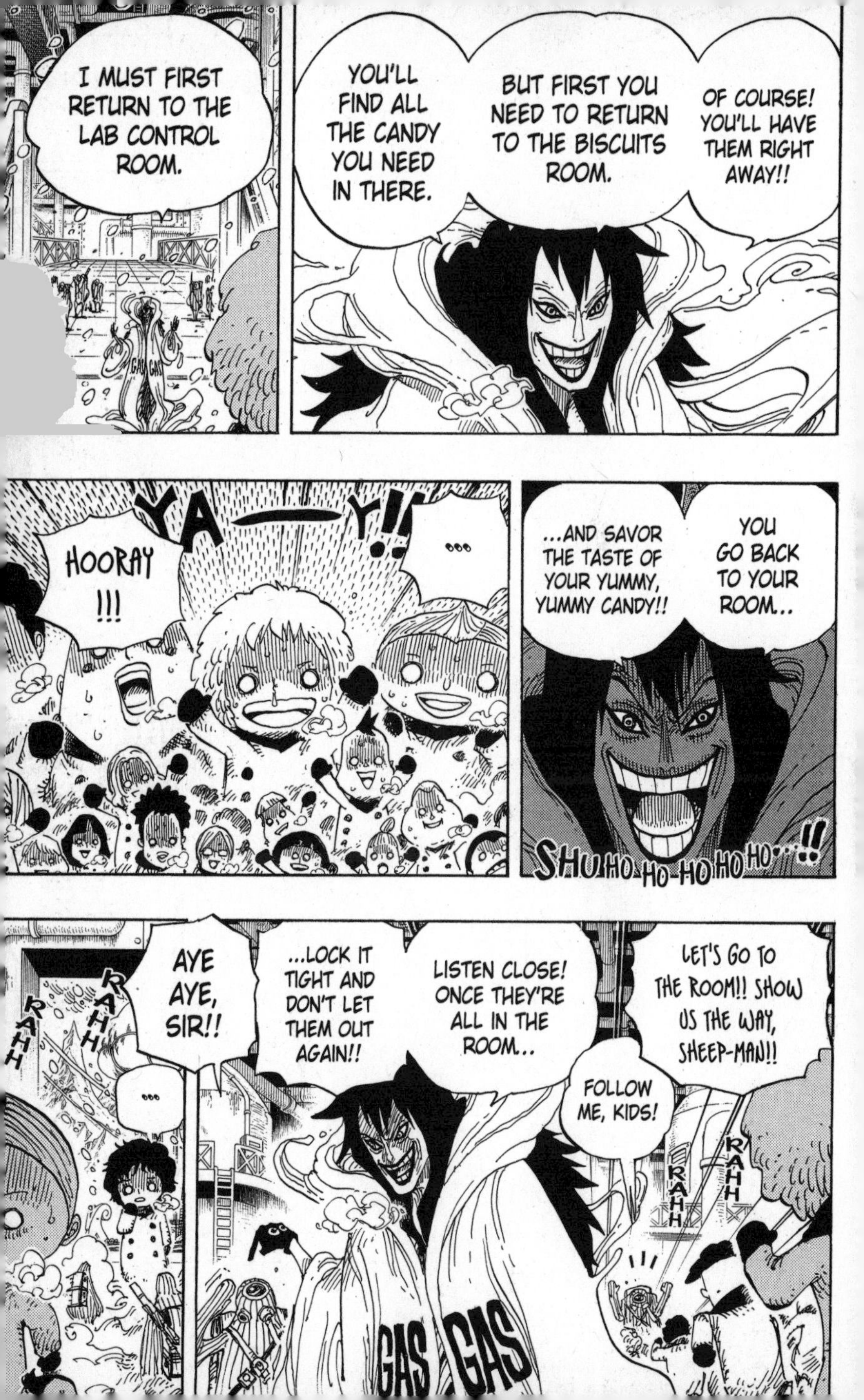
OF COURSE! YOU'LL HAVE THEM RIGHT AWAY!!
BUT FIRST YOU NEED TO RETURN TO THE BISCUITS ROOM.
YOU'LL FIND ALL THE CANDY YOU NEED IN THERE.
I MUST FIRST RETURN TO THE LAB CONTROL ROOM.
GAS GAS
YOU GO BACK TO YOUR ROOM..
...AND SAVOR THE TASTE OF YOUR YUMMY, YUMMY CANDY!!
SHUHOHOHOHOHOHO...!!
...
YA—Y!!
HOORAY !!!
LET'S GO TO THE ROOM!! SHOW US THE WAY, SHEEP-MAN!!
RAHH
RAHH
FOLLOW ME, KIDS!
LISTEN CLOSE! ONCE THEY'RE ALL IN THE ROOM..
...LOCK IT TIGHT AND DON'T LET THEM OUT AGAIN!!
GAS GAS
AYE AYE, SIR!!
...
RAHH
RAHH

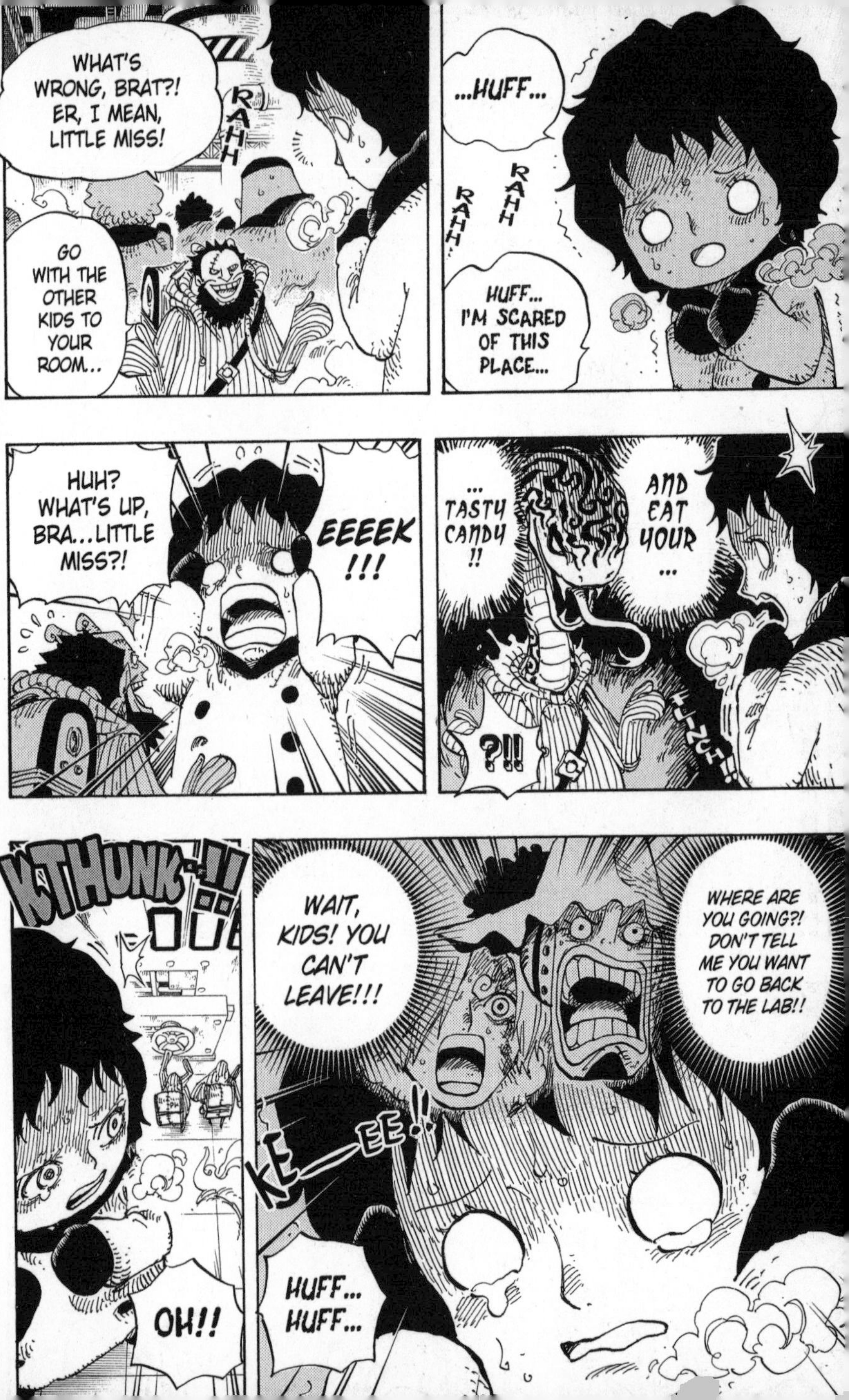
...HUFF...
RAHH
RAHH
HUFF... I'M SCARED OF THIS PLACE...
WHAT'S WRONG, BRAT?! ER, I MEAN, LITTLE MISS!
RAHH
GO WITH THE OTHER KIDS TO YOUR ROOM...
AND EAT YOUR ...
... TASTY CANDY !!
?!!
HUH? WHAT'S UP, BRA...LITTLE MISS?!
EEEEK !!!
WHERE ARE YOU GOING?! DON'T TELL ME YOU WANT TO GO BACK TO THE LAB!!
WAIT, KIDS! YOU CAN'T LEAVE!!!
KE—EE!!
HUFF... HUFF...
KATHUNK!!
OH!!

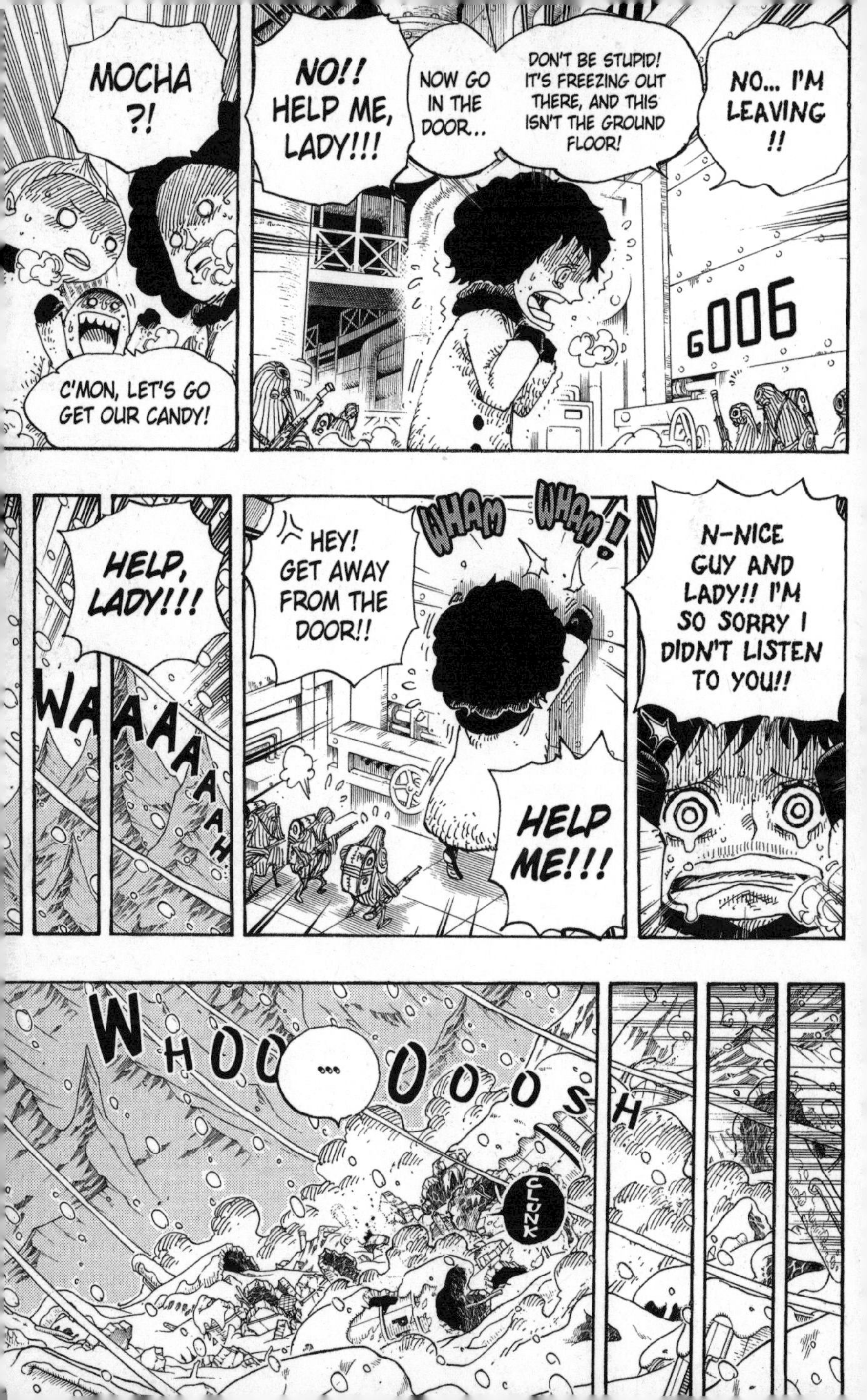

NO... I'M LEAVING !!
DON'T BE STUPID! IT'S FREEZING OUT THERE, AND THIS ISN'T THE GROUND FLOOR!
NOW GO IN THE DOOR...
NO!! HELP ME, LADY!!!
G006
MOCHA ?!
C'MON, LET'S GO GET OUR CANDY!
N-NICE GUY AND LADY!! I'M SO SORRY I DIDN'T LISTEN TO YOU!!
WHAM WHAM!
HEY! GET AWAY FROM THE DOOR!!
HELP ME!!!
HELP, LADY!!!
WAAAAAAAH
WHOOOOOOSH
...
CLUNK

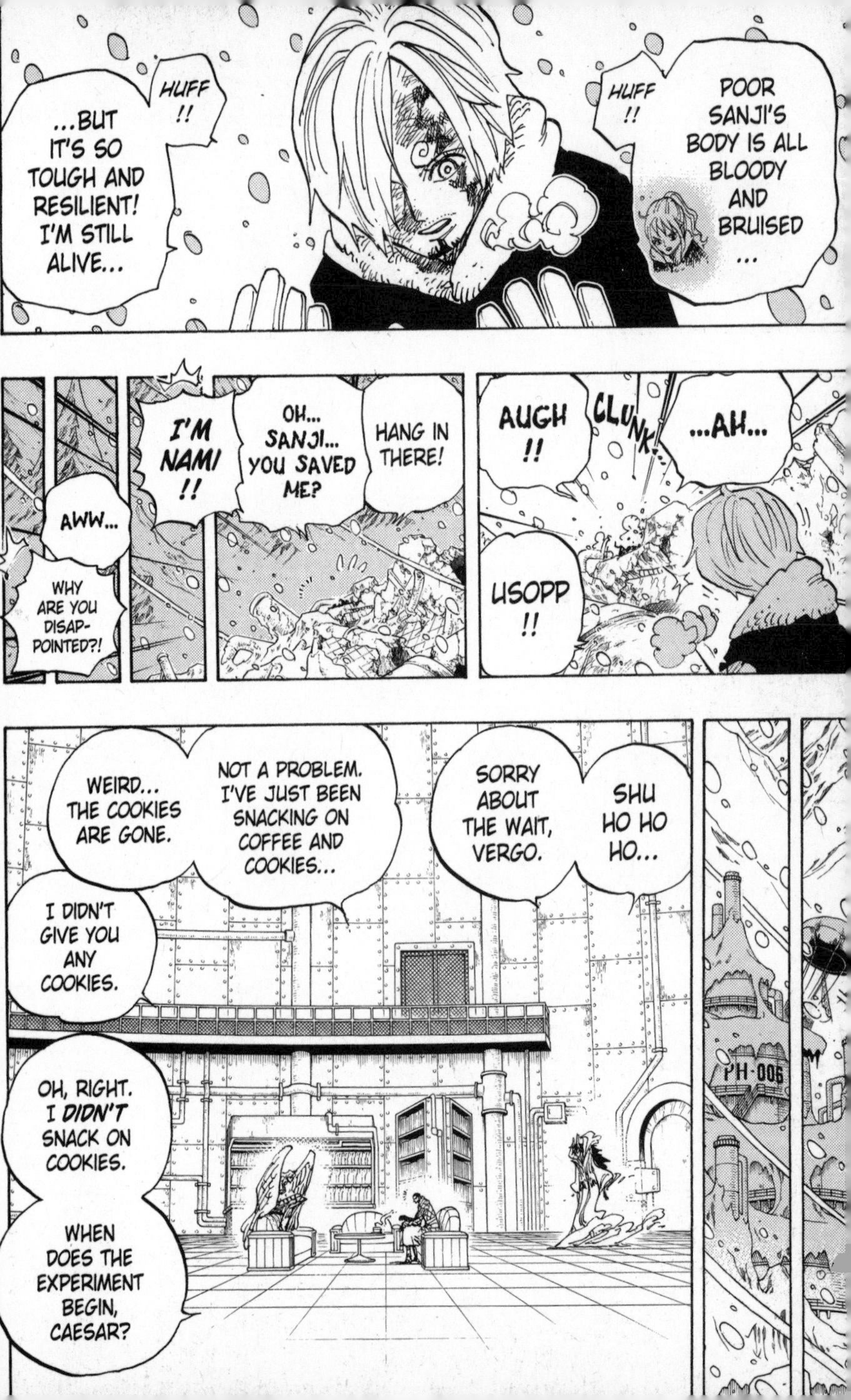
POOR SANJI'S BODY IS ALL BLOODY AND BRUISED ...
HUFF !!
HUFF !!
...BUT IT'S SO TOUGH AND RESILIENT! I'M STILL ALIVE...
...AH...
CLUNK
AUGH !!
USOPP !!
HANG IN THERE!
OH... SANJI... YOU SAVED ME?
I'M NAMI !!
AWW...
WHY ARE YOU DISAP-POINTED?!
PH-006
SHU HO HO HO...
SORRY ABOUT THE WAIT, VERGO.
NOT A PROBLEM. I'VE JUST BEEN SNACKING ON COFFEE AND COOKIES...
WEIRD... THE COOKIES ARE GONE.
I DIDN'T GIVE YOU ANY COOKIES.
OH, RIGHT. I *DIDN'T* SNACK ON COOKIES.
WHEN DOES THE EXPERIMENT BEGIN, CAESAR?

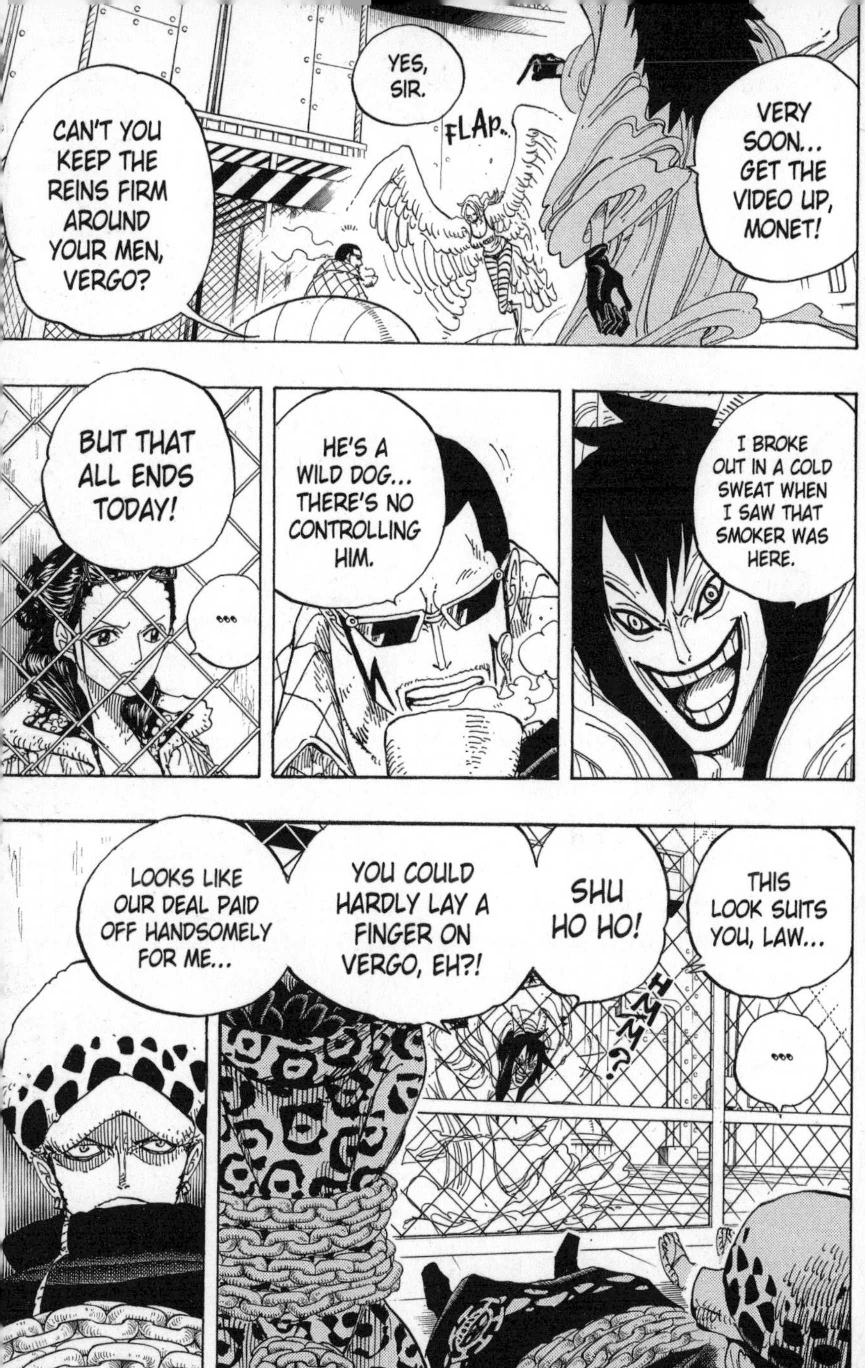
VERY SOON... GET THE VIDEO UP, MONET!
YES, SIR.
FLAP..
CAN'T YOU KEEP THE REINS FIRM AROUND YOUR MEN, VERGO?
I BROKE OUT IN A COLD SWEAT WHEN I SAW THAT SMOKER WAS HERE.
HE'S A WILD DOG... THERE'S NO CONTROLLING HIM.
BUT THAT ALL ENDS TODAY!
...
THIS LOOK SUITS YOU, LAW...
SHU HO HO!
YOU COULD HARDLY LAY A FINGER ON VERGO, EH?!
LOOKS LIKE OUR DEAL PAID OFF HANDSOMELY FOR ME...
HMMM?
...

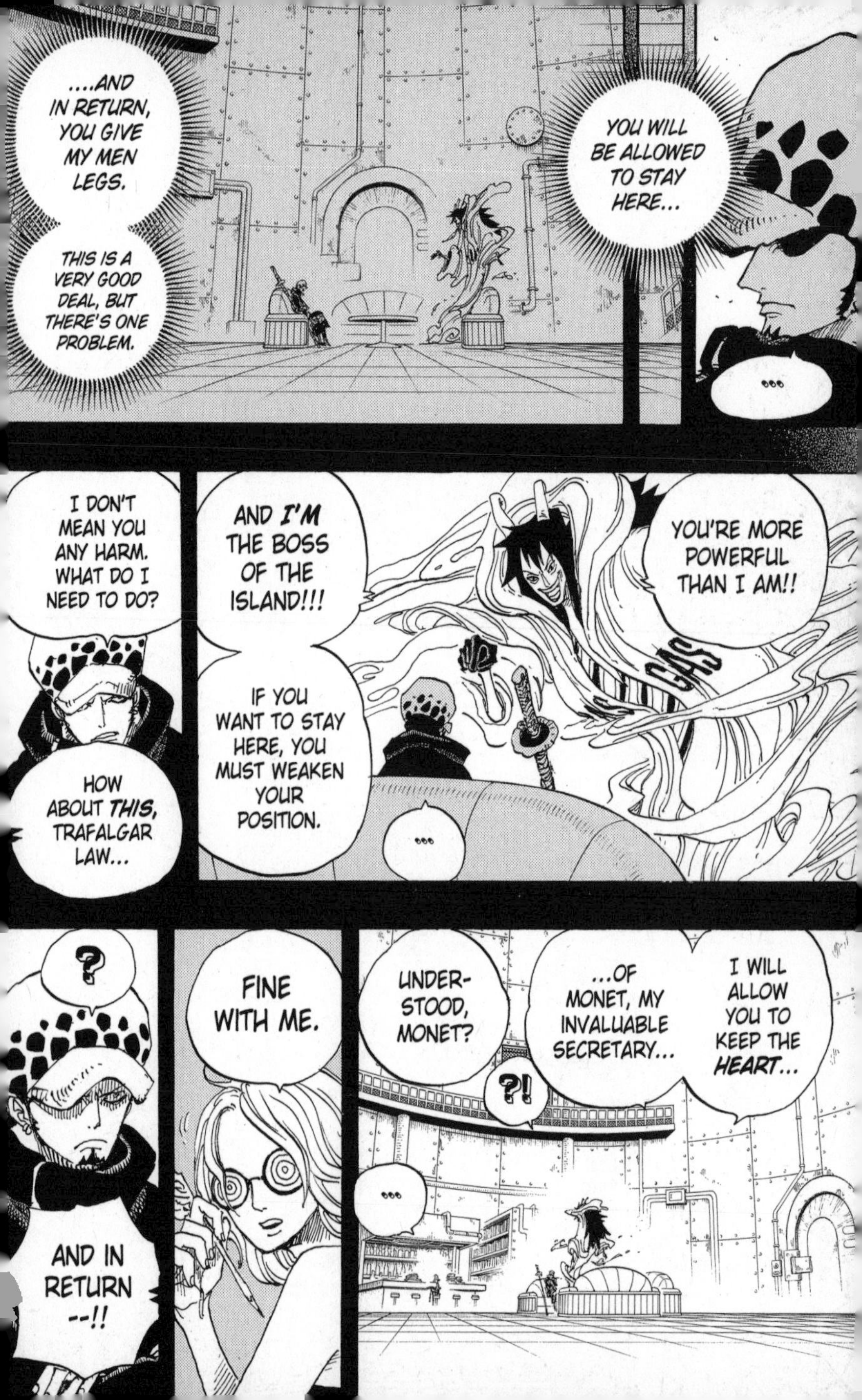
YOU WILL BE ALLOWED TO STAY HERE...
....AND IN RETURN, YOU GIVE MY MEN LEGS.
THIS IS A VERY GOOD DEAL, BUT THERE'S ONE PROBLEM.
...
YOU'RE MORE POWERFUL THAN I AM!!
AND *I'M* THE BOSS OF THE ISLAND!!!
IF YOU WANT TO STAY HERE, YOU MUST WEAKEN YOUR POSITION.
GAS
...
I DON'T MEAN YOU ANY HARM. WHAT DO I NEED TO DO?
HOW ABOUT *THIS*, TRAFALGAR LAW...
I WILL ALLOW YOU TO KEEP THE *HEART*...
...OF MONET, MY INVALUABLE SECRETARY...
UNDER-STOOD, MONET?
?!
...
FINE WITH ME.
?
AND IN RETURN --!!

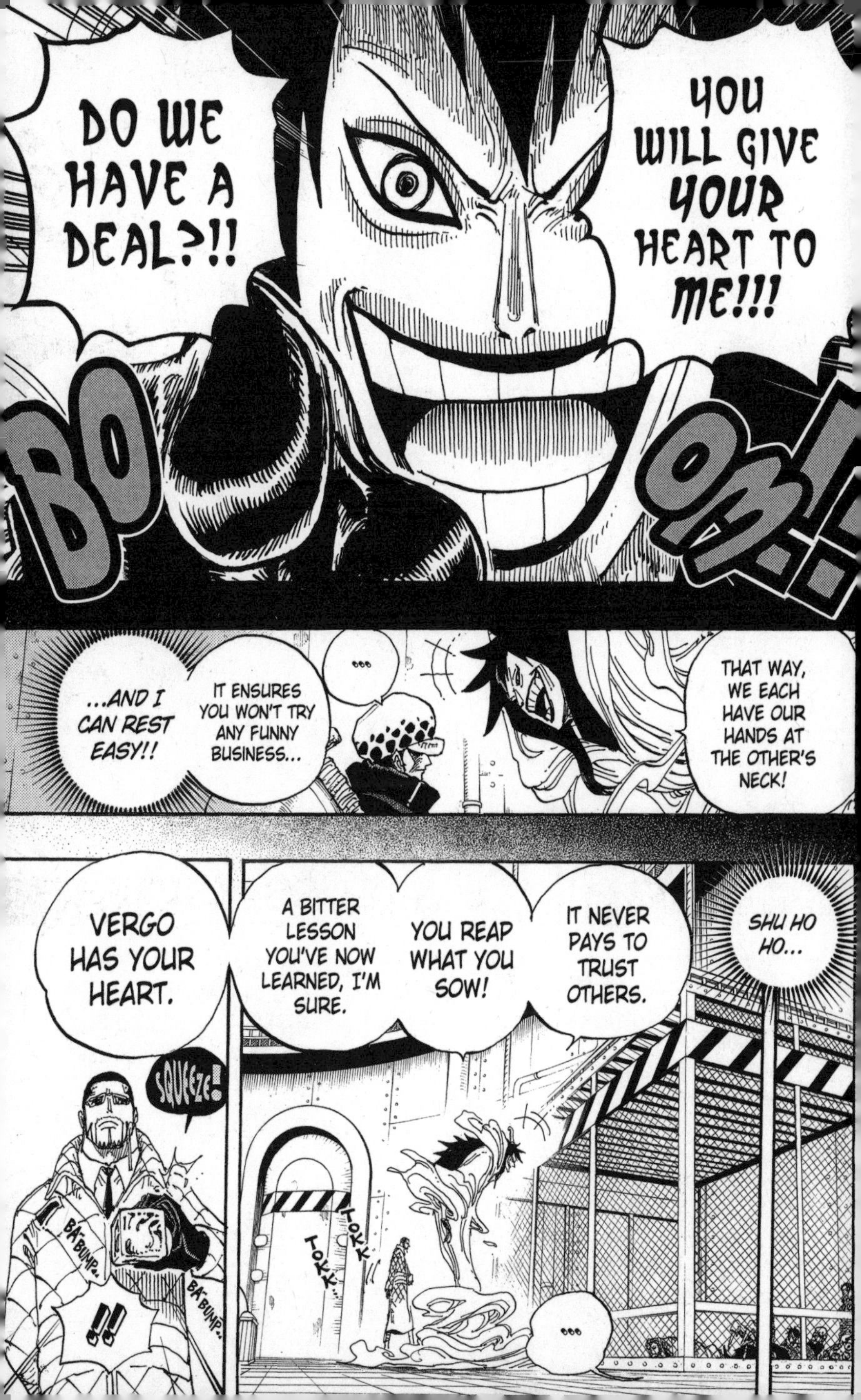
YOU WILL GIVE YOUR HEART TO ME!!!
DO WE HAVE A DEAL?!!
BOOM!!
THAT WAY, WE EACH HAVE OUR HANDS AT THE OTHER'S NECK!
...
IT ENSURES YOU WON'T TRY ANY FUNNY BUSINESS...
...AND I CAN REST EASY!!
SHU HO HO...
IT NEVER PAYS TO TRUST OTHERS.
YOU REAP WHAT YOU SOW!
A BITTER LESSON YOU'VE NOW LEARNED, I'M SURE.
TOKK
TOKK...
...
VERGO HAS YOUR HEART.
SQUEEZE!
BA-BUMP..
BA-BUMP..
!!

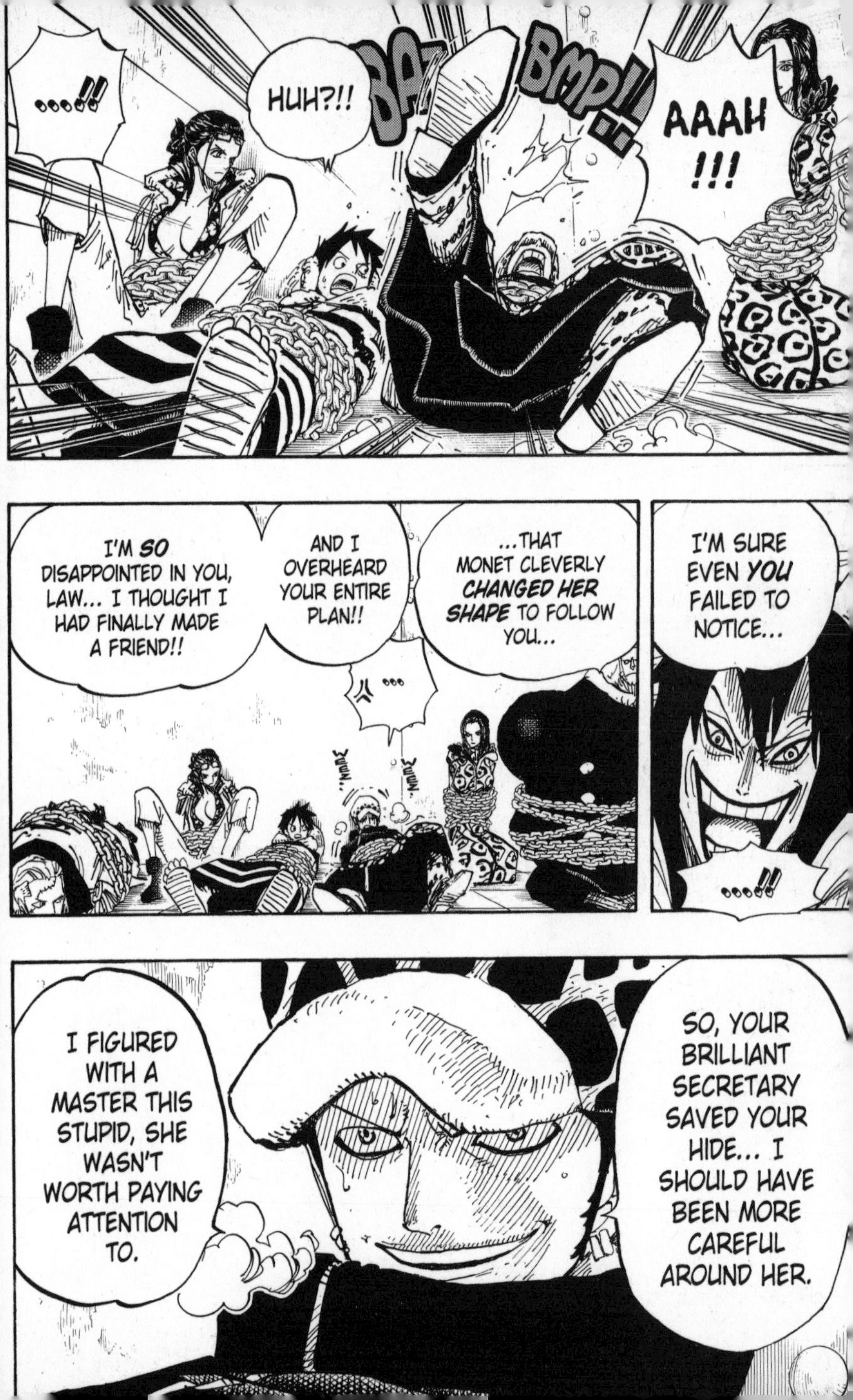

AAAH!!!
BMP!!
HUH?!!
...!!
I'M SURE EVEN YOU FAILED TO NOTICE...
...!!
...THAT MONET CLEVERLY CHANGED HER SHAPE TO FOLLOW YOU...
AND I OVERHEARD YOUR ENTIRE PLAN!!
I'M SO DISAPPOINTED IN YOU, LAW... I THOUGHT I HAD FINALLY MADE A FRIEND!!
...
SO, YOUR BRILLIANT SECRETARY SAVED YOUR HIDE... I SHOULD HAVE BEEN MORE CAREFUL AROUND HER.
I FIGURED WITH A MASTER THIS STUPID, SHE WASN'T WORTH PAYING ATTENTION TO.

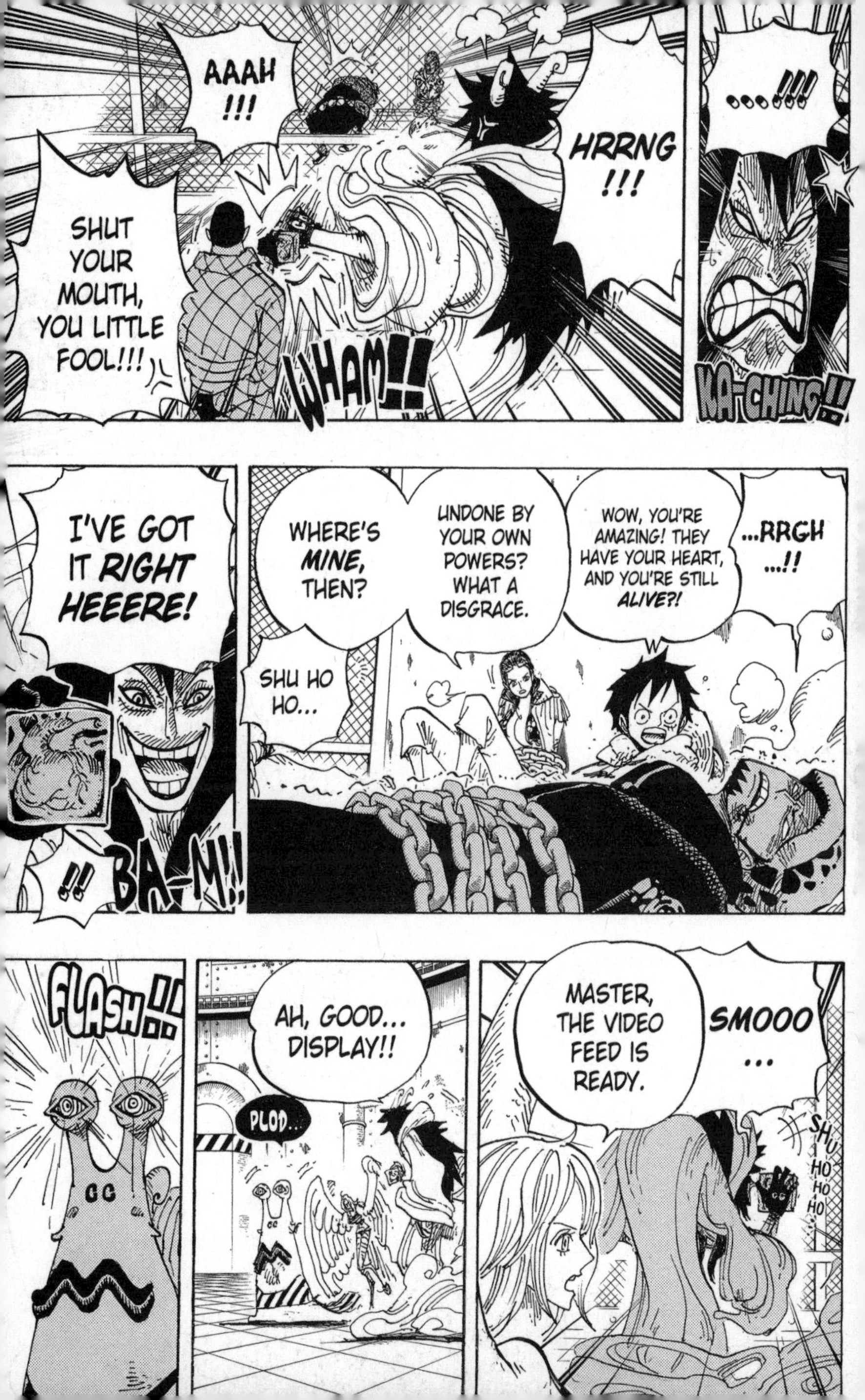
...!!!
KA-CHING!!
HRRNG !!!
AAAH !!!
SHUT YOUR MOUTH, YOU LITTLE FOOL!!!
WHAM!!
...RRGH ...!!
WOW, YOU'RE AMAZING! THEY HAVE YOUR HEART, AND YOU'RE STILL ALIVE?!
UNDONE BY YOUR OWN POWERS? WHAT A DISGRACE.
WHERE'S MINE, THEN?
SHU HO HO...
I'VE GOT IT RIGHT HEEERE!
!!
BA-M!!
SMOOO ...
MASTER, THE VIDEO FEED IS READY.
SHU HO HO HO
AH, GOOD... DISPLAY!!
PLOD...
FLASH!!

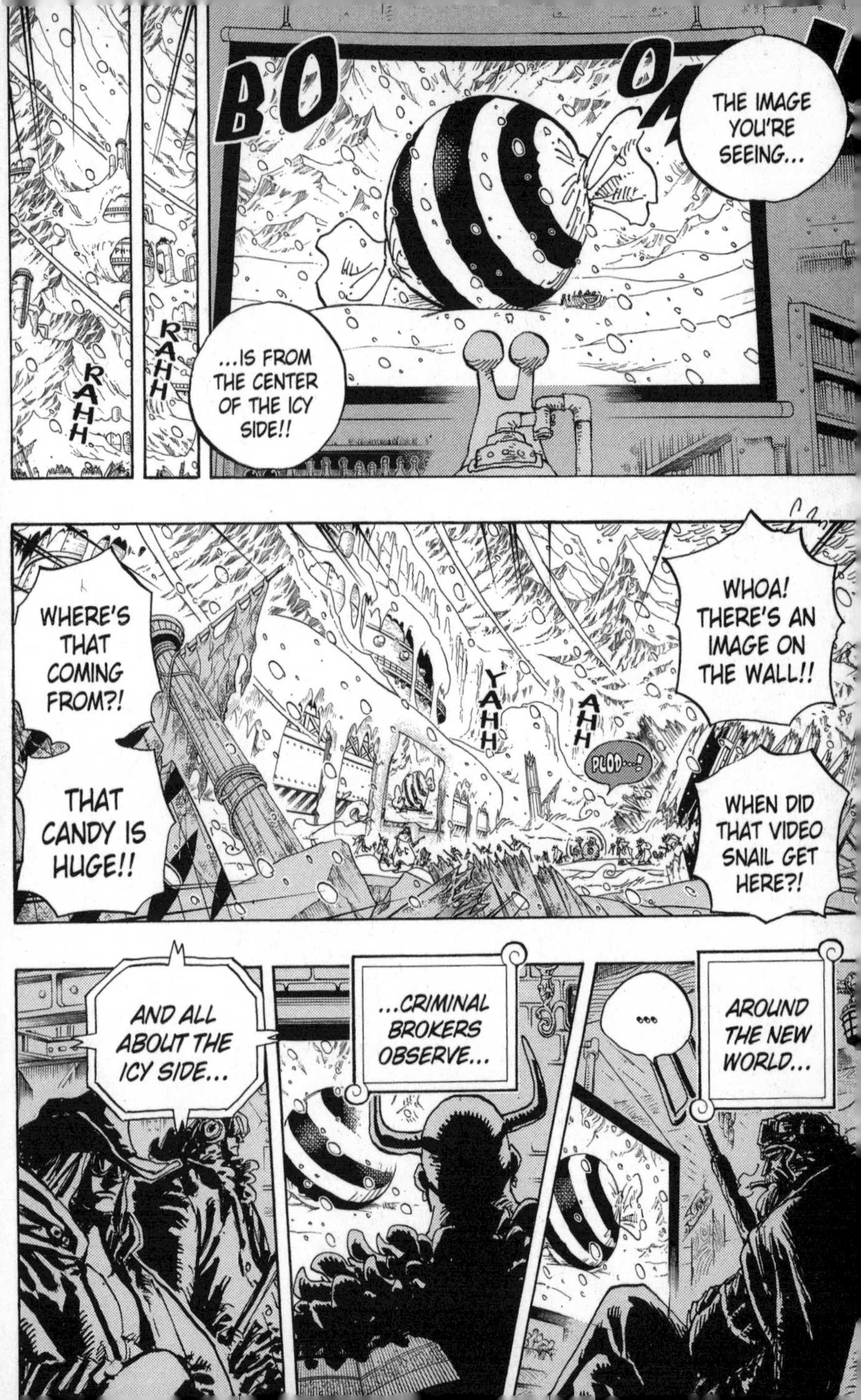
BOO
THE IMAGE YOU'RE SEEING...
...IS FROM THE CENTER OF THE ICY SIDE!!
RAHH
RAHH
WHOA! THERE'S AN IMAGE ON THE WALL!!
WHEN DID THAT VIDEO SNAIL GET HERE?!
PLOD...!
AHH
YAHH
WHERE'S THAT COMING FROM?!
THAT CANDY IS HUGE!!
AROUND THE NEW WORLD...
...
...CRIMINAL BROKERS OBSERVE...
AND ALL ABOUT THE ICY SIDE...

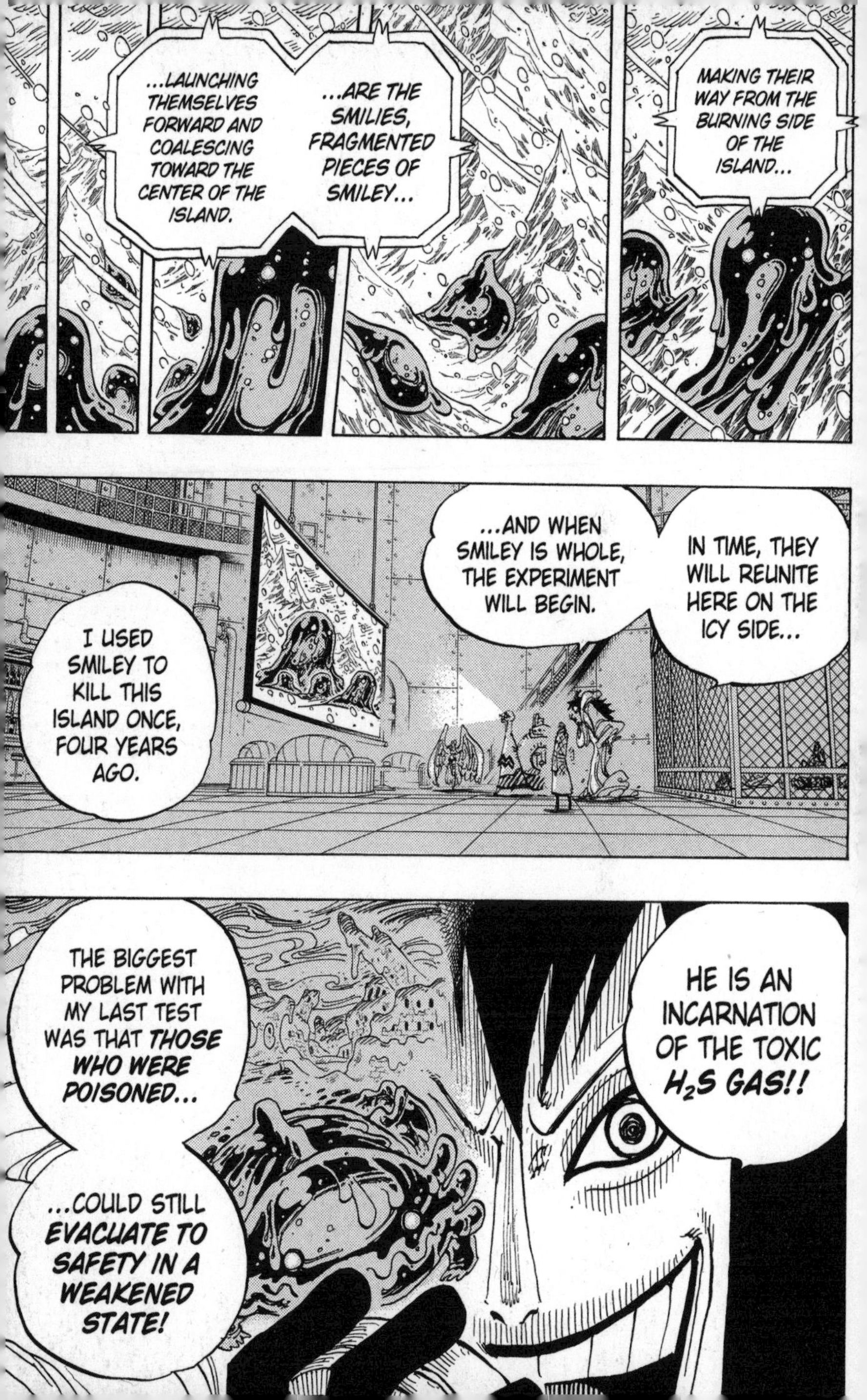
MAKING THEIR WAY FROM THE BURNING SIDE OF THE ISLAND...
...ARE THE SMILIES, FRAGMENTED PIECES OF SMILEY...
...LAUNCHING THEMSELVES FORWARD AND COALESCING TOWARD THE CENTER OF THE ISLAND.
IN TIME, THEY WILL REUNITE HERE ON THE ICY SIDE...
...AND WHEN SMILEY IS WHOLE, THE EXPERIMENT WILL BEGIN.
I USED SMILEY TO KILL THIS ISLAND ONCE, FOUR YEARS AGO.
HE IS AN INCARNATION OF THE TOXIC H_2S GAS!!
THE BIGGEST PROBLEM WITH MY LAST TEST WAS THAT *THOSE WHO WERE POISONED...*
...COULD STILL *EVACUATE TO SAFETY IN A WEAKENED STATE!*

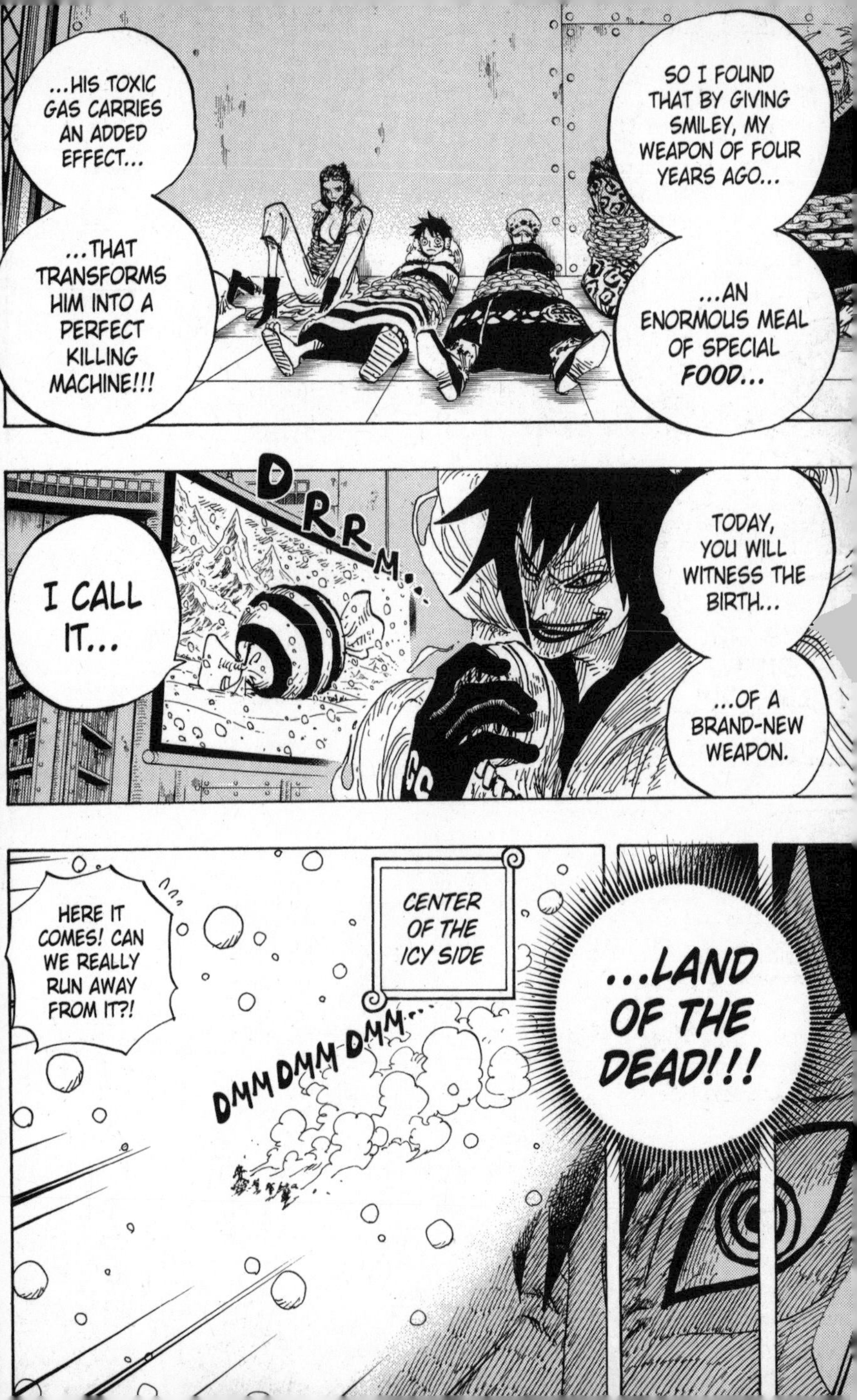

SO I FOUND THAT BY GIVING SMILEY, MY WEAPON OF FOUR YEARS AGO...
...AN ENORMOUS MEAL OF SPECIAL FOOD...
...HIS TOXIC GAS CARRIES AN ADDED EFFECT...
...THAT TRANSFORMS HIM INTO A PERFECT KILLING MACHINE!!!
TODAY, YOU WILL WITNESS THE BIRTH...
...OF A BRAND-NEW WEAPON.
DRRRM...
I CALL IT...
...LAND OF THE DEAD!!!
CENTER OF THE ICY SIDE
HERE IT COMES! CAN WE REALLY RUN AWAY FROM IT?!
DMM DMM DMM...

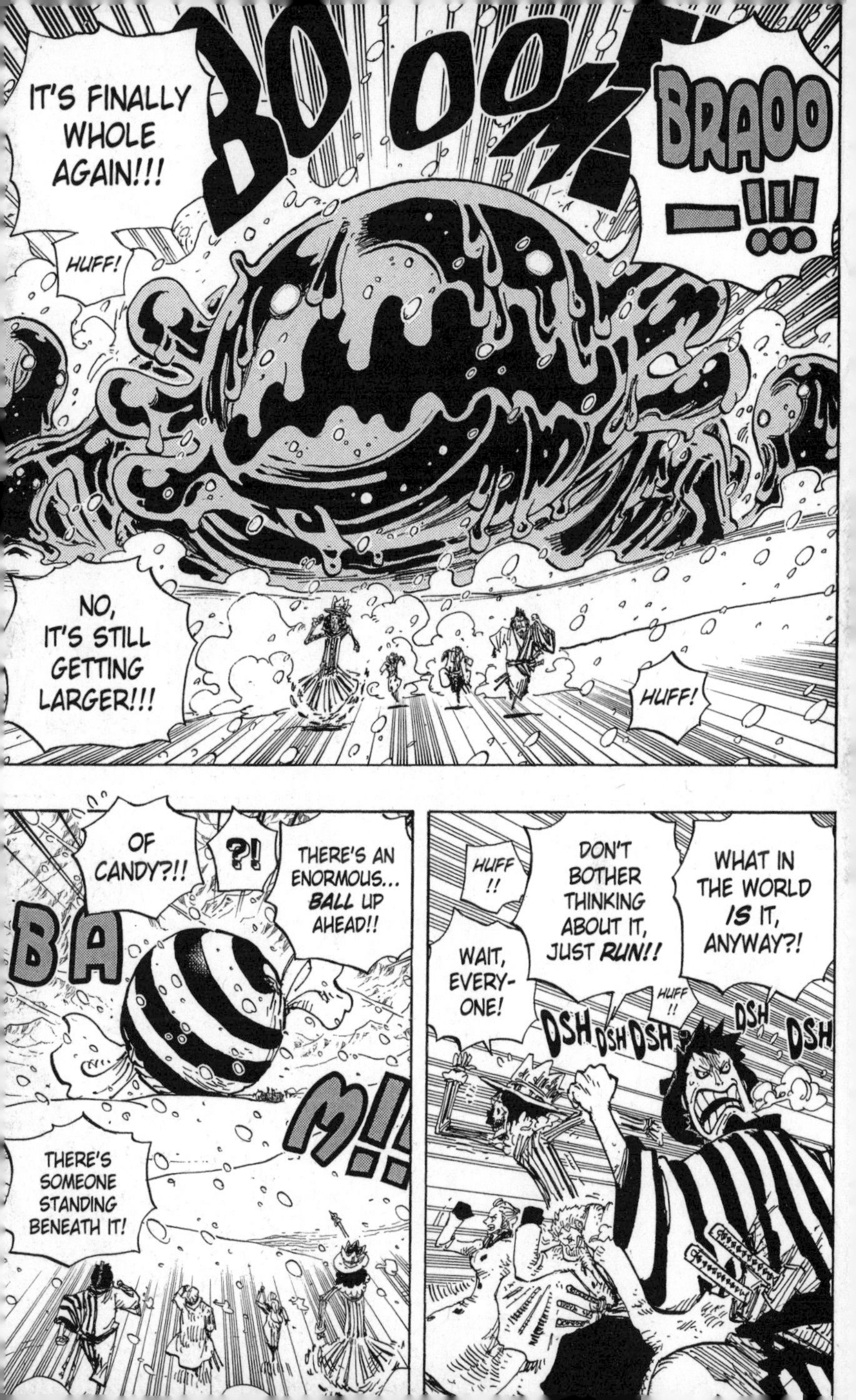
BRAOO —!!!
IT'S FINALLY WHOLE AGAIN!!!
HUFF!
HUFF!
NO, IT'S STILL GETTING LARGER!!!
WHAT IN THE WORLD *IS* IT, ANYWAY?!
DON'T BOTHER THINKING ABOUT IT, JUST *RUN!!*
HUFF !!
HUFF !!
WAIT, EVERY-ONE!
DSH DSH DSH DSH DSH DSH
THERE'S AN ENORMOUS... *BALL* UP AHEAD!!
?!
OF CANDY?!!
BA
M!!
THERE'S SOMEONE STANDING BENEATH IT!

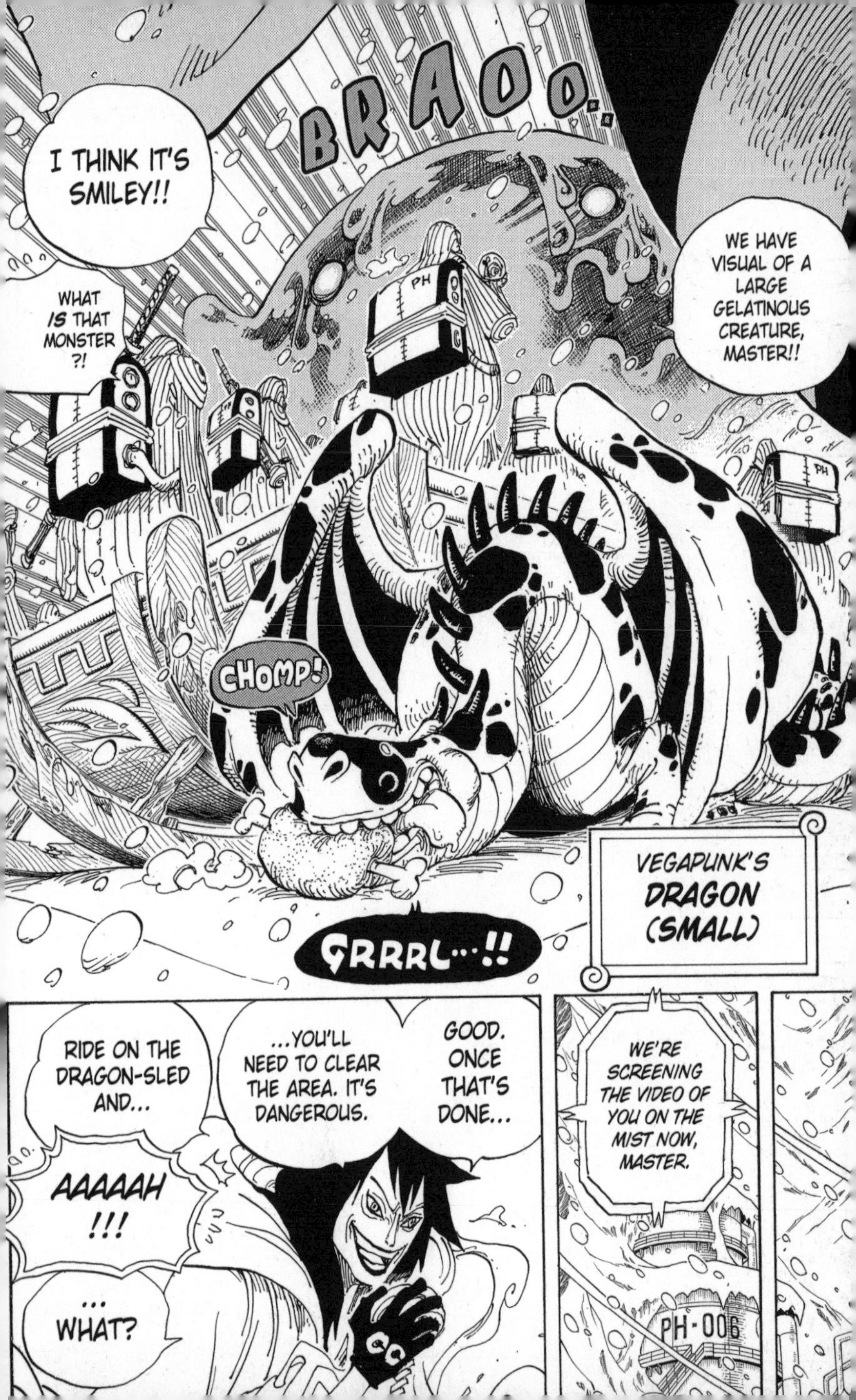
BRAOO..
WE HAVE VISUAL OF A LARGE GELATINOUS CREATURE, MASTER!!
I THINK IT'S SMILEY!!
WHAT *IS* THAT MONSTER?!
CHOMP!
VEGAPUNK'S **DRAGON (SMALL)**
GRRRL...!!
WE'RE SCREENING THE VIDEO OF YOU ON THE MIST NOW, MASTER.
PH-006
GOOD. ONCE THAT'S DONE...
...YOU'LL NEED TO CLEAR THE AREA. IT'S DANGEROUS.
RIDE ON THE DRAGON-SLED AND...
AAAAAH!!!
...WHAT?

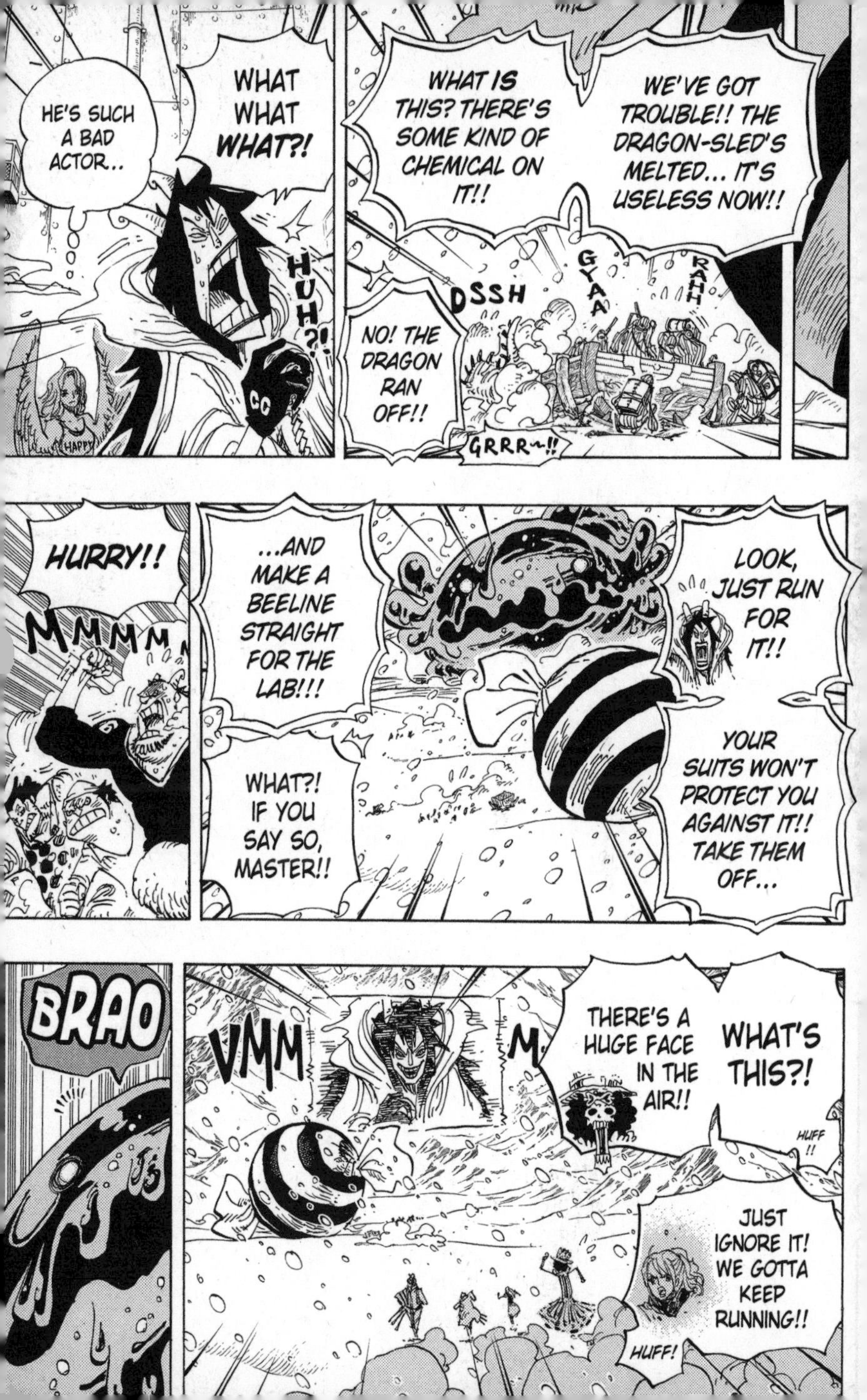
WE'VE GOT TROUBLE!! THE DRAGON-SLED'S MELTED... IT'S USELESS NOW!!
WHAT IS THIS? THERE'S SOME KIND OF CHEMICAL ON IT!!
RAHH
GYAA
DSSH
NO! THE DRAGON RAN OFF!!
GRRR~!!
WHAT WHAT WHAT?!
HUH?!
HE'S SUCH A BAD ACTOR...
LOOK, JUST RUN FOR IT!!
YOUR SUITS WON'T PROTECT YOU AGAINST IT!! TAKE THEM OFF...
...AND MAKE A BEELINE STRAIGHT FOR THE LAB!!!
WHAT?! IF YOU SAY SO, MASTER!!
HURRY!!
MMMM
WHAT'S THIS?!
THERE'S A HUGE FACE IN THE AIR!!
HUFF!!
M
VMM
JUST IGNORE IT! WE GOTTA KEEP RUNNING!!
HUFF!
BRAO

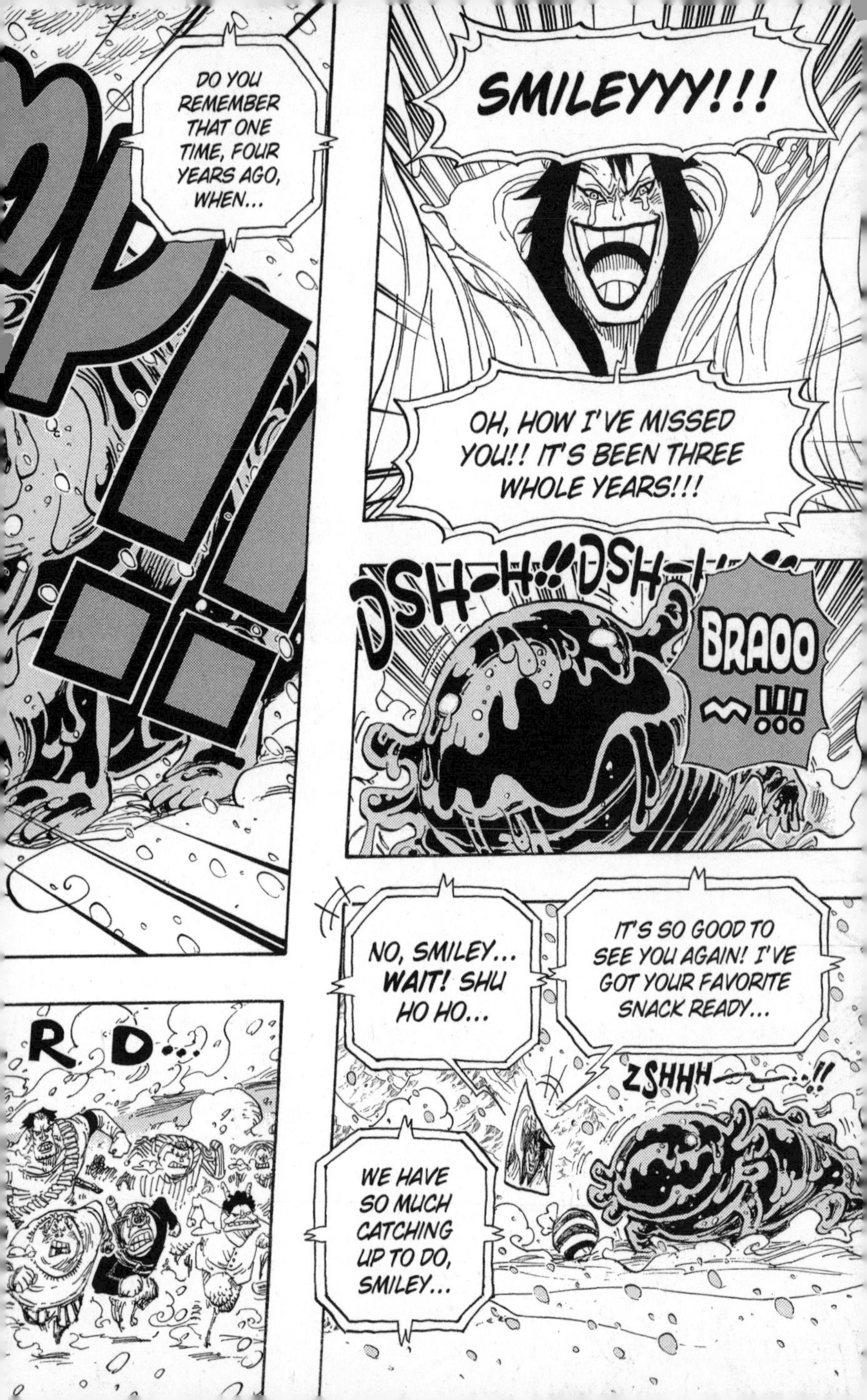
SMILEYYY!!!
OH, HOW I'VE MISSED YOU!! IT'S BEEN THREE WHOLE YEARS!!!
DSH-H!! DSH-H
BRAOO~!!!
DO YOU REMEMBER THAT ONE TIME, FOUR YEARS AGO, WHEN...
IT'S SO GOOD TO SEE YOU AGAIN! I'VE GOT YOUR FAVORITE SNACK READY...
NO, SMILEY... **WAIT!** SHU HO HO...
ZSHHH~~...!!
WE HAVE SO MUCH CATCHING UP TO DO, SMILEY...
R. D.

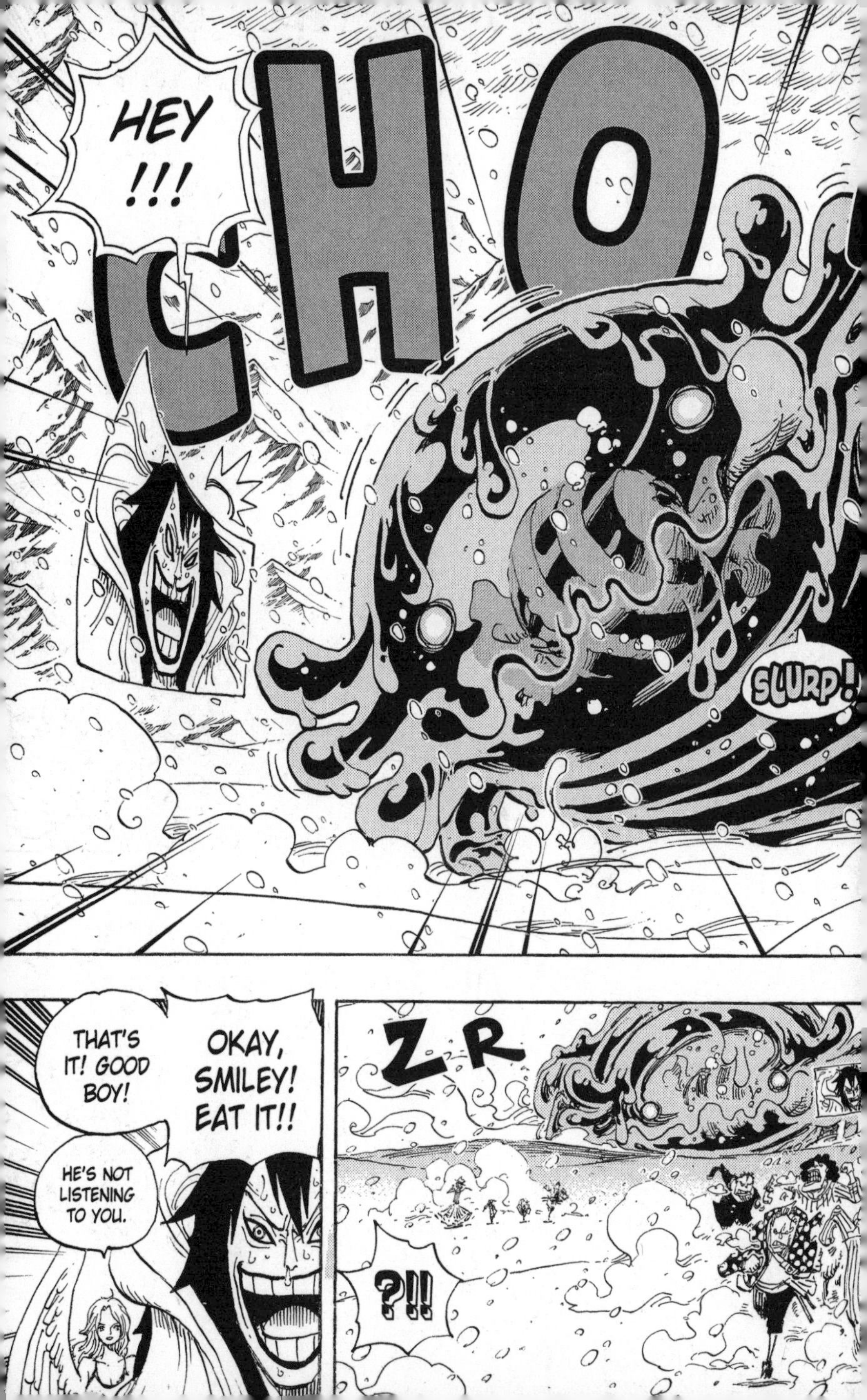
CHO
HEY !!!
SLURP !
ZR
?!!
OKAY, SMILEY! EAT IT!!
THAT'S IT! GOOD BOY!
HE'S NOT LISTENING TO YOU.

WEAPON OF MASS MURDER

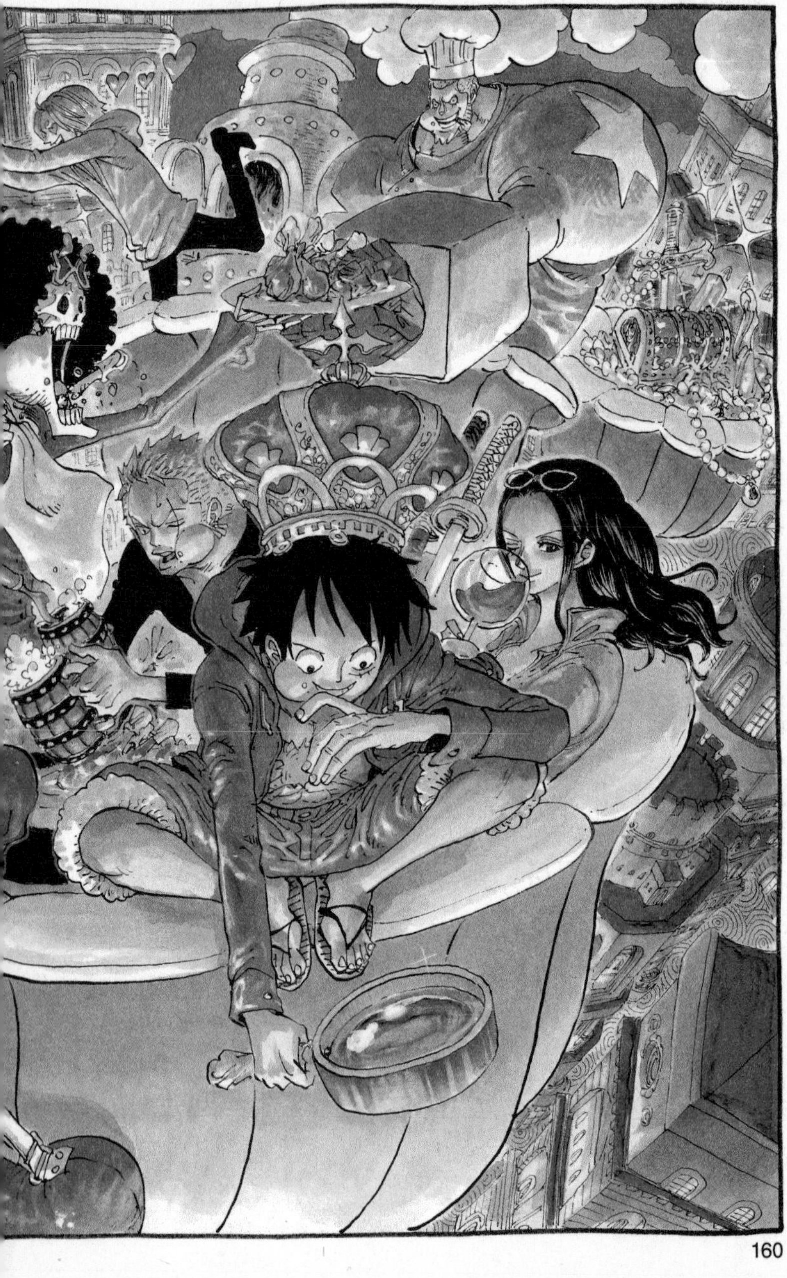

Chapter 676: THE PERFECT

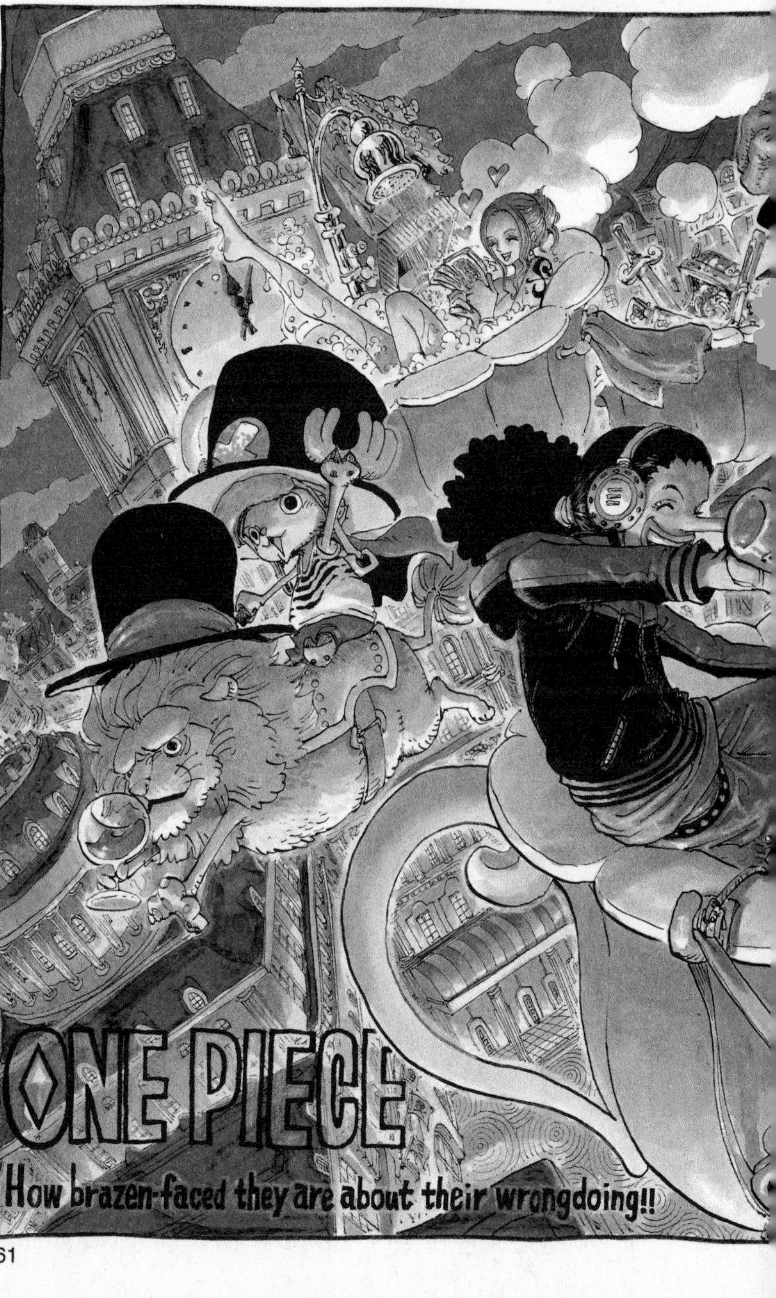
ONE PIECE
How brazen-faced they are about their wrongdoing!!

vol.68
ONE PIECE

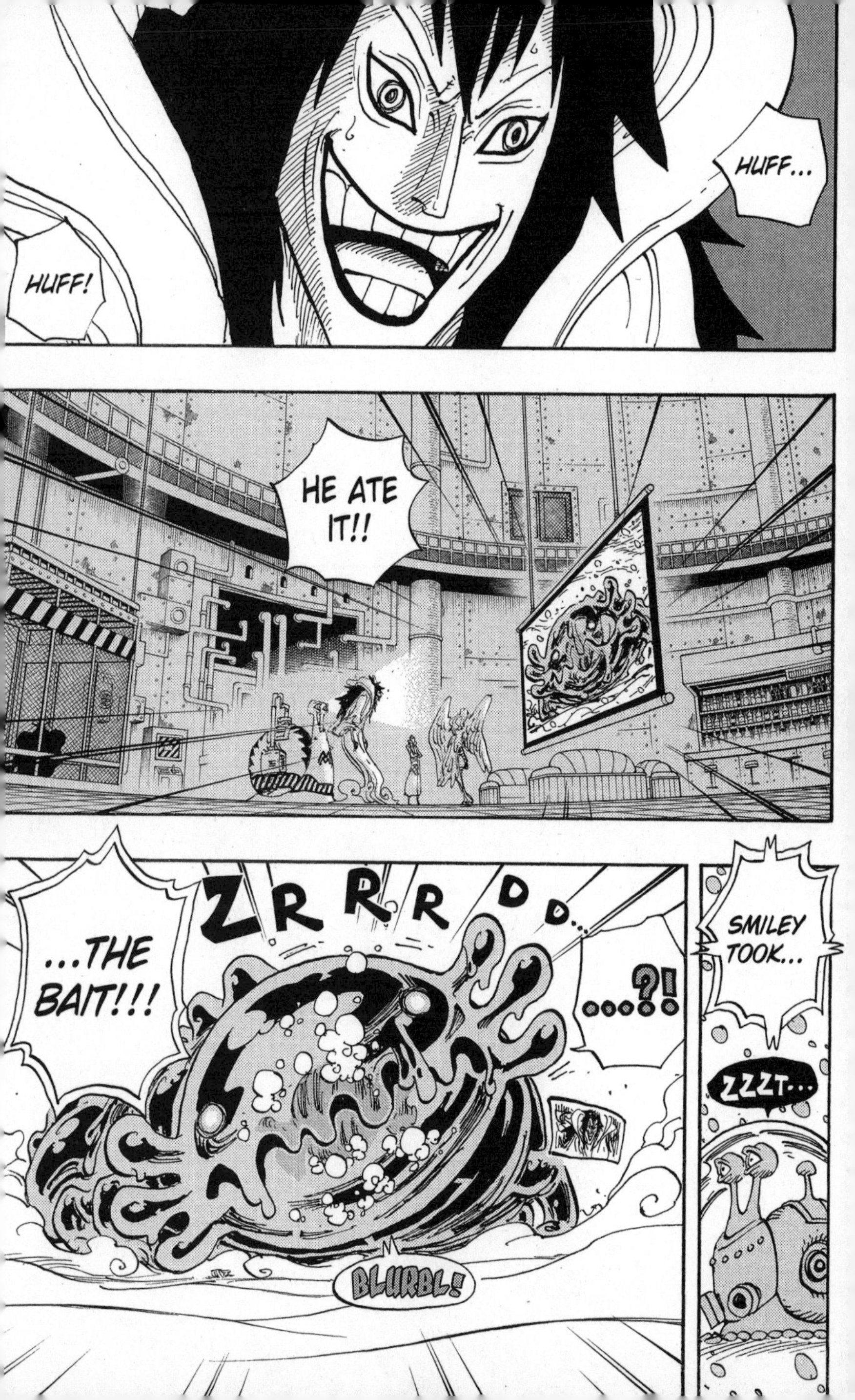

HUFF...
HUFF!
HE ATE IT!!
SMILEY TOOK...
ZZZT...
...?!
ZRRRDD...
...THE BAIT!!!
BLURBL!

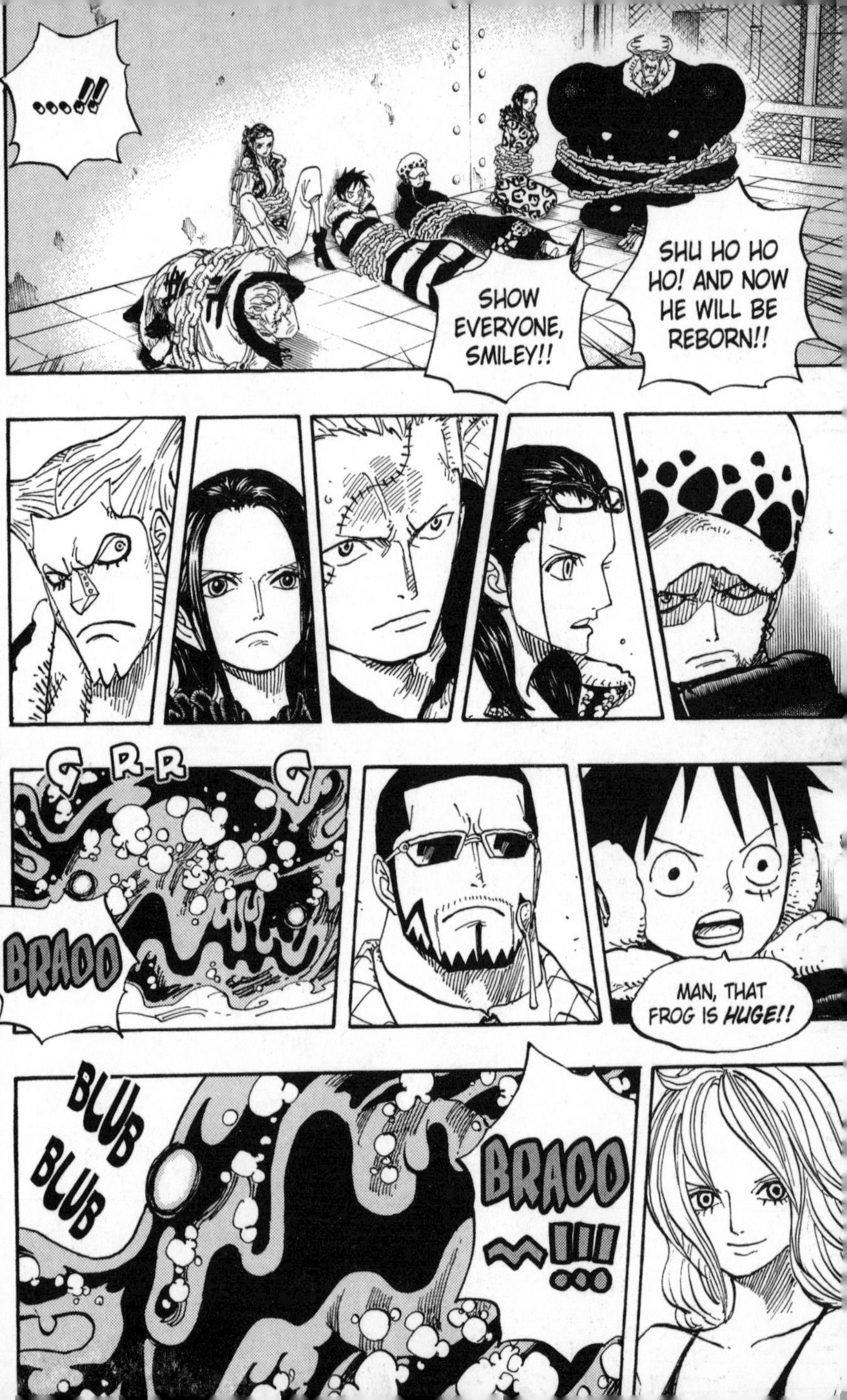
SHU HO HO HO! AND NOW HE WILL BE REBORN!!
SHOW EVERYONE, SMILEY!!
....!!
MAN, THAT FROG IS HUGE!!
G R R G
BRADO
BRADO ~!!!...
BLUB BLUB BLUB

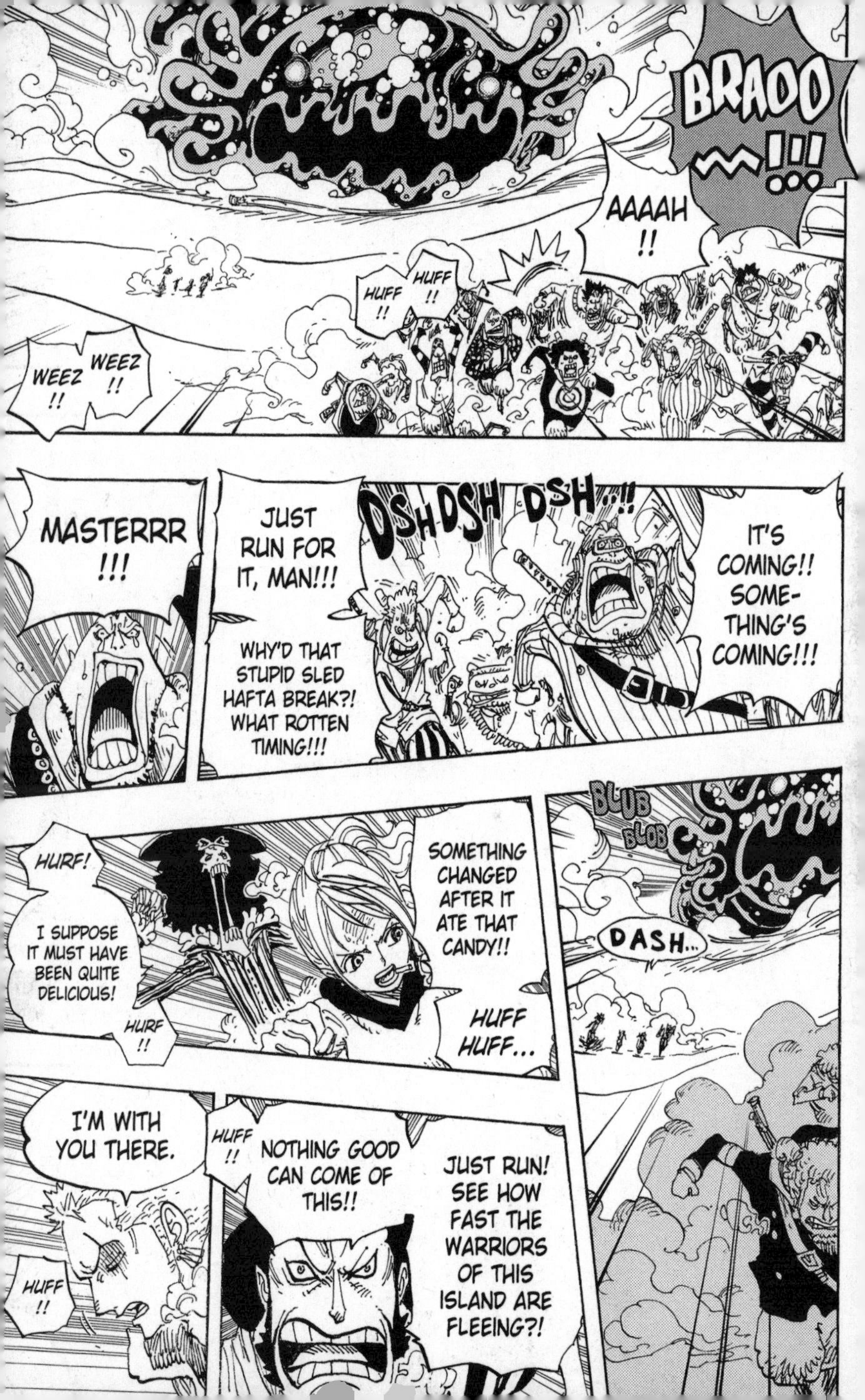
BRADOO~!!!
AAAAH!!
HUFF!!
HUFF!!
WEEZ!!
WEEZ!!
DSHDSH DSH..!!
IT'S COMING!! SOME-THING'S COMING!!!
JUST RUN FOR IT, MAN!!!
WHY'D THAT STUPID SLED HAFTA BREAK?! WHAT ROTTEN TIMING!!!
MASTERRR!!!
BLUB BLOB
DASH...
SOMETHING CHANGED AFTER IT ATE THAT CANDY!!
HUFF HUFF...
HURF!
I SUPPOSE IT MUST HAVE BEEN QUITE DELICIOUS!
HURF!!
JUST RUN! SEE HOW FAST THE WARRIORS OF THIS ISLAND ARE FLEEING?!
NOTHING GOOD CAN COME OF THIS!!
HUFF!!
I'M WITH YOU THERE.
HUFF!!

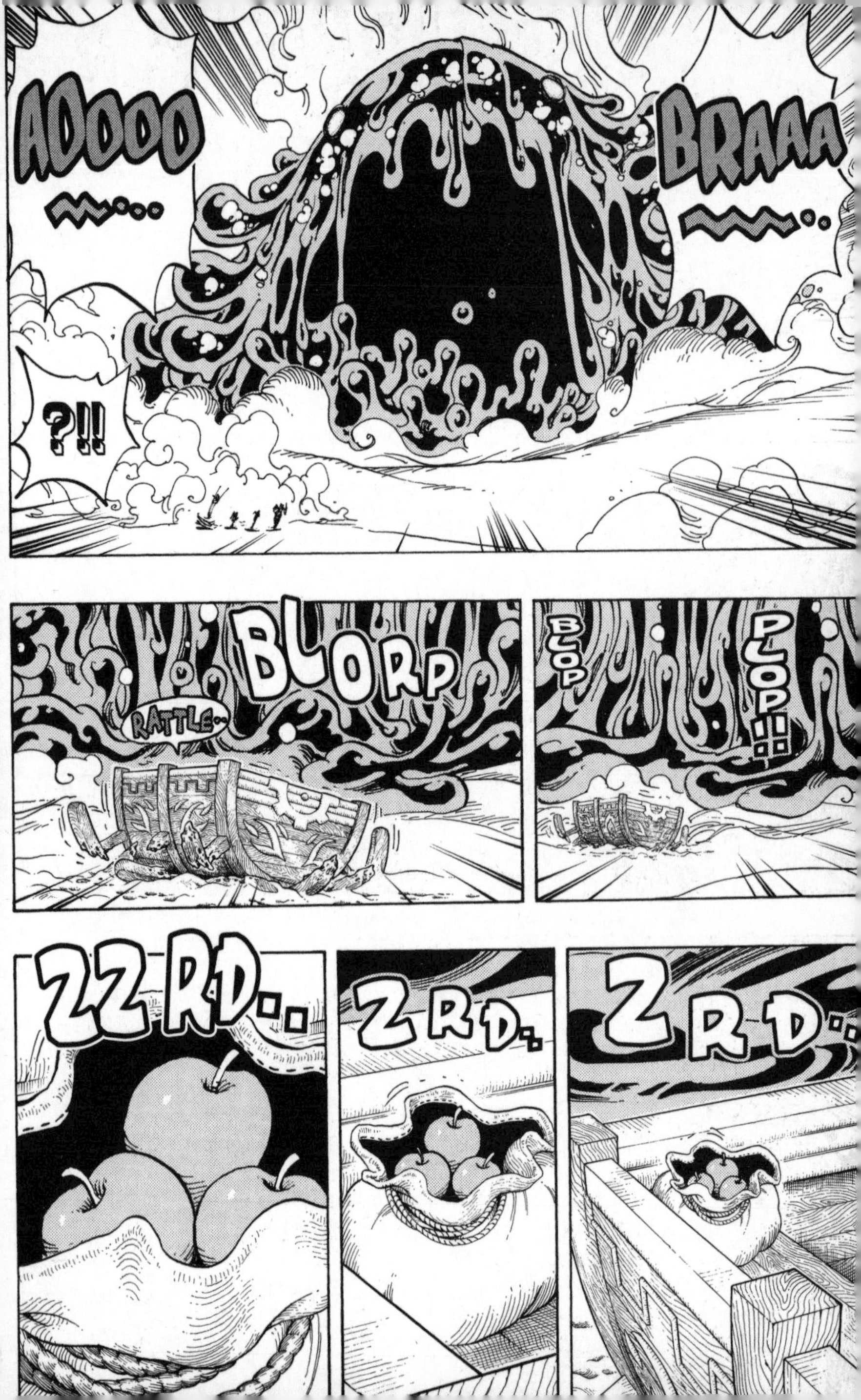
BRAAA
~~..
ADOOO
~...
?!!
BLOP
PLOP!!
BLORP
RATTLE..
ZRD..
ZRD.
ZZRD..

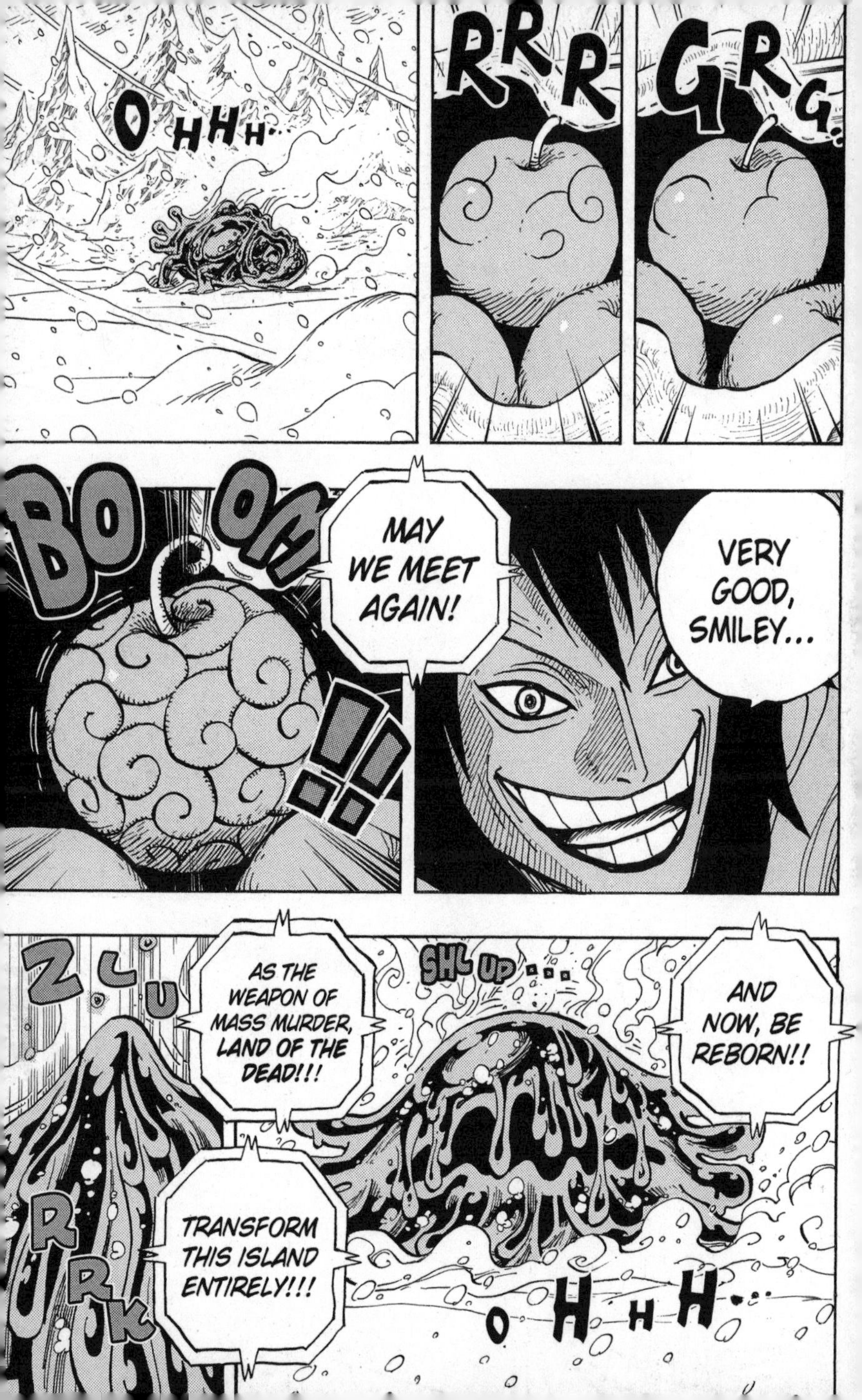
RRRGRG...
OHHH...
VERY GOOD, SMILEY...
MAY WE MEET AGAIN!
BOOM!!
AND NOW, BE REBORN!!
SHLUP...
AS THE WEAPON OF MASS MURDER, LAND OF THE DEAD!!!
ZLU
TRANSFORM THIS ISLAND ENTIRELY!!!
OHHH...
RRK

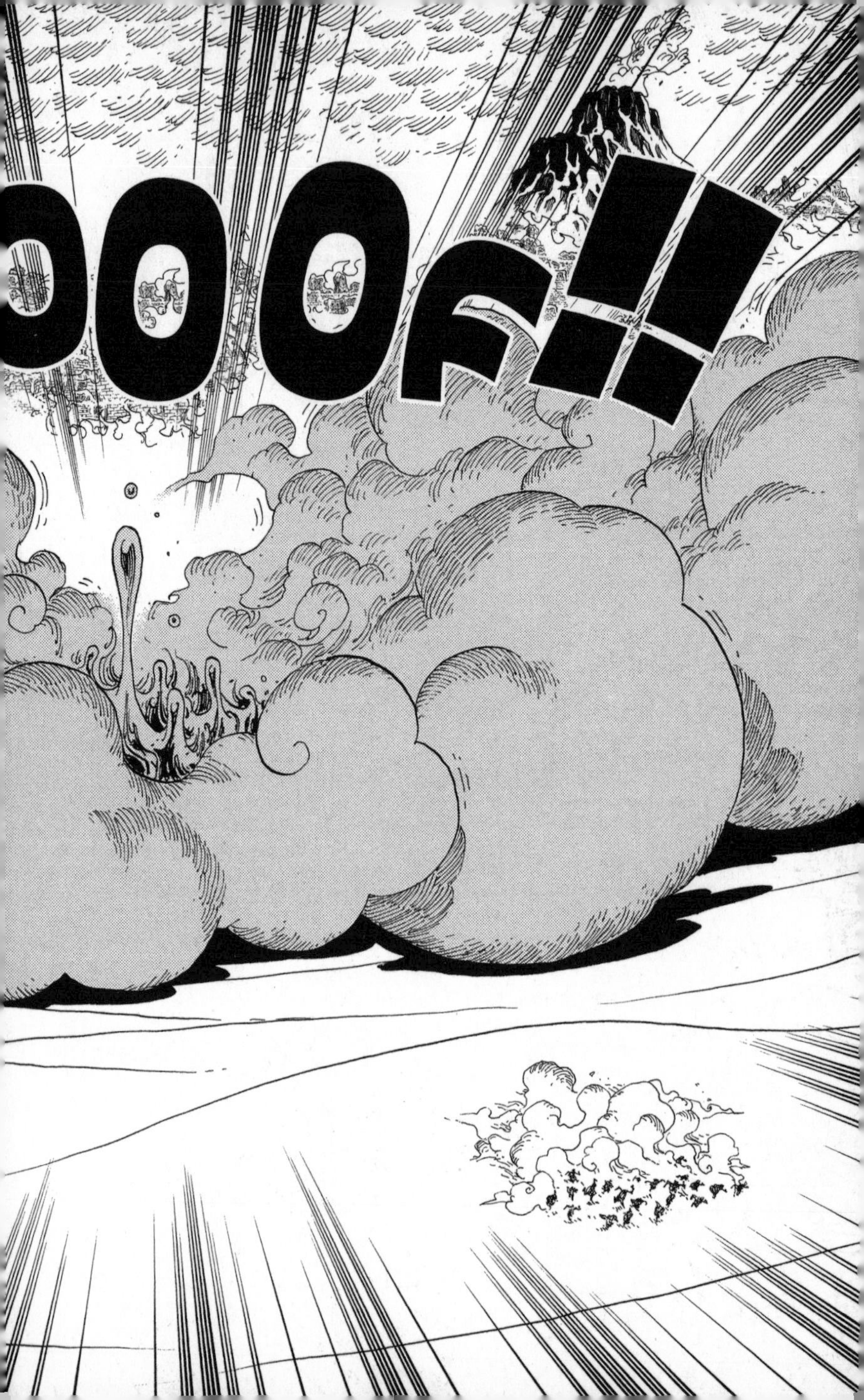
OOOA!!

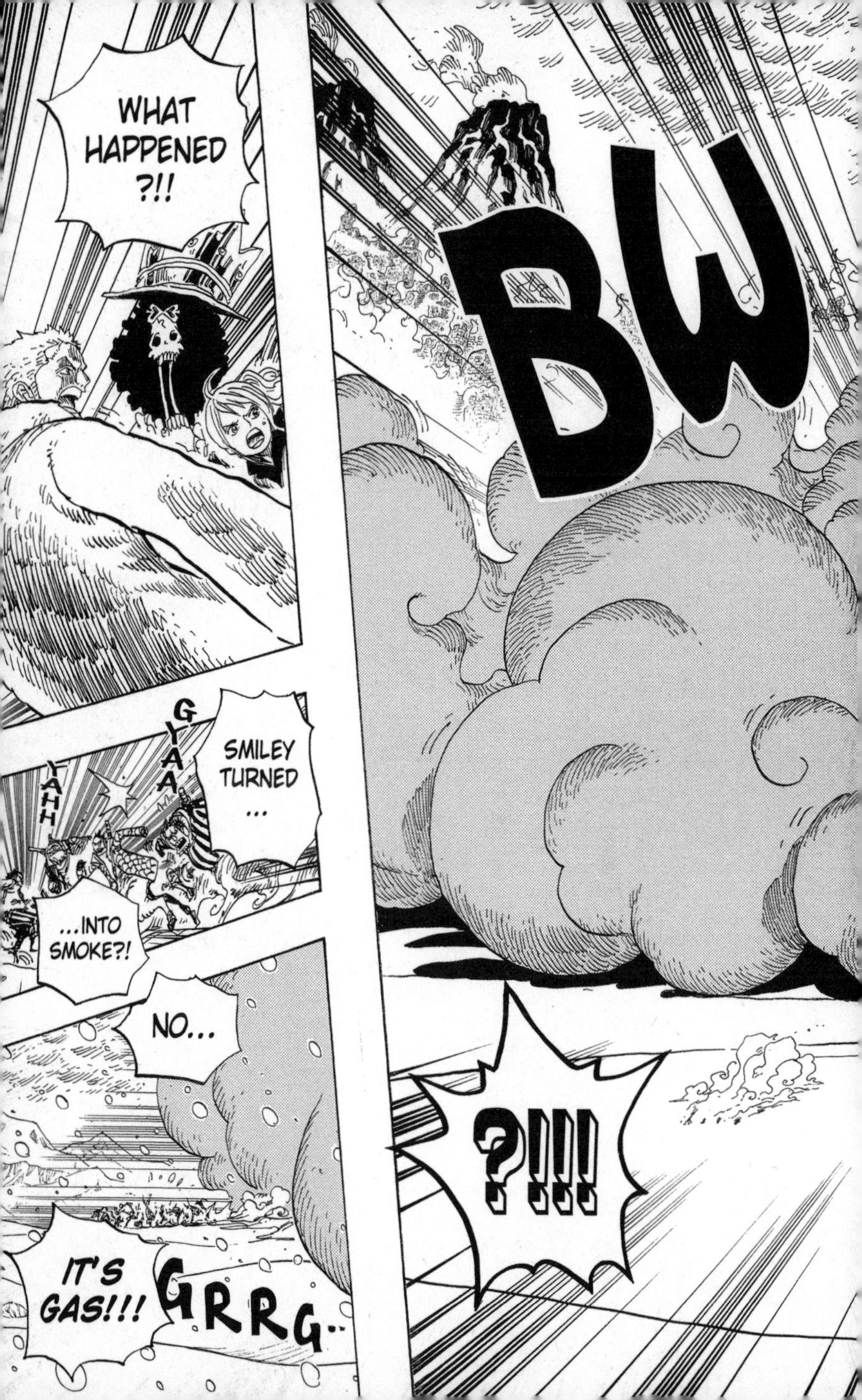
BW
?!!!
WHAT HAPPENED ?!!
GYAA
YAHH
SMILEY TURNED ...
...INTO SMOKE?!
NO...
IT'S GAS!!!
GRRG..

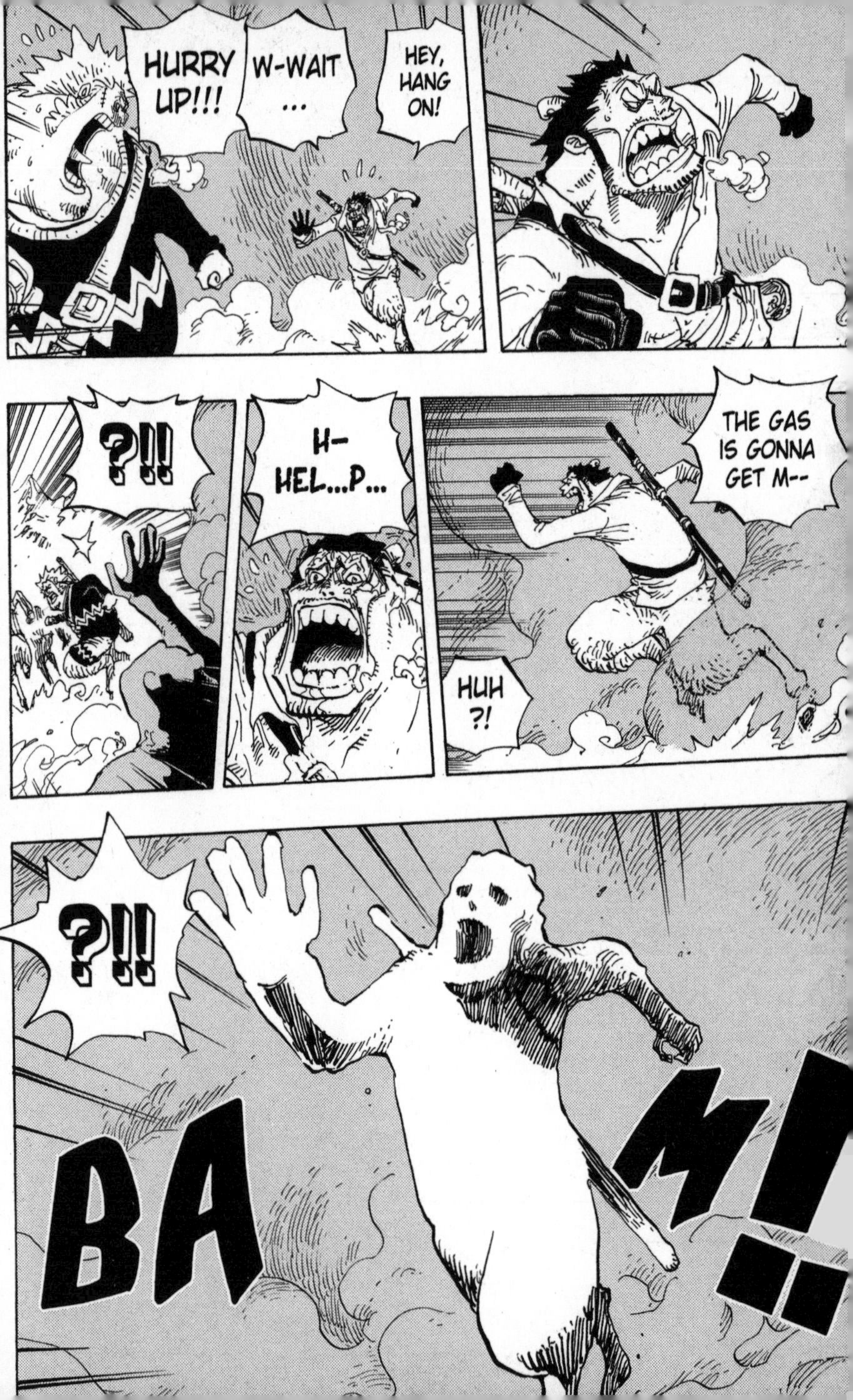
HEY, HANG ON!
W-WAIT ...
HURRY UP!!!
THE GAS IS GONNA GET M--
HUH ?!
H- HEL...P...
?!!
?!!
BAM!!

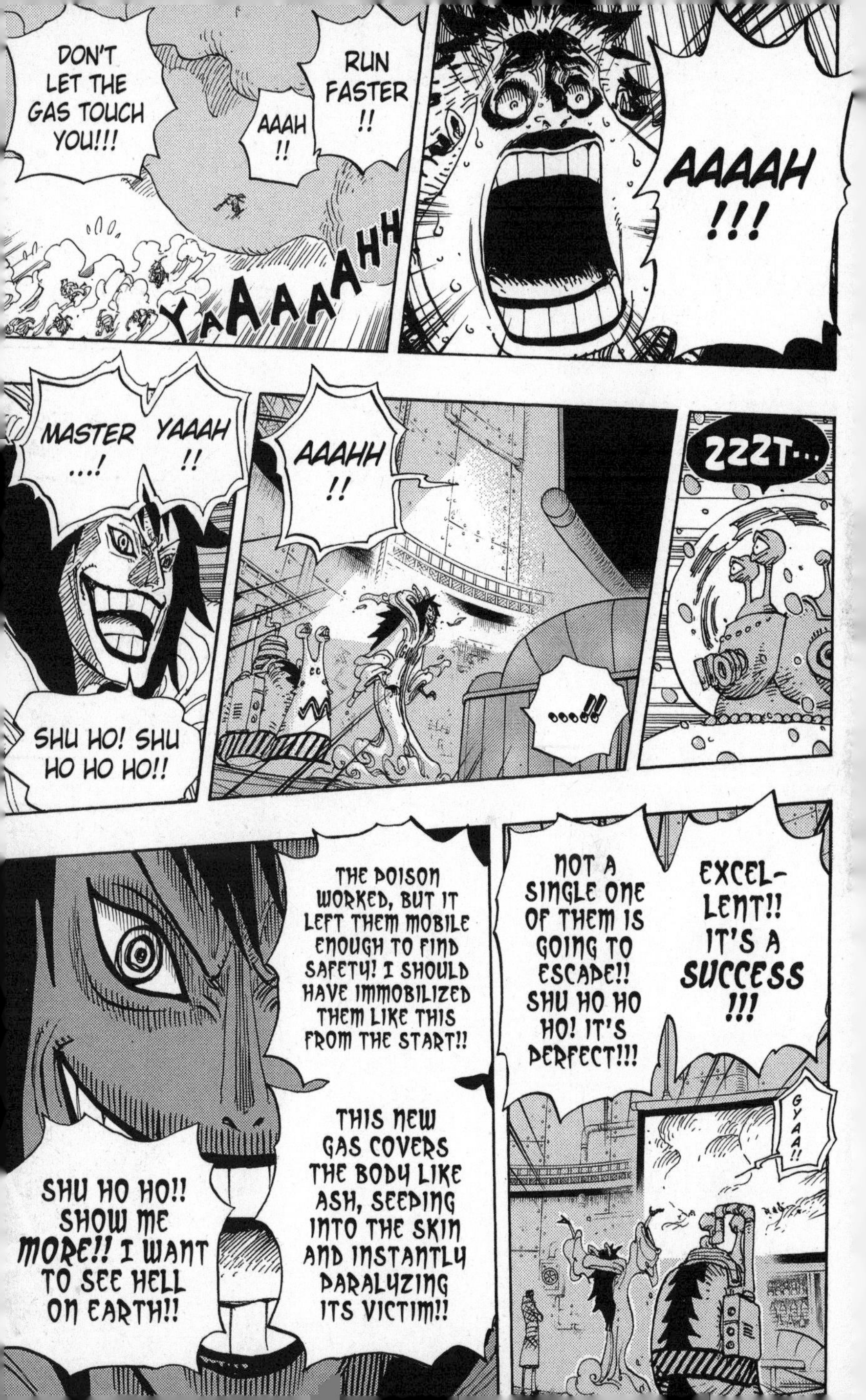

AAAAH!!!
RUN FASTER!!
AAAH!!
DON'T LET THE GAS TOUCH YOU!!!
YAAAAAAHH
ZZZT...
AAAHH!!
....!!
YAAAH!!
MASTER...!
SHU HO! SHU HO HO HO!!
EXCEL-LENT!! IT'S A SUCCESS!!!
NOT A SINGLE ONE OF THEM IS GOING TO ESCAPE!! SHU HO HO HO! IT'S PERFECT!!!
GYAA!!
THE POISON WORKED, BUT IT LEFT THEM MOBILE ENOUGH TO FIND SAFETY! I SHOULD HAVE IMMOBILIZED THEM LIKE THIS FROM THE START!!
THIS NEW GAS COVERS THE BODY LIKE ASH, SEEPING INTO THE SKIN AND INSTANTLY PARALYZING ITS VICTIM!!
SHU HO HO!! SHOW ME MORE!! I WANT TO SEE HELL ON EARTH!!

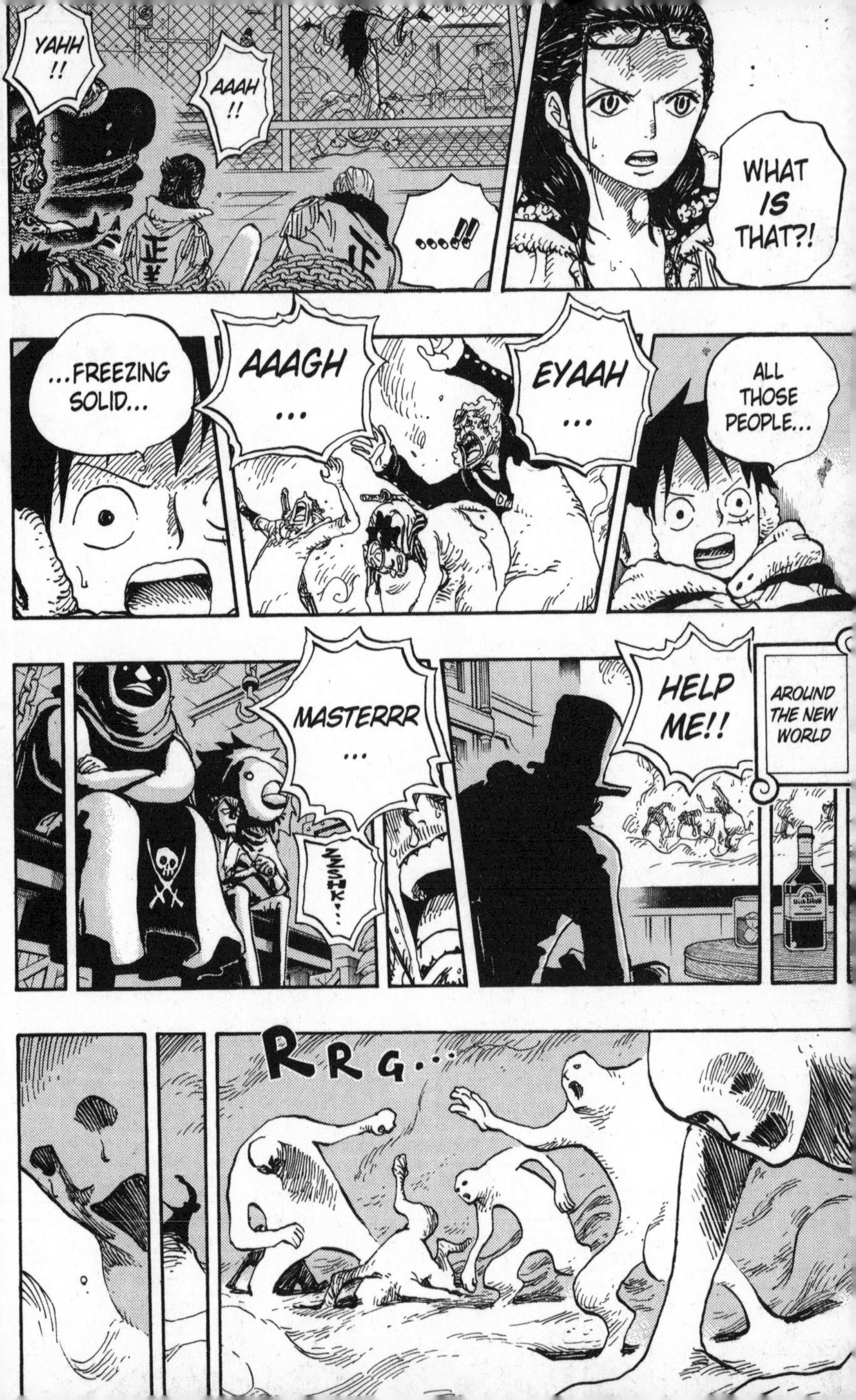
WHAT IS THAT?!
....!!
AAAH !!
YAHH !!
ALL THOSE PEOPLE...
EYAAH ...
AAAGH ...
...FREEZING SOLID...
AROUND THE NEW WORLD
HELP ME!!
MASTERRR ...
ZZSHK...
RRG...

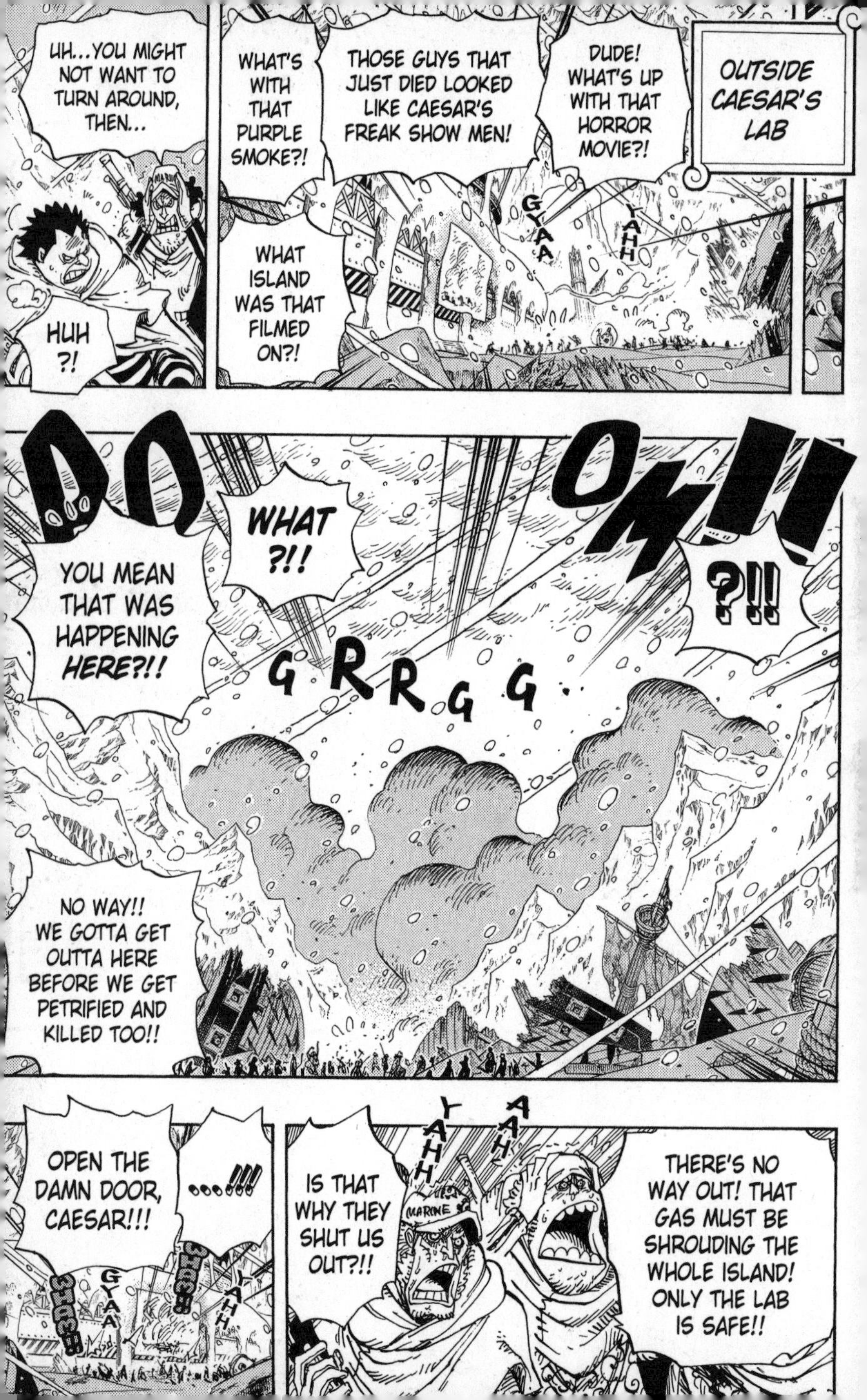
OUTSIDE CAESAR'S LAB
DUDE! WHAT'S UP WITH THAT HORROR MOVIE?!
GYAA
YAHH
THOSE GUYS THAT JUST DIED LOOKED LIKE CAESAR'S FREAK SHOW MEN!
WHAT'S WITH THAT PURPLE SMOKE?!
WHAT ISLAND WAS THAT FILMED ON?!
UH...YOU MIGHT NOT WANT TO TURN AROUND, THEN...
HUH ?!
DOOM!!
?!!
WHAT ?!!
YOU MEAN THAT WAS HAPPENING HERE?!!
GRRRGG
NO WAY!! WE GOTTA GET OUTTA HERE BEFORE WE GET PETRIFIED AND KILLED TOO!!
THERE'S NO WAY OUT! THAT GAS MUST BE SHROUDING THE WHOLE ISLAND! ONLY THE LAB IS SAFE!!
AAH
YAHH
MARINE
IS THAT WHY THEY SHUT US OUT?!!
...!!!
OPEN THE DAMN DOOR, CAESAR!!!
GYAA
YAHH

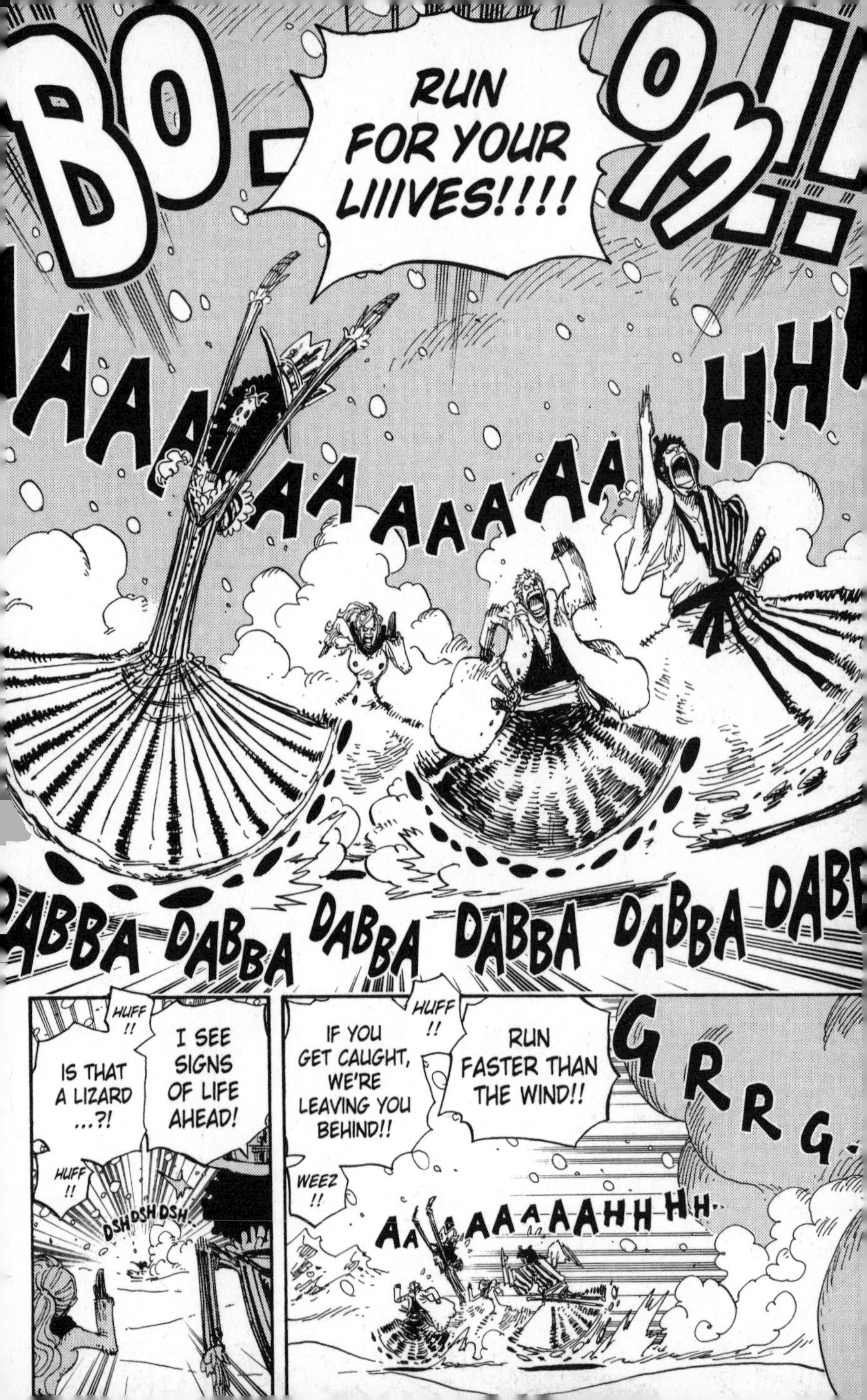
BO-
RUN FOR YOUR LIIIVES!!!!
AAAAAAAAAAAAHH
DABBA DABBA DABBA DABBA DABBA
GRRRG
RUN FASTER THAN THE WIND!!
HUFF !!
IF YOU GET CAUGHT, WE'RE LEAVING YOU BEHIND!!
WEEZ !!
AAAAAAAHHHHH
HUFF !!
I SEE SIGNS OF LIFE AHEAD!
IS THAT A LIZARD ...?!
HUFF !!
DSH DSH DSH

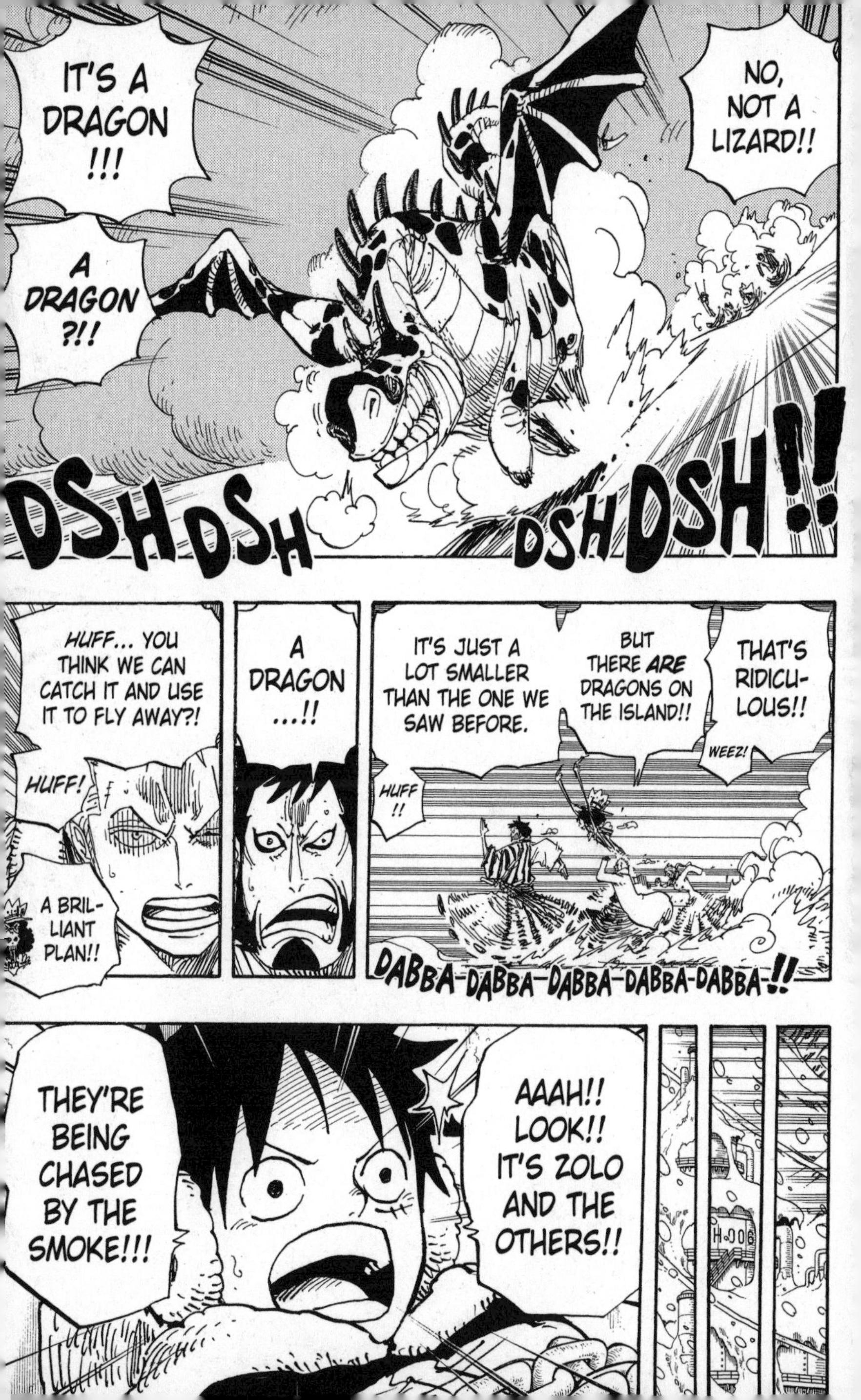

NO, NOT A LIZARD!!
IT'S A DRAGON!!!
A DRAGON?!!
DSHDSH!!
DSHDSH
THAT'S RIDICULOUS!!
WEEZ!
BUT THERE *ARE* DRAGONS ON THE ISLAND!!
IT'S JUST A LOT SMALLER THAN THE ONE WE SAW BEFORE.
HUFF!!
DABBA-DABBA-DABBA-DABBA-DABBA-!!
A DRAGON...!!
HUFF... YOU THINK WE CAN CATCH IT AND USE IT TO FLY AWAY?!
HUFF!
A BRILLIANT PLAN!!
AAAH!! LOOK!! IT'S ZOLO AND THE OTHERS!!
THEY'RE BEING CHASED BY THE SMOKE!!!

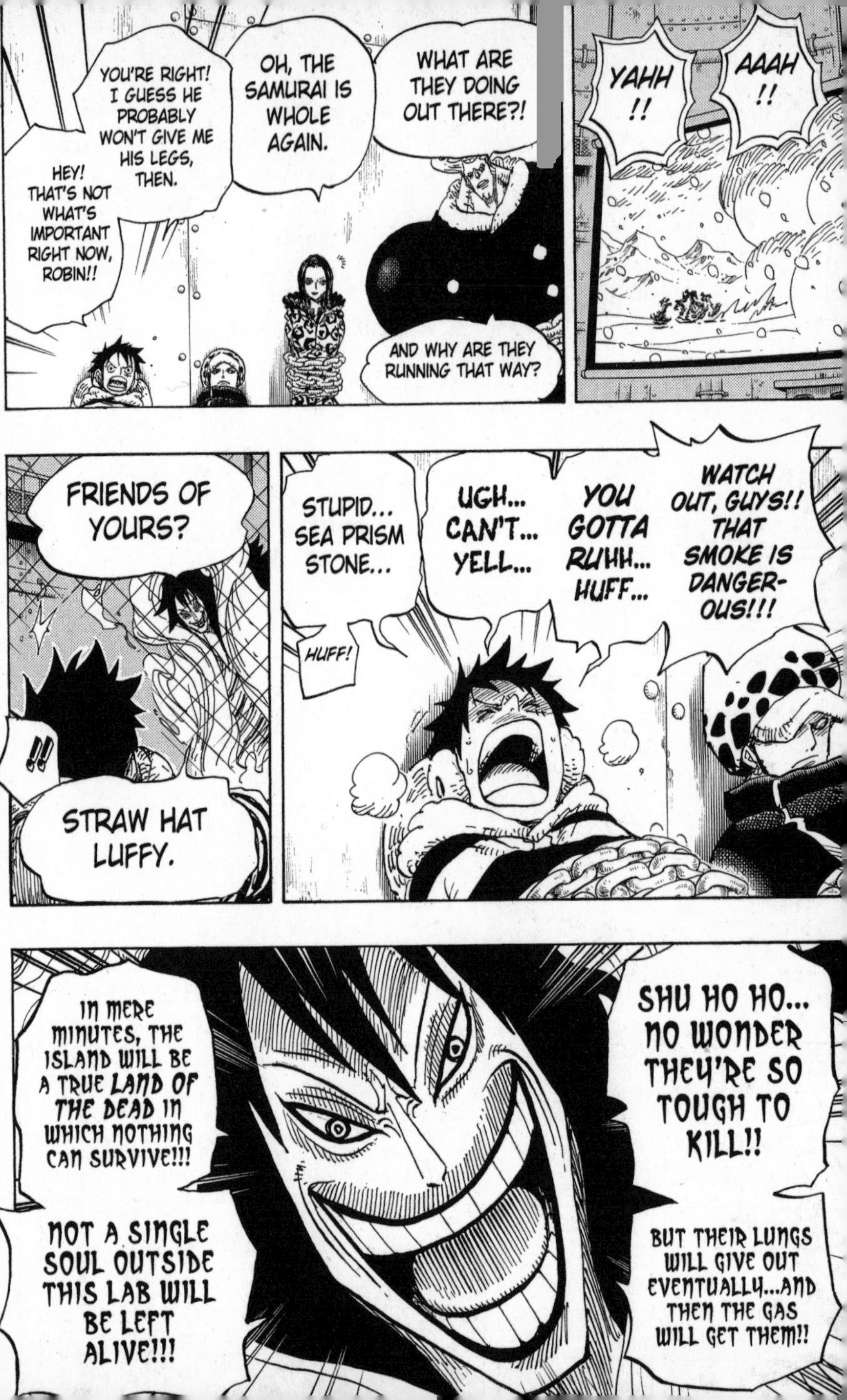
AAAH!!
YAHH!!
WHAT ARE THEY DOING OUT THERE?!
AND WHY ARE THEY RUNNING THAT WAY?
OH, THE SAMURAI IS WHOLE AGAIN.
YOU'RE RIGHT! I GUESS HE PROBABLY WON'T GIVE ME HIS LEGS, THEN.
HEY! THAT'S NOT WHAT'S IMPORTANT RIGHT NOW, ROBIN!!
WATCH OUT, GUYS!! THAT SMOKE IS DANGER-OUS!!!
YOU GOTTA RUHH... HUFF...
UGH... CAN'T... YELL...
STUPID... SEA PRISM STONE...
HUFF!
FRIENDS OF YOURS?
!!
STRAW HAT LUFFY.
SHU HO HO... NO WONDER THEY'RE SO TOUGH TO KILL!!
IN MERE MINUTES, THE ISLAND WILL BE A TRUE LAND OF THE DEAD IN WHICH NOTHING CAN SURVIVE!!!
BUT THEIR LUNGS WILL GIVE OUT EVENTUALLY...AND THEN THE GAS WILL GET THEM!!
NOT A SINGLE SOUL OUTSIDE THIS LAB WILL BE LEFT ALIVE!!!

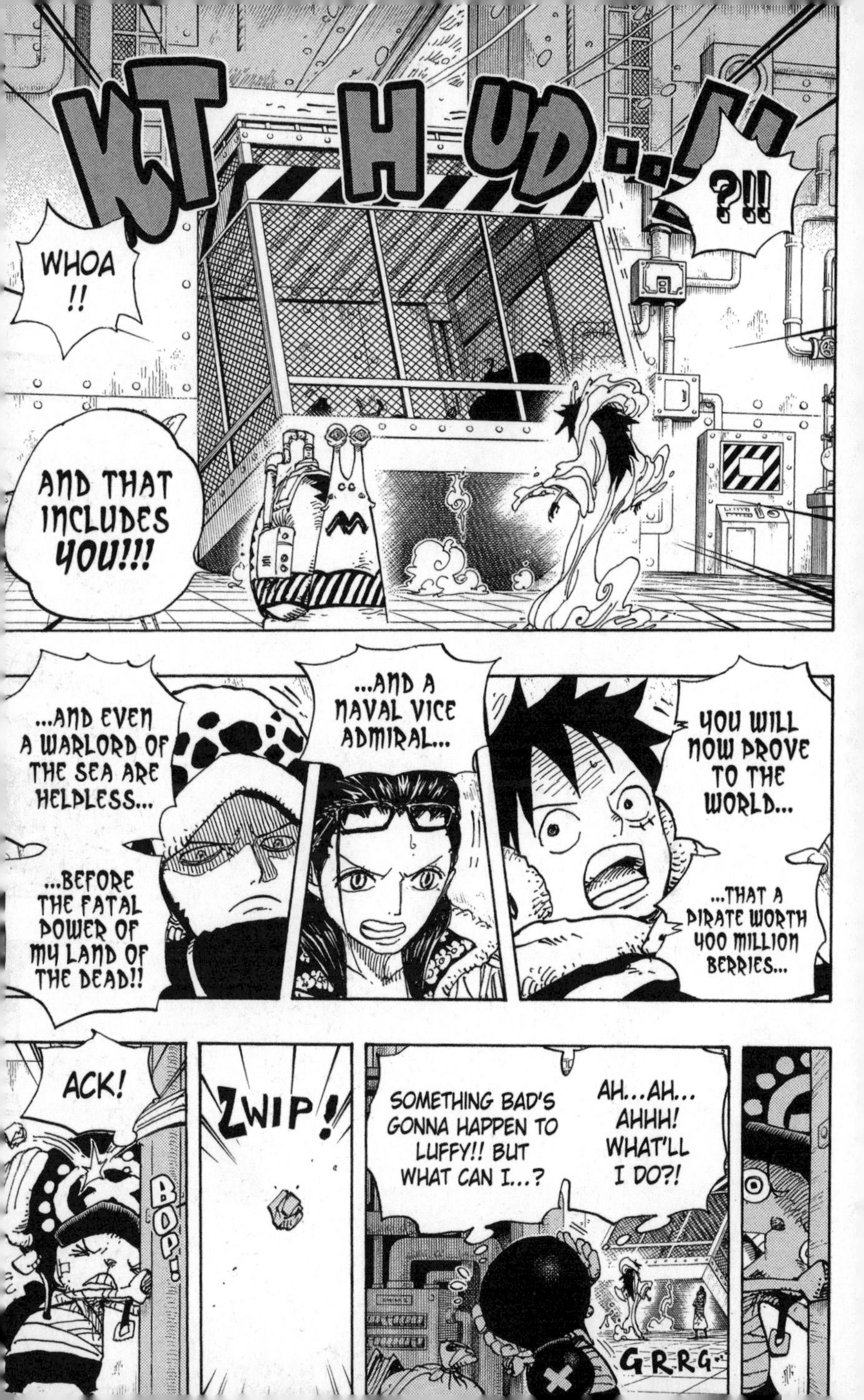
?!!
KTHUD..!!
WHOA !!
AND THAT INCLUDES YOU!!!
YOU WILL NOW PROVE TO THE WORLD...
...THAT A PIRATE WORTH 400 MILLION BERRIES...
...AND A NAVAL VICE ADMIRAL...
...AND EVEN A WARLORD OF THE SEA ARE HELPLESS...
...BEFORE THE FATAL POWER OF MY LAND OF THE DEAD!!
AH...AH... AHHH! WHAT'LL I DO?!
SOMETHING BAD'S GONNA HAPPEN TO LUFFY!! BUT WHAT CAN I...?
GRRG
ZWIP!
ACK!
BOP!

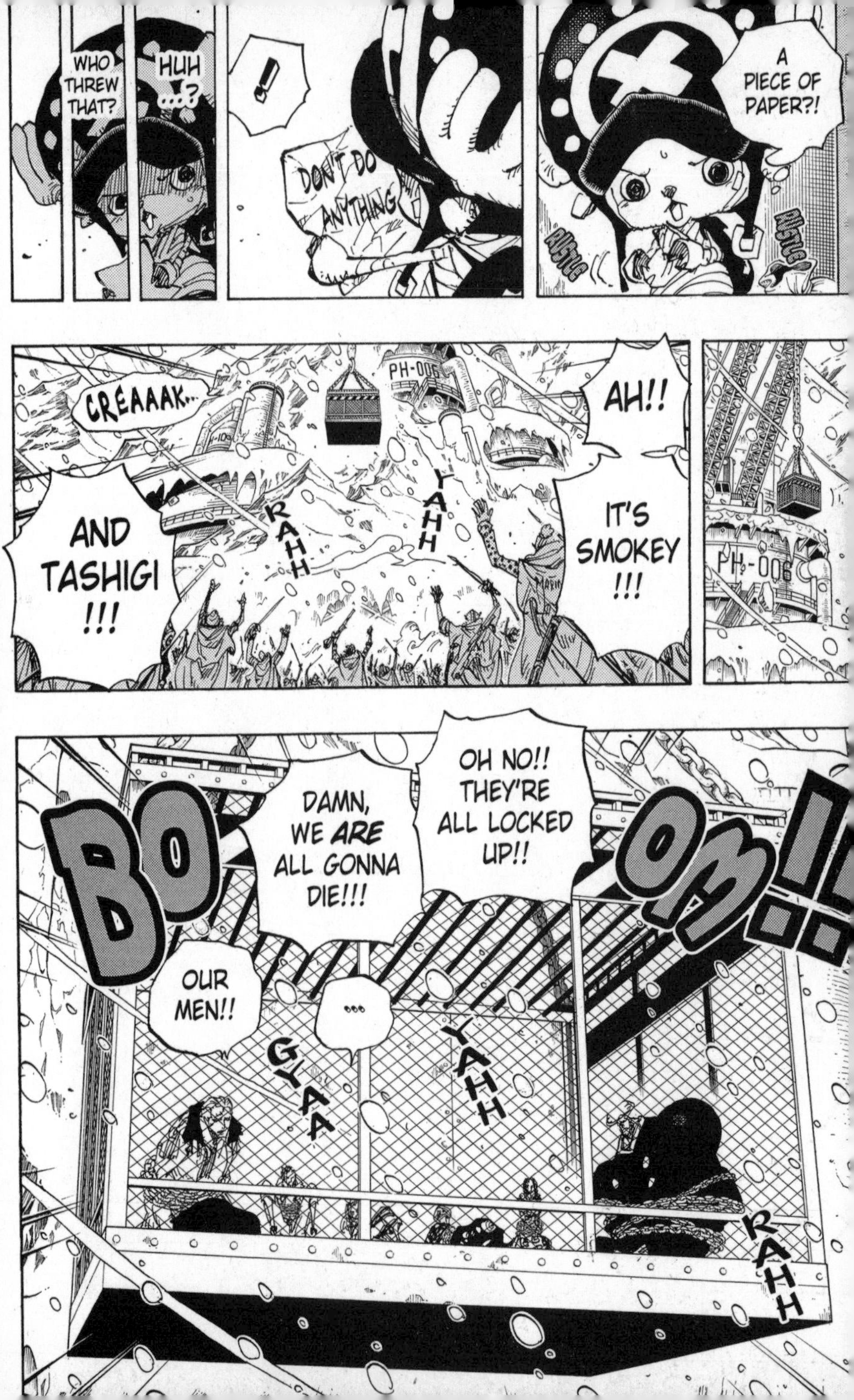
A PIECE OF PAPER?!
RUSTLE
RUSTLE
!
DON'T DO ANYTHING
HUH ...?
WHO THREW THAT?
AH!!
IT'S SMOKEY!!!
CREAAAK...
YAHH
RAHH
AND TASHIGI!!!
BOOM!!
OH NO!! THEY'RE ALL LOCKED UP!!
DAMN, WE *ARE* ALL GONNA DIE!!!
...
OUR MEN!!
YAHH
GYAA
RAHH

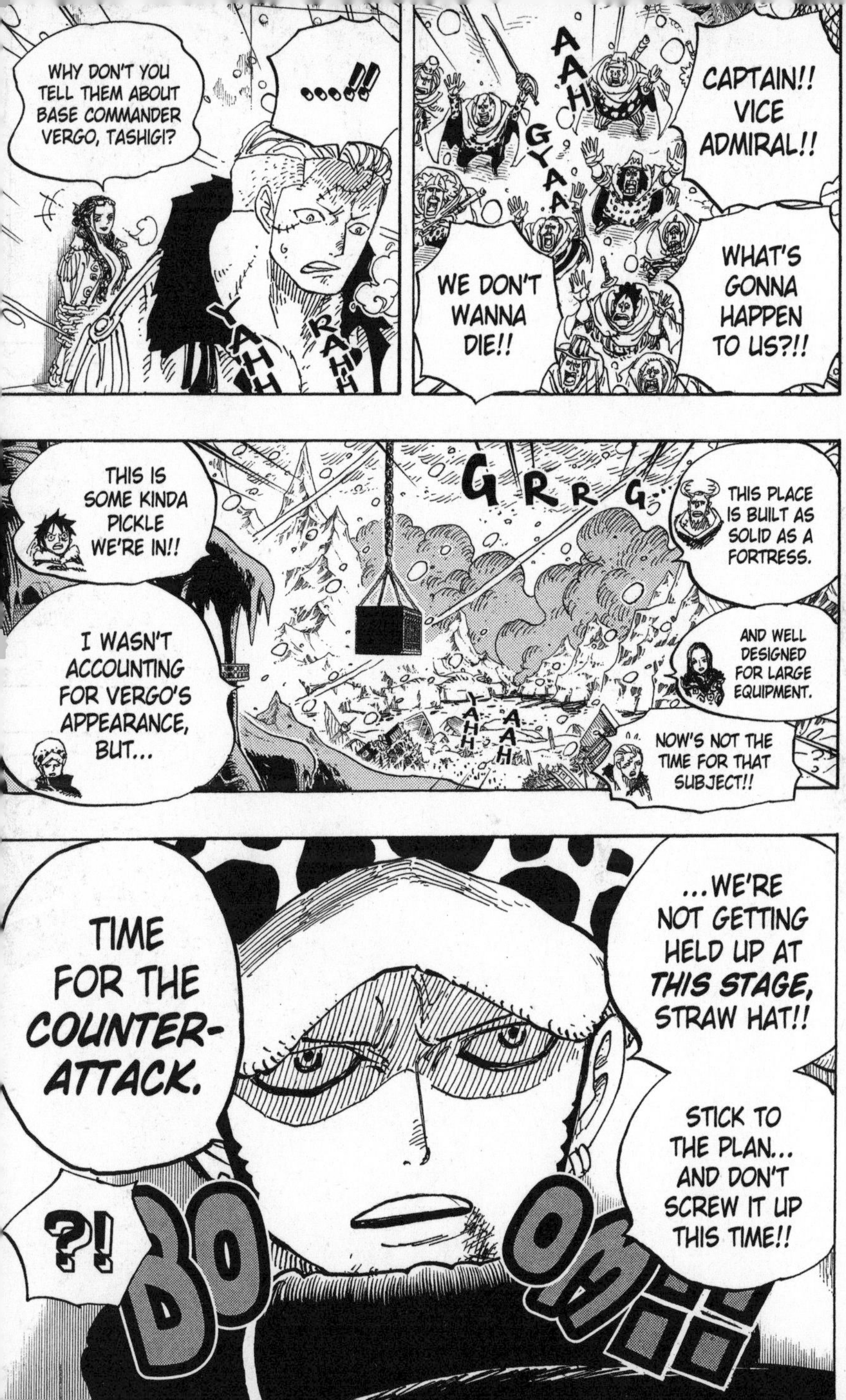
CAPTAIN!! VICE ADMIRAL!!
AAH
GYAAA
WHAT'S GONNA HAPPEN TO US?!!
WE DON'T WANNA DIE!!
....!!
WHY DON'T YOU TELL THEM ABOUT BASE COMMANDER VERGO, TASHIGI?
YAHHH
RAHHH
THIS PLACE IS BUILT AS SOLID AS A FORTRESS.
AND WELL DESIGNED FOR LARGE EQUIPMENT.
NOW'S NOT THE TIME FOR THAT SUBJECT!!
GRRRG...
YAHH
AAAH
THIS IS SOME KINDA PICKLE WE'RE IN!!
I WASN'T ACCOUNTING FOR VERGO'S APPEARANCE, BUT...
...WE'RE NOT GETTING HELD UP AT *THIS STAGE,* STRAW HAT!!
STICK TO THE PLAN... AND DON'T SCREW IT UP THIS TIME!!
TIME FOR THE COUNTER-ATTACK.
?!

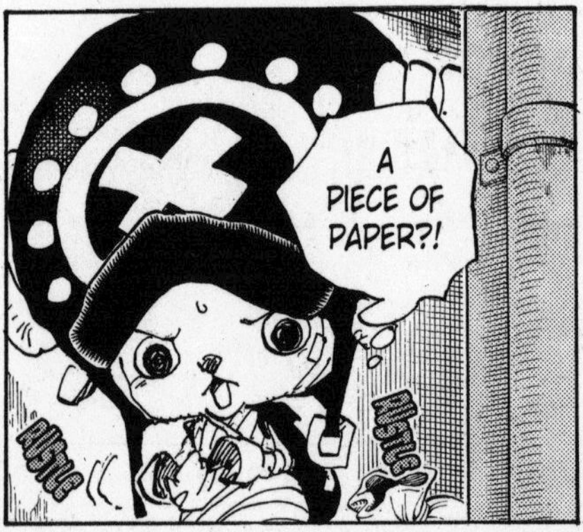
A PIECE OF PAPER?!
RUSTLE
RUSTLE

Chapter 677: COUNTER HAZARD!!

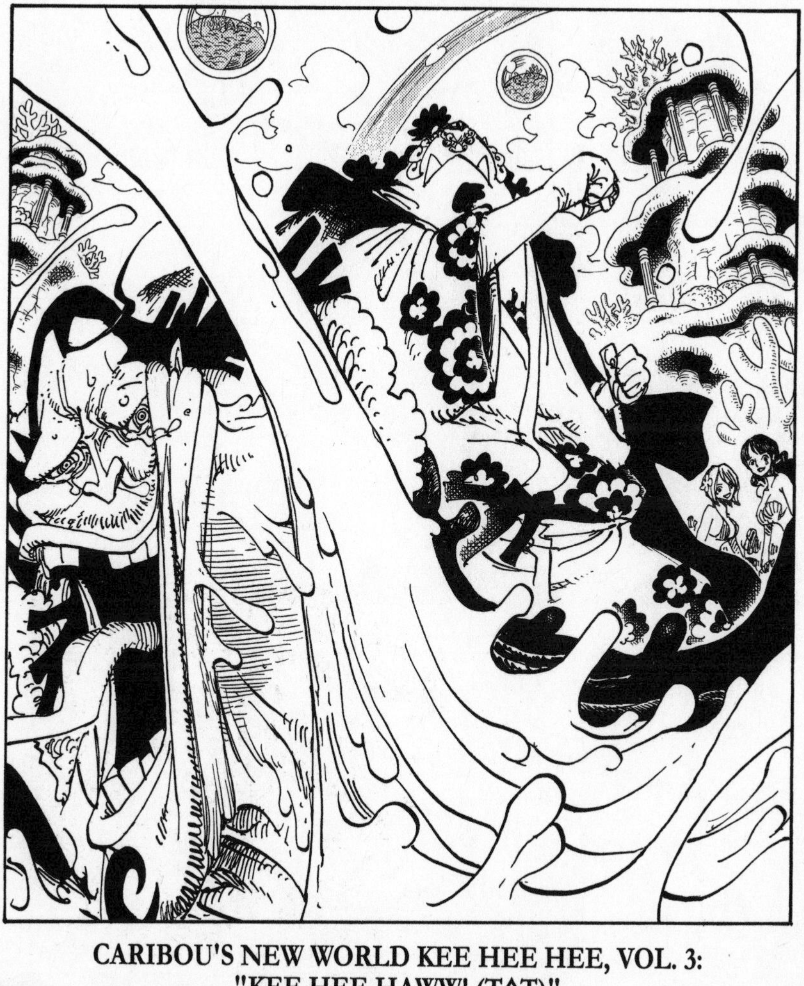

CARIBOU'S NEW WORLD KEE HEE HEE, VOL. 3:
"KEE HEE HAWW! (T◇T)"

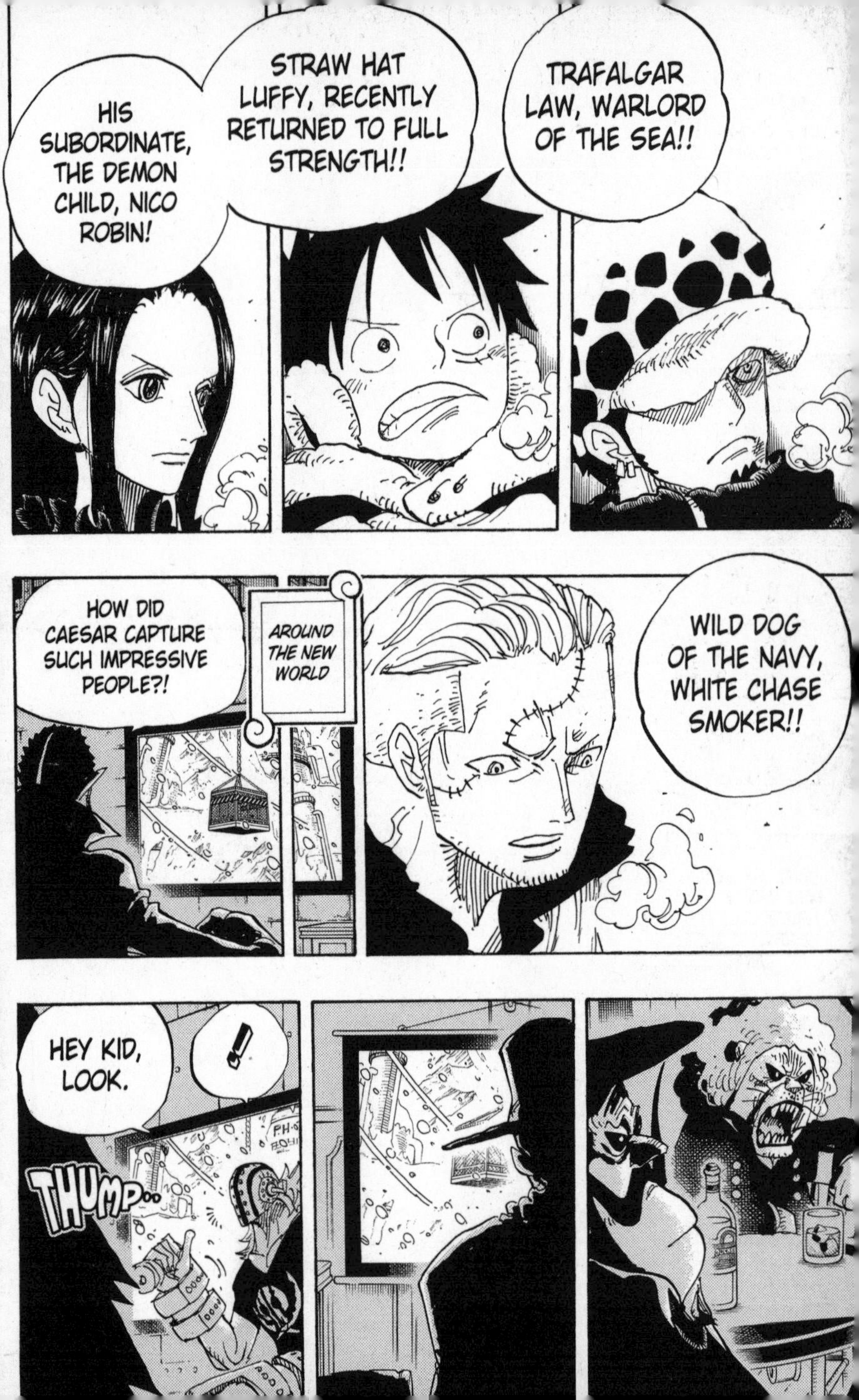
TRAFALGAR LAW, WARLORD OF THE SEA!!
STRAW HAT LUFFY, RECENTLY RETURNED TO FULL STRENGTH!!
HIS SUBORDINATE, THE DEMON CHILD, NICO ROBIN!
WILD DOG OF THE NAVY, WHITE CHASE SMOKER!!
AROUND THE NEW WORLD
HOW DID CAESAR CAPTURE SUCH IMPRESSIVE PEOPLE?!
!
HEY KID, LOOK.
THUMP

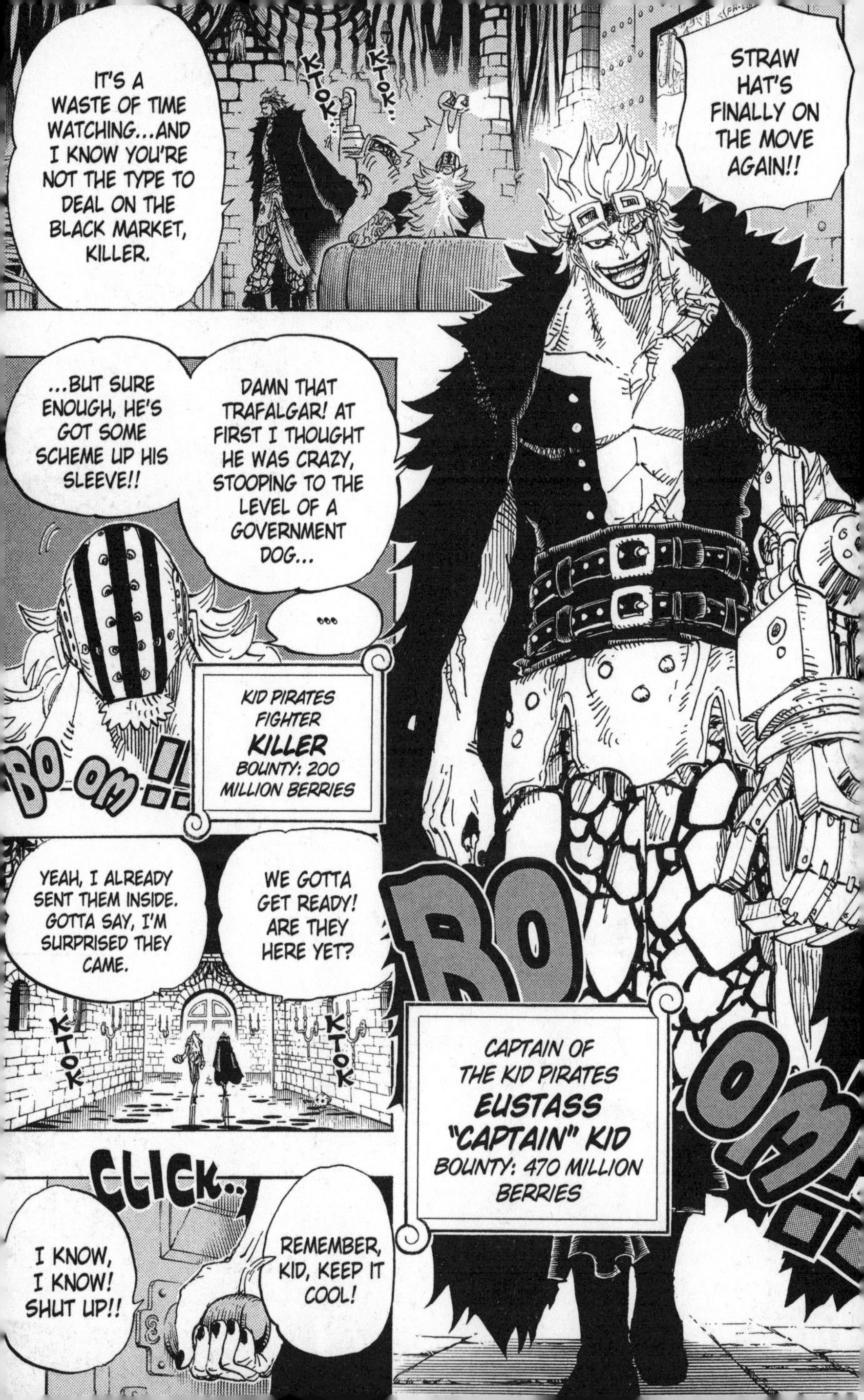
STRAW HAT'S FINALLY ON THE MOVE AGAIN!!
KTOK KTOK..
IT'S A WASTE OF TIME WATCHING...AND I KNOW YOU'RE NOT THE TYPE TO DEAL ON THE BLACK MARKET, KILLER.
BOOM!!
CAPTAIN OF THE KID PIRATES
EUSTASS "CAPTAIN" KID
BOUNTY: 470 MILLION BERRIES
DAMN THAT TRAFALGAR! AT FIRST I THOUGHT HE WAS CRAZY, STOOPING TO THE LEVEL OF A GOVERNMENT DOG...
...BUT SURE ENOUGH, HE'S GOT SOME SCHEME UP HIS SLEEVE!!
...
BOOM!!
KID PIRATES FIGHTER
KILLER
BOUNTY: 200 MILLION BERRIES
WE GOTTA GET READY! ARE THEY HERE YET?
YEAH, I ALREADY SENT THEM INSIDE. GOTTA SAY, I'M SURPRISED THEY CAME.
KTOK KTOK
CLICK..
REMEMBER, KID, KEEP IT COOL!
I KNOW, I KNOW! SHUT UP!!

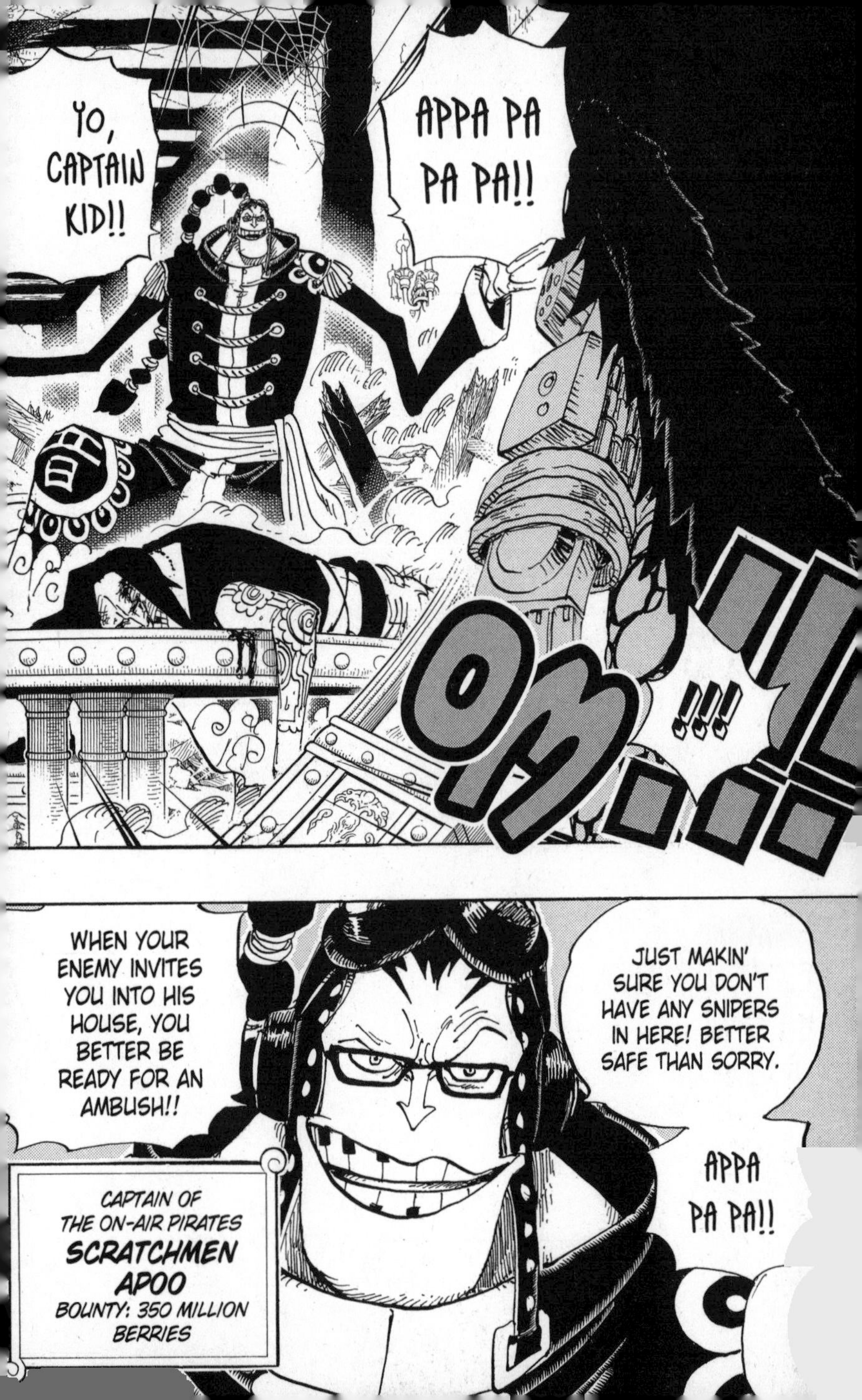
APPA PA PA PA!!
YO, CAPTAIN KID!!
OM..!!!
JUST MAKIN' SURE YOU DON'T HAVE ANY SNIPERS IN HERE! BETTER SAFE THAN SORRY.
WHEN YOUR ENEMY INVITES YOU INTO HIS HOUSE, YOU BETTER BE READY FOR AN AMBUSH!!
APPA PA PA!!
CAPTAIN OF THE ON-AIR PIRATES
SCRATCHMEN APOO
BOUNTY: 350 MILLION BERRIES

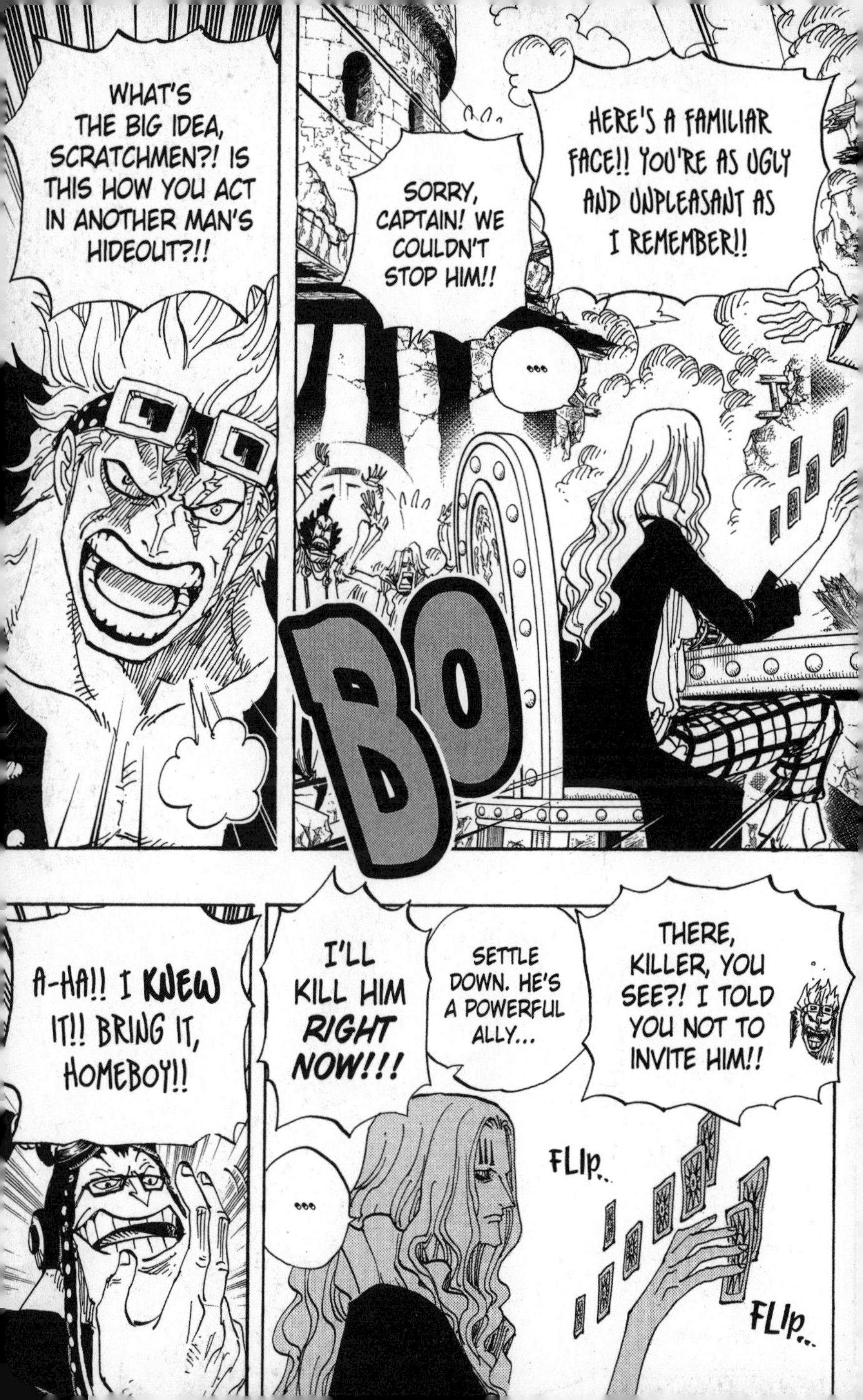
HERE'S A FAMILIAR FACE!! YOU'RE AS UGLY AND UNPLEASANT AS I REMEMBER!!
SORRY, CAPTAIN! WE COULDN'T STOP HIM!!
...
BO
WHAT'S THE BIG IDEA, SCRATCHMEN?! IS THIS HOW YOU ACT IN ANOTHER MAN'S HIDEOUT?!!
THERE, KILLER, YOU SEE?! I TOLD YOU NOT TO INVITE HIM!!
SETTLE DOWN. HE'S A POWERFUL ALLY...
I'LL KILL HIM RIGHT NOW!!!
...
FLIP..
FLIP...
A-HA!! I KNEW IT!! BRING IT, HOMEBOY!!

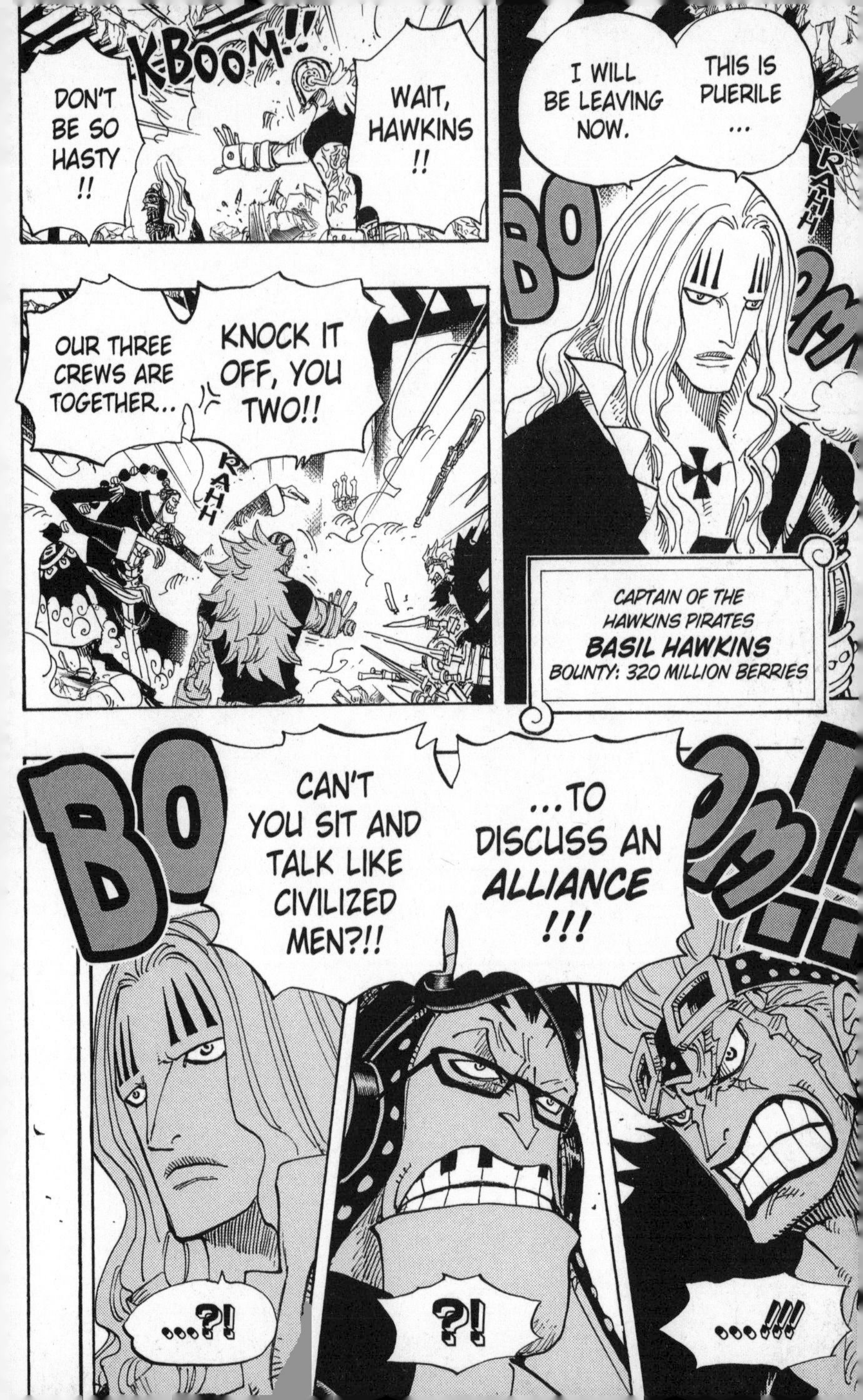
THIS IS PUERILE ...
I WILL BE LEAVING NOW.
BOOM
KRAHH
CAPTAIN OF THE HAWKINS PIRATES
BASIL HAWKINS
BOUNTY: 320 MILLION BERRIES
KBOOM!!
WAIT, HAWKINS !!
DON'T BE SO HASTY !!
KNOCK IT OFF, YOU TWO!!
OUR THREE CREWS ARE TOGETHER...
KRAHH
BOOM!!
...TO DISCUSS AN ALLIANCE !!!
CAN'T YOU SIT AND TALK LIKE CIVILIZED MEN?!!
...!!!
?!
...?!

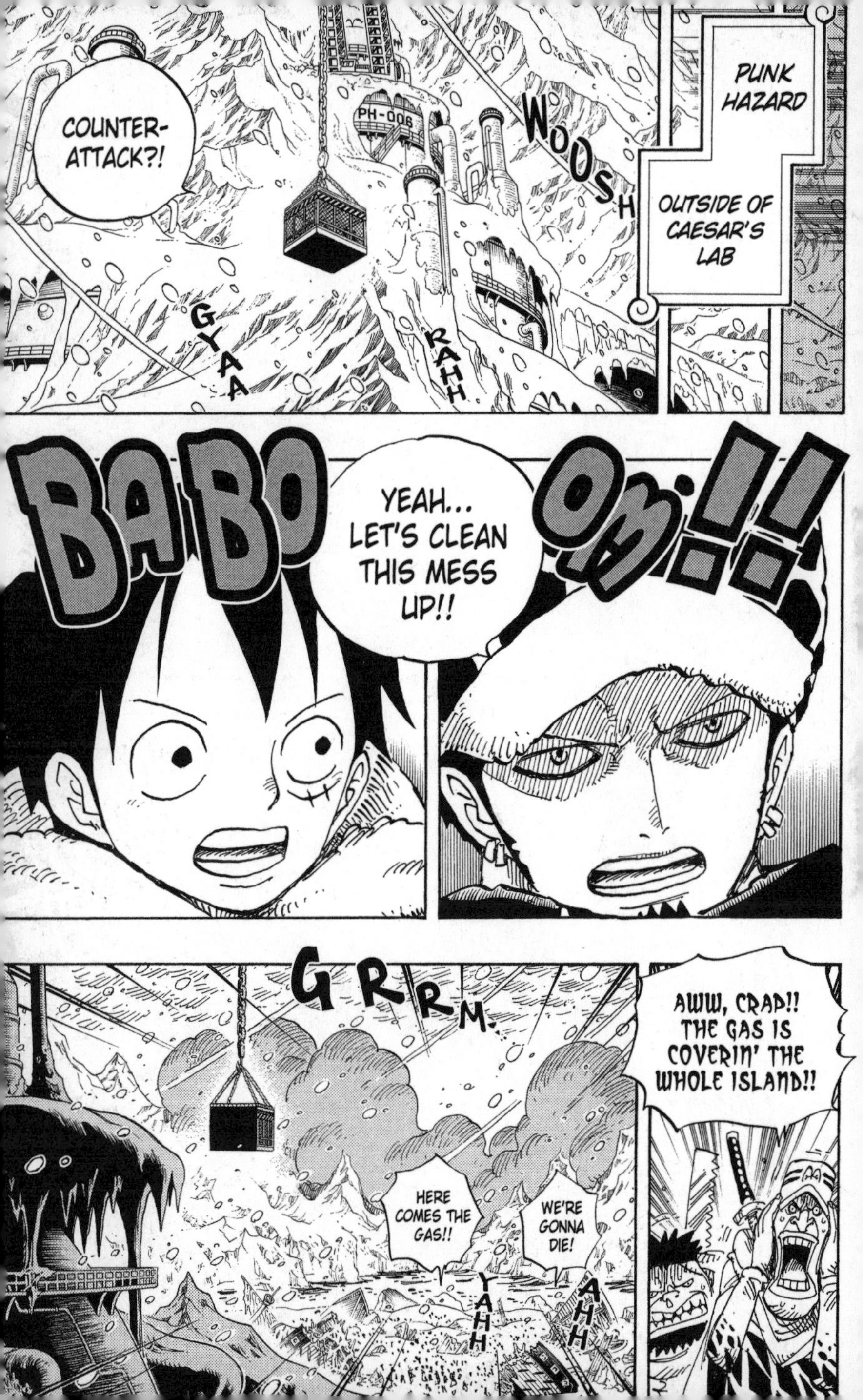
PUNK HAZARD
OUTSIDE OF CAESAR'S LAB
WOOOSH
COUNTER-ATTACK?!
GYAA
RAHH
PH-006
BABOOM!!
YEAH... LET'S CLEAN THIS MESS UP!!
AWW, CRAP!! THE GAS IS COVERIN' THE WHOLE ISLAND!!
GRRRM
WE'RE GONNA DIE!
AHH
HERE COMES THE GAS!!
YAHH

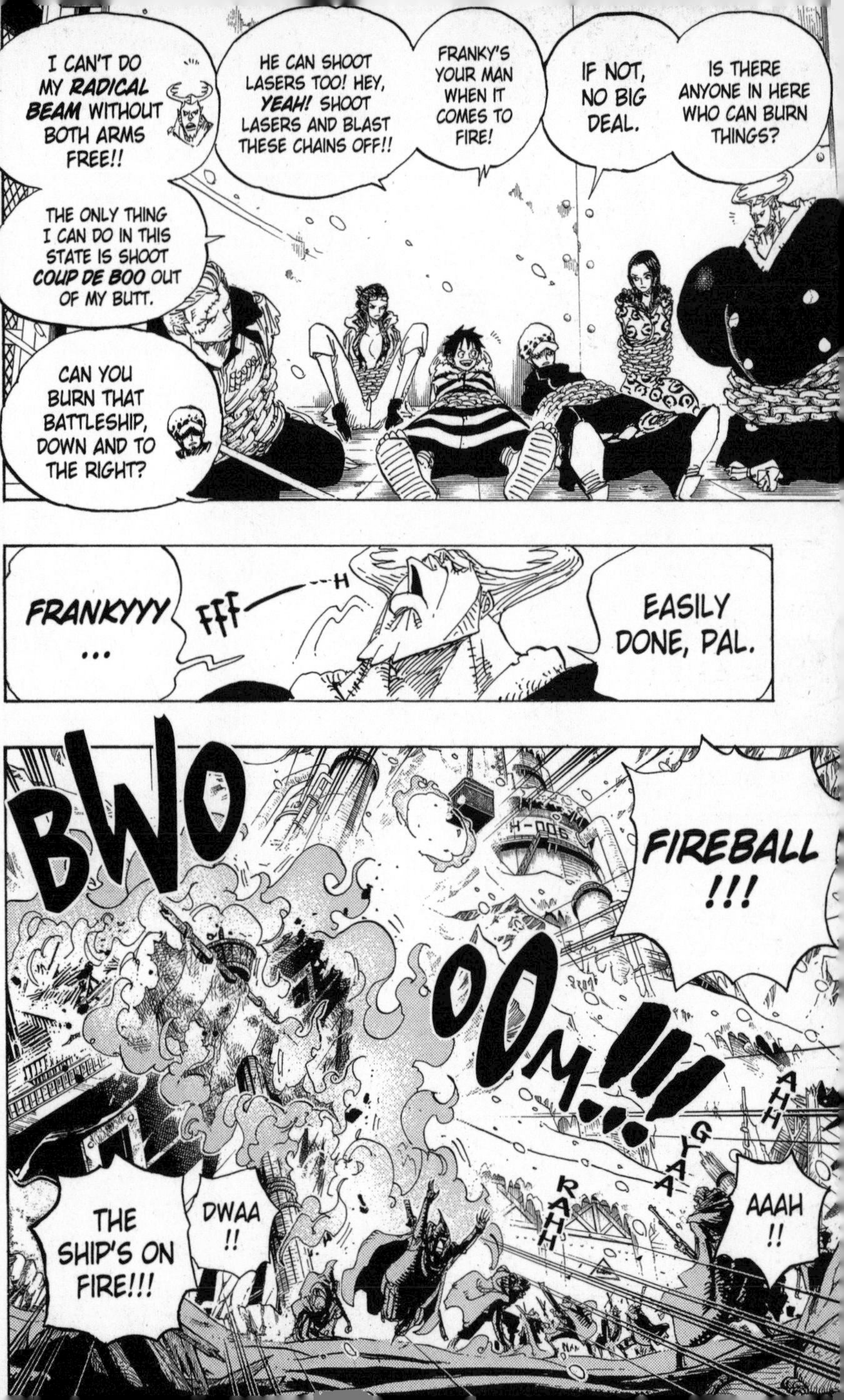
IS THERE ANYONE IN HERE WHO CAN BURN THINGS?
IF NOT, NO BIG DEAL.
FRANKY'S YOUR MAN WHEN IT COMES TO FIRE!
HE CAN SHOOT LASERS TOO! HEY, YEAH! SHOOT LASERS AND BLAST THESE CHAINS OFF!!
I CAN'T DO MY RADICAL BEAM WITHOUT BOTH ARMS FREE!!
THE ONLY THING I CAN DO IN THIS STATE IS SHOOT COUP DE BOO OUT OF MY BUTT.
CAN YOU BURN THAT BATTLESHIP, DOWN AND TO THE RIGHT?
EASILY DONE, PAL.
FFF---H
FRANKYYY ...
FIREBALL !!!
BWOOOM!!!
AHHH
GYAAA
RAHHH
AAAH !!
DWAA !!
THE SHIP'S ON FIRE!!!

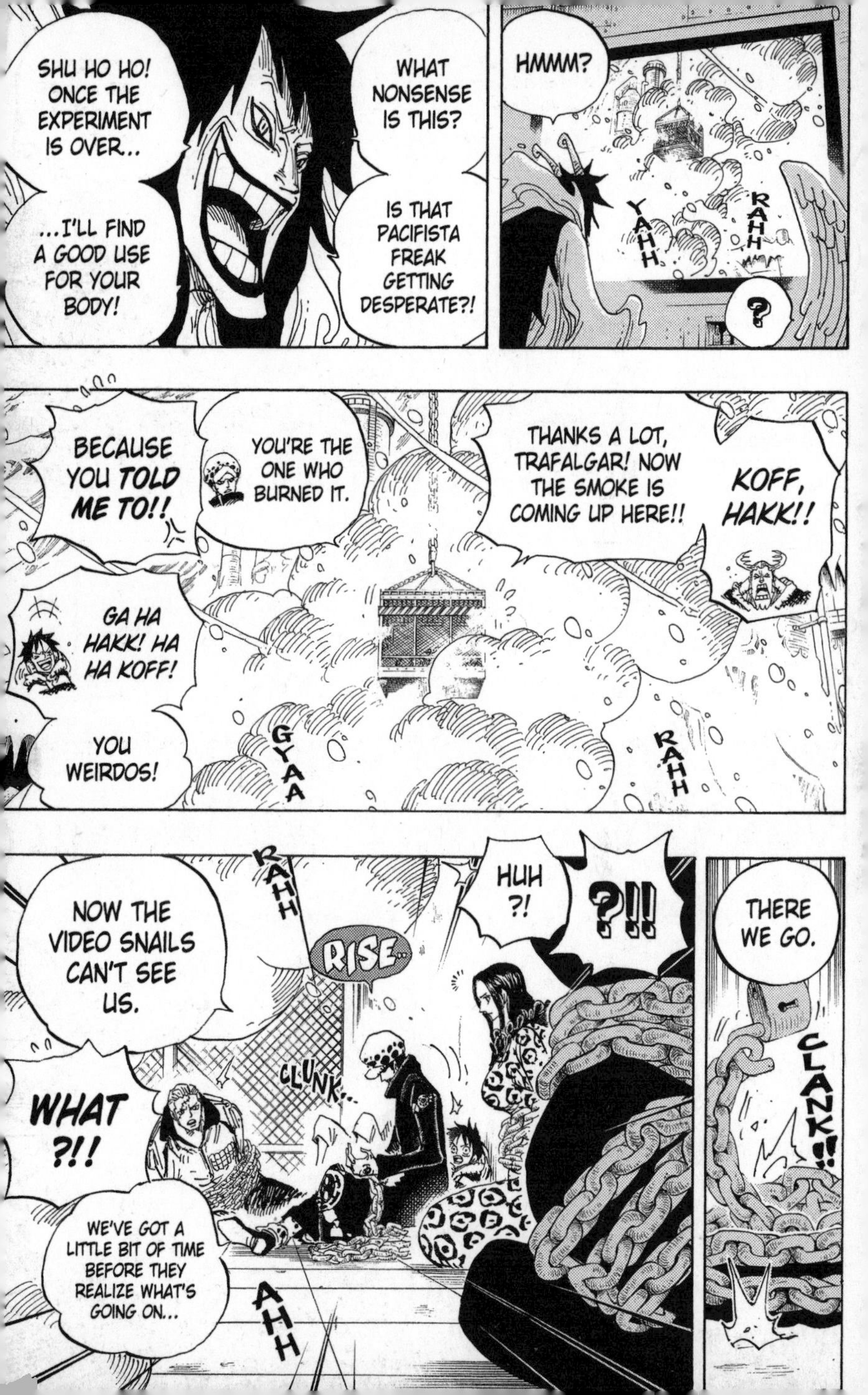
HMMM?
YAHH
RAHH
?
WHAT NONSENSE IS THIS?
IS THAT PACIFISTA FREAK GETTING DESPERATE?!
SHU HO HO! ONCE THE EXPERIMENT IS OVER...
...I'LL FIND A GOOD USE FOR YOUR BODY!
KOFF, HAKK!!
THANKS A LOT, TRAFALGAR! NOW THE SMOKE IS COMING UP HERE!!
YOU'RE THE ONE WHO BURNED IT.
BECAUSE YOU TOLD ME TO!!
GA HA HAKK! HA HA KOFF!
RAHH
GYAA
YOU WEIRDOS!
THERE WE GO.
CLANK!!
?!!
HUH ?!
RAHH
RISE..
NOW THE VIDEO SNAILS CAN'T SEE US.
CLUNK...
WHAT ?!!
WE'VE GOT A LITTLE BIT OF TIME BEFORE THEY REALIZE WHAT'S GOING ON...
AHH

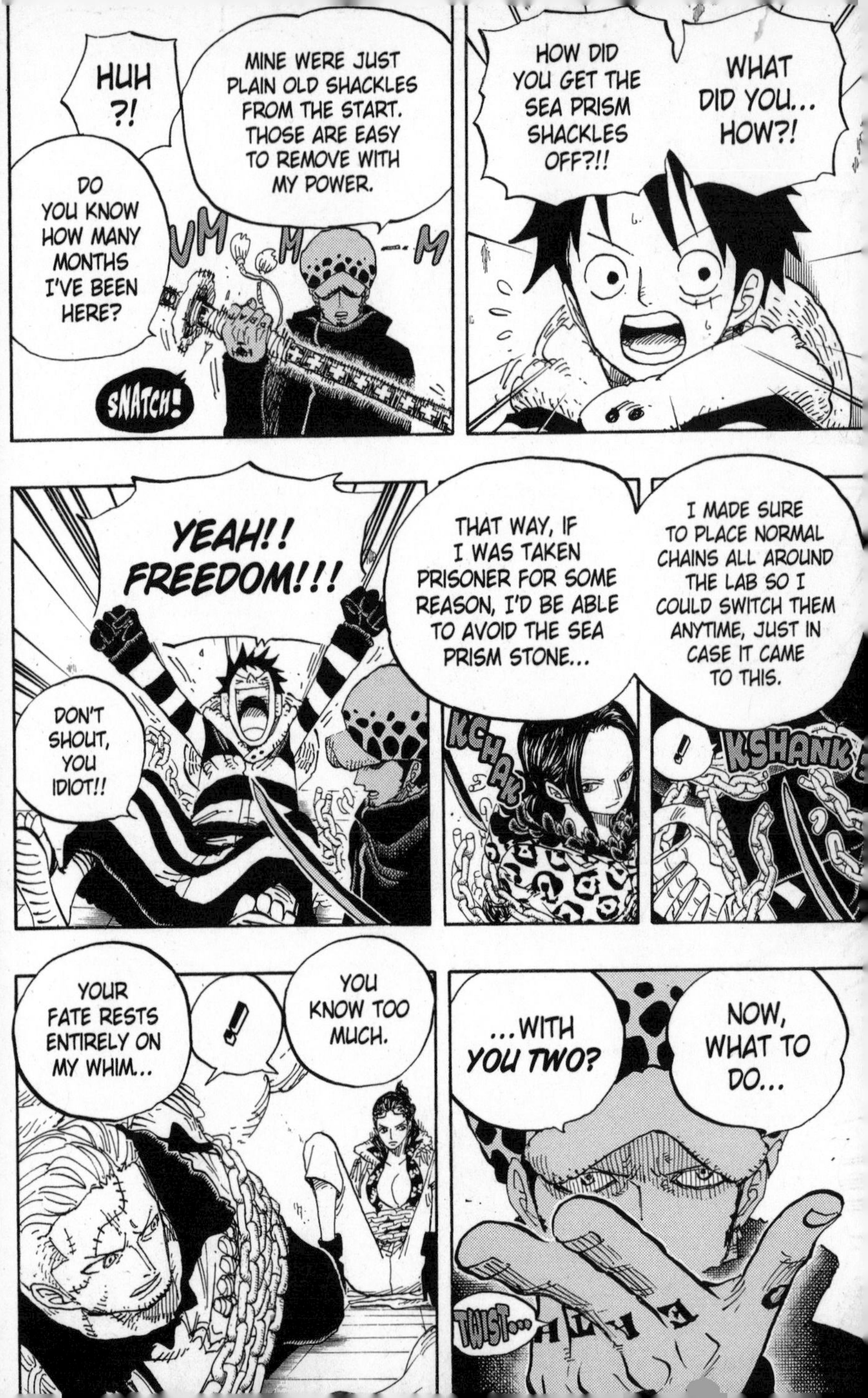
WHAT DID YOU... HOW?!
HOW DID YOU GET THE SEA PRISM SHACKLES OFF?!!
MINE WERE JUST PLAIN OLD SHACKLES FROM THE START. THOSE ARE EASY TO REMOVE WITH MY POWER.
HUH ?!
DO YOU KNOW HOW MANY MONTHS I'VE BEEN HERE?
SNATCH!
I MADE SURE TO PLACE NORMAL CHAINS ALL AROUND THE LAB SO I COULD SWITCH THEM ANYTIME, JUST IN CASE IT CAME TO THIS.
!
KSHANK
THAT WAY, IF I WAS TAKEN PRISONER FOR SOME REASON, I'D BE ABLE TO AVOID THE SEA PRISM STONE...
KCHAK
YEAH!! FREEDOM!!!
DON'T SHOUT, YOU IDIOT!!
NOW, WHAT TO DO...
...WITH YOU TWO?
TWIST...
YOU KNOW TOO MUCH.
!
YOUR FATE RESTS ENTIRELY ON MY WHIM...

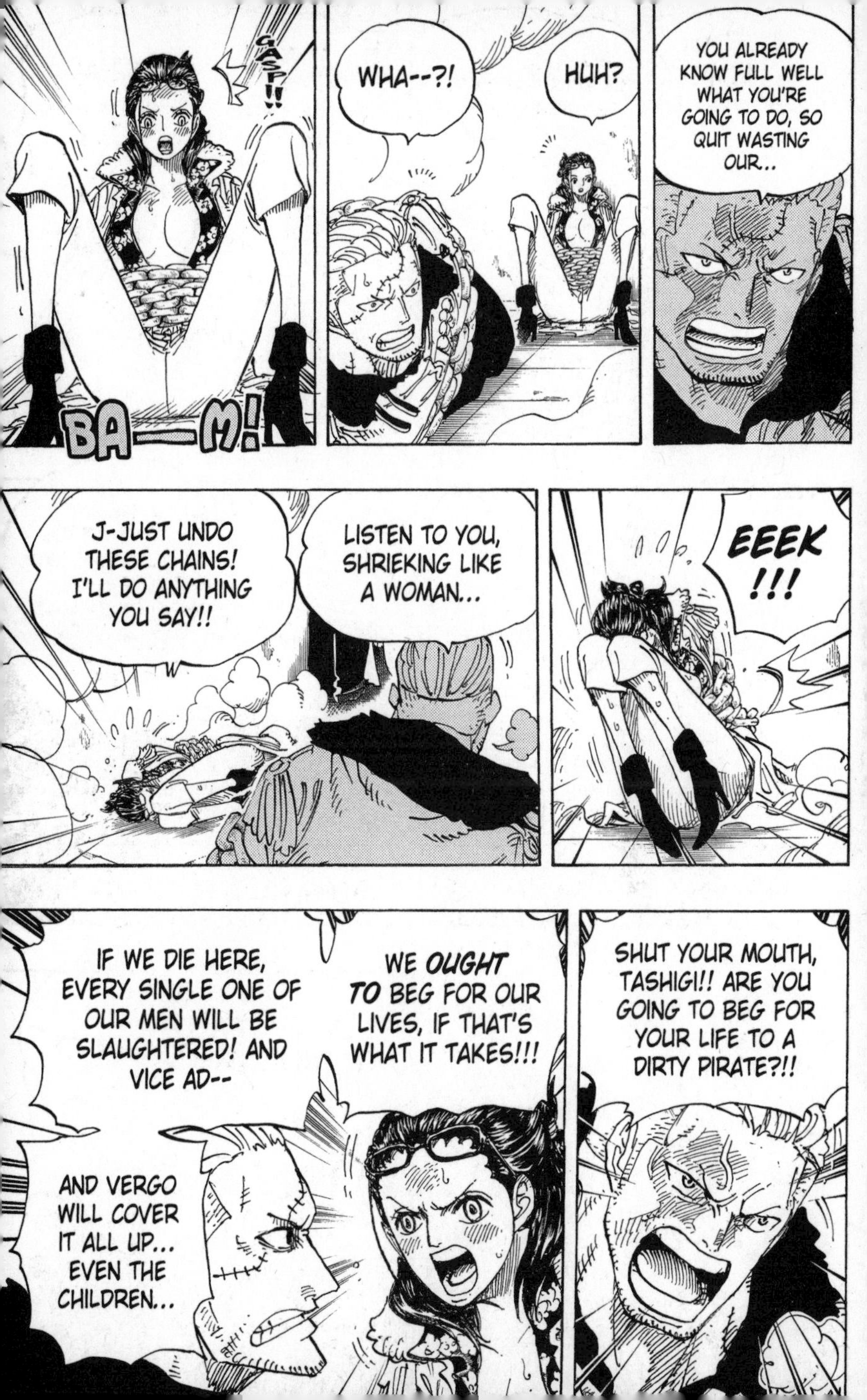
YOU ALREADY KNOW FULL WELL WHAT YOU'RE GOING TO DO, SO QUIT WASTING OUR...
HUH?
WHA--?!
GASP!!
BA——M!
EEEK !!!
LISTEN TO YOU, SHRIEKING LIKE A WOMAN...
J-JUST UNDO THESE CHAINS! I'LL DO ANYTHING YOU SAY!!
SHUT YOUR MOUTH, TASHIGI!! ARE YOU GOING TO BEG FOR YOUR LIFE TO A DIRTY PIRATE?!!
WE *OUGHT TO* BEG FOR OUR LIVES, IF THAT'S WHAT IT TAKES!!!
IF WE DIE HERE, EVERY SINGLE ONE OF OUR MEN WILL BE SLAUGHTERED! AND VICE AD--
AND VERGO WILL COVER IT ALL UP... EVEN THE CHILDREN...

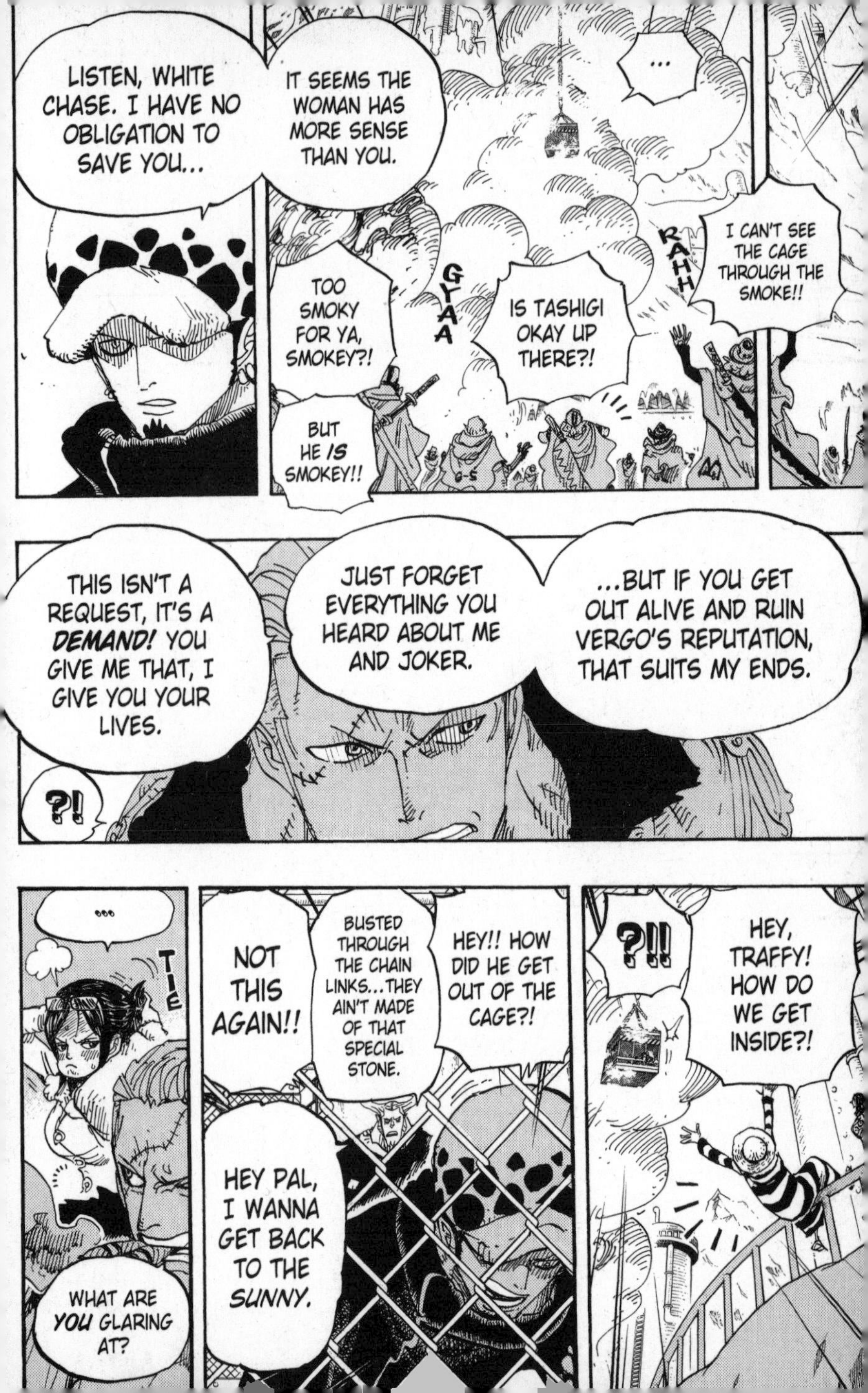
I CAN'T SEE THE CAGE THROUGH THE SMOKE!!
RAHH
...
IT SEEMS THE WOMAN HAS MORE SENSE THAN YOU.
IS TASHIGI OKAY UP THERE?!
GYAA
TOO SMOKY FOR YA, SMOKEY?!
BUT HE *IS* SMOKEY!!
LISTEN, WHITE CHASE. I HAVE NO OBLIGATION TO SAVE YOU...
...BUT IF YOU GET OUT ALIVE AND RUIN VERGO'S REPUTATION, THAT SUITS MY ENDS.
JUST FORGET EVERYTHING YOU HEARD ABOUT ME AND JOKER.
THIS ISN'T A REQUEST, IT'S A *DEMAND!* YOU GIVE ME THAT, I GIVE YOU YOUR LIVES.
?!
?!!
HEY, TRAFFY! HOW DO WE GET INSIDE?!
HEY!! HOW DID HE GET OUT OF THE CAGE?!
BUSTED THROUGH THE CHAIN LINKS...THEY AIN'T MADE OF THAT SPECIAL STONE.
NOT THIS AGAIN!!
HEY PAL, I WANNA GET BACK TO THE *SUNNY.*
...
TIE
WHAT ARE *YOU* GLARING AT?

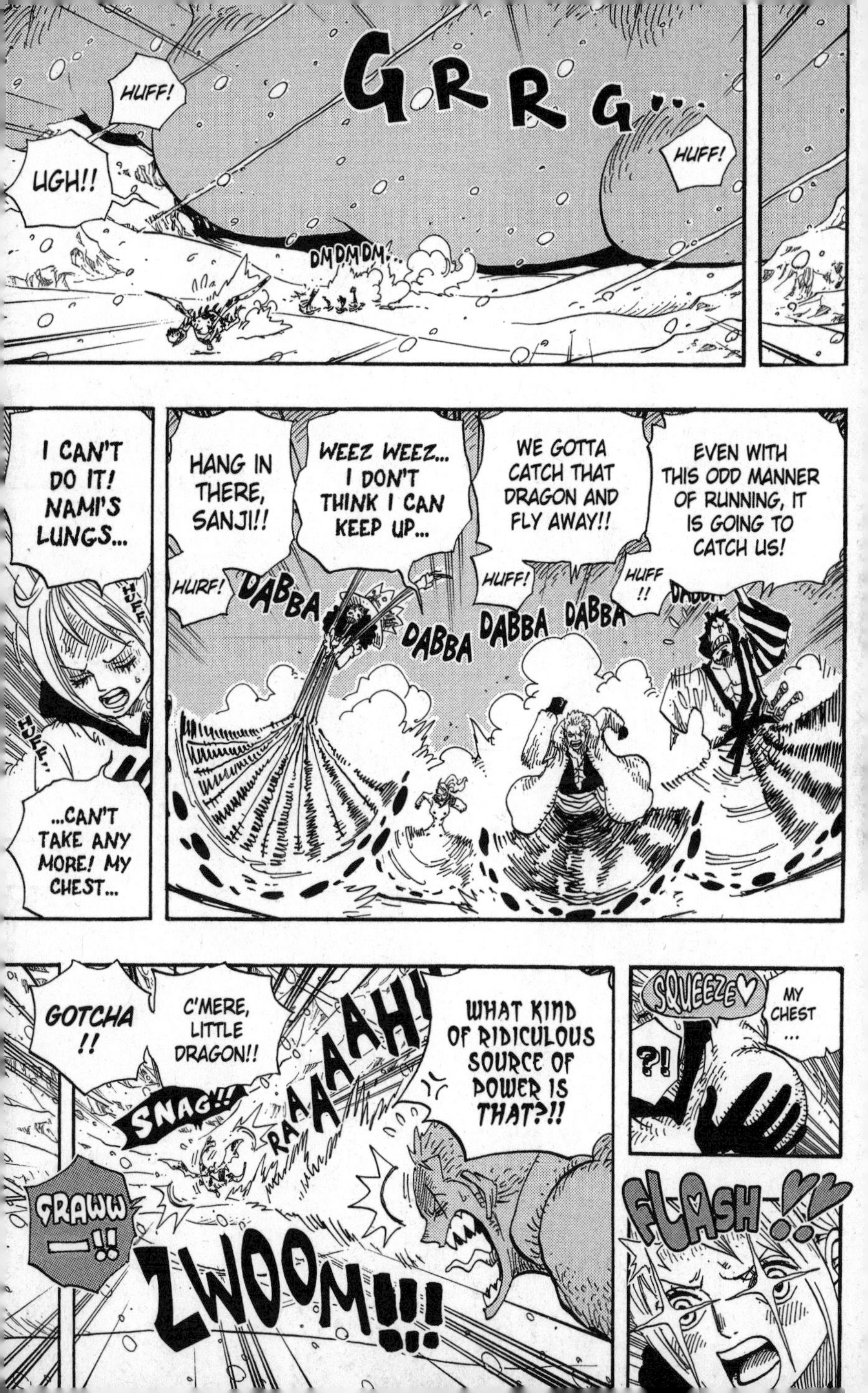
GRRRG...
HUFF!
HUFF!
UGH!!
DMDMDM...
EVEN WITH THIS ODD MANNER OF RUNNING, IT IS GOING TO CATCH US!
HUFF !!
WE GOTTA CATCH THAT DRAGON AND FLY AWAY!!
HUFF!
DABBA DABBA
WEEZ WEEZ... I DON'T THINK I CAN KEEP UP...
HANG IN THERE, SANJI!!
HURF!
DABBA DABBA
I CAN'T DO IT! NAMI'S LUNGS...
HUFF
HUFF...
...CAN'T TAKE ANY MORE! MY CHEST...
MY CHEST ...
SQUEEZE♥
?!
FLASH-!!♥♥
WHAT KIND OF RIDICULOUS SOURCE OF POWER IS THAT?!!
RAAAAAH
C'MERE, LITTLE DRAGON!!
GOTCHA !!
SNAG!!
GRAWW—!!
ZWOOM!!!

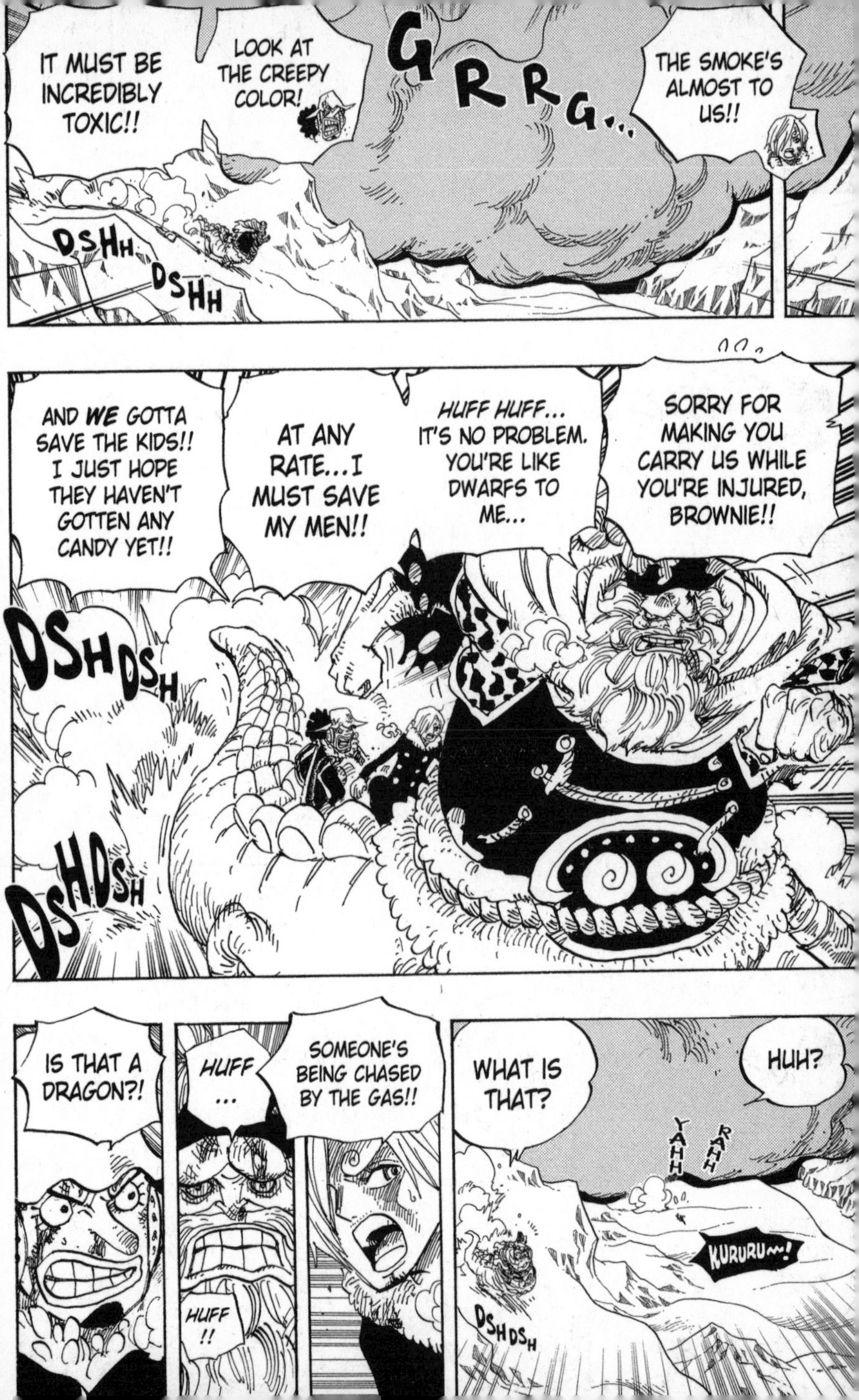
THE SMOKE'S ALMOST TO US!!
GRRG...
LOOK AT THE CREEPY COLOR!
IT MUST BE INCREDIBLY TOXIC!!
DSHH
DSHH
SORRY FOR MAKING YOU CARRY US WHILE YOU'RE INJURED, BROWNIE!!
HUFF HUFF... IT'S NO PROBLEM. YOU'RE LIKE DWARFS TO ME...
AT ANY RATE...I MUST SAVE MY MEN!!
AND **WE** GOTTA SAVE THE KIDS!! I JUST HOPE THEY HAVEN'T GOTTEN ANY CANDY YET!!
DSHDSH
DSHDSH
HUH?
WHAT IS THAT?
YAHH
RAHH
KURURU~!
DSHDSH
SOMEONE'S BEING CHASED BY THE GAS!!
HUFF ...
HUFF !!
IS THAT A DRAGON?!

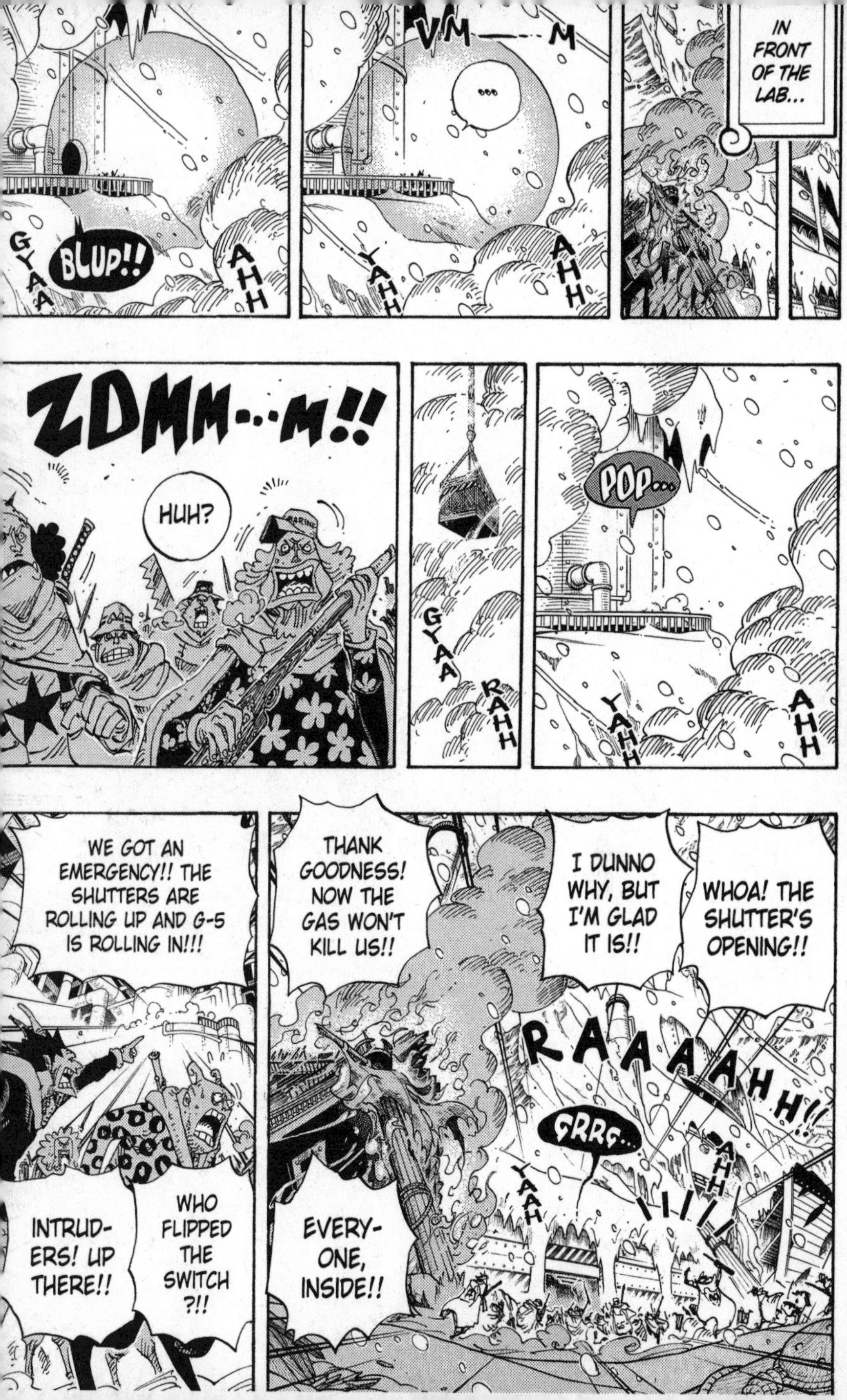
IN FRONT OF THE LAB...
VM——M
...
AHH
YAHH
AHH
BLUP!!
GYAA
POP...
AHH
YAHH
GYAA
RAHH
ZDMM...M!!
HUH?
WHOA! THE SHUTTER'S OPENING!!
I DUNNO WHY, BUT I'M GLAD IT IS!!
THANK GOODNESS! NOW THE GAS WON'T KILL US!!
RAAAAAHH!!
AHH
GRRG...
YAAH
EVERY-ONE, INSIDE!!
WE GOT AN EMERGENCY!! THE SHUTTERS ARE ROLLING UP AND G-5 IS ROLLING IN!!!
WHO FLIPPED THE SWITCH ?!!
INTRUD-ERS! UP THERE!!

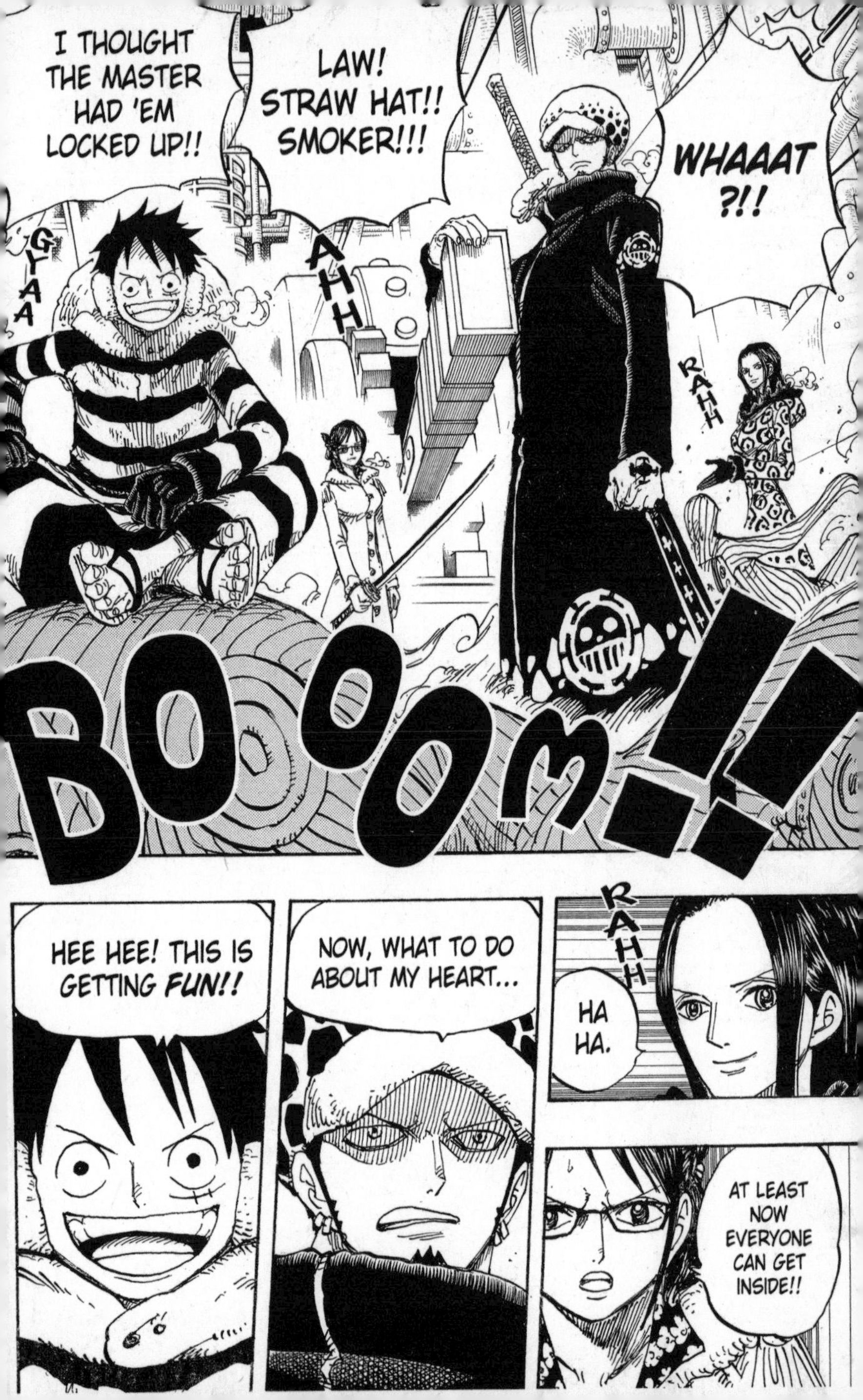
WHAAAT ?!!
LAW! STRAW HAT!! SMOKER!!!
I THOUGHT THE MASTER HAD 'EM LOCKED UP!!
RAHH
AHH
GYAA
BOOOM!!
RAHH
HA HA.
AT LEAST NOW EVERYONE CAN GET INSIDE!!
NOW, WHAT TO DO ABOUT MY HEART...
HEE HEE! THIS IS GETTING FUN!!

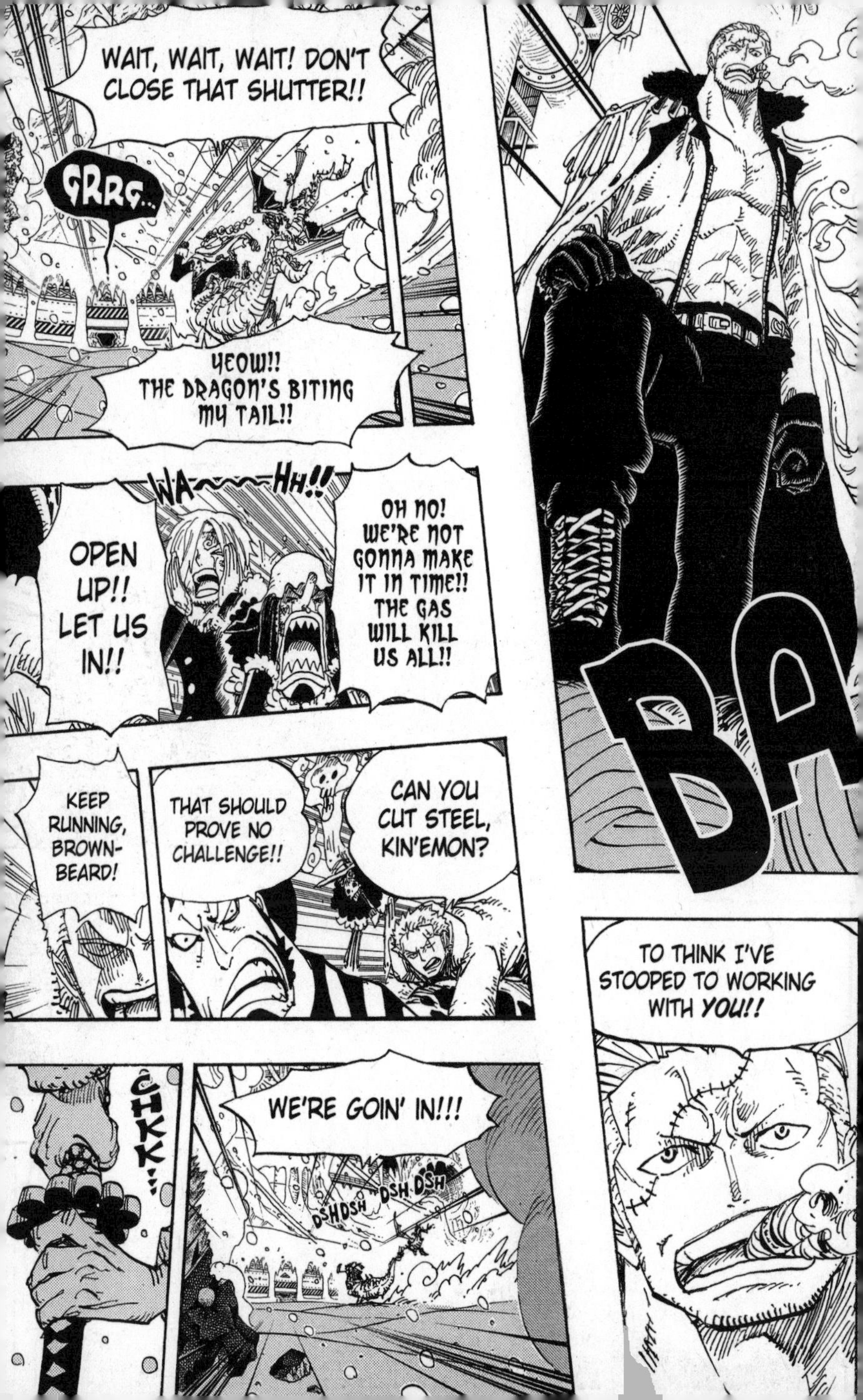
BA
TO THINK I'VE STOOPED TO WORKING WITH YOU!!
WAIT, WAIT, WAIT! DON'T CLOSE THAT SHUTTER!!
GRRG...
YEOW!! THE DRAGON'S BITING MY TAIL!!
OH NO! WE'RE NOT GONNA MAKE IT IN TIME!! THE GAS WILL KILL US ALL!!
WA~~~HH!!
OPEN UP!! LET US IN!!
CAN YOU CUT STEEL, KIN'EMON?
THAT SHOULD PROVE NO CHALLENGE!!
KEEP RUNNING, BROWN-BEARD!
WE'RE GOIN' IN!!!
DSH DSH
DSHDSH
CHKK!!

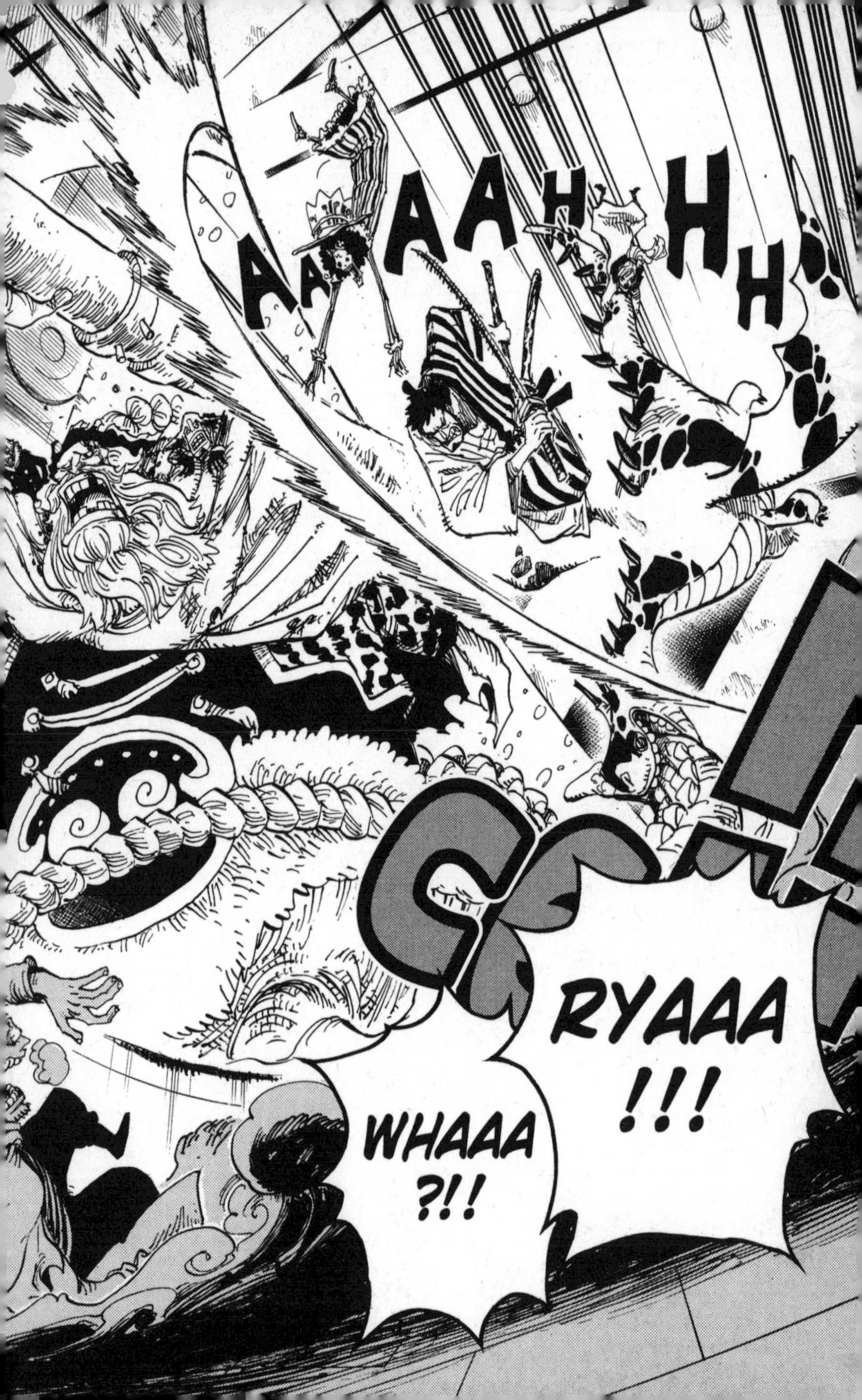
AAAAHHHH!!
RYAAA!!!
WHAAA?!!

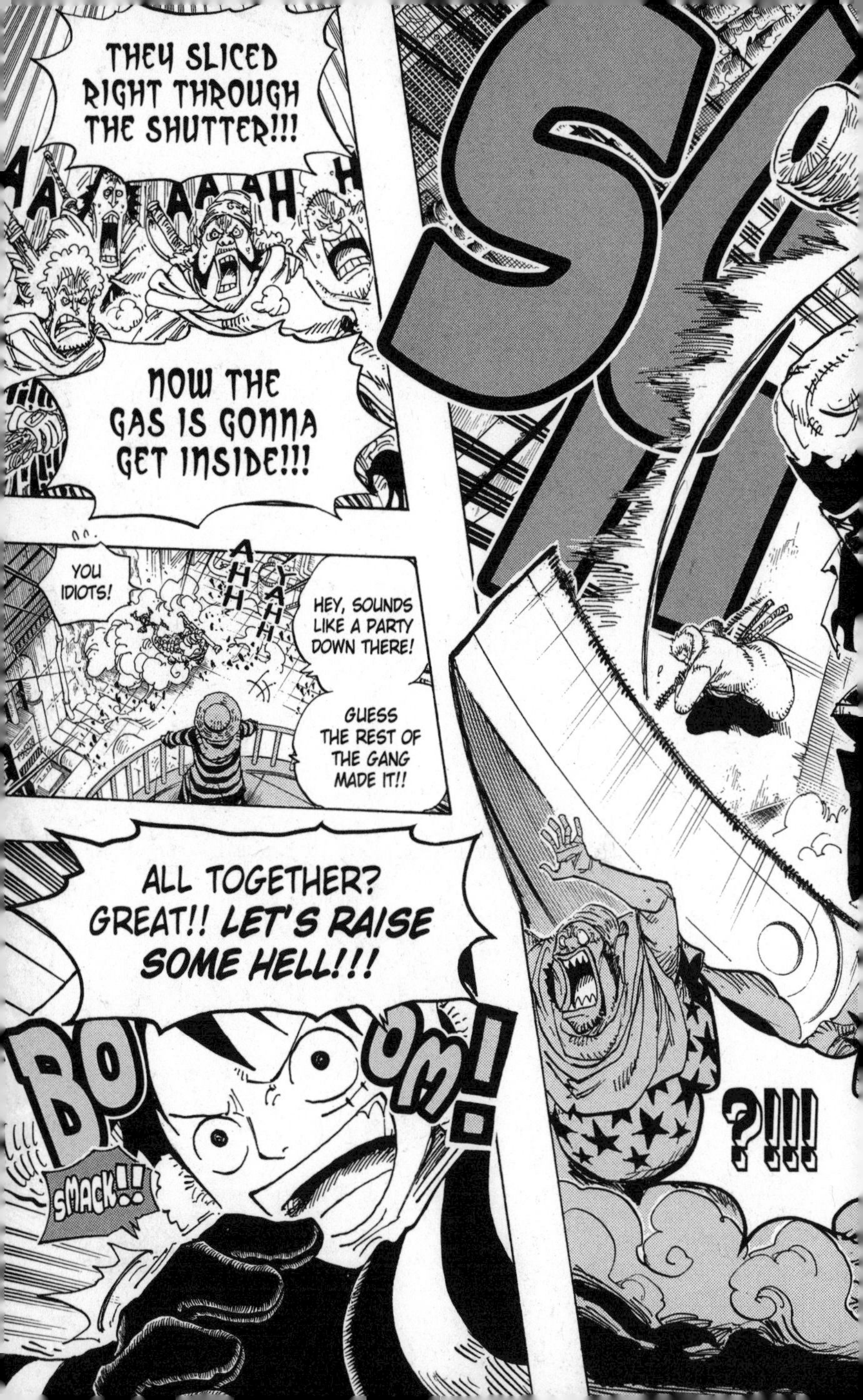
?!!!
THEY SLICED RIGHT THROUGH THE SHUTTER!!!
NOW THE GAS IS GONNA GET INSIDE!!!
HEY, SOUNDS LIKE A PARTY DOWN THERE!
GUESS THE REST OF THE GANG MADE IT!!
AHH
YAHH
YOU IDIOTS!
ALL TOGETHER? GREAT!! LET'S RAISE SOME HELL!!!
BOOM!
SMACK!!

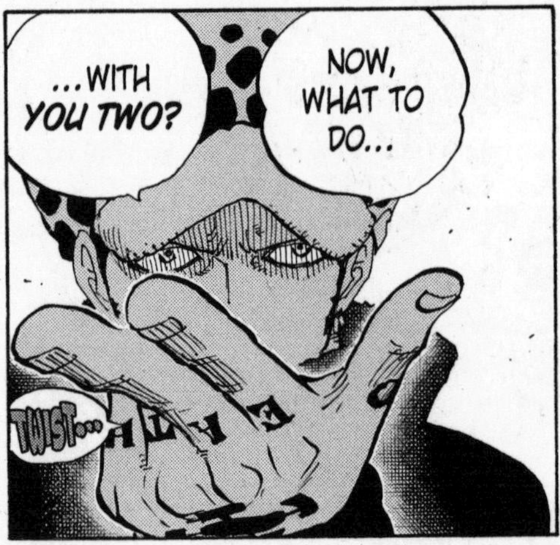
NOW, WHAT TO DO...
...WITH YOU TWO?
TWIST...

Chapter 678: LOBBY OF LABORATORY BUILDING A

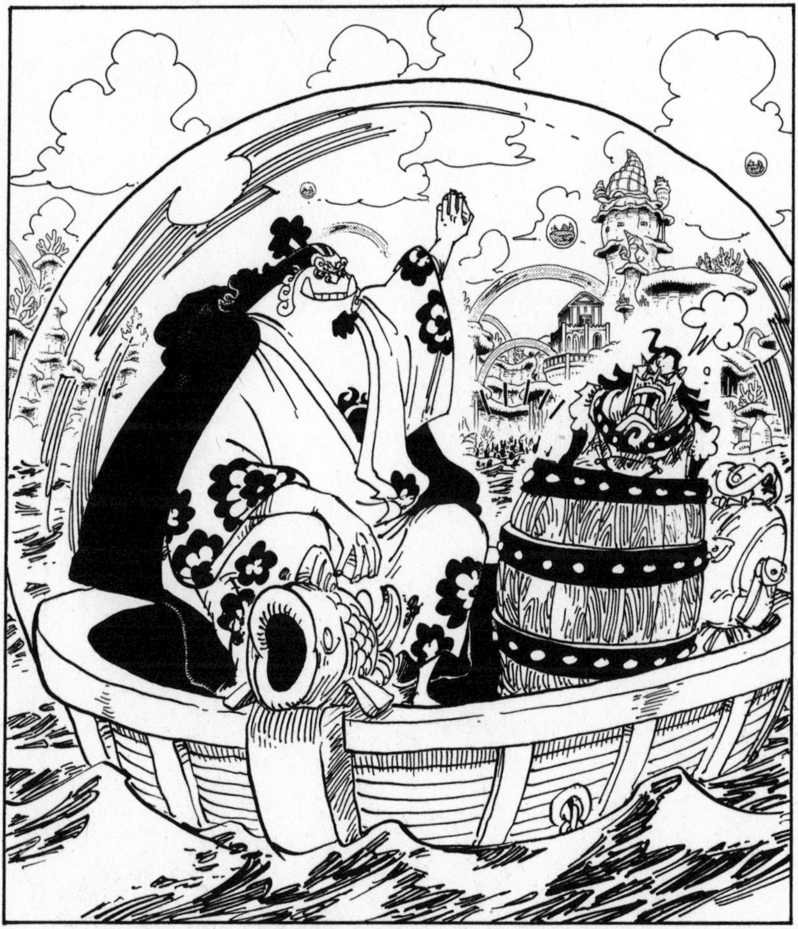

CARIBOU'S NEW WORLD KEE HEE HEE, VOL. 4:
"ESCORTED BY JIMBEI"

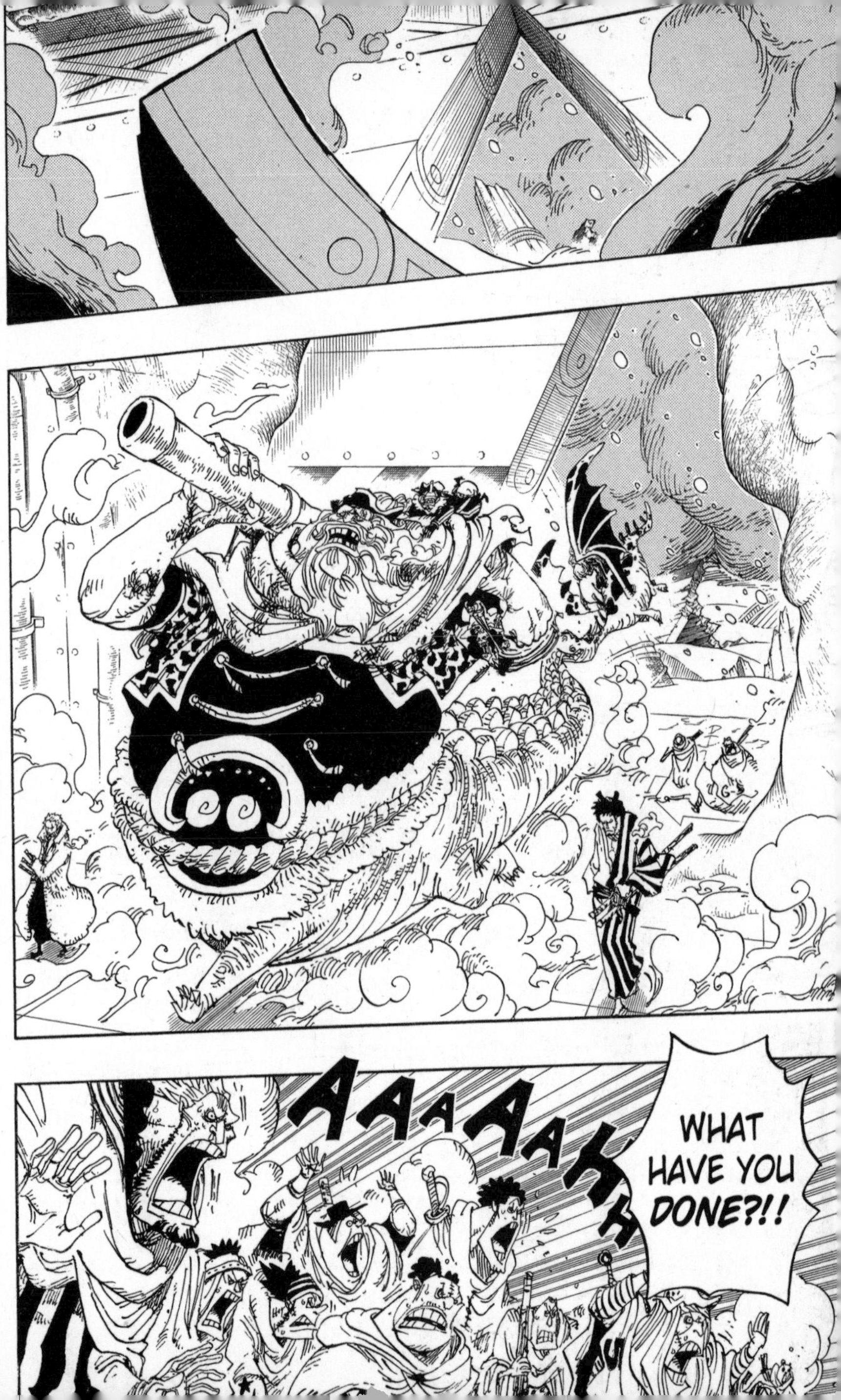
AAAAAAAAH
WHAT HAVE YOU DONE?!!

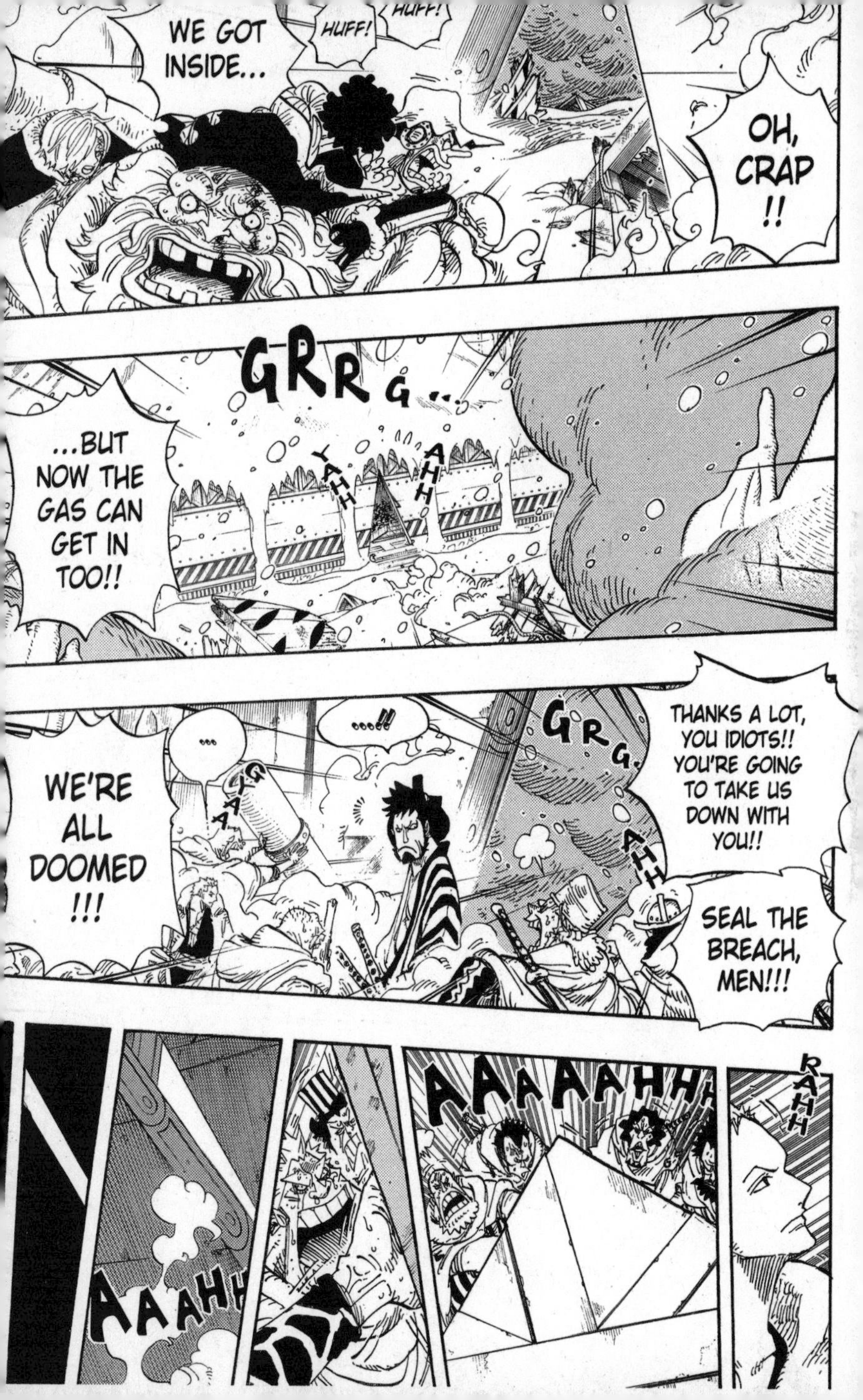

HUFF!
HUFF!
OH, CRAP!!
WE GOT INSIDE...
GRRRG...
AHH
YAHH
...BUT NOW THE GAS CAN GET IN TOO!!
THANKS A LOT, YOU IDIOTS!! YOU'RE GOING TO TAKE US DOWN WITH YOU!!
GRG
SEAL THE BREACH, MEN!!!
AHH
...!!
...
WE'RE ALL DOOMED!!!
RAHH
AAAAAHH
AAAHH

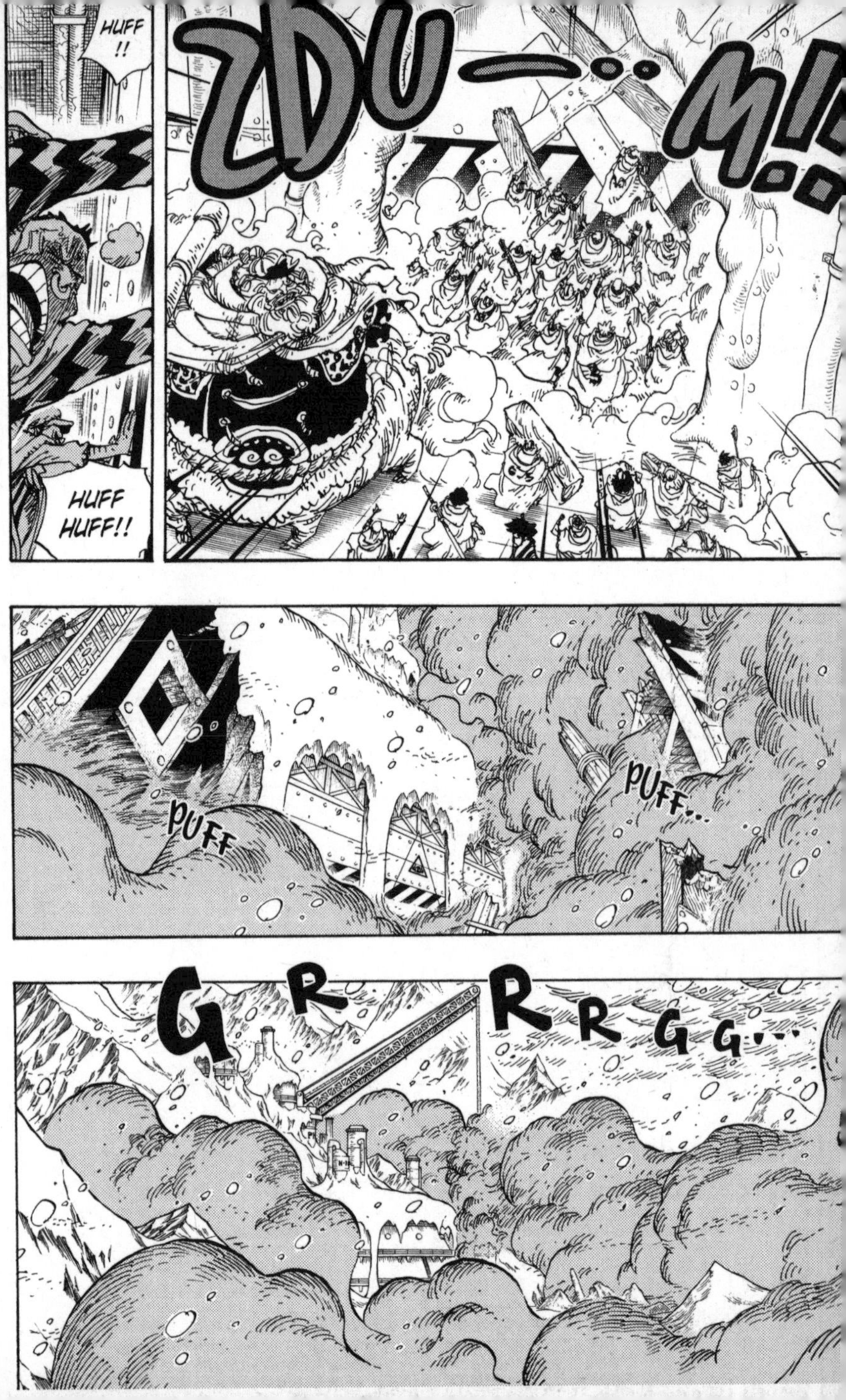
ZDU—..M!!...
HUFF!!
HUFF HUFF!!
PUFF...
PUFF
GRRRRGG...

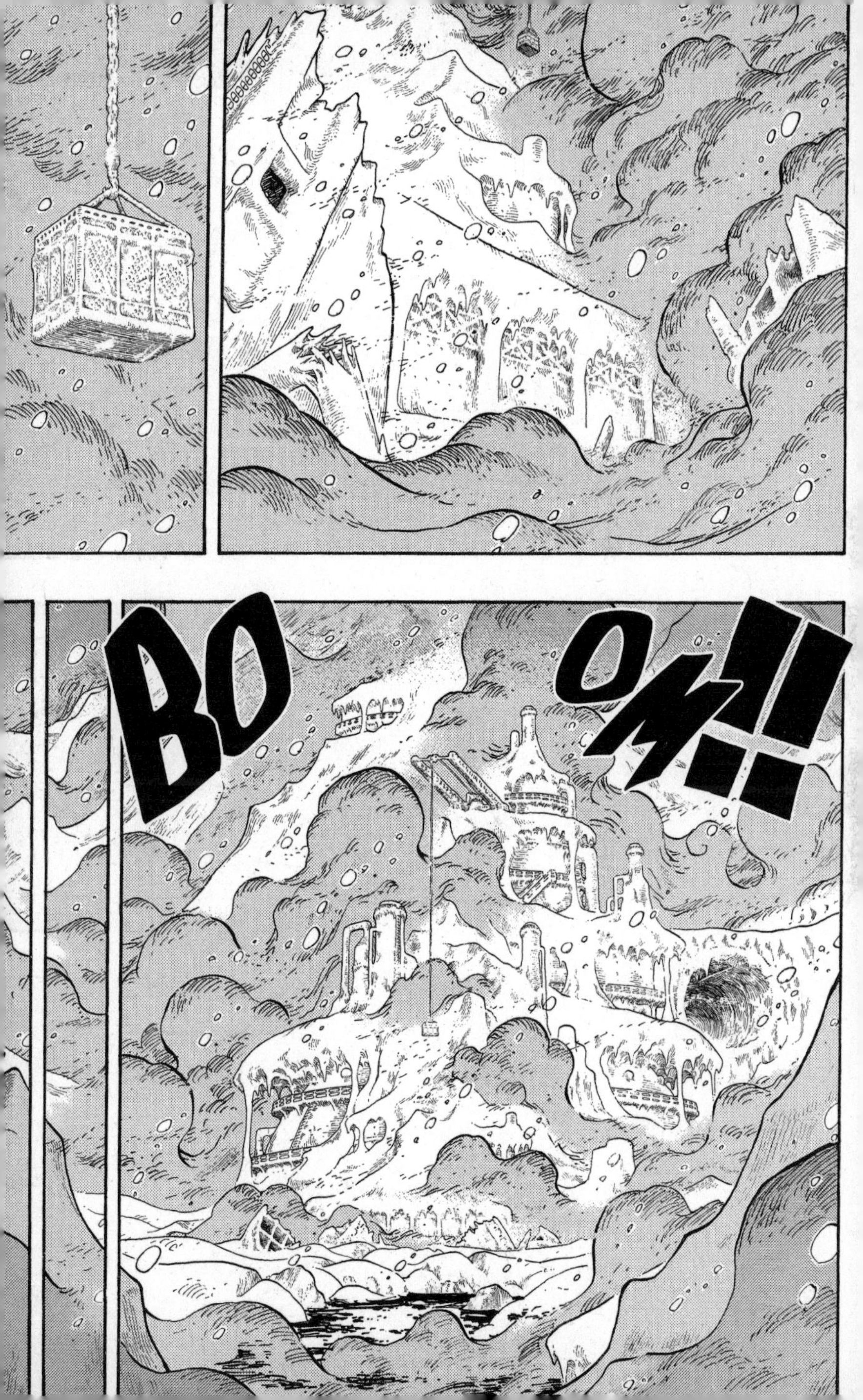
BOOM!!

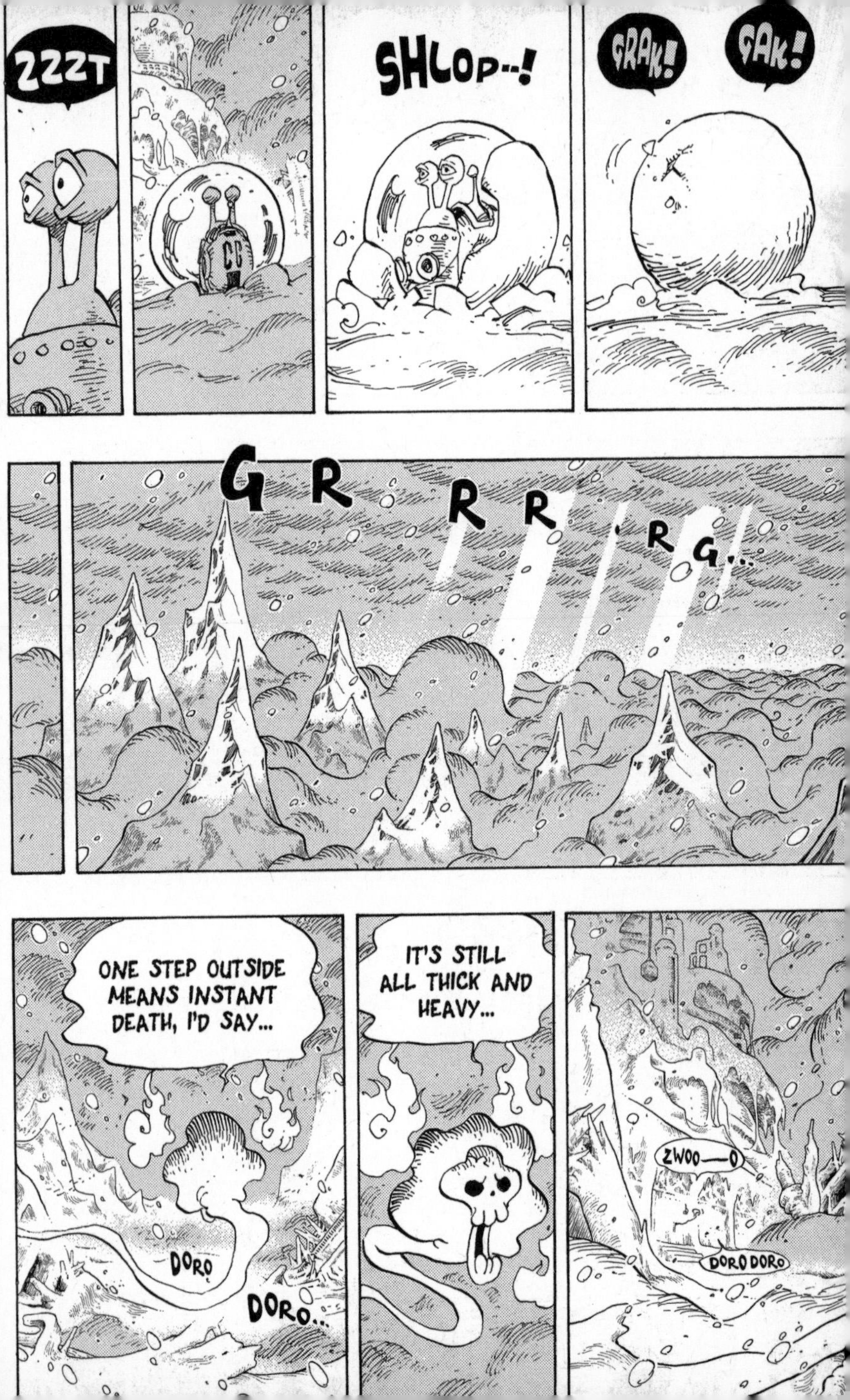
GAK!
GRAK!
SHLOP--!
ZZZT
GRRRRG...
ZWOO—O
DORODORO
IT'S STILL ALL THICK AND HEAVY...
ONE STEP OUTSIDE MEANS INSTANT DEATH, I'D SAY...
DORO
DORO...

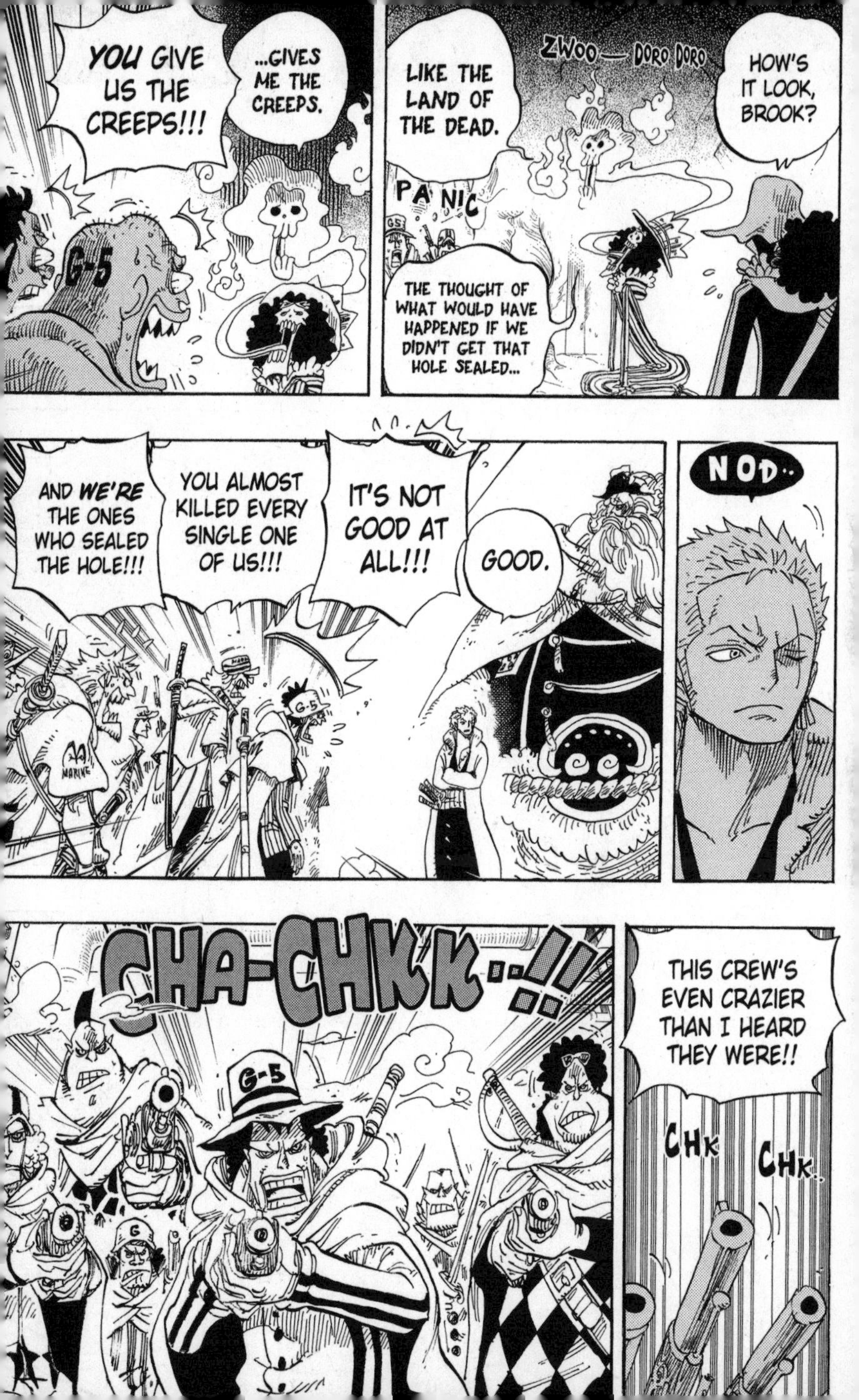
HOW'S IT LOOK, BROOK?
ZWOO— DORO DORO
LIKE THE LAND OF THE DEAD.
PANIC
THE THOUGHT OF WHAT WOULD HAVE HAPPENED IF WE DIDN'T GET THAT HOLE SEALED...
...GIVES ME THE CREEPS.
YOU GIVE US THE CREEPS!!!
G-5
NOD..
GOOD.
IT'S NOT GOOD AT ALL!!!
YOU ALMOST KILLED EVERY SINGLE ONE OF US!!!
AND *WE'RE* THE ONES WHO SEALED THE HOLE!!!
G-5
MARINE
THIS CREW'S EVEN CRAZIER THAN I HEARD THEY WERE!!
CHK
CHK..
CHA-CHKK..!!
G-5

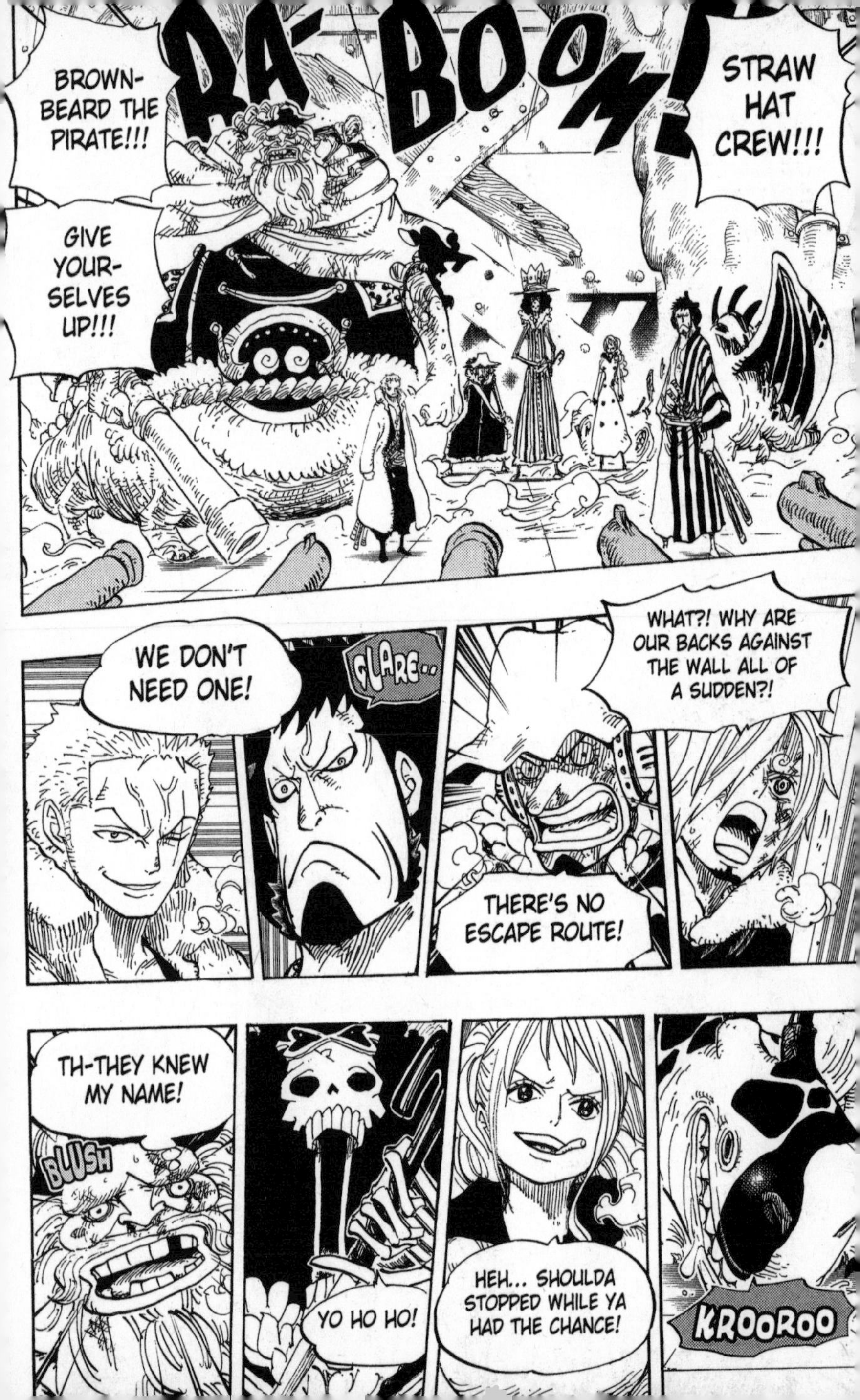
STRAW HAT CREW!!!
RA-BOOM!
BROWNBEARD THE PIRATE!!!
GIVE YOURSELVES UP!!!
WHAT?! WHY ARE OUR BACKS AGAINST THE WALL ALL OF A SUDDEN?!
THERE'S NO ESCAPE ROUTE!
GLARE..
WE DON'T NEED ONE!
KROOROO
HEH... SHOULDA STOPPED WHILE YA HAD THE CHANCE!
YO HO HO!
TH-THEY KNEW MY NAME!
BLUSH

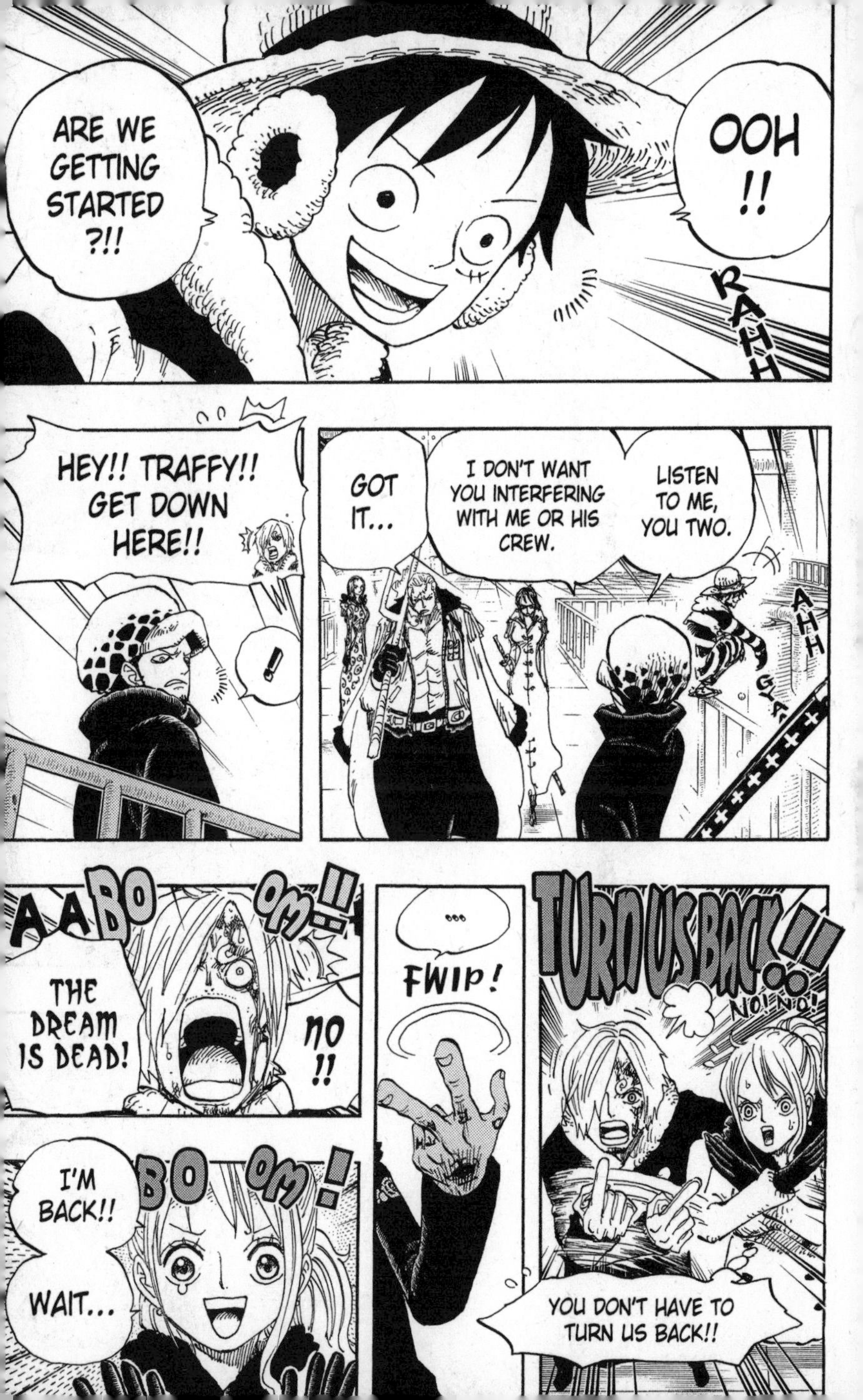
OOH !!
RAHHH
ARE WE GETTING STARTED ?!!
LISTEN TO ME, YOU TWO.
I DON'T WANT YOU INTERFERING WITH ME OR HIS CREW.
GOT IT...
AHH
GYA
HEY!! TRAFFY!! GET DOWN HERE!!
!
TURN US BACK!!
NO! NO!
YOU DON'T HAVE TO TURN US BACK!!
...
FWIP!
AABOOM!!
THE DREAM IS DEAD!
NO !!
BOOM!
I'M BACK!!
WAIT...

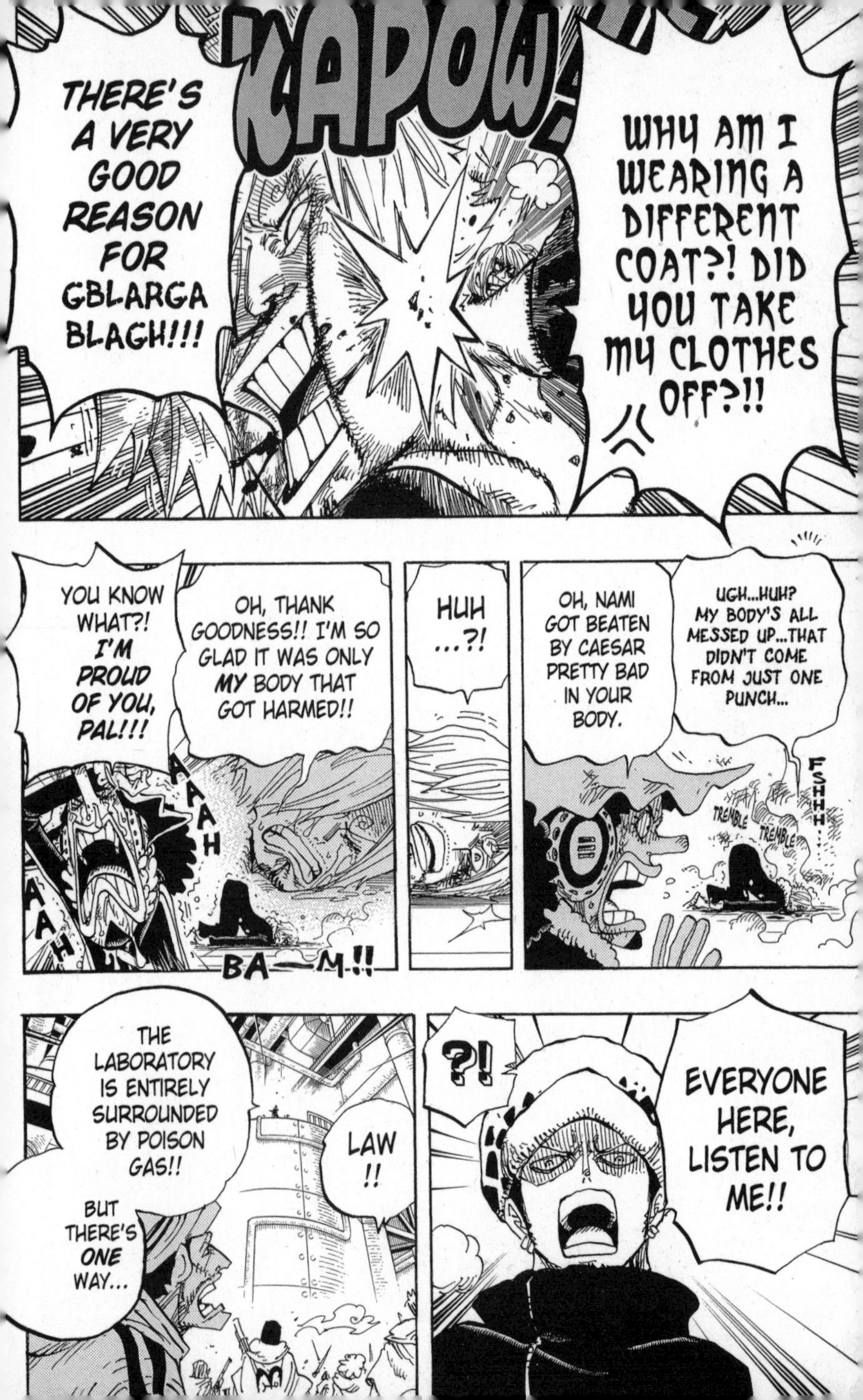
KAPOW!!
WHY AM I WEARING A DIFFERENT COAT?! DID YOU TAKE MY CLOTHES OFF?!!
THERE'S A VERY GOOD REASON FOR GBLARGA BLAGH!!!
UGH...HUH? MY BODY'S ALL MESSED UP...THAT DIDN'T COME FROM JUST ONE PUNCH...
OH, NAMI GOT BEATEN BY CAESAR PRETTY BAD IN YOUR BODY.
FSHHH...
TREMBLE
TREMBLE
HUH ...?!
OH, THANK GOODNESS!! I'M SO GLAD IT WAS ONLY MY BODY THAT GOT HARMED!!
YOU KNOW WHAT?! I'M PROUD OF YOU, PAL!!!
AAAH
AAAH
BA—M!!
?!
EVERYONE HERE, LISTEN TO ME!!
LAW !!
THE LABORATORY IS ENTIRELY SURROUNDED BY POISON GAS!!
BUT THERE'S ONE WAY...

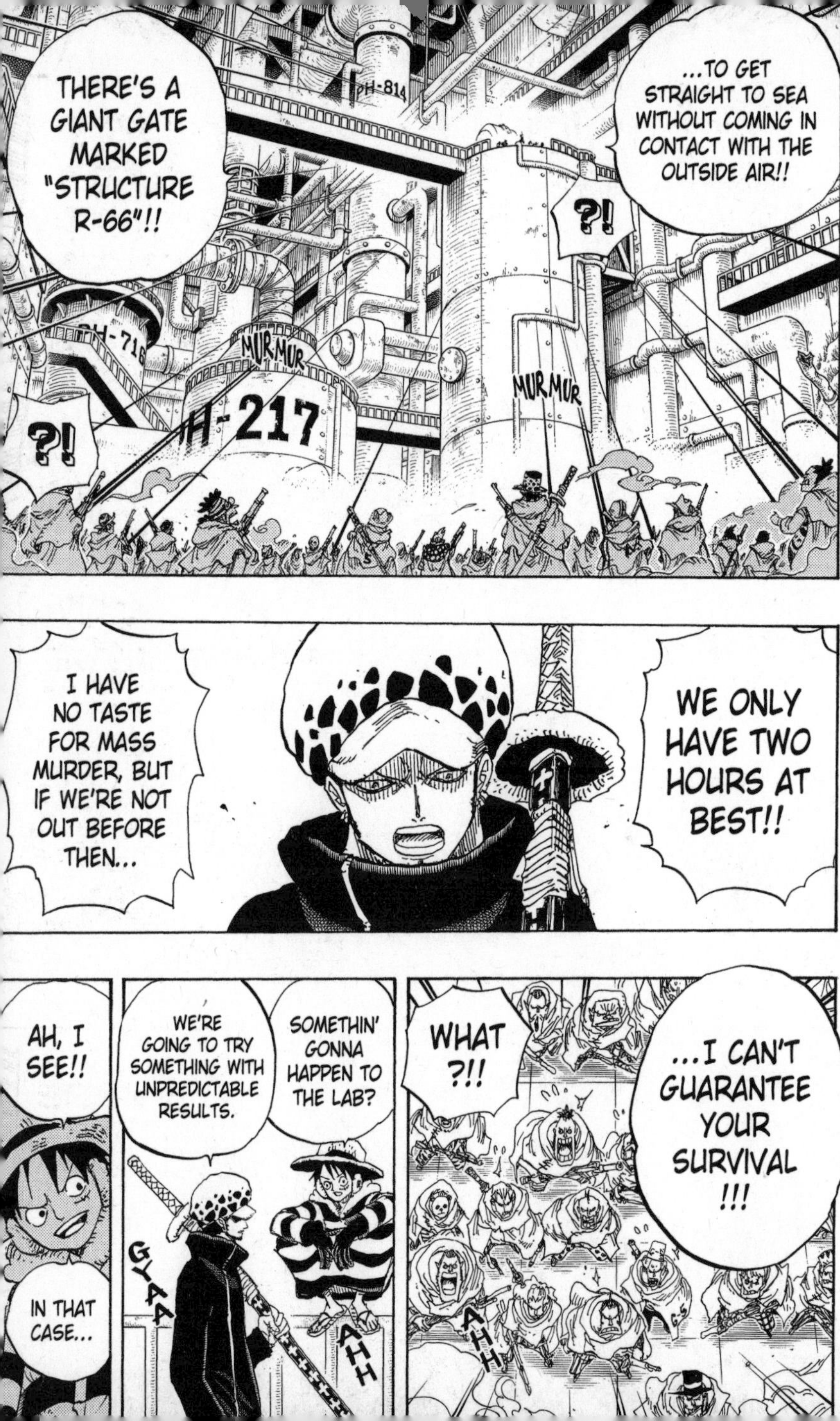
...TO GET STRAIGHT TO SEA WITHOUT COMING IN CONTACT WITH THE OUTSIDE AIR!!
?!
PH-814
THERE'S A GIANT GATE MARKED "STRUCTURE R-66"!!
MURMUR
MURMUR
H-217
?!
WE ONLY HAVE TWO HOURS AT BEST!!
I HAVE NO TASTE FOR MASS MURDER, BUT IF WE'RE NOT OUT BEFORE THEN...
...I CAN'T GUARANTEE YOUR SURVIVAL!!!
WHAT ?!!
AHH
SOMETHIN' GONNA HAPPEN TO THE LAB?
WE'RE GOING TO TRY SOMETHING WITH UNPREDICTABLE RESULTS.
AHH
GYAA
AH, I SEE!!
IN THAT CASE...

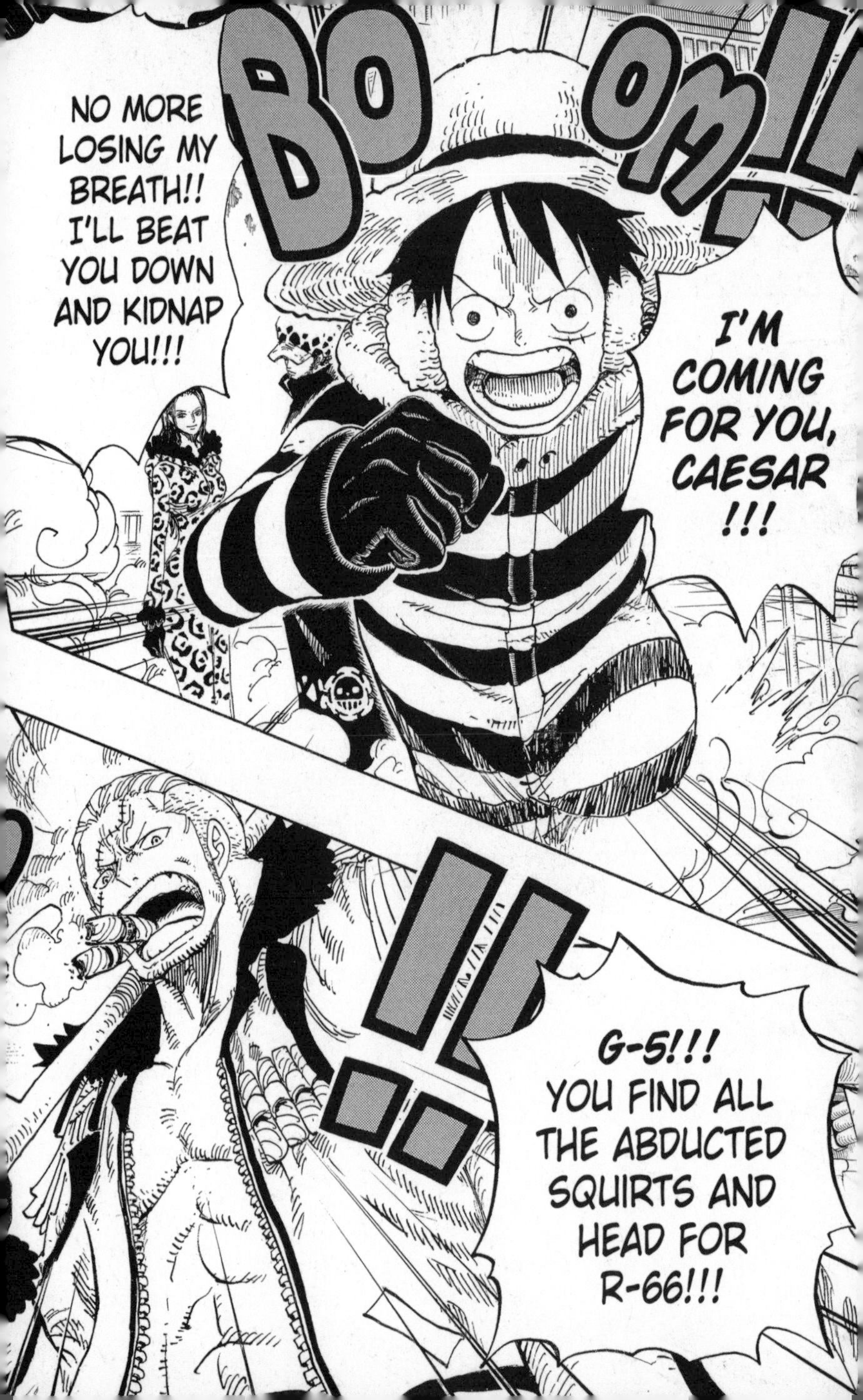
BOOM!!
I'M COMING FOR YOU, CAESAR!!!
NO MORE LOSING MY BREATH!! I'LL BEAT YOU DOWN AND KIDNAP YOU!!!
!!
G-5!!! YOU FIND ALL THE ABDUCTED SQUIRTS AND HEAD FOR R-66!!!

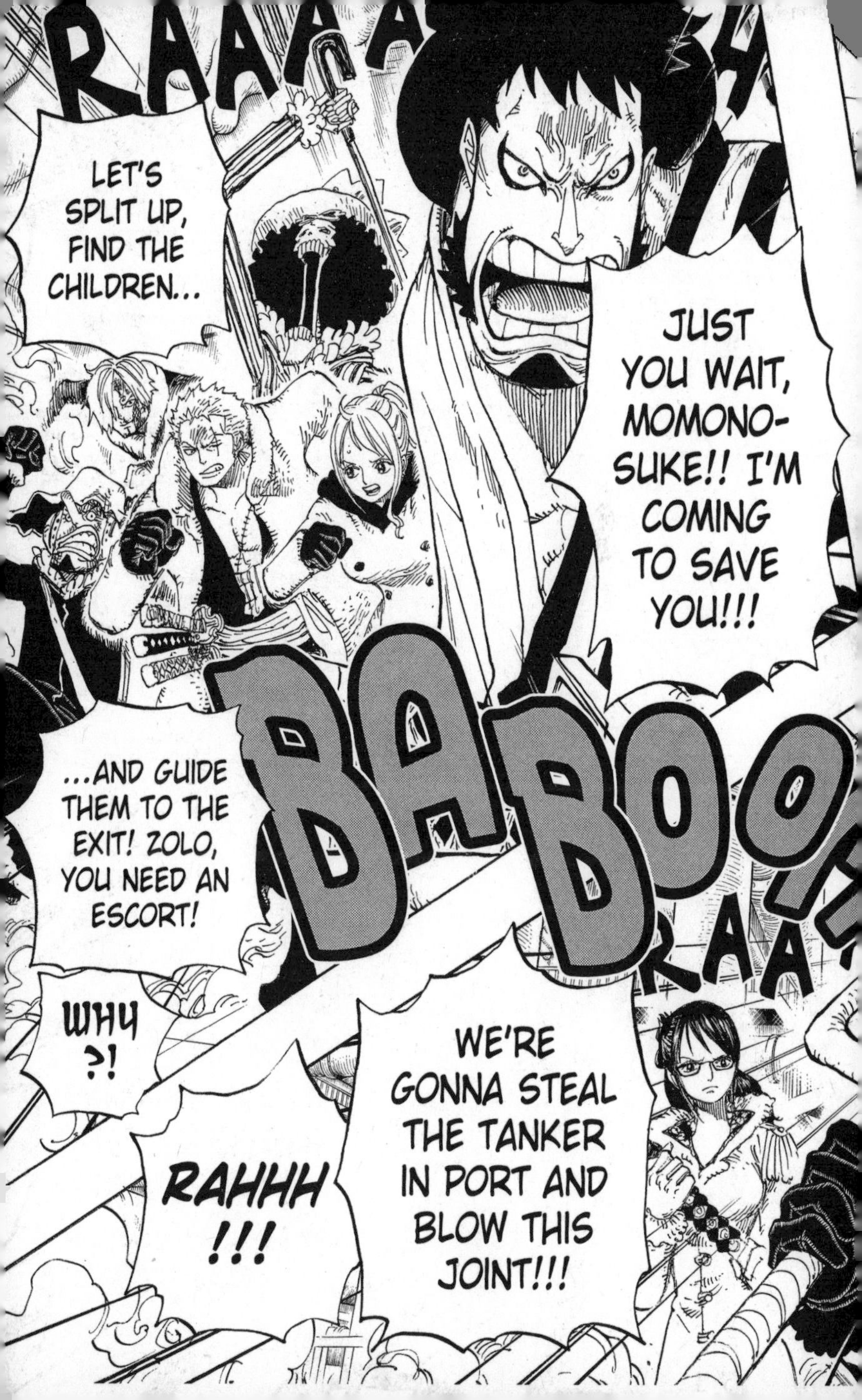
JUST YOU WAIT, MOMONOSUKE!! I'M COMING TO SAVE YOU!!!
LET'S SPLIT UP, FIND THE CHILDREN...
...AND GUIDE THEM TO THE EXIT! ZOLO, YOU NEED AN ESCORT!
WE'RE GONNA STEAL THE TANKER IN PORT AND BLOW THIS JOINT!!!
RAHHH !!!
WHY ?!

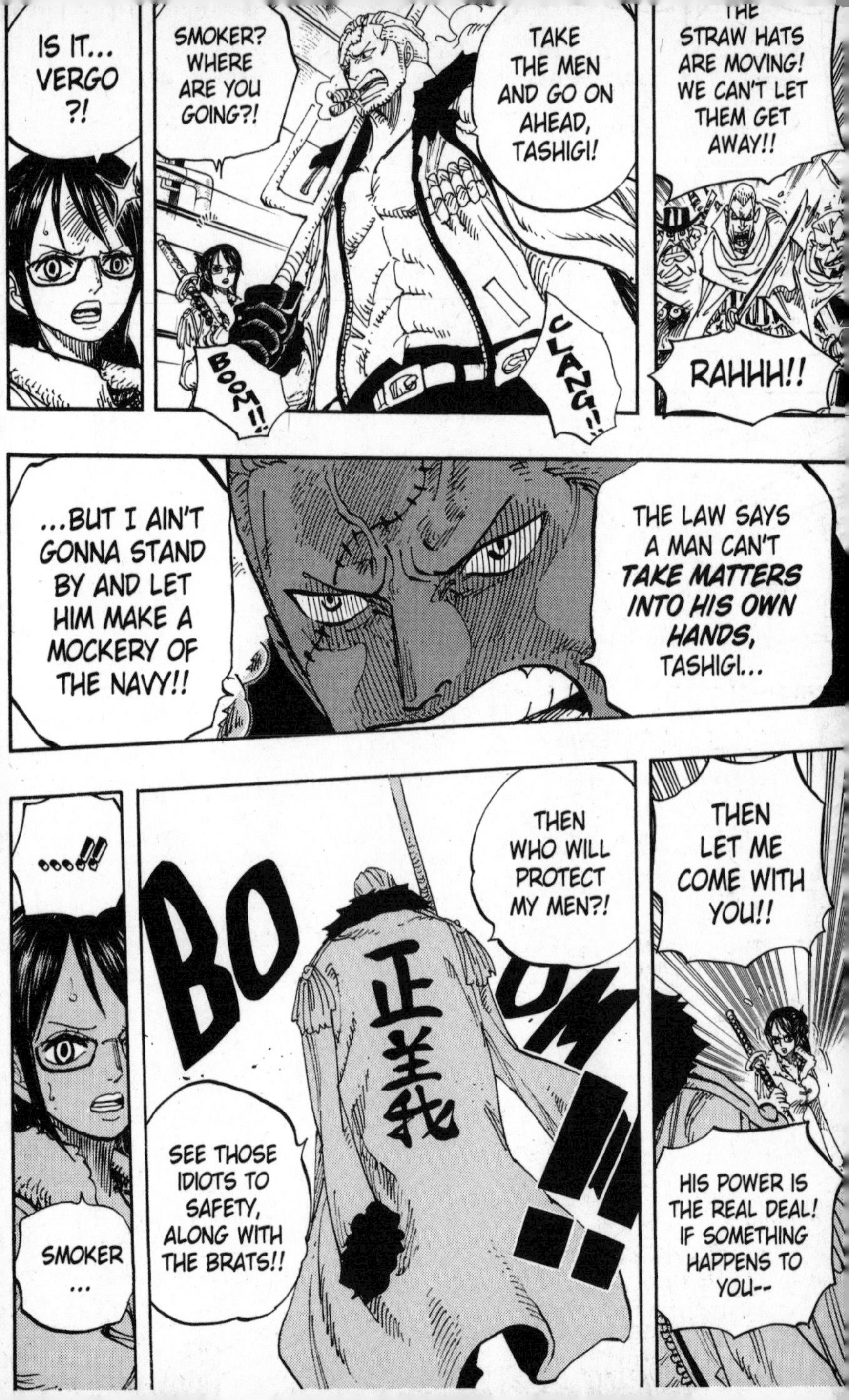
THE STRAW HATS ARE MOVING! WE CAN'T LET THEM GET AWAY!!
RAHHH!!
TAKE THE MEN AND GO ON AHEAD, TASHIGI!
SMOKER? WHERE ARE YOU GOING?!
CLANG!!
BOOM!!
IS IT... VERGO?!
THE LAW SAYS A MAN CAN'T TAKE MATTERS INTO HIS OWN HANDS, TASHIGI...
...BUT I AIN'T GONNA STAND BY AND LET HIM MAKE A MOCKERY OF THE NAVY!!
THEN LET ME COME WITH YOU!!
HIS POWER IS THE REAL DEAL! IF SOMETHING HAPPENS TO YOU--
THEN WHO WILL PROTECT MY MEN?!
BOOM!!
正義
SEE THOSE IDIOTS TO SAFETY, ALONG WITH THE BRATS!!
...!!
SMOKER ...

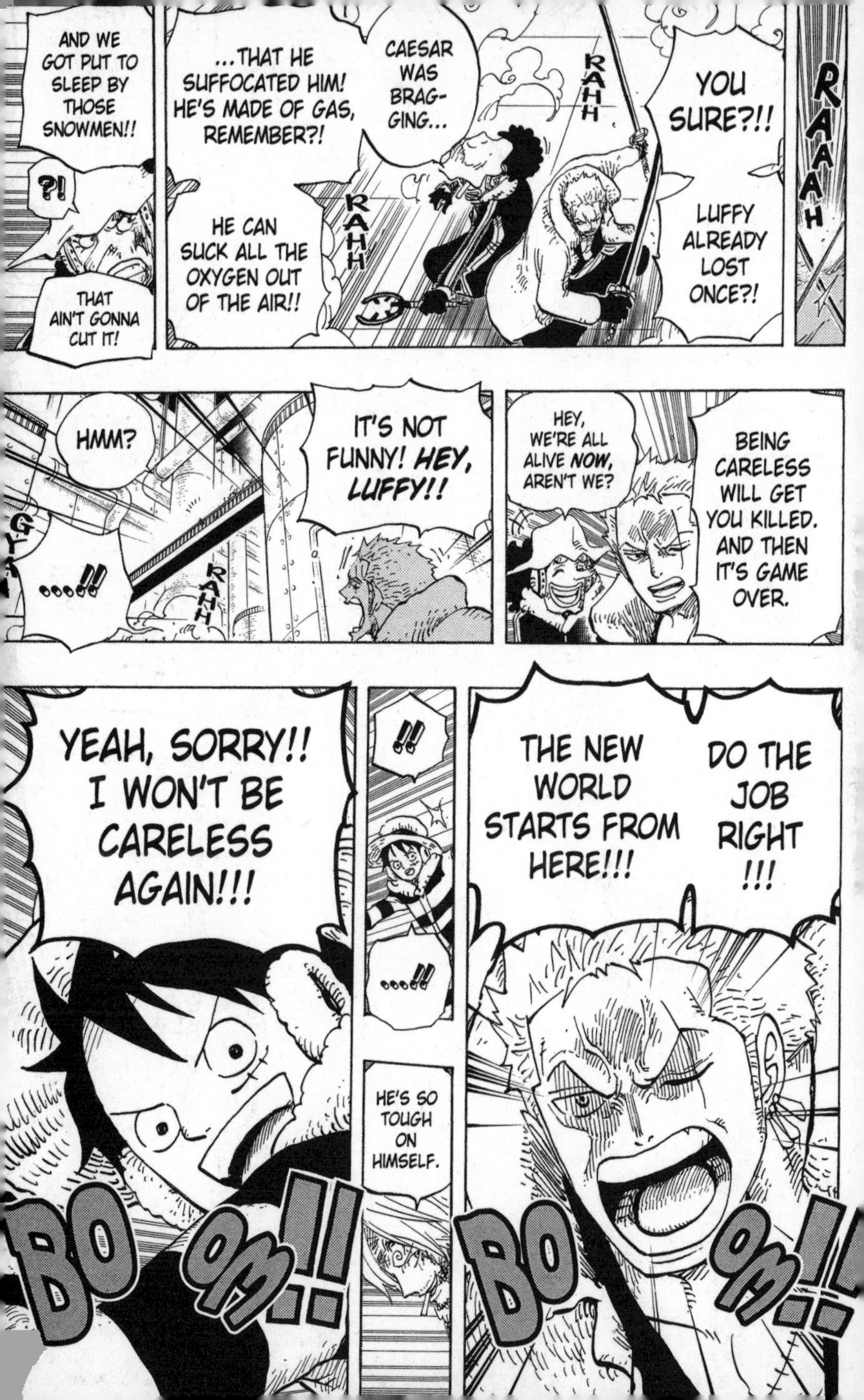
RAAAAH
YOU SURE?!!
LUFFY ALREADY LOST ONCE?!
RAHH
CAESAR WAS BRAG-GING...
...THAT HE SUFFOCATED HIM! HE'S MADE OF GAS, REMEMBER?!
HE CAN SUCK ALL THE OXYGEN OUT OF THE AIR!!
RAHH
AND WE GOT PUT TO SLEEP BY THOSE SNOWMEN!!
?!
THAT AIN'T GONNA CUT IT!
BEING CARELESS WILL GET YOU KILLED. AND THEN IT'S GAME OVER.
HEY, WE'RE ALL ALIVE *NOW*, AREN'T WE?
IT'S NOT FUNNY! ***HEY, LUFFY!!***
RAHH
HMM?
...!!
DO THE JOB RIGHT!!!
THE NEW WORLD STARTS FROM HERE!!!
BOOM!!
!!
...!!
HE'S SO TOUGH ON HIMSELF.
YEAH, SORRY!! I WON'T BE CARELESS AGAIN!!!
BOOM!!

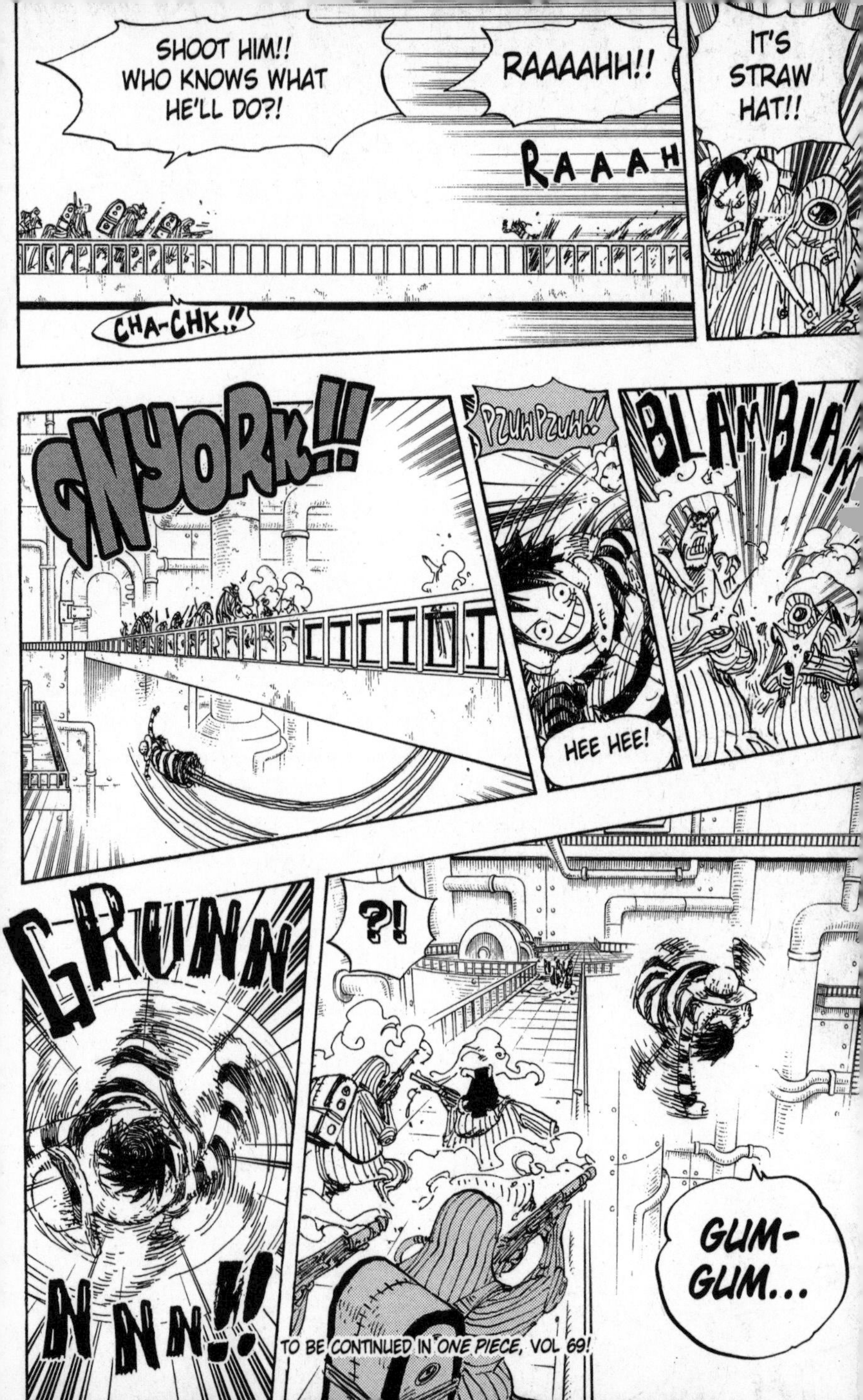
IT'S STRAW HAT!!
RAAAAHH!!
SHOOT HIM!! WHO KNOWS WHAT HE'LL DO?!
RAAAH
CHA-CHK.!!
BLAM BLAM
PZUHPZUH!!
HEE HEE!
GNYORK!!
?!
GUM-GUM...
GRUNN
NNN!!
TO BE CONTINUED IN ONE PIECE, VOL 69!

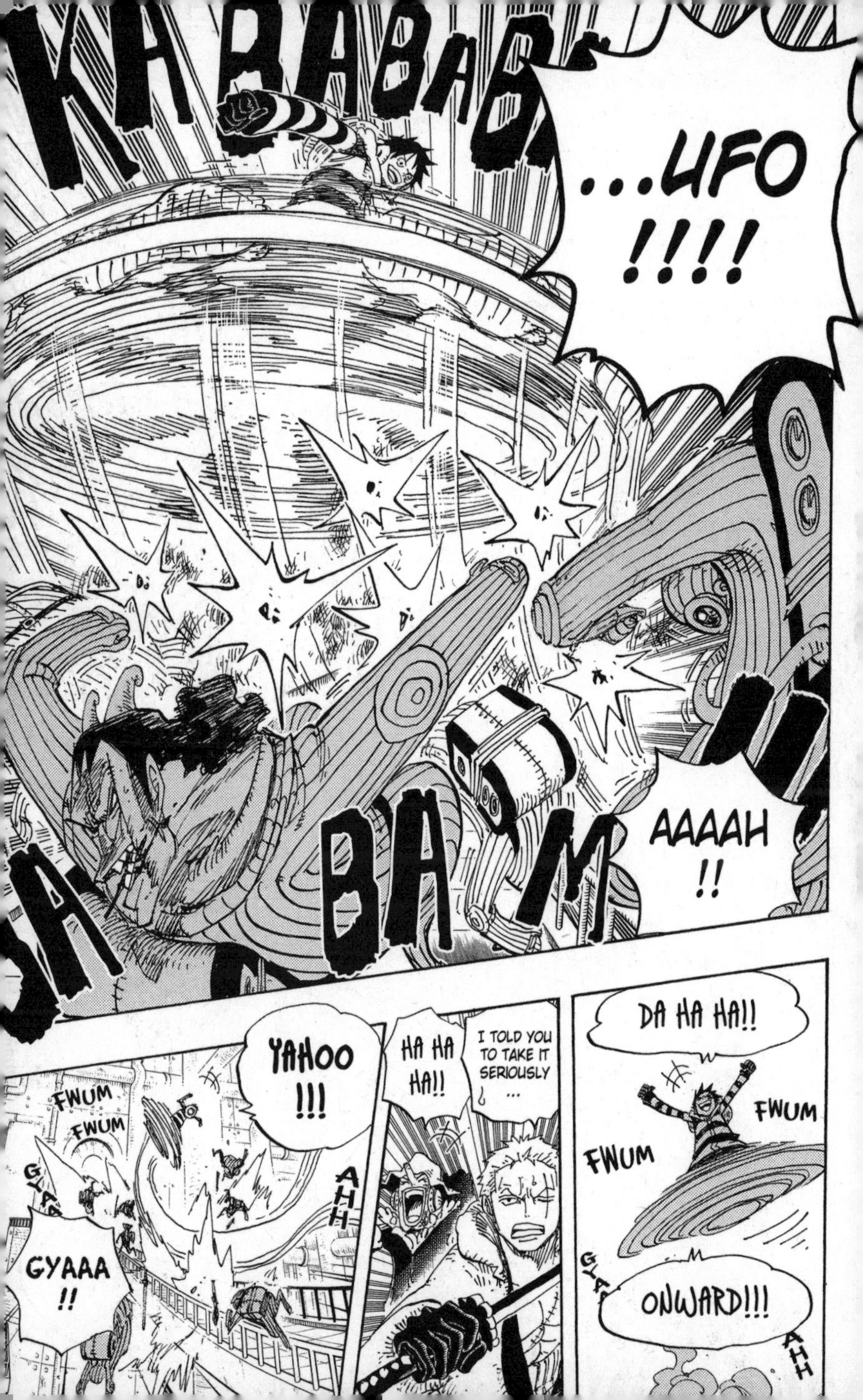
...UFO!!!!
KABABAB
AAAAH!!
BAM
DA HA HA!!
FWUM
FWUM
GYA
ONWARD!!!
AHH
I TOLD YOU TO TAKE IT SERIOUSLY...
HA HA HA!!
YAHOO!!!
AHH
FWUM
FWUM
GYA
GYAAA!!

COMING NEXT VOLUME:

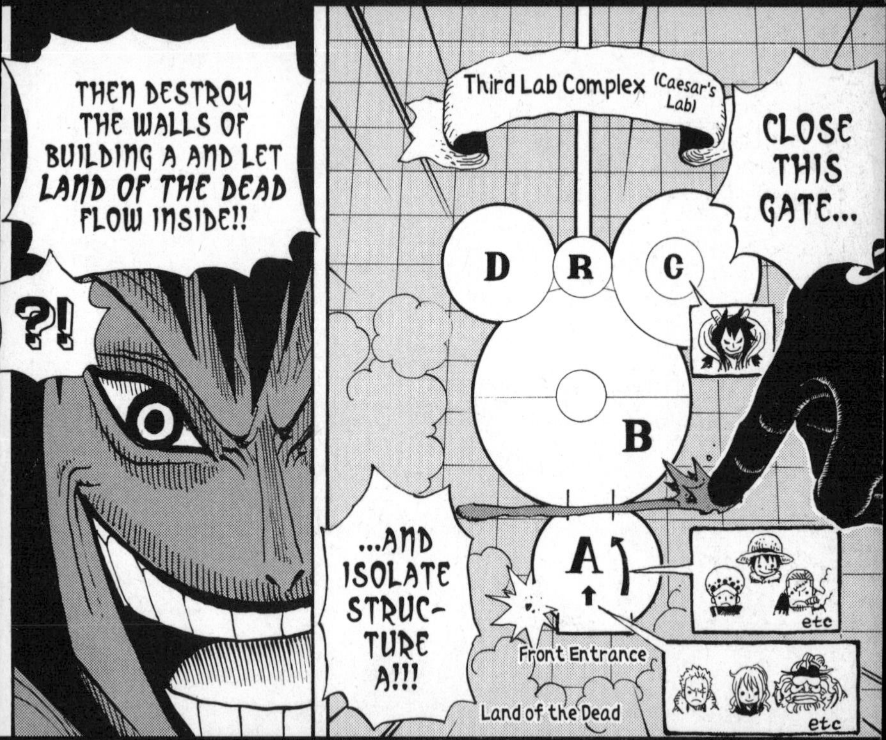
CLOSE THIS GATE...
Third Lab Complex (Caesar's Lab)
D
R
C
B
A
etc
Front Entrance
etc
...AND ISOLATE STRUCTURE A!!!
Land of the Dead
THEN DESTROY THE WALLS OF BUILDING A AND LET LAND OF THE DEAD FLOW INSIDE!!
?!

Now that the Straw Hats all have their old bodies back, it's time to storm Caesar Clown's lab and take down the mad scientist! They'll need to avoid Caesar's deadly gas if they hope to survive Punk Hazard.

ON SALE NOW!

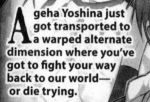

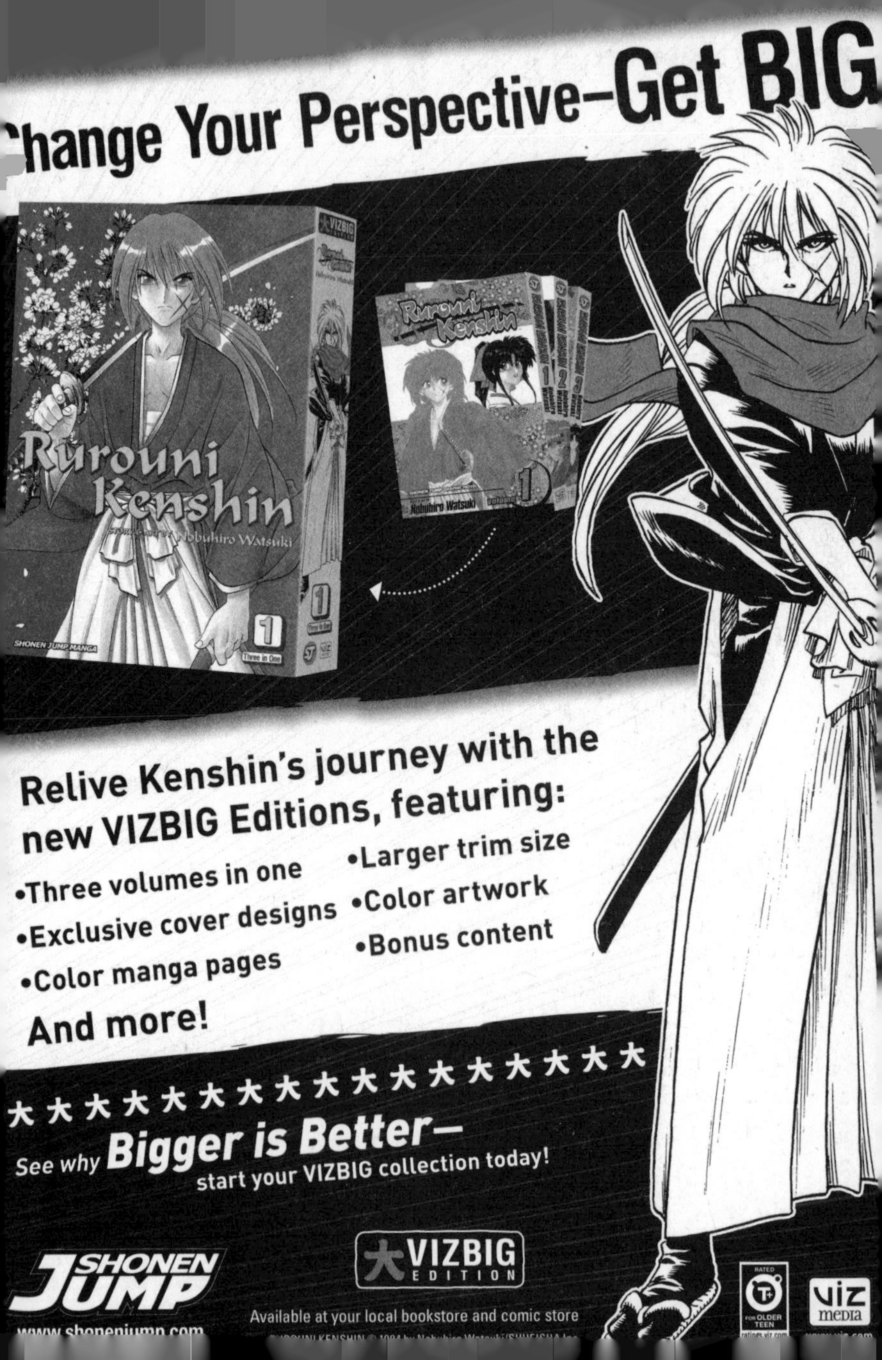
Change Your Perspective–Get BIG
Rurouni Kenshin
Nobuhiro Watsuki
SHONEN JUMP MANGA
Three in One
Relive Kenshin's journey with the new VIZBIG Editions, featuring:
•Three volumes in one
•Exclusive cover designs
•Color manga pages
•Larger trim size
•Color artwork
•Bonus content
And more!
See why Bigger is Better—
start your VIZBIG collection today!
SHONEN JUMP
VIZBIG EDITION
Available at your local bookstore and comic store
RATED T+ FOR OLDER TEEN
VIZ media

BAKUMAN。

STORY BY TSUGUMI OHBA
ART BY TAKESHI OBATA

From the creators of *Death Note*

The mystery behind manga making REVEALED!

Average student Moritaka Mashiro enjoys drawing for fun. When his classmate and aspiring writer Akito Takagi discovers his talent, he begs to team up. But what exactly does it take to make it in the manga-publishing world?

Bakuman。 Vol. 1
ISBN: 978-1-4215-3513-5
$9.99 US / $12.99 CAN *

You're Reading in the Wrong Direction!!

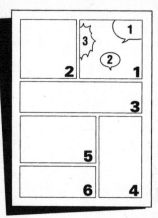

Whoops! Guess what? You're starting at the wrong end of the comic!

…It's true! In keeping with the original Japanese format, **One Piece** is meant to be read from right to left, starting in the upper-right corner.

Unlike English, which is read from left to right, Japanese is read from right to left, meaning that action, sound effects and word-balloon order are completely reversed…something which can make readers unfamiliar with Japanese feel pretty backwards themselves. For this reason, manga or Japanese comics published in the U.S. in English have sometimes been published "flopped"— that is, printed in exact reverse order, as though seen from the other side of a mirror.

By flopping pages, U.S. publishers can avoid confusing readers, but the compromise is not without its downside. For one thing, a character in a flopped manga series who once wore in the original Japanese version a T-shirt emblazoned with "M A Y" (as in "the merry month of") now wears one which reads "Y A M"! Additionally, many manga creators in Japan are themselves unhappy with the process, as some feel the mirror-imaging of their art skews their original intentions.

We are proud to bring you Eiichiro Oda's **One Piece** in the original unflopped format. For now, though, turn to the other side of the book and let the journey begin…!

—Editor ◀ • • •